HARVARD

MEMORIAL BIOGRAPHIES.

VOL. I.

CAMBRIDGE:
SEVER AND FRANCIS.
1867.

"Ὅθεν δὴ ἐν πάσῃ ἐλευθερίᾳ τεθραμμένοι οἵ τῶνδε πατέρες καὶ οἱ ἡμέτεροι καὶ αὐτοὶ οὗτοι, καὶ καλῶς φύντες, πολλὰ δὴ καὶ καλὰ ἔργα ἀπεφήναντο εἰς πάντας ἀνθρώπους καὶ ἰδίᾳ καὶ δημοσίᾳ, οἰόμενοι δεῖν ὑπὲρ τῆς ἐλευθερίας καὶ Ἕλλησιν ὑπὲρ Ἑλλήνων μάχεσθαι."

PLATO'S MENEXENUS, § 9.

"Hence it is that the fathers of these men, and ours also, and themselves too, being thus nurtured in all freedom and well-born, have shown before all men deeds many and glorious, in public and private, — deeming it their duty to fight for freedom and the Greeks, even against Greeks."

UNIVERSITY PRESS: WELCH, BIGELOW, & CO.,
CAMBRIDGE.

PREFACE.

THOSE of us whose fortunate lot it was to enlist in the army, during that magic epoch of adventure which has just passed by, will never again find in life a day of such strange excitement as that when they first put on uniform and went into camp. It was a day absolutely broken off from all that had gone before it. To say that it brought a sense of utter novelty, is nothing; the transformation seemed as perfect as if, by some suddenly revealed process, one had learned to swim in air, and were striking out for some new planet. The past was annihilated, the future was all. Now that dimly-visioned future has itself become a portion of the past; that new cycle of existence is ended; already its memories grow dim; and, after all that seeming metamorphosis, the survivors still find themselves with their feet upon the familiar earth, and pursue once more the quiet paths they left. The *auréole* is vanished from their lives, but it still lingers round the heads of the fallen. No time, no change, can restore them to the old ways, or take them from the enchanted sphere in which they henceforth dwell.

This is a series of memoirs of those graduates and former undergraduates of Harvard University who fell in battle during the recent war, or who died in consequence of services rendered in the contest. Former members of the Professional Schools of the University are not included. There are ninety-five of these memoirs, more than three quarters of which were prepared by Harvard graduates, and more than one quarter by graduates who have themselves served in the army. The work is, therefore, in a very thorough sense, a Harvard Memorial. Every memoir is here first published in its present form; and every memoir, with one exception, is the most elaborate yet printed upon the subject which it treats. Each was written, so far as practicable, by the person who seemed best adapted to that particular task, through personal intimacy or kinship; and if the results sometimes seem inadequate, they are like those unavoidable failures of a military campaign, which have often cost more labor than its successes.

The work not being a history, but a collection of biographies, historic interest has been kept subordinate to the exhibition of personal character. "The best thing we have from history," said Goethe, "is the enthusiasm which it excites"; and any light here thrown on military movements is only an indirect result, the main object being simply the delineation of the men. It was felt that if they could be truly pictured, and if vague superlatives could be rigidly excluded, then there would be no monotony in the book, since no two of these lives were in reality alike; and it would contain nothing superfluous, because the humblest of these lives was still given for our country at last.

If there is any one inference to be fairly drawn from these memoirs, as a whole, it is this: that there is no class of men in this republic from whom the response of patriotism comes more promptly and surely than from its most highly educated class. All those delusions which pass current in Europe, dating back to De Tocqueville, in regard to some supposed torpor or alienation prevailing among cultivated Americans, should be swept away forever by this one book. The lives here narrated undoubtedly represent on the whole those classes, favored in worldly fortune, which would elsewhere form an aristocracy, — with only an admixture, such as all aristocracies now show, of what are called self-made men. It is surprising to notice how large is the proportion of Puritan and Revolutionary descent. Yet these young men threw themselves promptly and heartily into the war; and that not in recklessness or bravado, — not merely won by the dazzle of a uniform, or allured by the charm of personal power, or controlled even by "that last infirmity," ambition, — but evidently governed, above all things else, by solid conviction and the absolute law of conscience. To have established incontestably this one point, is worth the costly sacrifice which completed the demonstration.

And if there is another inference that may justly be deduced from these pages, it is this: that our system of collegiate education must be on the whole healthy and sound, when it sends forth a race of young men who are prepared, at the most sudden summons, to transfer their energies to a new and alien sphere, and to prove the worth of their training in wholly unexpected applications. So readily have the Harvard graduates done this, and with such noble and unquestioned success, that I do not see how any one can read these memoirs without being left with fresh confidence in our institutions, in the American people, and indeed in human nature itself. Either there was a most rare and exceptional combination in the lives which Harvard University gave to the nation, or else—if they fairly represent their race and their time—then the work and the traditions of our fathers are safe in the hands of their descendants. The best monument that we can build to these our heroes, is to show that they have renewed our faith, and made nobler the years that are to come.

THOMAS WENTWORTH HIGGINSON.

CONTENTS OF VOL. I.

ODE

RECITED AT THE HARVARD COMMEMORATION,

JULY 21, 1865.

BY JAMES RUSSELL LOWELL.

[REPRINTED BY PERMISSION.]

I.

WEAK-WINGED is song,
Nor aims at that clear-ethered height
Whither the brave deed climbs for light:
We seem to do them wrong,
Bringing our robin's-leaf to deck their hearse
Who in warm life-blood wrote their nobler verse,
Our trivial song to honor those who come
With ears attuned to strenuous trump and drum,
And shaped in squadron-strophes their desire,
Live battle-odes whose lines were steel and fire:
Yet sometimes feathered words are strong,
A gracious memory to buoy up and save
From Lethe's dreamless ooze, the common grave
Of the unventurous throng.

II.

To-day our Reverend Mother welcomes home
Her wisest Scholars, those who understood
The deeper teaching of her mystic tome,
And offered their fresh lives to make it good:
No lore of Greece or Rome,
No science peddling with the names of things,
Or reading stars to find inglorious fates,
Can lift our life with wings

Far from Death's idle gulf that for the many waits,
And lengthen out our dates
With that clear fame whose memory sings
In manly hearts to come, and nerves them and dilates:
Nor such thy teaching, Mother of us all!
Not such the trumpet-call
Of thy diviner mood,
That could thy sons entice
From happy homes and toils, the fruitful nest
Of those half-virtues which the world calls best,
Into War's tumult rude;
But rather far that stern device
The sponsors chose that round thy cradle stood
In the dim, unventured wood,
The VERITAS that lurks beneath
The letter's unprolific sheath,
Life of whate'er makes life worth living,
Seed-grain of high emprise, immortal food,
One heavenly thing whereof earth hath the giving.

III.

Many loved Truth, and lavished life's best oil
Amid the dust of books to find her,
Content at last, for guerdon of their toil,
With the cast mantle she hath left behind her.
Many in sad faith sought for her,
Many with crossed hands sighed for her;
But these, our brothers, fought for her,
At life's dear peril wrought for her,
So loved her that they died for her,
Tasting the raptured fleetness
Of her divine completeness:
Their higher instinct knew
Those love her best who to themselves are true,
And what they dare to dream of dare to do;
They followed her and found her
Where all may hope to find,
Not in the ashes of the burnt-out mind,
But beautiful, with danger's sweetness round her;

Where faith made whole with deed
Breathes its awakening breath
Into the lifeless creed,
They saw her plumed and mailed,
With sweet, stern face unveiled,
And all-repaying eyes, look proud on them in death.

IV.

Our slender life runs rippling by, and glides
Into the silent hollow of the past;
What is there that abides
To make the next age better for the last?
Is earth too poor to give us
Something to live for here that shall outlive us, —
Some more substantial boon
Than such as flows and ebbs with Fortune's fickle moon?
The little that we see
From doubt is never free;
The little that we do
Is but half-nobly true;
With our laborious hiving
What men call treasure, and the gods call dross,
Life seems a jest of Fate's contriving,
Only secure in every one's conniving,
A long account of nothings paid with loss,
Where we poor puppets, jerked by unseen wires,
After our little hour of strut and rave,
With all our pasteboard passions and desires,
Loves, hates, ambitions, and immortal fires,
Are tossed pell-mell together in the grave.
But stay! No age was e'er degenerate
Unless men held it at too cheap a rate,
For in our image still is shaped our fate:
Ah, there is something here
Unfathomed by the cynic's sneer,
Something that gives our feeble light
A high immunity from Night,
Something that leaps life's narrow bars
To claim its birthright with the hosts of heaven;

A seed of sunshine that doth leaven
Our earthly dulness with the beams of stars,
And glorify our clay
With light from fountains elder than the Day;
A conscience more divine than we,
A gladness fed with secret tears,
A vexing, forward-reaching sense
Of some more noble permanence;
A light across the sea,
Which haunts the soul and will not let it be,
Still glimmering from the heights of undegenerate years.

V.

Whither leads the path
To ampler fates that leads?
Not down through flowery meads,
To reap an aftermath
Of youth's vainglorious weeds,
But up the steep, amid the wrath
And shock of deadly-hostile creeds,
Where the world's best hope and stay
By battle's flashes gropes a desperate way,
And every turf the fierce foot clings to bleeds.
Peace hath her not ignoble wreath,
Ere yet the sharp, decisive word
Reddens the cannon's lips, and while the sword
Dreams in its easeful sheath:
But some day the live coal behind the thought,
Whether from Baäl's stone obscene,
Or from the shrine serene
Of God's pure altar brought,
Bursts up in flame; the war of tongue and pen
Learns with what deadly purpose it was fraught,
And, helpless in the fiery passion caught,
Shakes all the pillared state with shock of men:
Some day the soft Ideal that we wooed
Confronts us fiercely, foe-beset, pursued,
And cries reproachful, "Was it, then, my praise,
And not myself was loved? Prove now thy truth;

I claim of thee the promise of thy youth;
Give me thy life, or cower in empty phrase,
The victim of thy genius, not its mate!"
  Life may be given in many ways,
  And loyalty to Truth be sealed
As bravely in the closet as the field,
    So generous is Fate;
    But then to stand beside her,
    When craven churls deride her,
To front a lie in arms and not to yield, —
    This shows, methinks, God's plan
    And measure of a stalwart man,
    Limbed like the old heroic breeds,
    Who stands self-poised on manhood's solid earth,
    Not forced to frame excuses for his birth,
Fed from within with all the strength he needs.

VI.

Such was he, our Martyr-Chief,
  Whom late the Nation he had led,
  With ashes on her head,
Wept with the passion of an angry grief:
Forgive me, if from present things I turn
To speak what in my heart will beat and burn,
And hang my wreath on his world-honored urn.
    Nature, they say, doth dote,
    And cannot make a man
    Save on some worn-out plan,
    Repeating us by rote:
For him her Old-World mould aside she threw,
  And, choosing sweet clay from the breast
    Of the unexhausted West,
With stuff untainted shaped a hero new,
Wise, steadfast in the strength of God, and true.
    How beautiful to see
Once more a shepherd of mankind indeed,
Who loved his charge, but never loved to lead;
One whose meek flock the people joyed to be,
  Not lured by any cheat of birth,

But by his clear-grained human worth,
And brave old wisdom of sincerity!
They knew that outward grace is dust;
They could not choose but trust
In that sure-footed mind's unfaltering skill,
And supple-tempered will
That bent like perfect steel to spring again and thrust.
Nothing of Europe here,
Or, then, of Europe fronting mornward still,
Ere any names of Serf and Peer
Could Nature's equal scheme deface;
Here was a type of the true elder race,
And one of Plutarch's men talked with us face to face.
His was no lonely mountain-peak of mind,
Thrusting to thin air o'er our cloudy bars,
A seamark now, now lost in vapors blind;
Broad prairie rather, genial, level-lined,
Fruitful and friendly for his humankind,
Yet also known to Heaven and friend with all its stars.
I praise him not; it were too late;
And some innative weakness there must be
In him who condescends to victory
Such as the Present gives, and cannot wait,
Safe in himself as in a fate.
So always firmly he:
He knew to bide his time,
And can his fame abide,
Still patient in his simple faith sublime,
Till the wise years decide.
Great captains, with their guns and drums,
Disturb our judgment for the hour,
But at last silence comes:
These all are gone, and, standing like a tower,
Our children shall behold his fame,
The kindly-earnest, brave, foreseeing man,
Sagacious, patient, dreading praise, not blame,
New birth of our new soil, the first American.

VII.

Long as man's hope insatiate can discern
  Or only guess some more inspiring goal
  Outside of Self, enduring as the pole,
Along whose course the flying axles burn
Of spirits bravely pitched, earth's manlier brood;
  Long as below we cannot find
The meed that stills the inexorable mind;
So long this faith to some ideal Good,
  Under whatever mortal names it masks,
  Freedom, Law, Country, this ethereal mood
That thanks the Fates for their severer tasks,
  Feeling its challenged pulses leap,
  While others skulk in subterfuges cheap,
And, set in Danger's van, has all the boon it asks,
  Shall win man's praise and woman's love,
  Shall be a wisdom that we set above
All other skills and gifts to culture dear,
  A virtue round whose forehead we enwreathe
  Laurels that with a living passion breathe
When other crowns are cold and soon grow sear.
  What brings us thronging these high rites to pay,
And seal these hours the noblest of our year,
  Save that our brothers found this better way?

VIII.

  We sit here in the Promised Land
  That flows with Freedom's honey and milk;
  But 't was they won it, sword in hand,
Making the nettle danger soft for us as silk.
  We welcome back our bravest and our best; —
  Ah me! not all! some come not with the rest,
Who went forth brave and bright as any here!
I strive to mix some gladness with my strain,
        But the sad strings complain,
        And will not please the ear;
I sweep them for a pæan, but they wane
        Again and yet again

Into a dirge, and die away in pain.
In these brave ranks I only see the gaps,
Thinking of dear ones whom the dumb turf wraps,
Dark to the triumph which they died to gain:
    Fitlier may others greet the living,
    For me the past is unforgiving;
        I with uncovered head
        Salute the sacred dead,
Who went, and who return not.— Say not so!
'T is not the grapes of Canaan that repay,
But the high faith that failed not by the way;
Virtue treads paths that end not in the grave;
No ban of endless night exiles the brave;
        And to the saner mind
We rather seem the dead that stayed behind.
Blow, trumpets, all your exultations blow!
For never shall their aureoled presence lack:
I see them muster in a gleaming row,
With ever-youthful brows that nobler show;
We find in our dull road their shining track;
        In every nobler mood
We feel the orient of their spirit glow,
Part of our life's unalterable good,
Of all our saintlier aspiration;
        They come transfigured back,
Secure from change in their high-hearted ways,
Beautiful evermore, and with the rays
Of morn on their white Shields of Expectation!

IX.

        Who now shall sneer?
    Who dare again to say we trace
    Our lines to a plebeian race?
            Roundhead and Cavalier!
Dreams are those names erewhile in battle loud;
Forceless as is the shadow of a cloud,
        They live but in the ear:
That is best blood that hath most iron in 't
To edge resolve with, pouring without stint

For what makes manhood dear.
Tell us not of Plantagenets,
Hapsburgs, and Guelfs, whose thin bloods crawl
Down from some victor in a border brawl!
How poor their outworn coronets,
Matched with one leaf of that plain civic wreath
Our brave for honor's blazon shall bequeath,
Through whose desert a rescued Nation sets
Her heel on treason, and the trumpet hears
Shout victory, tingling Europe's sullen ears
With vain resentments and more vain regrets!

X.

Not in anger, not in pride,
Pure from passion's mixture rude
Ever to base earth allied,
But with far-heard gratitude,
Still with heart and voice renewed,
To heroes living and dear martyrs dead,
The strain should close that consecrates our brave.
Lift the heart and lift the head!
Lofty be its mood and grave,
Not without a martial ring,
Not without a prouder tread
And a peal of exultation:
Little right has he to sing
Through whose heart in such an hour
Beats no march of conscious power,
Sweeps no tumult of elation!
'Tis no Man we celebrate,
By his country's victories great,
A hero half, and half the whim of Fate,
But the pith and marrow of a Nation
Drawing force from all her men,
Highest, humblest, weakest, all,
For her day of need, and then
Pulsing it again through them,
Till the basest can no longer cower,
Feeling his soul spring up divinely tall,

Touched but in passing by her mantle-hem.
Come back, then, noble pride, for 't is her dower!
How could poet ever tower,
If his passions, hopes, and fears,
If his triumphs and his tears,
Kept not measure with his people?
Boom, cannon, boom to all the winds and waves!
Clash out, glad bells, from every rocking steeple!
Banners, adance with triumph, bend your staves!
And from every mountain-peak
Let beacon-fire to answering beacon speak,
Katahdin tell Monadnock, Whiteface he,
And so leap on in light from sea to sea,
Till the glad news be sent
Across a kindling continent,
Making earth feel more firm and air breathe braver: —
"Be proud! for she is saved, and all have helped to save her!
She that lifts up the manhood of the poor,
She of the open soul and open door,
With room about her hearth for all mankind!
The helm from her bold front she may unbind,
Send all her handmaid armies back to spin,
And bids her navies, that so lately hurled
Their crashing battle, hold their thunders in:
No challenge sends she to the elder world,
That looked askance and hated; a light scorn
Plays on her mouth, as round her mighty knees
She calls her children back, and waits the morn
Of nobler day, enthroned between her subject seas."

XI.

Bow down, dear Land, for thou hast found release!
Thy God, in these distempered days,
Hath taught thee the sure wisdom of His ways,
And through thine enemies hath wrought thy peace!
Bow down in prayer and praise!
O Beautiful! my Country! ours once more!
Smoothing thy gold of war-dishevelled hair
O'er such sweet brows as never other wore,

And letting thy set lips,
Freed from wrath's pale eclipse,
The rosy edges of their smile lay bare,
What words divine of lover or of poet
Could tell our love and make thee know it,
Among the Nations bright beyond compare?
What were our lives without thee?
What all our lives to save thee?
We reck not what we gave thee;
We will not dare to doubt thee,
But ask whatever else, and we will dare!

HARVARD MEMORIAL BIOGRAPHIES.

1828.

JAMES SAMUEL WADSWORTH.

Vol. A. D. C., rank of Major, Gen. McDowell's staff, June, 1861; Brig.-Gen. Vols., Aug. 9, 1861; died May 8, 1864, of a wound received at the battle of the Wilderness, May 6.

IT has been well said that the people of the North were themselves the true heroes of the War for the Union. They were brave, generous, hopeful, and constant; while some, to whom they had a right to look for counsel and example, were cowardly, despondent, unstable, and selfish. An intelligent foreigner declared with great truth that General Wadsworth was "a noble incarnation of the American people." He certainly displayed throughout the same earnest, self-sacrificing, undismayed spirit which they collectively manifested.

James Samuel Wadsworth was born at Geneseo, New York, October 30, 1807. He was the eldest son of James Wadsworth, who had emigrated from Durham, in Connecticut, and whose family was among the most ancient and respectable in that State. It is said that one of his ancestors was that sturdy Puritan, Joseph Wadsworth, the captain of train-bands who concealed in the famous oak at Hartford, in defiance of the authority of the tyrant Andros, the precious charter which Charles II. had given to the Colony; and who afterwards, when another intruding governor, Colonel Fletcher of New York, attempted to exercise illegal rule over the Connecticut militia, caused his drums to beat and drown the reading of the royal commission, saying to Fletcher, "If I am interrupted, I will make the daylight shine through your body."

James Wadsworth of Durham, and his brother William, made their way to the banks of the Genesee in the year 1790, when that whole region was a rude wilderness, from which the Indians had scarcely been expelled. They opened their path, in some places, by their own axes, and established themselves at a point called "Big Tree," which is now the village of Geneseo. They were the agents of many of the proprietors, whose lands they cleared and brought into market; and they themselves, in process of time, became the most extensive and wealthy landholders of that neighborhood. Mr. Lewis F. Allen, to whose excellent Memorial of General Wadsworth I am indebted for some of the information contained in this paper, intimates that they owed this success to the happy union of their own personal qualities. William, who had a more hardy nature than his brother, carried on all the out-of-door operations, while James, who had received an excellent education at the East, and acquired habits of system and order, managed the finances, entertained the guests, and, by his sound judgment and fine taste, contributed not only to the material prosperity, but to the picturesque beauty of that famous valley. He had graduated at Yale College, and he took into the wild country to which he emigrated a love for letters and refined social intercourse, which made it blossom early with the sweet flowers of mental and moral culture. After the population had sufficiently increased, he caused tracts upon the subject of popular education to be printed and circulated at his own expense; he offered premiums to the towns which should first establish school libraries; he procured the passage of the school-library law, in 1808; he suggested the establishment of Normal Schools in 1811; he founded and endowed a library and system of lectures at Geneseo; and he provided that in all his sales a tract of one hundred and twenty-five acres in every township should be reserved for a church, and as much more for a school. When he died, in 1844, his gifts to the cause of education alone had exceeded the sum of ninety thousand dollars.

His wife, the mother of General Wadsworth, who is said to have been a most intelligent and amiable woman, was Naomi Walcott, of Windsor, in Connecticut, one of a family of importance in the history of that State.

This was the stock from which he sprung, and he proved his descent by the intrepidity and vigor of his character, as well as by that frank courtesy of manners and princely generosity which always distinguished him.

He received the first rudiments of his education at the common schools of Geneseo, although much of his youth must have been given to those rough employments in the open air which the border-life of those days required, even of the sons of rich fathers. Some of his friends in New York remember him well when he was a boy of twelve or thirteen, and made a visit to the city in company with his uncle William. They had come all the way on horseback, driving a herd of cattle; and Wadsworth was then a hardy, vigorous stripling, intelligent, manly, and self-possessed.

He entered Hamilton College, near Utica; but after a short residence there went to Harvard, where he remained a longer time, but never graduated. About the year 1829 he became a student of law at Yale College, where he stayed a few months, and then continued his course with Mr. Webster at Boston, and finished it in the office of McKeon and Deniston at Albany. He was in due time called to the bar, but he never practised law as a profession. He preferred to assist his father in the care of the family estate, which had been increased by the property devised by his uncle William, who died a bachelor in 1833.

Wadsworth was married about this time to Miss Wharton of Philadelphia. They went abroad soon after their marriage, and upon his return Wadsworth applied himself with great spirit and success to agricultural affairs. In 1842 he was elected President of the State Society, and he always manifested a lively interest in its prosperity. He repeatedly took prizes from this and the County Society for the excellence of his farm stock.

In 1844 he had the misfortune to lose his worthy father, and was thus left in sole charge of the greater part of the property, embracing, in addition to his own share, the estates of his two sisters. He continued to make Geneseo his chief residence, and was induced, both by self-interest and affection, to promote its prosperity by every means in his power. Among other generous acts, he caused the works which supply the village with water to be constructed. He was intending to erect a building there for the purposes of the literary institution which his father had founded, when the breaking out of the war prevented the execution of the project, for which, however, he provided in his will.

He made another visit to Europe, with his family, in 1854; and shortly after his return purchased a house in Sixteenth Street, in the city of New York, which he made his permanent town residence.

I now approach the time when Wadsworth's name became interwoven with the history of the nation. He had been chiefly known as a wealthy landholder, — a hospitable country gentleman, — a leading agriculturist. But the day had come which was to develop nobler aims and larger capacity than he had ever manifested before. The metal of every man's character was to be tested. None came out of the furnace purer and brighter than his.

Let me attempt to describe him as those who knew him best remember him to have been at that time. And let me first speak of his home in Geneseo; for this is necessary that we may understand the purity of his motives, the greatness of his sacrifices, and the value of his example.

His country house, as it has been represented to me by one of our most honored landscape artists, was large, but not ostentatious, — embosomed in trees, and commanding, on its western side, a prospect of the beautiful valley of the Genesee, which, with its glimpses of sparkling water, its cultivated fields shut in by rich masses of foliage, and its scattered groups of oaks and elms, partook of the character of an English landscape, and reminded my artist friend of the famous view of the valley of the Thames from Richmond Hill. All these trees were relics of the primeval forest, had been preserved by the pioneer who first opened these solitudes, and had been since protected with pride and reverence by his descendants. Near the mansion was the home-farm of two thousand acres, which received the special attention of Wadsworth, and was well stocked with flocks and herds. Beyond and around, in Livingston and the neighboring counties, lay the leased lands of the estate, a domain of fifteen thousand acres altogether, — and, if regarded as one tract, as large as some German principalities.

I may not intrude upon the interior of the homestead, made charming by all that wealth and taste and affection could collect, — books, pictures, music, — the conversation of intelligent guests, and the exercise of graceful and refined hospitality. Here Wadsworth lived, in the midst of numerous, contented, and thriving tenants, two thirds of whom, or their fathers, had also been the tenants of the first James Wadsworth, and thus proved, by their continuing the relation, the justice and liberality of their landlords.

I will not attempt to give a minute analysis of the character of our friend, but only to describe some of its more striking qualities. One of these seems to me to have been his direct, straightforward manliness. He never knew fear himself, and he despised all cowards. He was also eminently true and just. He hated all shams, and loved whatever was open, frank, and genuine. Perhaps he might have seemed to some a little unsympathetic, — a little wanting in tenderness. But this arose from absent-mindedness or the preoccupation of engrossing business. There was an inner source of gentleness and sympathy in his nature which they discovered who knew him best, and saw him at times when the secret doors of the heart were unlocked. That he was thoroughly benevolent and generous is proved, not only by the alacrity and profusion with which he contributed to the Irish famine fund and other public and splendid charities, but also by the readiness with which, when the crops failed, he constantly forgave the rent to those small farmers who paid in kind, and thus quietly abridged his own income to the extent, sometimes, of tens of thousands of dollars.

Wadsworth had excellent natural powers of mind, but little academic cultivation. His intellectual ability was developed rapidly in the latter years of his life. He was an original thinker. His judgment was always clear and sound ; but he disliked the details of business and the petty cares of an office. He seized with great quickness the point of a law question, or any other matter which was the subject of his reading or conversation. He also was a capital judge of character, and had the art, which distinguishes many leading minds, of sifting the knowledge of those who engaged in discussions with him, by putting a few pointed questions. No one had more tact than he in talking with the farmers of his neighborhood. He rode about among them on his small pony in the most simple and unpretending manner, and his advice had always an important influence in forming and directing their opinions.

He was entirely free from all false pride. He never, directly or indirectly, boasted of his wealth or his connections. In his manners he was simple, cordial, and unaffected. Mr. Lothrop Motley says of him, in a letter which I have read : "I have often thought and spoken of him as the true, original type of the American gentleman, — not the pale, washed-out copy of the European aristocrat." In his dress and equipage he observed a simplicity which was almost Spartan. He had no trinkets or curiosities of the toilet. He was extremely temperate in eating and drinking, and despised all the epicureanism of the table.

He was now in the flower of his age. His figure was tall, well-proportioned, and firmly knit. The glance of his gray eye was keen and determined. His Roman features were well rounded, and his hair, which had become prematurely white, added to the nobility of his expression.

Such is an imperfect outline sketch of the man and of his

home in Geneseo, as they appeared in the autumn of 1860, when the great conspiracy, which had for many years been plotting at the South to destroy the national government, proceeded from seditious language to treasonable acts, and finally dared to inaugurate civil war. James Wadsworth took at once the most open, manly, and decided stand on the side of the Union. From that moment till the day of his death he postponed all private affairs to public duties, and devoted his time, his thoughts, his wealth, and all the power which his position gave him, to the service of his country.

To this he was impelled by his political principles, no less than his personal character. He had come of old Federalist stock, and learned from his father to respect the Constitution and the national government which the people had created under it. So long ago as 1848 he had supported the Free-Soil party, which had proposed his name as a District Elector. He was consistent and persevering afterwards in his efforts on the same side. In 1856 he had received the nomination of State Elector from the Republicans; and now, in November, 1860, he was chosen a District Elector for Lincoln and Hamlin.

He owned immense tracts of land and had numerous tenants; and this, to a superficial observer, might seem likely to have diverted his sympathies toward the Southern slaveholders. He was also connected, by the marriage of one of his sisters, with a noble English family, and his associates and intimate friends had been chiefly formed among the wealthy classes, and in circles where the fires of patriotism were burning very low, if they had not gone out altogether. Some of his closest friends were indeed representatives of the best Southern society, — men possessing that refined and winning manner, the faint tradition of Huguenot politeness, which seems, in a few instances, to have survived the adverse influences that surrounded it, and which has been nowhere more unduly praised than at the North. But notwithstanding all these hindrances, Wadsworth remained a true, brave, Northern democrat. Mr. Lothrop Motley, in the letter from which I have already quoted, says of him: "He believed, honestly, frankly, and unhesitatingly, in democracy, as the only possible government for our hemisphere, and as the inevitable tendency of the whole world, so far as it is able to shake off the fetters of former and present tyrannies. He honored and believed in the people with his whole heart, and it is for this reason the people honored and believed in him. . . . . It has always seemed to me that he was the truest and most thoroughly loyal American I ever knew; and this, to my mind, is his highest eulogy, feeling as I do how immeasurably higher the political and intellectual level of America is than that of any other country in the world!"

No man valued his fellow-beings more than Wadsworth for the high qualities of mind and heart, and, I may add, the strong right-arms which God had given them, and no man less for their clothes, their trivial accomplishments, or the company they kept. No man more thoroughly despised that counterfeit chivalry which was neither truthful nor merciful, but repudiated its promises to pay, and, instead of defending the oppressed, hunted its trembling fugitives with bloodhounds.

He had opposed the extension of slavery into the Territories, and he befriended the negro as he did any other unhappy human being who needed his assistance. For this he was called by that name which then seemed to some persons the most opprobrious which party ingenuity could invent, — the name of "Abolitionist." Perhaps the application of this name to him may add another to those examples in history, where that which was devised as the instrument of shame became afterwards the badge of immortal honor. Wadsworth saw with his clear eye that a deadly struggle had now begun between systems of society entirely repugnant to each other, — between the civilized democracy of the nineteenth century and that ferocious spirit of bastard feudalism which, strangely enough, found a more congenial home on the banks of the Mississippi than it had ever enjoyed on the Neva or the Danube. No charms of social intercourse, no claims of private friendship, obscured the clearness of his vision on this point. He attributed at once to the Southern conspirators a spirit of determined aggression, a calculating, comprehensive treason, which Northern optimists were at first reluctant to admit. He saw that the laws of population and the irresistible opinion of the world forbade them from delaying an enterprise which their mad ambition had long before planned, and that all temporizing measures on our part would be idiotic and pusillanimous.

Accordingly, in that *comédie larmoyante*, created by crafty Virginia politicians, and misnamed the Peace Conference, upon whose doors should have been written Claudian's words,

> *Mars gravior sub pace latet,*
> "Under the show of peace a sterner war lies hidden," —

in that assembly, in which he took his seat on the 8th of February, 1861, he wasted no time in speeches, but constantly voted against all measures that seemed to jeopard the honor and independence of the loyal States. On the 17th of February, upon his motion, the delegation of New York virtually resolved to vote "No" upon the chief sections of the report of the committee which summed up the action of the Conference; and the State of New York was spared the mortification of assenting to overtures which weakened the position of the North, while they failed to propitiate the Southern conspirators.

For the time was now at hand when the action of deliberative bodies was to be of no account, and the safety of the nation to depend upon military measures alone. Fort Sumter was attacked and captured. The soldiers of Massachusetts were assaulted in the streets of Baltimore. The railroad communication with the capital was interrupted, and the supplies for the troops there were nearly cut off. In respect to this latter danger, the clear, practical mind of Wadsworth seized at once the difficulties of the situation, and devised the remedy. With great promptness and energy, he caused two vessels to be loaded at New York, on his own account, with provisions for the army, and accompanied them to Annapolis, attending personally to their delivery. During that interval of great anxiety between the first demonstration of the enemy against Washington and the commencement of General McDowell's campaign, Wadsworth was in constant communication with Lieutenant-General Scott, and was employed by him in executing delicate and important commissions. But he was not content with the performance of duties which, however difficult and responsible, made his example less valuable than in the more dangerous service of the field. He soon determined to enter upon this, notwithstanding the sacrifices it involved. Let us remember that he was now considerably past the military age; that his private affairs were numerous and engrossing; that he was able to give wise counsel and large pecuniary aid to government, and fulfil, in this way, every duty which the most exacting patriotism might be supposed to require. He had, as we have seen, a home made attractive by everything which wealth and taste and the love of friends could supply. He had six children, — three sons and three daughters, — some of whom were just coming into the active duties of life; and, while they needed his careful supervision, their affection and high promise made the parting from them all the more difficult and trying. Wadsworth resisted all these temptations, and rejected all these excuses. In June, 1861, he became a volunteer aid on the staff of General McDowell, and fought his first battle in the disastrous affair of Bull Run. His intimate friends declared, when they heard of his resolution to take military service, that this was equivalent to the sacrifice of his life. They knew his bravery was so impetuous that he would court every peril and exposure, and that he would never survive the war. These predictions, alas! were too surely to be accomplished, but not until a later day. They were, indeed, very nearly fulfilled at Bull Run. Nobody was more conspicuous than Wadsworth in every post of danger. He had a horse shot under him in his efforts to rally the panic-stricken troops. He seized the colors of the New York Fourteenth, and adjured that brave regiment to stand up for the old flag. As cool and collected as a veteran, he was one of the last to leave the field, and was most active in restoring order on the retreat, and in assisting, at Fairfax Court-House, to preserve the government property and to relieve the wounded.

In the organization of the national army, Governor Morgan, supposing he had a right to propose the names of two major-generals from his State, sent Wadsworth's and Dix's to the President. Wadsworth, however, upon learning that but one was allowed, immediately declined the intended honor, considering General Dix to be better qualified for the service. Afterwards, in the summer of 1861, Wadsworth was made a brigadier.

Whatever may be the judgment of intelligent critics upon the expediency of taking generals from civil life, and however unsatisfactory they may consider the reasons which influence the government in making such appointments, it is admitted by all that Wadsworth received his commission with diffidence, and that his genius, which was essentially military, coupled with his attention to his duties, soon made him an efficient officer. His brigade was attached to the Army of the Potomac, and stationed in the advance, near Upton's Hill. He lay there during the autumn of 1861 and the succeeding winter, impatient at the delay of the Commander-in-Chief in moving upon Manassas, and always insisting upon what has since been proved to be true, that the enemy's force there was for a long time too weak to resist any serious attack upon it, if we had made one. He asked, indeed, permission to follow the retreating enemy, but was refused.

In March, 1862, General Wadsworth was appointed Military Governor of Washington, and for nine months discharged the very delicate and responsible duties of that office with great satisfaction to the government. A competent writer, who served under him, says: —

> "While he gave the citizens all the liberties consistent with public safety, he took vigorous measures against traitors, spies, blockade-runners, and kidnappers. He seized the slave-pen, discharged the captives, and permanently established the rule that no negro should be taken out of the District of Columbia, under color of the Fugitive Slave Law, without an examination on the part of the military authorities respecting the loyalty of the master. . . .

Great pains were taken by General Wadsworth to facilitate the change of these people from bondage to freedom. He organized a contraband bureau, established permanent quarters, taught the poor blacks how to work for themselves, and made the confiscated goods of the blockade supply their wants. Amid political and military embarrassments, he succeeded in pioneering the way to practical emancipation while commanding the fortifications and twenty-four thousand troops."

Gurowski says, in his Diary, that he was the good genius of the fugitive negroes. But for him, great numbers of them would have been remanded to the slave-whip.

In the autumn of 1862, and while he was still in command of Washington, he received the Union nomination for Governor of New York. This had been offered to him, in 1848, by the Free-Soil Democrats, and again, in 1856, by the Republicans, but he had declined it on both occasions. He now thought it to be his duty to accept the position, and, in his letter to the President of the Convention, stated in a clear and forcible manner his opinions of the questions involved in the canvass. He assumed that the election would turn upon the necessity of sustaining the national government in its effort to maintain its territorial integrity, and upon the Proclamation of Emancipation; and he showed that to carry out the latter measure would be the most effectual, as well as humane, method of putting down the Rebellion.

He afterwards came to New York and made a speech, which had a homely earnestness and force about it that was better than all the polished elegance of the schools. It was full of quaint, outspoken honesty, which reminds us of Abraham Lincoln. "I stand before you," he said, "a candidate for your suffrages, but, if I know my own heart, I come with no personal aspirations. I have seen with pain the undue and exaggerated commendations with which my friends have referred to me. . . . . The man who pauses to think of himself, of his affairs, of his family even, when he has public duties to perform, and his country lies prostrate, almost in the agonies of dissolution, is not the man to save it." It seems strange now, when we can view this election in the light of subsequent events, that

Mr. Seymour should have defeated General Wadsworth by a majority of more than ten thousand.

General Wadsworth's term of service in Washington lasted for nine months. A friend who saw him constantly at that time says that he felt more deeply and more painfully the disasters of the country than almost any one he met. He suggested certain movements to the President which were disapproved by more experienced military minds; but they showed, at any rate, his personal courage and his restless patriotism. He constantly applied for more active duty, and in December, 1862, the government ordered him to report to Major-General Reynolds, then in command of the First Corps. General Reynolds gave him his First Division, and this he led, with great galantry, at Fredericksburg and Chancellorsville.

The experience of the last four years has proved the truth of the assertion of military men, that war is a science which must be studied like any other, and that civilians cannot be extemporized into generals. It must be confessed, however, that the genius of some civilians eminently fits them for command; and a campaign or two may supply the want of early professional study. As I have already stated, Wadsworth seems to have been one of these natural soldiers. He manifested decided ability in conducting the retreat of his troops at Chancellorsville. After effecting a difficult crossing of the river, he was ordered to recross. It was intended that this should have been done in the night, but the order did not reach him until after daylight. He got three or four regiments over without being observed, owing to the cover of earthworks; but the enemy soon after saw the movement, and opened upon him with shot and shell. One bridge had been taken up the day before. The remaining one was lost three times during the recrossing. General Reynolds ordered the movement to be suspended as impracticable, but Wadsworth convinced him it was not, and completed it with a loss of only about twenty killed and wounded, and the same number of artillery horses. He remained until the last regiment crossed, preceding only the skirmishers and pickets.

General Wadsworth was very successful in gaining the love of his men. His high sense of justice and true republican respect for manliness, wherever he found it, soon convinced them that, if they did their duty, they should be rewarded. They knew, too, that he made their comfort his constant study. These qualities endeared him greatly to his troops, and when, before the battle of Fredericksburg, he rode with his staff unexpectedly into the encampment of his old brigade, the soldiers of all the four regiments rushed tumultuously towards him and made the skies ring with their shouts of welcome. But there was another and a better reason why his soldiers loved him, and also why he was always a reliable officer: he was so cool and collected under fire. "He had a habit," says an intelligent writer, who saw him at the front just before his death, "of riding about the foremost line, and even among his skirmishers, which somewhat unnecessarily exposed his life. He knew very well how to handle his division, and he knew how to hold a line of battle, — how to order and lead a charge, — how to do the plain work which he liked best; and at Gettysburg he showed how much a plucky, tenacious leader can do with a handful of troops in keeping back and making cautious an overwhelming force of the enemy. He was pertinacious; did not like to give up or back out; and was not a man safely to be pressed, even by a force much superior to his own."

General Meade writes of him: "The moral effect of his example, his years, and high social position, his distinguished personal gallantry and daring bravery, all tended to place him in a most conspicuous position, and to give him an influence over the soldiers which few other men possess."

And General Humphreys, General Meade's chief of staff, in speaking of the qualities he showed on the field on which he lost his life, writes: "In the two days of desperate fighting that followed our crossing the Rapidan, he was conspicuous *beyond all others* for his gallantry, prompter than all others in leading his troops again and again into action. In all these combats he literally *led* his men, who, inspired by his heroic bearing, continually renewed the contest, which, but for him, they would have yielded."

This is high praise, and from the most competent sources, to be given to a man who had never been under fire until he had passed his fifty-third year, and whose life had been occupied in quiet agricultural pursuits. It was the blood of the old Puritan captain which tingled in his veins in those days of trial: better than that, it was the inextinguishable love of country, — the reverence for right and truth, — the inborn hatred of everything false, and mean, and treacherous, which made him content to exchange the delights of such a home as I have attempted to describe, for the unspeakable horrors of the battle-field.

It may well be supposed that, with qualities like these, he was not allowed to remain inactive in the campaign which succeeded the battles of Fredericksburg and Chancellorsville. At Gettysburg he commanded the First Division of the First Corps until the fall of General Reynolds, when he assumed charge of the corps. Before that, however, his division had received the brunt of the enemy's attack. It went into action at nine in the morning, and continued under fire until four in the afternoon, suffering heavier loss than any other in the army. He had several horses shot under him, and he animated the fight everywhere by his noble presence. At the council of war held after the victory, Wadsworth, who, as the temporary commander of a corps, had a seat at the board, was one of three who, with decided earnestness, favored the pursuit of the enemy; but his advice was overruled, and Lee escaped. A competent military authority says: "No doubt now exists in the mind of any unprejudiced observer, that, had this course been adopted, the army of Lee would have been entirely captured or put to rout." The war has seen no better instance of good judgment in civilian officers than Wadsworth's on this occasion.

After General Grant was ordered to the Eastern Division, Wadsworth was constantly employed in assisting in the arrangements for the campaign. Before it was undertaken, however, and about the beginning of the year 1864, he was sent upon special service to the Mississippi Valley, and made an extensive tour through the Western and Southwestern States. It was on the eve of his departure that he made to the paymaster from whom he had always drawn his pay the remarkable declaration, that he desired to have his accounts with government kept by one and the same officer, because it was his purpose, at the close of the war, to call for an accurate statement of all the money he should have received, and then to give it, whatever might be the amount, to some permanent institution founded for the relief of invalid soldiers. "This is the least invidious way," said he, "in which I can refuse pay for fighting for my country in her hour of danger."

When General Grant finally began his campaign, Wadsworth was placed in command of the Fourth Divison of the Fifth Corps, which was composed of his old division of the First Corps, with the addition of the Third Brigade. He crossed the Rapidan on Wednesday, the 4th of May. On the 5th and 6th the battle of the Wilderness was fought. It was here that the event occurred which his friends, knowing his impetuous valor, had feared from the first. Wadsworth was mortally wounded. This heroic termination of a noble career, and its attendant circumstances, are described in simple and touching language by his son, Captain Craig Wadsworth, in a letter which is published in Mr. Allen's Memorial. Captain Wadsworth was attached to the cavalry division, which was guarding the wagon-train; but, by permission of his commanding officer, he went to the front, and remained with his father for two or three hours on the morning of the memorable 6th, and while the fight was going on. There is also an interesting description of it by a Confederate officer, which has been communicated to the family, but never yet published.

It seems from these accounts that General Wadsworth's command had been engaged for several hours on the evening of the 5th, and had lost heavily. Early the next morning General Hancock ordered it again into action on the right of the Second Corps. The enemy's division opposed to it was at first Heth's and afterwards Anderson's, which were strongly posted in thick woods, and supported by artillery placed in a small open field about two hundred yards in the rear. The ground declined gently from this field to Heth's position.

Wadsworth charged repeatedly with his division, and drove the enemy back in disorder, but he was unable to retain his advantage. He was afterwards reinforced, and with six brigades made several other assaults. He fought with the most conspicuous bravery, and had two horses killed under him. At eleven o'clock General Hancock ordered him to withdraw, and there was a lull in the battle until about noon, when Longstreet, who had in the mean time come up, precipitated his force upon Wadsworth's left, and drove back Ward's brigade at that point in some confusion. Wadsworth immediately threw forward his second line, and formed it on the Orange and Fredericksburg Plank-Road, at right angles with his original position. It was while he was trying to hold this line with his own division, then reduced to about sixteen hundred men, that his third horse was shot under him, and he was himself struck in the head by a bullet. The enemy were charging at the time, and took the ground before General Wadsworth could be removed.

The Confederate officer, to whose account allusion has been made, states that he found him in the woods about fifteen paces to the left of the Plank-Road. None of the Federal dead or wounded were more than twenty or thirty yards nearer than he was to the open field toward which the attack had been directed. He was lying upon his back under a shelter-tent, which was extended over him at about three feet from the ground, the two upper corners being attached to boughs of trees, and the lower ones and the sides supported by muskets. The officer recognized him by a paper with his name on it, which had been pinned to his coat. His appearance was perfectly natural, and his left hand grasped the stock of one of the supporting muskets near the guard. His fingers played with the trigger, and he occasionally pushed the piece from him as far as he could reach, still grasping it in his hand. Supposing he might wish to send some message to his family, the officer addressed him. The General, however, paid no attention to the words, and it was soon evident that he was unconscious of what was passing around him, although the expression of his face was calm and natural, and his eyes indicated intelligence. It was in this state that he was taken to one of the Confederate hospitals. No medical skill could save his life. He lingered from Friday until Sunday morning, the 8th of May, and then yielded his brave spirit into the hands of its Maker.

There is something touching in the manner in which his remains were recovered. One Patrick McCracken, who had been a prisoner for nine weeks in the Old Capitol, while the General was Military Governor of Washington, and had known how just and true a man he was to foes as well as to friends, saw him as he lay in the hospital on the day of his death, and, by permission of the surgeon in charge, carefully interred the body in a family burial-ground. A few weeks afterwards, through his information and assistance, it was restored to his friends, and removed with every demonstration of love and respect to his native town, where it was finally buried.

Thus died James Samuel Wadsworth, in the fifty-seventh year of his age, and in the full strength of his manhood. Many a true, and brave, and noble soldier fell on that bloody field, but none truer, or braver, or nobler than he. Many a patriot consummated there the long record of his sacrifices, but none left a brighter and purer record of sacrifices than his. In this war, which has been illustrated by so many instances of heroism, it seems almost unjust to compare one man's services with another's; and Wadsworth, with his unaffected modesty, and his reverence for worth wherever it existed, if his spirit could sit in judgment on our words, would rebuke us for attributing to him a more genuine loyalty than that which animated many a poor private who fell by his side. But when we remember how entirely impossible it was in his case that his worldly advantages should have been increased by military service, and how often it is that a mixture of motives impels men to undertake such duty, we feel that we can give our praise to him with fuller hearts, in unstinted measure, and with no reservations or perplexing doubts.

As he lay upon the field, in the midst of the dead and the dying, in that awful interval between the retreat of his own men and the advance of the enemy, if any gleam of consciousness was vouchsafed to him, may we not feel confident that the recollection of his noble fidelity to his country assuaged the bitterness of that solemn hour?

"Who is the happy warrior?" asks a famous English poet; and the poet answers, — He is the happy warrior

"Whom neither shape of danger can dismay,
Nor thought of tender happiness betray; . . . .
Who, whether praise of him must walk the earth
Forever, and to noble deeds give birth,
Or he must fall and sleep without his fame,
And leave a dead, unprofitable name, —
Finds comfort in himself and in his cause;
And, while the mortal mist is gathering, draws
His breath in confidence of Heaven's applause:
This is the happy warrior, this is he
Whom every man in arms should wish to be!"

1833.

FLETCHER WEBSTER.

Colonel 12th Mass. Vols. (Infantry), June 26, 1861; killed at the battle of Bull Run, Va., August 30, 1862.

FLETCHER WEBSTER, son of Daniel and Grace (Fletcher) Webster, was born in Portsmouth, New Hampshire, July 23, 1813. He was fitted for college at the Public Latin School in Boston, his father having removed to that city in 1816. He entered Harvard College in 1829, and graduated in 1833. Though not of studious habits, he held a respectable rank as a scholar. His generous character and cordial manners made him a general favorite with his classmates, and he was selected by them to deliver the class oration at the close of their collegiate life, — a distinction more gratifying to a social and sympathetic nature like his than the highest honors of scholarship would have been.

After leaving college he studied law, partly with Mr. Samuel B. Walcott, at Hopkinton, Mass., and partly with his father, in Boston, and was in due time admitted to the Suffolk bar, and began the practice of his profession in Boston. In the autumn of 1836 he was married to Miss Caroline Story White, daughter of Stephen White, Esq., of Salem, and immediately after his marriage put in execution a plan he had previously formed of trying his professional fortunes at the West, — a change which at that time required more enterprise and involved greater sacrifices than now. He went first to Detroit, where he remained till the close of 1837 in the practice of his profession, and then removed to La Salle, in Illinois, where he remained till 1840. During his residence in Illinois, he made the acquaintance of Mr. Abraham Lincoln, who immediately recognized Colonel Webster when they met in Washington in 1861, and recalled their former intercourse to his memory.

Colonel Webster met with fair success in the practice of the law, but the profession was not congenial to his tastes or in harmony with his temperament. He had the quick perceptions, the ready tact, and the easy elocution which are so important in the trial of causes, but he disliked the drudgery of preparation and was not patient in the investigation of legal questions. This repugnance might have been overcome, had he continued a few years longer in the practice of his profession, but such was not destined to be his fate. His whole course of life received a new direction in consequence of the election of General Harrison to the office of President of the United States in the autumn of 1840. Mr. Daniel Webster became Secretary of State, and Colonel Webster removed to Washington, where he acted as private secretary to his father, and occasionally as assistant Secretary of State. This was a sphere of duty congenial to his tastes. He was a clear and ready writer, and was fond of the discussion of political questions. His father has said that no one could prepare a paper, in conformity with verbal instructions received from him, more to his satisfaction than his son Fletcher; and this was a point on which Mr. Daniel Webster's parental affection would not have blinded him. He was very fond of his son, and was not only happy in having him near him, but his happiness was always imperfect if his son were absent from him. So far as the son's advancement in life was concerned, it might have been better that he should have been left to make his way alone, and that his father should have consented to the sacrifice of affection which such a separation would have required; but, now that both are gone from earth, who will not pardon a mistake — if mistake it was — which had its source in the best affections of the human heart?

In 1843 Mr. Caleb Cushing was appointed Commissioner to China, and Colonel Webster accompanied him as Secretary of Legation. He remained in China till the objects of the mission were accomplished, and reached home on his return in January, 1845. In the course of the year after his return, he frequently lectured in public on the subject of China, and gave interesting reminiscences of his own residence there.

In 1850 he was appointed, by President Taylor, Surveyor of the Port of Boston, an office which he held by successive appointments till March, 1861, when a successor was nominated by President Lincoln.

Immediately after the firing upon Fort Sumter, and the attack by a lawless mob in Baltimore upon the Sixth Massachusetts Regiment, he responded to an appeal made to the patriotic citizens of Massachusetts by the following notice, which appeared in the Boston papers of Saturday, April 20, 1861.

"FELLOW-CITIZENS, — I have been assured by the Executive Department that the State will accept at once an additional regiment of infantry. I therefore propose to meet to-morrow at ten o'clock, in front of the Merchants' Exchange, State Street, such of my fellow-citizens as will join in raising this new regiment. The muster-roll will be ready to be signed then and there.

"Respectfully,

"FLETCHER WEBSTER."

The above call was seconded by the following notice, subscribed by the names of twenty-eight well-known gentlemen.

"There will be a public meeting to-morrow, Sunday, in front of the Exchange, State Street, at ten o'clock, A. M., to aid in the enrolment of the new regiment of volunteer militia called for by Fletcher Webster. Come all."

At the appointed hour on Sunday, April 21st, an immense crowd appeared in State Street in front of the Exchange. Colonel Webster attempted to address them, but the place where he stood made it impossible for him to be heard except by those who were near him. Some one proposed to go to the Old State-House, at the head of the street, a few rods distant, and the suggestion was received with acclamation and immediately carried into effect. Colonel Webster then spoke from the balcony of the Old State-House, and, among other things, said he could see no better use to which the day could be put than for us to take the opportunity to show our gratitude to Divine Providence for bestowing upon us the best government in the world, and to pledge ourselves to stand by and maintain it. He whose name he bore had the good fortune to defend the Union and the Constitution in the forum. This he could not do, but he was ready to defend them in the field. He closed his remarks with an allusion to his father's devotion to the country, and expressed a hope that we should yet see the nation united, and our flag remain without a star dimmed or a stripe obliterated. He then announced that all who desired to enlist would find papers ready for signatures at the surveyor's office, at the Custom-House.

The meeting was then addressed by other gentlemen in a similar strain. Nothing could surpass the enthusiasm with which the remarks of all the speakers, and especially those of Colonel Webster, were received by the audience. And this was in no small degree owing to the impression made by the fact that it was the son of Daniel Webster who was ready to risk his life for the defence of the Union and the Constitution. The illustrious statesman had been but nine years in his grave; and, of the audience which listened to the son, probably nine tenths at least had seen the father and heard him speak. The scene before them recalled him. To the mind's eye, that majestic form and grand countenance seemed standing by the side of his son, and in the mind's ear they heard again the deep music of that voice which had so often charmed and instructed them. And there was yet another reason for the strong feeling that was awakened. Colonel Webster had been for some years identified with the great party which had been defeated in the election of 1860, and he had been removed from a lucrative office by the administration of President Lincoln. But none the less zealously did he come forward in aid of his country in her hour of peril and distress, and the value of his example was appreciated and felt.

The enthusiasm of the meeting was not a transient flame, but a steady fire. The next day a committee of one hundred persons was organized to co-operate with Colonel Webster in forming and providing for his regiment, and among them were some of his own warmest personal friends, and some of the most zealous and devoted of the political disciples of his father. Money was contributed with lavish hand. So rapidly were the ranks of the regiment filed, that in three days the enlistment was completed and the lists closed. Five companies were enlisted in Boston, one in North Bridgewater, one in Abington, one in Weymouth, one in Stoughton, and one in Gloucester. Colonel Fessenden, a graduate of West Point, offered his services as military instructor, which were gratefully accepted. The classmates of Colonel Webster presented him with a valuable horse and equipments. The young ladies of Mr. Emerson's school in Boston made liberal donations to the company commanded by Captain Saltmarsh, which, in their honor, was called the Emerson Guard. The pupils of the Latin School made most generous provision for the equipment of the company commanded by Captain Shurtleff, a graduate of the school, and, in acknowledgment, the company was named the Latin-School Guard.

The three months after the organization of the regiment were spent in Fort Warren, in the harbor of Boston, in the discipline and drill requisite to convert fresh recruits into steady soldiers. This was dull work for ardent young men, burning for actual service in the field; but the event showed that it was time well spent. On the 26th of June the regiment was mustered into service. On the 18th of July a splendid standard was presented to the regiment, on behalf of the ladies of Boston, by Edward Everett, who accompanied the gift with a patriotic and soul-stirring address, to which Colonel Webster made an appropriate reply.

On the afternoon of the 23d of July, the regiment left Fort Warren for the seat of war. They were received with enthusiastic welcome on their arrival at New York the next day. The officers were entertained at the Astor House by the sons of Massachusetts resident in New York. With a few stoppages, the regiment arrived at Baltimore about noon on Friday, July 26th, and were cordially received. Colonel Webster and his command proceeded to Harper's Ferry, where they arrived on Saturday, July 27th, and pitched tents on the Maryland side of the Potomac, about a mile from the ferry, calling their encampment Camp Banks. The regiment was soon after removed to Darnestown, where it remained until it was transferred to Cantonment Hicks, about four miles east of Frederick City, in Maryland, arriving there on Thursday, December 5, 1861. At that place the regiment remained in camp until February 27, 1862, when it marched into Virginia for more active service.

For the next four or five months the Webster regiment, forming part of the division of the army under Major-General Banks, was mainly employed in guarding the Upper Potomac, and keeping vigilant watch upon the enemy, so as to prevent him from crossing the river into Maryland. It was an important though not an exciting service, and was of essential value in completing their military training, and giving them that efficiency which is the result of mutual knowledge and mutual confidence.

During all this time Colonel Webster showed himself possessed, in no common measure, of the qualities of a good commander. His discipline was firm and uniform, but not alloyed by petulance or passion. His regiment acquired a good name from the neat and soldier-like appearance of the men, the quickness and accuracy of their drill, and the orderly arrangements of their camp. His men were warmly attached to their Colonel. They appreciated his manly frankness, his simplicity of character, his kindness of heart, and the cheerfulness with which he bore the hardships and privations of the service, though he had no longer the unworn energies of youth to sustain him.

In the early part of August, 1862, Colonel Webster obtained leave of absence for a few days, and came home. This was in consequence of the death of his youngest daughter, Julia, to whom he was tenderly attached, and whose death overwhelmed him with grief, and awakened in him an irresistible longing to mingle his tears with those of his wife and surviving children. It was during this brief absence that his regiment was for the first time set upon the perilous edge of battle in the disastrous affair of Cedar Mountain, August 9th, where that gallant and promising young officer, Captain Shurtleff, was killed, and where so many of our "beautiful and brave" of the Second Massachusetts Regiment poured out their precious blood. It was a source of regret to Colonel Webster that his regiment should have been led into their first battle by any one but himself; but, on the other hand, he had a right to be proud of their excellent conduct and steadiness under a hot fire of two or three hours.

Colonel Webster, on the 16th of August, rejoined his regiment, which was then encamped upon the Rapidan, near Mitchell's Station. It was a part of Hartsuff's brigade, Ricketts's division, and McDowell's corps, forming a portion of the Army of Virginia, under the command of General Pope. On the 18th of August, the army began a movement towards the North Fork of the Rappahannock, and by the 20th the main body was behind the river and prepared to hold its passes.

On the 24th of August, General McDowell's corps was at or near Warrenton. On the morning of the 27th of August, he was directed to move forward rapidly on Gainesville, by the Warrenton Turnpike. And the required position was reached before the next day. On the next evening a brisk engagement took place at Thoroughfare Gap between the advance of the Rebel force under General Longstreet and the division under General Ricketts, in which the Twelfth Massachusetts Regiment took part, and behaved well, having six men wounded. "The Colonel did splendidly," said one of his officers, writing home immediately after.

The regiment was not on the field on the 29th of August, the first day of the second battle of Bull Run, but in the perils and disasters of the next day it bore a conspicuous part. It was stationed on the left, against which the main attack of the Rebel force was directed, where the fight was most severe and the slaughter most terrible. Colonel Webster led his men into battle with the utmost gallantry; and, encouraged by his voice and presence, they behaved admirably well. Many of them fell, but the survivors did not flinch. Late in the afternoon, some of the regiments on their left, overborne by superior numbers, began to give way, and the Twelfth fell back some twenty paces, to avoid being placed between the fire of advancing foes and retreating friends, but in good order and without breaking their ranks. Not long after this Colonel Webster was shot through the body. Lieutenant Haviland was near him when he fell, and with two men went with him to the rear. They had gone but a few paces when one of the men was shot, and the other, seeing the enemy close upon him, sought safety in flight. Colonel Webster was perfectly helpless, and Lieutenant Haviland, still suffering from an injury received from his horse having fallen upon him at Cedar Mountain, could do no more than find a place of shelter for the dying man under a bush in a little hollow. No one could be found to carry him away, and messages sent for a surgeon proved ineffectual. Colonel Webster desired his friend to leave him, but Lieutenant Haviland was determined to save him if possible; at any rate, not to desert him. Within a short time, a body of Rebel troops came upon them and took them prisoners. They would not carry away Colonel Webster from the spot where he lay, nor yet allow Lieutenant Haviland to remain with him. The officer in command promised to send an ambulance for him, but his pledge was not redeemed.* He died on the spot where he was left, and we can only hope that his suffering was not long or severe. His body was recovered and sent home by the generous and courageous efforts of Lieutenant Arthur Dehon, as is told in the memoir of that promising officer and most amiable young man. His funeral services were held at the church on Church Green, Boston, on Tuesday, September 9, 1862. The building was filled with a large body of mourning and sympathizing friends, who listened with deep feeling to the well-chosen words of the officiating clergyman, the Rev. Chandler Robbins, and the solemn and appropriate music of the choir. At the close of the services his body was taken to

* Since the publication of the first edition I have learned through Captain Pritchard of Petersburg, who was serving in one of the Virginia regiments, that this statement is not correct. An ambulance was sent, after some unavoidable delay, but Colonel Webster breathed his last at the moment they were raising him in order to place him in it.

Marshfield and committed to the dust, in the family cemetery, by the side of his illustrious father.

Colonel Webster was long mourned and affectionately remembered by the officers and men who had served under him. And there were others, too, who grieved for his loss; for though not widely known, he had many faithful friends who had known and loved him from boyhood, and had stood by him in all the changes and chances of life. His own heart was warm, his nature was generous and open, and his temperament cordial and frank. His tastes were strongly social, and his powers of social entertainment were such as few men possess. He had an unerring sense of the ludicrous, his wit was ready and responsive, and no man could relate an amusing incident or tell a humorous story with more dramatic power. Nor was he without faculties of a higher order. His perceptions were quick and accurate, he was an able and forcible speaker, and he wrote with the clearness and strength which belonged to him by right of inheritance. The value which his friends had for him was higher than the mark which he made upon his times. The course of his life had not in all respects been favorable to his growth and influence, and he had not the iron resolution and robust purpose which make will triumph over circumstance. But when the golden opportunity came, he grasped it with heroic hand. He rose to the height of the demand made upon him, and dormant powers and reserved energies started into vigorous life as the occasion required them. Had he lived, he might have had a higher place, but it is enough for his friends to know that in the providence of God he was permitted to die a glorious death, at the head of his regiment, with his face to the foe, calmly confronting the shock of adverse battle, in defence of the Union, the Constitution, and the laws, for which his father had lived. Who could ask more for the friend of one's heart or the child of one's love?

Colonel Webster left a widow and three children, — two sons and a daughter. His eldest son has since died.

1834.

CHARLES HENRY WHEELWRIGHT.

Assistant Surgeon, U. S. Navy, October 17, 1839; Surgeon, April 5, 1854; died July 30, 1862, at Pilotstown, S. W. Pass, La., of disease contracted in the service.

CHARLES HENRY WHEELWRIGHT, late surgeon in the Navy of the United States, was born in Purchase Street, in the city of Boston, May 29, 1813, in a house which was built by his father on the spot where the Sailors' Home now stands. His father, Lot Wheelwright, a native of Cohasset, Massachusetts, was originally a ship-builder, and afterwards a ship-owner and merchant in Boston, and was in 1813, and for many years afterwards, a man of wealth. His mother was Susannah (Wilson) Wheelwright, of West Cambridge. They were married in 1793, and Charles was the youngest of their six children.

When about ten years old Charles was sent to the Round Hill Academy, at Northampton, then a celebrated school, kept by Dr. Cogswell, late of the Astor Library, and by Mr. George Bancroft, the historian; but in consequence of failing health (for his constitution was naturally delicate), he remained there only about a year. He went next to the well-known school at Jamaica Plain, near Boston, kept by Mr. Green, where he remained for some time; but his final preparation for college was made under the private tuition of the late Jonathan Chapman, afterwards Mayor of Boston, who, at the request of an older brother, undertook to direct his studies. Before he entered college, however, his health being still delicate, he was sent abroad in a vessel commanded by a brother-in-law, and travelled through various parts of England, Scotland, Wales, and Ireland. This was the beginning of those wanderings which occupied the greater part of his life; and though in after days he often complained of his long absences from home, and of separation from friends and relatives to whom he was strongly attached, yet there was in his nature a certain restlessness and fondness for new scenes and places, which had something to do with his final choice of a profession.

He entered college in 1831, becoming a member of the class which graduated in 1834. After a little more than a year of college life, his health again became impaired, and his lungs appeared so much affected that he obtained leave of absence, and passed the winter in Mobile and New Orleans. At Cambridge he was a general favorite, and formed many intimate friendships which lasted through life. His popularity with his friends and acquaintances arose not only from the sterling qualities of his character, his warm-heartedness, and the general kindness of his disposition, but from his cheerfulness when in society, and the high spirits which seemed natural to him, although he was subject at intervals to very great depression. He was always animated in conversation, speaking in a rather loud tone. He sang a song acceptably, for he had a musical taste, though his voice was not melodious; and in convivial moments his spirits would rise as easily without artificial stimulants, as if the glasses, which he would quietly fill with water and then toss off, really contained the champagne he was supposed to be drinking. It seemed as if the mere presence of his friends was a sufficient stimulus to enable him to drive off that depression which many find it difficult to overcome without some excitement more potent than water.

In the latter part of the Senior year, in consequence of some disturbances which occurred in College, several members of his class were punished by expulsion or otherwise. This treatment was felt by their classmates to be unjust. A pamphlet of considerable ability, written under the authority of the class by one of their number, in which the character and conduct of the Faculty were rather severely handled, only added to the excitement, as it placed the government in the unpleasant dilemma of either suffering under its imputations in silence, or so far forgetting its dignity as to answer an attack made by boys. Finally a number of the class, considering themselves equally guilty with those who were punished, determined not to receive their degrees; and accordingly, when their names were called, agreeably to ancient custom, on Commencement day, they were not to be found.

At a later period, when the pamphlet and the causes which led to this youthful act of quixotism were forgotten, most of these recusants received their degrees, and were welcomed back to the bosom of their Alma Mater; but Dr. Wheelwright's absence on his professional duties, and some unavoidable delays, prevented him from being included in their number, as he had expected. Since his death his friends and classmates have regretted that the list of the Class of 1834, in the Triennial Catalogue, does not contain the name of one who was, to say the least, as much loved and appreciated in College and in after life as any whose name it bears.

There is a Catalogue, however, of at least one society in College, where his name is enrolled. This society is an ancient one, of a social character, composed at that time mostly of intimate friends, and his name appears as its presiding officer from 1833 to 1834. He was also Adjutant of the Harvard Washington Corps, a military company composed of the students of Harvard University, but now long extinct.

Shortly after leaving college, his taste for chemistry and other kindred studies induced him to select medicine as his profession; and he entered the office of the late Dr. George C. Shattuck, and became a member of his household. In 1837 he received the degree of M. D. from the Medical Department of Harvard University; and his father's property having become much reduced, if not entirely lost, he now stood ready to begin life with that advantage which his excellent preceptor, Dr. Shattuck, thought so important, and which in his peculiar style he was wont to term "the healthy stimulus of prospective want."

He decided to enter the Navy; and having first attended a course of medical lectures in Philadelphia, he was examined and commissioned as Assistant Surgeon, October 17, 1839.

He must have passed an excellent examination, as his name stood third on the list. He was soon after ordered to the sloop-of-war Marion, and remained in her on the Brazil station about three years. Much of the time was spent in the ports of Rio Janeiro, Buenos Ayres, and Monte Video, especially in the two latter. At Buenos Ayres the American officers were treated with much attention by Rosas, who was then at the height of his power; and Dr. Wheelwright saw a great deal of him and his family. In a letter written during this cruise he says: "I passed seven as happy months as I ever knew in Buenos Ayres, and perhaps, had the country been quiet, I had been there still. But Rosas is losing ground. . . . . These South American republics, like the Kilkenny cats, fight till nothing but their tails are left." He little thought, as he wrote this letter, that he should, in a comparatively few years, see his own country engaged in a civil war in which more valuable lives would be lost on each side than Rosas and his antagonist had enrolled in their respective armies, and that his own would be among the number.

On his return, in 1843, he was for some time in the receiving-ship Ohio, at Boston, and the frigate Independence, one of the Home Squadron. In this year he passed the usual examination, and took the rank of Passed Assistant Surgeon.

In 1844 he left the Home Squadron; and after a short leave of absence, he was ordered, in 1845, to the Naval Hospital at Pensacola. The government was at this time constructing a new hospital at that station, and orders came from Washington, for some reason, to cut down the trees which grew on a marsh in the vicinity. The medical officers at Pensacola remonstrated against this measure, as being likely to cause malaria by exposing so much wet ground to the rays of the sun, but without effect. The summer of 1845 was dry, but the winter and spring succeeding were very wet and rainy; and after the heat of summer came on, a most violent form of bilious or yellow fever showed itself, and soon began to rage with great severity. The gentleman who held the position of surgeon during the first part of the sickly season was in very delicate health. There were no hospital nurses except ignorant negroes, and almost the whole responsibility and labor fell upon Dr. Wheelwright, as assistant surgeon. The mortality was very great, for all the invalids of the Gulf Squadron were sent to the hospital. It soon became almost impossible to procure and retain servants; and he was obliged, in many cases, to perform the duties of surgeon and nurse for the dying, and then to render the last offices to the dead. The surgeon who succeeded the one first in charge took the fever himself, and the poor assistant was worse off than ever; but he continued to perform his duties with his usual energy and spirit, even after the time had passed when, by the usages of the navy, he had a right to ask to be relieved from the post. At last he was taken ill himself. The fever ran high, and for some days his life was despaired of; and though he finally rallied, he never afterwards enjoyed the same degree of health as before.

After his recovery from the fever, he had leave of absence for some months, which he employed in travelling in Europe and in visiting the hospitals of Paris and other Continental cities; and he then joined the Mediterranean Squadron in January, 1848. In February, 1849, he returned to this country; and in the spring of 1850 he was ordered to California, by way of the Isthmus. The agitation caused by the gold discoveries had extended to our naval vessels on that station, and they were for some time unable to move for want of crews: the men deserted, and not a few of the officers resigned. Dr. Wheelwright was attached to one of these vessels for many tedious months. As the pay of a naval officer then hardly equalled that of a waiter in a hotel, a visit to San Francisco was too expensive to be often undertaken; and Congress, too, evidently disapproved of such visits, and refused to increase the pay of the officers on that station. This monotonous course of life was at last ended by his being ordered to the Falmouth, in which vessel he visited Oregon and Vancouver's Island, and finally returned to the Atlantic States in February, 1852.

In the following August he joined at Norfolk the steamer

Powhatan, which made a part of Commodore Perry's famous Japan expedition. Doctor Wheelwright was not present at the signing of the treaty between the United States and Japan, for he was ordered to the Plymouth, which left for China before that ceremony took place. During this cruise he was promoted to a surgeoncy, his commission being dated April 5th, 1854. On his arrival at home, after being a few months in the receiving-ship at Boston, he was ordered to the Home Squadron in the Cyane, and visited Newfoundland and other places on the northeast coast of America. In 1859 he was again in the Gulf of Mexico, exposed to the bad influence which the climate now had upon his constitution.

In 1860, at Philadelphia, and again in 1861, at the Brooklyn Navy-Yard, he was a member of the Board to examine Surgeons for admittance to the Navy. In 1861 this service was very fatiguing, owing to the great increase of the medical corps required by the civil war. The Board sat for many hours daily during several months; and when he returned to the receiving-ship at Boston, where he was then stationed, he was much exhausted. Anxious, however, to perform his duty, and probably not aware of his own state of health, he applied for active servive, and was in consequence ordered to the steamer San Jacinto, which sailed March 5th, 1862, in search of the ship-of-the-line Vermont, reported to be drifting about dismasted off the South Shoal. After a vain search (for the report afterwards proved incorrect) the San Jacinto returned to Boston, and had hardly arrived when orders were received (on March 9th) to sail at once for Hampton Roads, to assist in the expected sea-fight with the famous Merrimack. Dr. Wheelwright came on shore for an hour, on the afternoon of that day, to take leave of his friends. They never saw him again.

The San Jacinto remained in Hampton Roads until Norfolk was taken, and in May joined the Gulf Squadron. This squadron consisted of about twenty-three vessels, and for several weeks Dr. Wheelwright performed the duties of fleet surgeon. He was at this time much reduced in consequence of having had a severe attack of dengue, or break-bone fever, on his passage from Norfolk to Key West. It was evident from his letters that he looked forward with dread to another summer in the Gulf, and had a sick man's longing for home; but he did not ask to be relieved. Just at this time he received orders to go North in the Colorado, but most unfortunately the orders reached him forty-eight hours after she had sailed. This was a terrible disappointment. Surgeons could not be spared in those days, and new orders came for him to take charge of the Naval Hospital recently established at Pilotstown, a little village on the southwest pass of the Mississippi. This hospital received the sick and wounded from the squadron in the river; and as it had been established but a short time, and in a hurried manner, was poorly provided with the necessary articles for the suffering patients. The responsibility and labor of the post weighed heavily upon the surgeon. He had been there about a week when he thus wrote to a relative:—

"My duties here are like those at Pensacola, only infinitely greater. I was young and strong then, and came away, as you remember, much shattered. There are about sixty patients, many terribly wounded, or sick with fever, and most limited means to treat them. Except beds, no furniture that we have not taken by force from the dozen or more houses here. Conflicting orders come to the captains of the transport steamers relative to receiving men from the hospital without their accounts, and these are not sent with them to the hospital. So here I have to keep them, and many die in consequence. It is distressing to have those in charge who ought to be sent home; and yet my hands are tied, and I cannot send them. I have been here a week, have only one assistant, am weak from want of sleep and a diarrhœa. There is no way to get relief from my situation. I shall do my duty to the last."

He was not only weakened by a constantly increasing diarrhœa, and worn down by his incessant labor and want of sleep, but the feeling that he could not properly provide for those under his charge, and that many lives were lost on this account, depressed his spirits, and left him the less energy to resist his disorder. Till the 30th of July, however, he continued to perform his duties, but on the morning of that day he was unable to get up. He grew rapidly worse; and though all means were used which the place afforded, it was too late to save him. Before the day closed he was quietly relieved of his post. His death, though far removed from his home and relatives, was in some respects such as he himself would have preferred; for up to the last possible moment that his strength permitted, and till within twenty-four hours of his death, he was engaged in the discharge of the most satisfactory duty which any man can perform, — the relief of the sick, the wounded, and the dying; and he fell a sacrifice to his own exertions and anxiety in behalf of those whom his country had committed to his charge.

In his last letter he alludes to his being no longer young and strong, but years had made no change in the qualities of his heart or in the general characteristics of the man. He had still the same slender, erect figure, the same hearty, ringing tones in his voice, the same animated and confident manner, and the same kindness and good-will expressed in his whole bearing. Any one who saw much of him, even if not an intimate friend, must have perceived his strong, plain common-sense, his contempt for everything mean and underhand, his resolution, firmness, and courage in the performance of his duty, the great purity of his character, and, above all, a manly straightforwardness in his every action, word, and look; for there never seemed to be the slightest disguise about him. His friends, of course, understood the generosity of his character and the strength of his attachments; but few could know how devoted he was to the interests of some whom he looked upon as especially committed to his protection, what acts of generous kindness he was constantly performing for them, and how much they and their home mingled in all his thoughts and plans.

The following extract from a letter written by the distinguished commander whose vessel, the Cayuga, led the fleet in the famous passage of the forts below New Orleans, and who had known him since his first entrance into the Navy, indicates in what estimation he was held in that service where the best years of his life were spent.

"The character of Dr. Wheelwright was singularly free from reproach of any kind. He had the love and respect of all who ever sailed with him. He ranked high in his own corps as a skilful and thorough physician, and was distinguished always for his sympathy with, and careful attention to, the sick. He adorned our profession by many noble qualities. With winning and affable manners, he combined firmness, a high conscientiousness, a firm adherence to whatever was right, and an uncompromising resistance to injustice and wrong.

"He lived for others more than for himself; and this is proved by the manner of his death, which was caused by his devotion to our sick and wounded sailors after the battle of New Orleans. . . . .

"No one who knew Dr. Wheelwright speaks of his loss without emotion; but to those who were intimately associated with him, his loss is beyond repair. His life was as gallant and costly a sacrifice as any which the Rebellion entailed on our country."

Dr. Wheelwright was never married. His remains were buried at Mount Auburn, August 14, 1862.

1837.

JAMES RICHARDSON.

Private Twentieth Connecticut Vols. (Infantry), August 2, 1862; died at Washington, D. C., November 10, 1863, of disease contracted in the service.

IN portraying most of the younger men whose memoirs are contained in this volume, one is naturally led to compare them with what they would, perhaps, have been in times of peace. But in writing of the men of middle age, one compares them with what they previously were. To some the war only supplied a new direction for powers already developed and mature. To some, on the other hand, it brought a complete transformation; or if not quite that, yet a consummation so rapid and perfect as to seem like transformation, giving roundness and completeness to lives previously erratic or fragmentary. Of this there was no more striking instance than in the case of James Richardson.

"A prophet is never called of God until the age of forty," says the Arab proverb. James Richardson had all his life been loved and blamed, criticised and idolized, without ever finding his precise or proper working-place on earth. When at forty-five he left his preaching and his farm, to enlist as a private soldier, then his true and triumphant Christian ministry began, and he continued in it till his death.

I remember watching his college eccentricities when I was a boy in Cambridge, and was largely occupied, like most Cambridge boys, in studying human nature as exhibited among the undergraduates. Long after, I was associated with him in post-graduate studies at the same university, where he lingered long; and I have known him ever since. And any acquaintance with him came near to intimacy, because of his open and eager nature and his warmth of heart.

James Richardson was born in Dedham, Massachusetts, May 25, 1817. His mother's maiden name was Sarah Elizabeth Richards. His father was James Richardson, of Dedham, a man who had been a good deal in public life, and was in his old age quite an interesting relic of the stern Federalist days. I remember his fighting his battles over by the fireside, and telling me anecdotes of my grandfather, a warm Federalist like himself. The old man and his son seemed as intimate with each other as two school-boys, and it was easy to see whence the latter had inherited some of his marked qualities.

In his autobiography in the Class Book, he says: —

"The earliest event of importance, in my mental and spiritual education, was the death of a mother, when I was but three years old. An epidemic had swept through the little village of Dedham, and three of our family, including myself, became its subjects. My mother and baby brother fell its victims; and though I survived, my constitution has not yet wholly regained its former healthy tone. The death of a mother at this tender age, when I most required her guarding love, was a circumstance of almost incalculable injury to me. Her form and features are indelibly impressed upon my mind; and the remembrance of her teachings in the holy quiet of the Sabbath mornings, when my heart was fresh in innocence and warm in happiness, even now oft fills my eyes with blissful tears. From her I inherited the love of harmonious sounds; and before I could utter articulate words, do I remember catching from her lips the notes of some simple melodies.

"After my mother's death, on account of my father's frequent absences on business connected with different public offices, I was left almost wholly to the care of a nurse and other family domestics, who governed me only by fear, and who rewarded me only with tales of murder, bloody-bones, ghosts, and hobgoblins. The best influence of such treatment was to excite the love of the marvellous to an undue degree of action.

"To my father . . . . I owe the cultivation of my imagination and my love of the beautiful. Added to his fine poetical taste was a deep love of nature; and after my fifth year my frequent rambles with him, especially on Sabbath evenings, imbued me, in some small degree, with his own spirit. The sports and games which boyhood so generally pursues had no interest for me. I loved to roam the fields, to commune with Nature in her sublimity and in her beauty, in her strength and in her cunning. I would sit for hours gazing upon the mountain rock, the giant oak, the leaping, dancing streamlet, admiring their simple grandeur or reclining under the shade of some ancient tree. I would listen to the sighing zephyr, as it made sad music among the fresh foliage, or to the low murmuring of the rippling stream, till my soul was lost in the misty maze of its own meditations. Or, again, I would watch the yellow-bird, as she lined her downy nest with the soft fur of the mullein-leaf, and the honey-bee, as she rolled herself in the farina of the rose's cup. Nature was my study, nature was my delight. By my father I was first introduced to the conversation of the English poets, and many of their sweetest verses I learned to repeat on his knee. It was in my sixth summer that I first fell to rhyming, and a happy boy was I ! — happy in that state of purity and innocence which had not yet fallen a prey to the passions and temptations of the world, — happy in an undisturbed peace, not in the triumph of spiritual victory. One evening, ere the light of the moon had displaced the last blush of fading day, as I pressed my early pillow, the thoughts of my great Father's bounty came rushing in a full tide of grateful feeling over my soul, and I gave that joy expression in poetic measure. At the returning day I repeated it to my sister, and as she had advanced a step beyond me, in learning to write, she kindly volunteered to put it on paper for me and hand it up to the schoolmistress among the compositions of her class. Of course the schoolmistress, the scholars, and other foolish friends gave me exaggerated and undue praise, which fostered still more my rhyming propensity, imbued me with a desire of praise, and puffed me up with a nonsensical vanity, which, without the balance of firmness and pride, has marked my character, and injured me no little, even up to the present day. The devotional character of my rhymes, my peculiar course of reading, and the character of my conversation and feelings, induced my friends to suppose that I had inherited the deep religious cast of mind that distinguished my mother, and I therefore received the name of the 'little minister.' It was my custom to assemble, in all sobriety and simplicity, my little playmates, and, imitating the parson's robe, to be their chorister and priest. In my sixth year I was attacked with lung-fever, which again brought me to death's door."

He was fitted for college chiefly by Rev. Daniel Kimball of Needham, and entered with his class in 1833. Rev. John Weiss was his first room-mate, and has told me that Richardson showed, within the very first week of his college career, that peculiar nervous excitability which never entirely left him, and which at that early period sometimes caused serious anxiety among his friends. "Mental labor would just a little unsettle his delicate temperament"; and this was combined with internal disorders, of which nobody could ever tell — either then or years afterward — how much was real or how much imaginary. These traits of constitution also made his college life less happy than his childhood; and his distaste to all regular study made him no favorite with the Faculty, though his aims were always high and his morals unstained. He had much facility as a writer and speaker, was a contributor to "Harvardiana," and always claimed to have written in that magazine the first American review of Carlyle.

His long and rambling autobiography in the Class Book closes with this expression of his purposes at graduation: "I shall most probably occupy myself in some literary pursuit in the West for six or seven years to come, and then, unless Heaven shall have given me some other pursuit, I shall return to Cambridge and study for the sacred office." He graduated with his Class in 1837; and a letter which he wrote to the Class Secretary, dated Haverhill, Massachusetts, November 4, 1847, bridges over the intervening years of his life: —

"Prior to the prosecution of my present profession I was from October, 1837, to December, 1838, Principal of the Academy at Milford, New Hampshire. The first young man whom I fitted for college is the Rev. L. Jarvis Livermore, now settled in East Boston. The famous Hutchinson singers were there my pupils. From December, 1838, to June, 1842, I was located in Rhode Island, being Principal of Kent Academy for the first year, and afterward of the Rhode Island Central School in East Greenwich, Rhode Island, where I had youth from all parts of the country under my care, receiving some fifteen into my family.

"To the question, 'What is your profession?' I reply, a public teacher, or preacher of theology and religion or righteousness, and also, in connection with it, that of minister, or servant in the great cause of human salvation from ignorance, malice, sin, disease, and suffering. To study this profession I stayed three years at Divinity College, Cambridge. I also was much with Dr. Lamson, editor of the Christian Examiner. But I really studied it as little at the college as anywhere. Nature and man were my books, the inward spirit my teacher. I left Divinity College in the summer of 1845; was soon settled in Central Connecticut, in the town of Southington, against my wishes, but from motives of benevolence and missionary duty. I was ordained in June, 1846. Herewith I transmit you an order of exercises. This ordination was the first occasion on which several hundred Unitarians ever sat down at dinner together in *Connecticut.* Dr. Parkman, of Boston, was president of the day. Dr. Dewey exchanged with me the Sunday before, and spent a week with me. At the collation, after the ordination services, delightful speeches were made by Messrs. Parkman, Dewey, Gray, Harrington, Hodges, Nightingale, Farley, Hale, Snow, &c., &c.

"On the 1st of September, 1847, for the sake of being near my father, and having some exchanges, which for two years I had been without, I settled in Haverhill, Massachusetts, though I did not get my dismission from Southington until September 19th, on account of the unwillingness of my people to let me go. When I left Southington my society had increased so as to more than fill their church, it having doubled in a year. I also left bodies of Liberal Christians in the neighboring towns of Berlin, Cheshire, Meriden, &c., — the Unitarian congregation of Berlin being as large as that of Southington.

"On the 26th of September, 1847, I preached my farewell sermon in Southington, comprising my views of the nature and services of theology, and my views of Christian religion, salvation by Christ. They are just being published by Crosby and Nichols, 111 Washington Street; and as the philosophy they contain is perhaps peculiar, and I think peculiarly important and worthy of attention and consideration at the present theological and religious crisis, I have a great desire that those of the class who take an interest in such discussions, and especially who favor the spiritual-rationalistic school, should peruse them.

"I am now residing at Haverhill, where, again, I was settled contrary to my inclination and sense of worldly interest, but from motives of Christian philanthropy and duty."

At this period James Richardson was a very noticeable person, and in fact seemed almost unique in style and temperament. Conspicuous rather than commanding in his aspect, he had a peculiarly formed head, with a forehead rather narrow and very prominent, thin, soft brown hair, pale blue eyes, and very mobile features. Incongruities seemed to meet in him, and he himself seemed to enjoy them, and liked to hear them mentioned. He was tall, erect, and well built, — yet his health was delicate, he had little physical strength, and seemed to move by his nerves rather than by his muscles. His face had always a youthful look, despite his increasing baldness. His voice, in speaking, was rather jarring and metallic, — I always fancied it might resemble Shelley's, — yet in singing it was melodious and beautiful. His verbal utterance was hurried and somewhat confused, yet his style of composition was rather elaborate, and his handwriting unusually clear and regular. In his manners an uneasy self-consciousness was singularly mingled with real power. And every peculiarity seemed to open the way to some other peculiarity, so that the very groundwork of his nature seemed bizarre and fantastic, while all its main tendencies were essentially noble.

He wrote verses easily and smoothly, had a good deal of musical taste, and a faculty for floriculture that seemed akin to genius. He was too vivacious and sociable to be a student; but his memory was well stored and ready for action, though rather loose and inaccurate. He hated argument, and always rather preferred the deferential society of men younger than himself, or his inferiors in culture. To such he was often very dazzling; for with great apparent mental activity and unbounded fluency he combined a real kindness of heart and desire to do everything for everybody, limited only by a decided love of change. He was easy of address, — perhaps too easy, — and had a horror of being thought dignified, of which, however, there was small danger. Of course, he was essentially a reformer. Moral courage cost him no effort, for he liked to be conspicuous and startling; and his free exercise of this virtue, together with his own taste for variety, kept him constantly in motion among the parishes, so that some one christened him "the flying prophet." As a preacher he was eloquent, rather than satisfactory, and was often the object of great enthusiasm among his congregations, especially during the first weeks of his stay. He was settled for periods varying in length, at

Haverhill, Kingston, and Groveland, Massachusetts, — at Southington and East Brooklyn, Connecticut, — and at Rochester, New York.

Most of the peculiarities which have been described were so very obvious that, however wide might be the discrepancies of judgment among comparative strangers, there could not be much variation in the estimates made of James Richardson by those who knew him well. I cannot refrain from matching my own sketch of him by some extracts from an admirable analysis of his character from the skilful pen of Octavius Frothingham, who was also a friend of many years' standing. The first sentence, especially, conveys so felicitous a statement, that it might almost take the place of all which I have said.

"I have just an impression of him as a wreath of fire-mist which seemed every moment to be on the point of becoming a star, but which never did, though it showed signs of solidity here and there, in spots of special effulgence. I remember him as all diffusiveness, loving everybody he knew, and wishing it believed that he loved everybody he did not know, and knew everybody that his friends loved. Was there any end to his cousins and intimates? Was there any end to his affectionateness, his obligingness, his desire to be of service to his fellow-men? His mental apprehension was so rapid, that reflection with him had no chance. He was hospitable to ideas, and entertained so many strangers that he had no bed to sleep on and no stool that he could call his own. Each guest monopolized him in turn. But through all his mutations of mind his spirit remained the same, always bright and buoyant and hopeful, always believing, always anticipating better things, always charitable and kind. If Richardson could have contained himself, he would, I think, have been a man of mark. He was a powerful stimulator, but his stimulus soon spent itself; and when those he had stirred looked for results, they not only did not find any, but they did not find him."

Such was James Richardson at the age of forty-five. He had gradually retired, however, from the active duties of his profession, and had devoted himself more and more to his favorite pursuit of horticulture, on a farm, which he had long owned, in Southington, Connecticut. He had also been married for a few years (since September 18, 1856), to Henrietta Harris, of Brooklyn, New York, but they had no children. The second year of the war had arrived, when, quite to the surprise of his friends, on the 2d of August, 1862, he enlisted as a private in the Twentieth Connecticut Infantry, Colonel Ross.

The regiment was encamped for about three weeks at New Haven, where he was detailed as clerk to his captain, sharing his tent. To this duty, after the regiment had reached Virginia, was added that of attendance in regimental hospital. He wrote after some months' absence: —

"I never go on drill or review or parade with the rest. It is understood that I have different and separate duties, — the captain's and company's business generally, and the care of the wounded and sick, so I have to submit and give up 'sojering.' I should like to have learned military tactics, drill, discipline, and the use of arms; but I resign myself to what seems a higher duty."

His remarkable combination of faculties, large and small, came rapidly into play. Among his domestic aptitudes, for instance, was a decided culinary talent, and so he superintended the cook-tent. He had picked up a good deal of medical knowledge, and so could be, in case of need, hospital steward or assistant surgeon. Rev. William Henry Channing, who saw him amidst these duties, thus defines his other functions, so far as they were definable: —

"In the absence of a chaplain, he became the sympathizing friend, the comforter and teacher; writing letters, receiving last messages of affection, transmitting moneys, and gradually fulfilling the varied functions of confidant, guardian, father, confessor, peacemaker, common friend. Then his fine social gifts of genial sympathy, cheerful good spirits, entertaining gossip, exhaustless anecdote, and love of music came in play to make his tent the centre and focus of brotherly kindness and good fellowship. And finally, when, at the time of a grand movement of the army, it became necessary to transfer the sick from the camps to hospitals in Washington, he was put in charge of these scores or hundreds of helpless men, and with unflagging energy discharged this duty till all were comfortably distributed and cared for or sent home."

It is an indirect illustration of the laborious life which Richardson must have led, that he, who had always before been a rather voluminous writer, now scarcely wrote letters or diary. "I have so much to do that I have no time," was all he could usually say. Again he wrote: —

"I shall try to get time soon to copy my journal; but it is hard to keep it up, as I literally have not a moment, between the wants of officers and men, to call my own. If I could know what my work for the day was to be, I could get some time for myself; but every day there are some new reports or records to make. Then all our sick boys come to me for help and comfort. As I am writing, two boys, one with a sprained foot and one with an ulcerated sore throat, are waiting for me."

Again he wrote, more despondingly: —

"Nothing, however, troubles me much that concerns myself. But for my country, at times, I almost despair. How terrible this nightmare of a war, that never seems to advance or accomplish anything! I sometimes feel that the day of grace has passed, that our repentance of our sin is too late, and that our nation is doomed. This defeat of Burnside, and butchery of the boys, the sufferings of the unpaid soldiers, without tents, poor rations, a single blanket each, with no bed but the hard, damp ground, — it is these things that kill me."

In February, 1863, he was detailed by Colonel Ross, his regimental commander, to report for duty to the "Sanitary Commission" at Washington. He was to serve in the "Special Relief" Department, planned and directed by his old friend, Rev. Frederick N. Knapp, whose name should be forever remembered in history as one of the "more than conquerors" in that great work of peace. This was a post entirely to his mind, and in this he labored until he died. "I have a great satisfaction," he says, "in having a place of usefulness, where I am conscious of doing great service to the soldiers, and where continually a large field is opening before me."

But the strain upon him proved very great. He wrote, for instance, after the battle of Chancellorsville: —

"I am worn down with the general grief and horror that has fallen upon us like a pall, — this slaughter of my regiment, of the boys in my own company, some of whom were just here; and then to go in the hospitals and see my own boys lying mutilated, maimed, and dying! O my God, all this is too horrible!"

Later in the summer he wrote: —

"The mental and physical labor of my work here is so great that I cannot bear an ounce more burden of anxiety and care, nor spare another minute from the continually narrowing time allotted to sleep."

He died of fever at Washington, November 10, 1863. But the rest can best be told in the eloquent words of William Henry Channing, who knew Richardson intimately at this period, and whose substitute the latter was, for a time, as chaplain of the Stanton Hospital at Washington. The narrative, from which the following is an extract, was written to be read at a meeting of the Class of 1837.

"'Only give me work enough to fill up eighteen hours of every day,' said he, as he entered on his new office, 'and I shall be satisfied.' And all but literally did he fulfil the ideal. Of all persons I have met with, during the trials of this civil war, I calmly think that James Richardson was the most indefatigable. Up at dawn, and off through storms on long walks to camps or hospitals, he was all day engaged in patient explorations of difficult and entangled cases; following up every clew through the mazes of different departments, and sitting up till after midnight in completing his records and registers, and finishing his correspondence. He never seemed to feel fatigue, or the want of food or sleep. And instead of being burdened by these accumulated toils, he grew light-hearted, buoyant, bright, and happy, according to the measure of his disinterested services. And in addition to these official duties in the Special Relief Department, Richardson found other spheres for activity, in erecting, arranging, and superintending 'Soldiers' Rests' and 'Temporary Homes,' for the sick and wounded, on their first arrival from the front, or in their transient residence in Washington on their way to their homes, when discharged or furloughed. In these 'homes' he was father, brother, friend to hundreds and thousands, distributing food, refreshing drinks, clothing, money, or whatever might be needed, with a good sense, overflowing kindness, and hearty cheerfulness, which were beautiful to witness. Finally, to all these works he voluntarily superadded the function of hospital chaplain, during the absence from his post of a friend. And thus engaged, through the heats of last summer, month in, month out, without one day's rest or intermission, did our humane and heroic brother labor on, with resistless energy, till he fell, fainting and fever-struck, in the midst of the wide harvest-field of charity, waiting for the husbandman to garner.

"A few days before he was called 'to come up higher,' he said to a fellow-laborer: 'I almost wish I was up yonder, to help our poor boys who are putting off mortality and seeking a soldier's rest in heaven. I should so rejoice to welcome them there.' The wish was very characteristic, — expressive at once of his glowing faith in the nearness of the spirit-world to earth, and the closeness of angelic ministries to man, and also of his generous disinterestedness. The prayer was heard, and he was promoted to higher services. He had fought a good fight, and won a crown, as a hero of humanity.

"Personally I never knew our friend till I met him in Washington; but I had often heard of him as extravagant in enthusiasm, and erratic through divergent tendencies. Like many richly endowed men, James Richardson had probably never found his true sphere till the scenes of suffering and sacrifice called his varied powers into action, and concentrated their influence into one glowing focus of good-will for the soldiers of freedom. Here was a bond of unity that gave harmony to otherwise discordant tastes. He could here be spiritualist and physiologist, architect and musician, good neighbor and preacher, reformer and man of business, all at once. The result was charming, in a rare blending of almost feminine sweetness with courageous energy, of poetic ardor with practical skill, of patient fidelity in minutest detail with a loving-kindness wide as the horizon, and hope high as the heavens. Moving swiftly and noiselessly to and fro, with his soft yet luminous blue eyes seeing all, penetrating all around him at a glance, — courteous and graceful in manner, while dauntless in sincerity, in speech and deed, — he suggested the thought of one ready to be translated from the struggles of earth to the blessed fellowship of guardian angels."

The manner of his departure seemed in harmony, not alone with the self-devotion of his life, but with the peculiar nervous quality which had always marked it. His wife, who was with him in Washington for some months before his death, says that, on November 3d, he was seized with a chill in dressing, but went out and attended to his duties as usual. In the evening he had another chill, followed by violent pains in the chest, which proved to be pneumonia. For several days he suffered extremely, but was afterwards more free from pain, though very weak. His mind was entirely occupied with his duties; and, in defiance of the advice of physicians and friends, he gave daily directions, and had reports brought to him. His nights were very restless; he was constantly talking in his sleep, and always on the one subject of his work, reiterating directions for the kind treatment of the soldiers. He had at that time the supervision of one of the Sanitary Commission "lodges" at Alexandria, Virginia, and of another at the Alexandria Railway Station in Washington, and had been quite annoyed by the difficulty of inducing the employees to treat the soldiers with proper consideration. This trouble seemed ever present with him; and while giving, in his dreams, directions for feeding the men, he would break out with the exclamation, "You *must* speak kindly to them."

On the morning of November 7th he thought himself better, and planned new work; in the afternoon he found himself weaker again, and said, that night, that he should never get well. A consultation of physicians was held, who thought that there was no cause for serious apprehension, if he would only give up all thoughts of labor, which he promised to do. He adhered to his original conviction, however, and made all his final arrangements. On the morning of November 10th he was seized with a violent chill, and after it had passed sank into a stupor, and passed away in such quietness that it could scarcely be known when his breathing ceased. It seemed as if his delicate organization, taxed to the utmost, had at last stopped its vital motion without struggle, — in such a death as he would have always predicted for himself, and such a death as he would have wished to die.

1841.

CHARLES FRANCIS SIMMONS.

First Lieutenant and Adjutant 14th Mass. Vols. (Infantry), July 15, 1861; discharged, on resignation, January 24, 1862; lost at sea, February, 1862, on a voyage to Cuba, undertaken on account of a fatal disease of the lungs contracted in the service.

AT the Freshman examination of Harvard University, in 1837, I will remember to have observed, among my future classmates, a tall, erect young man, of demure aspect and rather sedate motions, with blue eyes and closely curling fair hair, who was pointed out by some one as Charles Simmons, with the prediction that he would be our first scholar. He came with an intellectual prestige, based less upon his own abilities than upon those of his two elder brothers, both of whom had been accounted remarkable for gifts and culture. Such a reputation is often rather discouraging to a younger brother, if it demands from him a career in any degree alien to his temperament. Perhaps it was so with Simmons. He certainly seemed rather to shrink from the path of college ambition than to pursue it; and his academical career, though respectable, was never brilliant.

He was the youngest son of William and Lucia (Hammatt) Simmons, and was born January 27, 1821. His mother was a native of Plymouth, Massachusetts; his father was also born in Plymouth County, and was for many years one of the Justices of the Police Court in Boston. Charles was fitted for college partly at the Boston Latin School, and partly by his brother, Rev. George Frederick Simmons.

In college I had never much personal acquaintance with him, but vividly remember the implied contrast of his grave manners and fastidious air with the witty sayings and mirthful feats attributed to him by his few intimates. This partial antagonism had indeed a peculiar zest for the whole class, when exhibited in his public declamations, which were rather noted among us; since he usually selected some serio-comic passage, which was recited with the gravest face and the most irresistible humor.

He was shy, sensitive, proud, and reticent. But he was exceedingly faithful to his friends and to his avowed principles, manifesting in this way a sort of chivalrous spirit, which indeed brought upon him his only serious college censure. In some undergraduate disaffection, in our Senior year, he stepped forward to take a conspicuous position, from which the other leaders shrank, and he was deprived of his degree in consequence. It was bestowed upon him fourteen years after, on the earnest petition of his classmates.

He afterwards studied law with David A. Simmons, Esq., a relative, and was admitted to the Suffolk bar. For the rest of his life he had an office in Boston, with a moderate chamber practice. But apparently the same qualities which had impaired his collegiate success followed him into professional life also. Over-sensitiveness, ill health, and perhaps some want of resolute purpose, always kept him back, while other men more fortunately constituted won an easy success.

He remained unmarried, and rather shunned general society as well as public affairs. Yet he had excellent judgment in practical matters, and held decided views on the questions of the day; having become, for instance, strongly anti-slavery in his convictions. But he seemed by temperament a scholar and a critic rather than a man of affairs. He was especially a student of the natural sciences; had much knowledge of music, and a rare taste in all matters of art. His love of nature grew with his years; and his chief pleasures, beyond books and music, were found in country life, among "God's fresh creations," as he himself said. Never demonstrative in manner, he became less so as he grew older, and to strangers seemed cold and uninterested. He was reserved even with his intimates; and it was, as I am assured, a matter of surprise to his nearest friends when they heard of his enlistment, through his own letters from Fort Warren.

The attack on our troops in Baltimore had, indeed, seemed

to excite him very much. He had described hearing the departure of the regiments from Boston, in the middle of the night, two days after; was very much impressed by it, and he said then that, if he had not from boyhood "despised soldiering," — and so did not know the use of a gun, — he should have gone off with some of the three-months men. So he joined two different classes in Boston, for the purpose of drilling, and said that when he knew enough he should go. But he went at last very suddenly, in July, without having time to arrange his business affairs; for Colonel William B. Greene, who had been his friend for several years, came home from Paris to take part in the war, and, finding this recruit ready, made him his Adjutant at once in the Fourteenth Massachusetts.

His letters describe his interview with Colonel Greene, and his enlistment.

FORT WARREN, July 26, 1861.

"Then the first day I saw him, — the day he landed, — I told him I would go into the service myself, under him. Two days after he sent to me to know if I 'was serious' in what I had said. And the result was that he took me, green as I was; and says, after four weeks' trial, that he does not repent of his choice, and that he thought he could make a soldier of me then, and is sure of it now. So I am entirely satisfied. And if I should come to grief, be assured it will be with a light conscience; for I have no one dependent upon me, and have not been troubled with any conflict of duties."

In the same letter he thus speaks of the soldiers: —

"'Our regiment,' the Fourteenth Massachusetts, or 'Essex,' has as good material as ever marched out of the old Commonwealth. All from Essex County. Stalwart, sober men, all of them. Whether we succeed in drilling them to form squares, direct and oblique, or not, during the short ten days we have left, I will warrant every company of them to make face against cavalry, even in line, before turning their backs and taking to the woods. If they allow themselves to be 'cut up,' without killing man for man, call me no prophet."

The change in his mode of life seemed to transform his whole nature. This shy, contemplative, lonely, middle-aged man, for whose fastidious nature the daily intercourse of Court Street had been far too rough and harassing, entered with a sort of enthusiastic delight upon the duties of a regimental adjutant, — perhaps the most wearing and vexatious functions which the army has to offer, and such as seem to demand all the energy of youth and all the equanimity of health.

His first letters from camp were very ardent. The details of camp life, the noise and routine of military affairs, which before had appeared either absurd or tedious, now excited and interested him very much. The desire, as he expressed it, "to strike a blow for the old flag we were all born under," seemed to make him forget all annoyances; and he worked there, and through his whole military life, as he perhaps had never worked before. And though it ended in disappointment, both for the regiment and for himself, yet his duty was done with his accustomed thoroughness, as his letters show.

"FORT ALBANY, VA., August 19, 1861.

"Here we are at last, within four miles of the Rebels. We received sudden orders yesterday morning, at our camp at Meridian Hill, to strike our camp, and march with our whole baggage and equipage across the famous Long Bridge to this height by three o'clock, which was morally impossible; but we got here by five o'clock, with a mile of regimental wagons and ambulances bringing up the rear of our long line of men.

"The regiment really made a fine appearance going through Washington, and did honor to old Essex.

"We have been half drowned with rain ever since leaving home; and this last experience of last night makes the climax of everything disgusting you can conceive of, to those brought up as white men and Christians. The mud is so loathsome and universal, that the men are 'down' at last, and look sober to-day. These Essex men are splendid fellows for soldiers, — tough, cheerful, and persevering. They have seen nothing but the roughest side of soldiers' life ever since coming South, and yet the regiment is in a state of perfect subordination and good feeling. In striking our camp yesterday, all our tents but one fell at the tap of the drum, — pretty well for raw troops. I have to detail a strong guard every day to protect the mansion (in our immediate neighborhood) of a malignant Secessionist, which would be burnt in five minutes after removal of the guard, — not a specially agreeable interposition to a man of my ultraism."

"FORT ALBANY, September 14.

"This stationary life in camp, without any security that we shall be here to-morrow, and without any movement or incident, is the pure prose of war. We have all the solid discomforts which can be combined in camp life. The most sanguinary fighting would be a welcome change, — I had almost said another Bull Run, which was rather more disgraceful than bloody, but still exciting. The Colonel tries to reconcile me with our present inaction, or rather want of action, — for we have work enough, — by assuring me that our previous hardships are 'nothing' to those we shall have to face in the field. But I have no faith in it. I believe that no possibility of camp life in the field can take us by surprise. In fact, I suspect it is a general aspiration in the regiment, not confined to 'field and staff,' to take our chance of some hard knocks from the Rebels, rather than die of mildew in these wretched fens near the Potomac."

"FORT ALBANY, October 3.

"Your pleasant picture of placid, rural Concord takes me miles away from this war-blasted scene, and brings to my mind the murmuring pines and elms of the Avenue and North Branch, and the lowing of cattle and song of birds which usher in a Concord nightfall. Here no bird is heard, but a few desolate cat-owls in the night; all the rest of the feathered tribe have been frightened off by the laying bare to the glare of the sun their ancient shady retreats, where the woods were all felled, or by the firing of artillery and the rattle of drums. No ox or cow can live anywhere this side the Potomac, in presence of the interminable camps of the 'grand army.' On the Maryland side of the river there are many vistas of thick, green foliage in the dim distance; but all on this side is devoted to Mars or Pluto, and is appropriated to the one purpose of furnishing a great battle-field on which two hundred thousand men can decide with the sword the issues of this war. All smooth and level places have been scarred and dug in every direction with earthworks and defences, or have been trampled bare of every vestige of vegetation by the marching and manœuvring of regiments and batteries. Every hill-top has been stripped and cleared, and crowned with the inevitable fort; and every road has been bared of its sheltering trees, and even stripped of its fences and hedges, to remove every cover for the enemy. The whole country has a grim, ravaged look, as far as you can see."

The regiment had very hard service at first, and then was converted into heavy artillery, and kept at Fort Albany, with always a hope of being ordered into active service. The climate was formidable, in respect to fever and ague, and at one time they had a hundred and twenty men on the sick-list from this one cause. Simmons was also ill for a time with this disease, early in September, and perhaps never fully recovered from its effects. The change of armament and service necessarily threw very hard work upon the Adjutant, because of the great amount of writing required; and then, before having any opportunity to take part in active service, he was taken ill again, and felt that he could never do anything more. It was a bitter disappointment. Apparently he had never dreaded the thought of death, — certainly not of being killed in battle, — but to be a permanent invalid was an appalling prospect. After his return he said, indeed, that, had his position been one where an invalid could have been of any service, he would gladly have remained and have died in his place.

After a severe exposure, one October night, he was attacked with violent congestion of the lungs, followed by bleeding; but he tried for some time to convince himself that he was gaining, and would not apply for leave of absence, being at last decisively ordered away by the surgeons. The following letters tell the story: —

"FORT ALBANY, October 22, 1861.

"I am sick to-day. Have had to detail a lieutenant to perform my out-door duties. Had to ride to the other end of Long Bridge the other day, in a pouring rain, without cape or leggins. Have been out for a week together, since I was in camp, without damage, but this time am quite knocked up by it. Rode the same morning out to the Rebel lines near Fairfax Court-House; and perhaps that was the reason I took cold, being tired. You say, perhaps we shall not be here. I hope we shall not. It will be heart-breaking if we are. There is a great stir in our camp to-night. I feel just sick enough to care nothing about it; but if a kind Providence *should* inspire General McClellan to order us forward, with or without our guns, I should be very glad to go, sick or well."

"FORT ALBANY, (*toujours*,) October 31, 1861.

"I have checked my hemorrhage, in spite of constant horseback exercise. We are having fine, clear, wholesome weather, (almost for the first time,) and I keep out of doors and on my horse all the time. I have no doubt of receiving to-day General McClellan's permission to go off for thirty or sixty days to recruit, and expect to come back *well*, at least hope to. I am sorry to have to say that the Fourteenth Massachusetts is probably destined to hold these fortifications during the winter. So we must abandon all claim to occupy a prominent place in the attention or interest of the public, — and even of friends at home, — who are mainly interested in the *progress* of the great drama, and the *actors* in it. It was a great disappointment to most of the officers in the regiment when we found that *this* was the meaning of our being set to drilling at siege guns. But the disappointment would have been much more cruel to me, individually, if I had continued well. Now, I care very little about it. The annoyance of it is very trifling compared with that of falling sick."

He obtained leave for sixty days' absence at first; and after a short journey to one or two places, he decided to accept the invitation of a classmate and friend, and visit him in Minnesota. For a little while he seemed better, but it did not last long, as these letters show: —

"——, MINNESOTA, December 12, 1861.

"My visit to these distant regions is not for pleasure, but for life, as the air of this high plain was suggested to me by the doctors as affording the best chance — a rather slender one — of making me well again. I have had no further hemorrhage since I came here, but am harassed with a cough, which at the East I would expect to finish me in a very few months. I shall be driven to resign my commission in the army, I suppose, during this month. It is, of course, a great disappointment to me; and if I die this way, I shall be greatly chagrined that I had not been favored with a more soldierly death in Virginia, like poor William Putnam, and so many others in the Fifteenth and Twentieth, at Ball's Bluff."

"——, MINNESOTA, January 11, 1862.

"I find the air dry and bracing, but the cold and high winds make all out-of-doors exercise next to impossible, and I don't find myself bettered at all, in respect of this 'cough'; consequently I leave here, on Tuesday next, for the East. Mean to stop a few days in Detroit, and so come to Boston in about ten days, where I expect to embark in the first clean merchantman, with cheap rates of passage, either for Cuba or the Mediterranean. I should prefer the Mediterranean voyage, on general grounds, to one to Cuba or the Azores, for the reason that I do not go out with the idea of being cured at all, but feeling utterly indisposed for any kind of work, and not expecting a very long life, I feel an insuperable longing to enjoy myself for a few months. Emerson says, 'Give me health and a day, and I will make the pomp and luxury of emperors and kings ridiculous.' For 'health,' alas! I have not much to hope, and so trust it is not an indispensable ingredient. And I cling to the faith that I can enjoy a great many pleasant days yet, in rambling over the hills which look out on the blue Mediterranean, or walking the beaches by Nice, or Leghorn, or Genoa, and hearing the familiar murmur of the great waters so many leagues from Saco."

He at last offered his resignation, which was accepted, to date from January 24, 1862. It was the heaviest disappointment he had ever met, and at first it seemed more than he could bear with equanimity; but when it became certain that he was fatally diseased, he grew more cheerful and more like himself, as if feeling that it would have been useless for him to remain in the service. He never had seemed more thoughtful for others, more patient himself, than during these last days.

He finally sailed, on February 25th, for St. Jago de Cuba. All who saw him felt that they were never to see him again, although they anticipated no such sudden calamity as that which occurred. The vessel sailed with a fine breeze, but was never heard of again. The next day there were very high winds, and it was supposed that she had been struck by some gale, and had sunk at once, for no trace of her was ever found. A vessel which sailed a few days later was nearly wrecked near the Gulf Stream, and it was thought that this disaster might have proceeded from one end of the gale which had sunk the other vessel.

It is the impression of some of his most intimate friends, that, if he could have chosen, he would not have regretted his sudden departure in such a way; for he could feel that he was dying with the well and strong, and not in his character of invalid, which, as he himself said, he "particularly detested."

For the last month that he had remained in Massachusetts, while growing weaker all the time, he had retained all his interest in his regiment. He expressed peculiar pleasure in recalling his intercourse with the men; saying that he felt sure he had been useful to many of them, and that only the pleasantest relation had existed between them and him. Great as was his disappointment, he certainly never regretted his participation in the war. He said once that it was a great satisfaction to him to think that if he had stayed at home he should have been better off in money affairs, for his business had increased since he went; so that it was proved to himself that he went from patriotic motives. He also liked the thought that, had he stayed at home, he probably would not have been thus mortally diseased; for his lungs had been pronounced perfectly sound by the physicians of a Life Insurance Company before he entered the service. He could feel that it was a vigorous life and a prosperous fortune of which he had made the sacrifice. There was something noble, not selfish, in the feeling that led him thus to dwell, in what he knew to be the closing period of his life, on the offering thus given to his country, — to rejoice that he had been permitted to give it, and that he had possessed so much to give.

1842.

WILLIAM LOGAN RODMAN.

Major 38th Mass. Vols. (Infantry), August 19, 1862; Lieutenant-Colonel December 4, 1862; killed at Port Hudson, La., May 27, 1863.

THE many Boston and Cambridge boys who met thirty years ago at the boarding-school of that fine old-fashioned Englishman, William Wells, in the near neighborhood of Harvard University, can hardly have forgotten one schoolmate who came among us from New Bedford, in the year 1836. He was a large, heavy, rather unwieldy boy, of great personal strength and rather indolent habit, who possessed, by reason of physical proportions, a kind of brevet seniority among his compeers. Neither genius nor the reverse, neither eminent saint nor prominent sinner, he earned a permanent *sobriquet* from his size, and left behind him chiefly an impression of inertia, of good nature, and of good sense.

But those whose acquaintance with him continued through college life will also remember how that cumbrous frame gradually developed into a very powerful and commanding manhood; that rather heavy face into a handsome and noble aspect; and that rather indolent mind into clearness and vigor, though perhaps never into brilliancy. He became, in due time, and in his own way, a man of society, of culture, and of taste. But he studied no profession, developed no marked ambition. He was satisfied, perhaps too easily, with the competence and the pleasant surroundings to which he was born; and, retiring after graduation to his native city, he passed twenty years so quietly that his name was hardly mentioned beyond it, save among a small inner circle of his early companions, until the war called him forth for duty and for death.

William Logan Rodman was the only son of Benjamin and Susan (Morgan) Rodman, and was born March 7, 1822. He was descended, on the mother's side, from a prominent family in Philadelphia, and on the father's side from a line of worthy ancestors, all members of the Society of Friends, and numbering in their ranks the most influential merchants and shipowners of Nantucket and New Bedford. Joseph Rotch, his great-great-grandfather, William Rotch, his great-grandfather, Samuel Rodman, his grandfather, were all men of uncommon character and ability, who left a permanent impression on the community where they lived. The latter, especially, was a man of remarkable capacity, uprightness, and benevolence, and of physical appearance so striking as to attract attention everywhere. "All Boston," said his friend Josiah Bradlee, of that city, "would turn out to see Samuel Rodman walk down State Street." Something of this personal prestige belonged to his grandson, in middle life, as a mounted officer.

William Rodman spent five years at Friends' Academy in New Bedford, and two years under the care of Mr. William Wells. He entered college with his class in 1838, and graduated in 1842. He soon began mercantile life, being at first chiefly engaged in the oil trade. In 1849, during the California excitement, he sailed for San Francisco in the ship Florida, part of which he owned; but he went "before the mast," and did his full share of the ship's duty. Leaving the vessel at that port, he returned home by way of Calcutta and Europe, having been absent about two years in all. This was his only prolonged absence from home until he entered the army.

During the intermediate period his life was quiet and uneventful. He participated moderataly in business life, and in social and political activities; was never married, lived at home, and enjoyed his books and his gardening, with some admixture of genealogical researches and antiquarian pursuits. As a son and brother he was not merely irreproachable, but carried into those relations a rare tenderness and a loyal, almost romantic reverence. As a citizen he was public-spirited, honorable, and morally stainless. He was president of the local Horticultural Society, a trustee of Friends' Academy, and of the Five Cent Savings Bank; was a member of the Common Council in 1852, and one of the city representatives in the State Legislature in 1862, having been elected as a Conservative Republican. During all this period he kept a diary; and a few extracts from this will show, better than anything else, the manner in which his whole nature was roused and stimulated by the gathering alarm of war. The extracts begin with the day of President Lincoln's first election.

"*November* 7, 1860. — Was up until three o'clock, and came home with the assurance of a Republican victory. I have no fear of secession or revolution. The South will bluster and resolve, but cotton is seventeen and a half cents per pound, and all will be quiet. It is a great revolution, however, in one sense. Political power changes hands, and the most corrupt and degraded administration topples over, not, I hope, to be revived in my day. . . . .

"*November* 10. — The last three days, talking over returns. Today we have accounts of terrible import from Charleston and Savannah. They will have to submit to the will of the majority in the Union, or go to everlasting smash out of it. My own idea is, that, however the South may fume, fret, and bluster, just now, they will be very calm before next March. . . . .

"*November* 13. — Papers still full of Southern secession nonsense. . . . .

"*December* 5. — I cannot feel that this great confederacy is to be destroyed just yet, and I don't like to contemplate the fearful ruin that must overtake the South if they pursue their mad scheme. . . . .

"*December* 10. — Put on my skates this afternoon. Am aching all over. Two hundred and fifteen pounds is a heavy weight to be supported on two one-eighth-inch irons, but I love to mingle in these gay crowds. . . . .

"*December* 17. — Wonder what South Carolina is doing. Skating. . . . .

"*December* 28. — Great stir yesterday, owing to the despatch that Major Anderson had evacuated and destroyed Fort Moultrie. Some of the people talk blood and warfare, but this is easy talking far away from the probable scenes of danger. . . . .

"*January* 25, 1861. — What a short-sighted babydom prevails in Boston. The Mayor fears W. Phillips and the Abolitionists will make a riot, and so closes the Anti-slavery Convention. Boston gentlemen, or rather, Boston snobbery, must stop the mouths of the radicals and fanatics, because, forsooth, the traitors of South Carolina won't like it. — Bah! the fools make one sick! . . . .

"*March* 7.—Anniversary of D. Webster's fatal speech, and of *my birth*. . . . .

"*April* 15.—'T is true Sumter has fallen, and war has commenced. We accept the fact with mortification and anger. A severe accounting must follow. I don't fear the result. Stirring times. Governor Andrew issues orders for an assembling to-morrow of the Massachusetts volunteers, and the Guards are preparing to start in the morning. Two thousand must start for Washington to-morrow. . . . .

April 16.—The Guards went off this morning in good style. Thirty-five muskets,—some dozen more to follow this evening. They were addressed by Clifford, from the City Hall steps, in a beautiful little speech. The crowd was very large, and the scene was solemn. Tears rolled down many a rough face. We escorted them to the boat. We may all have to follow. . . . .

"*May* 24.—I have been occupied in soldiering, having become a high private in Company C, Home and Coast Guard. Drilling takes up my evenings, and all last week I did garrison duty at Fort Phenix. We had, upon the whole, a good time. Ours was the first squad from Company C detailed for service, and we acquired quite a reputation for soldierly bearing. The sneer at 'kid gloves' is wearing out, for we have done more real hard work, drilled more, and behaved better than any other company. Of course the gentleman will tell now, as it always has in the service."

It appears from this diary that he was sent for soon afterwards by Governor Andrew, who offered him the post of quartermaster in any regiment which he might choose. The offer did not satisfy him, as he wished for a position in the line; and so he waited awhile longer. Bull Run did not discourage him. He came home indignant from Boston, on the day the news arrived, and wrote, "I never did see such a set of croakers. . . . . For my own part, much as I regret the result, I see in it good to come."

In September he went to Washington to see about an appointment, but nothing came of it, though he enjoyed the visit very much. He says (October 8th, 1861): "I failed in the object of my visit to Washington, but saw, what every one ought to see, the capital in war time. I have new love for my country and new confidence in our rulers."

In November he was elected to the State Legislature, as a Conservative Republican. There he was an active member of the Committee on Finance, — no easy post in Massachusetts in war time. The session lasted until April 30th, 1862; and his services were thus mentioned, in a letter written after his death, by Honorable A. H. Bullock, then Speaker of the House, and now Governor: "In the session of 1862 I became warmly attached to Colonel Rodman, and our friendship ripened into intimacy. His frank and gallant bearing, as an associate among gentlemen, attracted the appreciation of all. His marked intelligence and honorable purposes commanded the respect of the House."

During the summer following, at a time when recruiting moved heavily in New Bedford, Rodman decided to raise a company for the war, and showed such zeal that he was ultimately commissioned Major of the Thirty-eighth Massachusetts, dating from August 19th, 1862. The regiment left the State on September 24th, and was encamped near Baltimore until November 10th, when it sailed for New Orleans, with General Banks's expedition. During the period of delay, Rodman wrote with his accustomed frankness: "I am green as a leek, but pick up constantly, and manage pretty well." This admission makes it the more interesting to read in his letters the record of steady progress and of final mastery.

"CAMP BELGER, BALTIMORE, MD., September 5, 1862.

"So you see we are not likely to have a mere picnic party out of our military life, but shall probably have our share of hard knocks before I see New Bedford again. I believe I am all ready to take my chance, come when it may. We are very unconcerned. You may have heard me remark upon the strange mental change enlistment makes. Being bound to go where sent, and resolved to do one's best, seems to calm one's excitement; and it is rather an effort than otherwise to read the newspaper, or look at maps. You have had a vast deal more of excitement of the recent battles than we have. . . . .

"*November* 4, 1862. [After orders to move.] — There is a thousand times more chance of making a reputation in one of these expeditionary corps, than if we were swamped in the large mass of regiments in the Army of the Potomac. These outside movements will be like pictures in the one-day-to-be-written history of the war. . . . .

"*December* 4. — How does the old Academy flourish? I hope for the Allens' sake, excellently well. I must resign my secretaryship of the Board. Tell Ned he must be my successor, and he must enter my *military rank* in the records somehow. It will be the first instance of such a record among the Quakers. I won't resign my trusteeship, however. . . . .

"*January* 16, 1863.—Every day this week I have been attending a court-martial, ... and it is a great nuisance; for it takes me from my regiment, and I am losing the invaluable opportunity of making myself a good commander. You can't imagine how it galls me. There is no escape, and it may last a month. . . . .

"*February* 4. — None did so well as the Thirty-eighth; we did not make a single mistake. Were twice complimented by General Emory. First, when we passed in review, he said, 'The Thirty-eighth is doing finely.' This to his staff; and subsequently in the drill, when we were the only regiment which went through an important movement all right, in a tone to be heard all over the field, 'Very well done, that Massachusetts regiment on the left.'

"These are little things, to be sure, but they are gratifying to officers and men. One great thing we have gained, and that is in the gratification experienced by the men, who have their regimental pride stimulated immensely. . . . .

"*February* 9. — We had made up our minds to a lively enterprise with danger in it, but one likely to be successful, and give us a little reputation; and now, after a week tied up to the levee, we are on our way down to Carrolton. . . . .

"*February* 23. — I find plenty to do in camp, and am never so contented as when attending to my duties here.

"As to the absurd twaddle about 'the Union as it was,' I am astonished that men of sense can indulge in such ridiculous nonsense. It is infernal humbug, all of it.

"People may argue and speechify as much as they please, they can't help it. This is a revolution, and must result in a complete reorganization of social systems, and all the old fogies in Christendom can't prevent it. . . . . Lord, how I wish I could put a few hundreds of the stay-at-homes into a regiment, and put them on knapsack drills whenever they opened their mouths to say a word on public affairs. . . . .

"*February* 24. — By the way, I see that Bob Shaw and Norwood Hallowell are to be field officers of the Massachusetts blacks. I suppose they are much laughed at. I can't say I want to have anything to do with black troops, but I respect these young men for the part they have taken. They do it from principle, and are worthy of admiration. The organization of a black army is a grand experiment, which may be productive of splendid results, not only to the negro race, but the country. I saw last night an extract from Higginson's report of his Florida expedition, which is certainly encouraging, and should disarm the sneering sceptic for a while at least. . . . .

"The balls, theatricals, and operas revive pleasant memories, but I don't want yet to join in them; but if the war is ever over, and I live to see the end, I have no doubt I shall enjoy again just such things, for I feel as young as ever. . . . . I never was better in my life. Life in the open air and sleeping in a tent are just suited to my case. I have hardly had an ache or a pain or a symptom of any kind whatever since I entered the service. . . . .

"*March* 9. — We have doubtless a hard fight before us, but the troops are in good order, and high spirits. The stir and movement of the day of final preparation have been exhilarating in the extreme, after the monotony of camp life. . . . . The Thirty-eighth is all ready. I mean to do my duty. I don't feel as if I were to suffer; but, come what may, be assured of my unalterable love for you. . . . .

"*March* 29. — It will be a disappointment to have to give up all idea of taking part in any of the great scenes which we hope will go far towards ending the war, but something may turn up for us, and it is consoling to know that not always those most conspicuous are most useful. I shall be content to play an insignificant part, if the war can be brought to a close. . . . .

"*April* 18. — On road to Opelousas. It was pitch-dark; we rolled ourselves in our blankets and slept in line of battle. . . . . [April 13, date included in the foregoing.] Their artillery sent a shower of shell over our heads, and the zip-zip of the bullets was ever in one's ears; but although some came near, none were hit. I had, like most men, expected to be a little scared; but somehow I was not in the least so, and our boys all made fun of every shot that came very near us. Meanwhile I had hard work to keep the men flat, as they wanted of course to see what was going on; and, moreover, we were in the midst of an abundance of very fine blackberries, to pick which required some wandering. . . . . At two o'clock I was ordered to prepare to advance, come what might, to a point within good musket-shot of the works.

"This time I found that uneasy might be the shoulder that wears a strap, for I should think I had a mighty good chance of being shot; for my passage across the field was greeted with particular attention, that I was willing to excuse for the future. I must have been in full sight, and was the only person mounted on the field. Then the former order was so far modified as to rescind the lying down part of it. Now the order stood, 'Go on, and if you reach the works go into them.' Charging more than three fourths of a mile of earthworks, with four thousand men at least, and eight pieces of artillery, with a line of skirmishers, let me tell you, is not a thing very often done; indeed, I do not think it was ever attempted. It looked like a forlorn hope at the start. My officers appreciated the nature of the attempt, and so did many of my men, — but no one thought of hesitating. I was, at twenty minutes past two, ordered to advance, and at the word 'Forward!' my men went off as if on skirmish drill. It was elegant! First my skirmishers, then my reserves. So handsome was the advance, that Colonel Currie, of the One Hundred and Thirty-third New York, who was in the thickest of the fight, on the other side of the bayou, and his men, gave three cheers. I heard the cheers, and thought it was some success over there. I had found, in my movement during the last quarter of an hour, that I was a spotted man. I was the only person mounted, and every now and then the bullets whistled round me thick, and I thought more of my gallant horse than I did of myself. I don't quite understand it now, but I did not feel afraid of being hit at all. I every now and then stopped to think about it, generally eating a few blackberries in a ditch, while cogitating upon the matter. The fact is, I don't think anybody was afraid, or if any, not more than one officer and a few men. . . . .

"*Tuesday, April* 14. — At the dawn of day the Fifty-third moved into the works and planted 'old glory' on the parapet, just about the time that Weitzel crowned the works on the other side. At seven o'clock we were ordered to go and do likewise, and our now baptized flag was placed on the lunette. . . . . At Franklin all went into a field to bivouac, very tired, but in high spirits. We learned that we have taken twelve hundred prisoners, and that the Diana was blown up by the Rebs themselves, while the Queen of the West was destroyed by the Arizona. We began to think ourselves becoming famous; and the boys forgot their sore feet, and ceased to grumble because they had not eaten meat twice since Saturday. . . . .

"*Friday, April* 17. — General Emory came up with me on the march the other day, and said, 'Colonel, I am glad to see you. How is my old Thirty-eighth to-day? You did elegantly, elegantly.' I thanked him and said, 'General, I am glad you are satisfied. We did what we could; but my regiment, deployed as skirmishers along a line of three fourths of a mile, could not take an equal length of earthworks.' The old fellow shrugged his shoulders, and with his pleasant smile said, in his prettiest way, 'You did all that was expected of you, and more.' . . . . I think we did as well as any regiment in the corps would have done. Not to do so would have been disgraceful to us all, and I would not have my darling mother and loving little sister blush for me. . . . .

"*May* 3. — Dr. Ward and I are the only really tough ones. My knock-about out-door life tells now, and I don't wilt down like these shade-grown men. Perhaps my time will come, but certes I was never better than now. . . . .

"*May* 7. — It is very hard to *blow up* the weary wretches, and make them believe you are very savage, when you are overflowing with sympathy. . . . .

"*May* 8. — With the breaking up of slavery, which I hope will follow this war, possibly these great places may be shorn of their magnificence. I don't wonder the owners deprecate such a fate. I can't, however, sympathize with them. May all these results of the vile system vanish, say I. . . . . I am told that strong signs of Union feeling are found in this vicinity. I doubt all such yarns. The chivalry are not to be trusted. . . . .

"*Tuesday, May* 26, 9 o'clock, A. M. — I have just had a stirring hour, occasioned by the arrival of Colonel Nelson with his native Louisianian (black) infantry, one thousand strong, who halted in our midst awhile, and attracted much attention. I was interested to see how my men would regard such neighbors, and was glad to see there was not much merriment and no contempt, even among the Irishmen. The general impression was that they were a fine lot of men, and will fight. Colonel Nelson and all his officers are convinced they are to distinguish themselves; and Nelson tells me he and his *niggers*, according to the programme, are to make the *assault*, and he has no doubt of his colors being taken into the town first. If they fight well, and Port Hudson falls, the great problem of 'Will the blacks fight?' will be solved forever. It is a question of vast interest. General Paine has just been down to see me, and has given me a fair idea of my position. I am on the extreme right of all."

This was his last letter. The last evening of his life was spent in entertaining these officers. The rest must be told in the words of others.

The two letters which follow are from his cousin, Captain Rodman of the Thirty-eighth Massachusetts, and from Adjutant Loring of the same regiment.

"BEFORE PORT HUDSON, June 7, 1863.

"MY DEAR UNCLE, — I wrote you and Aunt S. a few lines on the 28th ultimo, giving you the particulars of William's death on the 27th. I think it best now to give such a connected account of matters that you may know the whole.

"On the 22d of May we landed at Bayou Sara and marched towards Port Hudson. On the 23d we encamped in an old cornfield about three miles from the fortifications. On the 25th we encamped at a bayou, where we met the Rebel pickets, and had two men killed and one wounded, — none of them my men. On the morning of the 27th we marched to the left, through the woods, into the open space about the works, where the enemy had felled trees to give the batteries range. Then we supported Duryea's regular battery, lying down in the ravine behind the ridge where they were posted, the enemy's works being about six hundred yards distant. Up to about eleven o'clock we had met with but one casualty.

"About eleven, Generals Grover and Paine ordered us to charge the works. The Twelfth Maine was in front of us. We marched forward on what may be called a natural causeway, which ran winding to the fort, having dark ravines on each side of it. We had passed half the distance between our first position and the work, when we heard a cheer and saw the skirmishers, who had deployed in the ravine, struggling up the slope of the works and fighting hand to hand with the Rebels. So we went forward at the double-quick, to meet the next instant a perfect storm of bullets. The order to 'Lie down' was given, and we lay down on the causeway, while our artillery played upon the enemy's works. About twelve o'clock General Paine gave the order for the five right companies to skirmish, the five left to storm the works. A few moments before, I saw William sitting behind a stump a dozen yards in my rear, when a bullet whizzed over me. I heard some one say 'Wounded,' and inquired 'Who?' and was told, Colonel Rodman.

By the time I got to him he was already dead, supported in Lieutenant Howland's arms. He was in the act of rising to transmit to the regiment General Paine's order, when the fatal bullet struck him in the left shoulder, and thence, passing obliquely down through his heart, made its exit at the right side. He only said, 'My God, I am hit,' and then I have no doubt life was extinguished instantaneously.

"We remained in the causeway until six o'clock, in close proximity to his dead body, when, the order to fall back having been given, the men of his old company put their muskets under him and carried him to the hospital, where Dr. N. Ward had all the necessary arrangements made. He was laid in a box, wearing, except the coat, the clothes he wore when slain, — wrapped in a blanket, and the coffin filled and covered with green leaves. Our good Quartermaster Mason endeavored to have him carried to New Orleans, to be sent North from that city, but found this was forbidden at this season by general orders. So he was laid in a beautiful little space near our camping-ground of a few nights previous, and by his side Captain Bailey, of the Fifty-third Massachusetts, and Lieutenant —— of the ——.

"Our Quartermaster and Dr. Thompson were the only officers who attended the funeral; all the others being compelled, by their duty, to be at the front. Lieutenant Mason tells me that his face had its most natural expression, — one of perfect tranquillity and repose.

"At the grave a few remarks were made by the chaplain of the Fifty-third Massachusetts, Mr. Whittemore. . . . .

"Your affectionate nephew,

"THOMAS R. RODMAN."

"HEAD-QUARTERS, DEFENCES OF NEW ORLEANS,
NEW ORLEANS, June 5, 1863.

"DEAR SIR, — I had hoped to obtain some of the details of your son's death in time to send by the last mail, knowing that it would be a comfort, though a sad one, for you to know how and where he fell.

"It is, however, only since the steamer sailed that I have heard anything which I could venture to write as reliable.

"The regiment was lying down in a line of rifle-pits, to protect itself from the fire of sharpshooters.

"A messenger rode up with orders ; and as Colonel Rodman impulsively rose to receive them, he was shot through the heart, dying instantly and without pain.

"The Thirty-eighth is on the north side of Port Hudson, so far (twenty miles) from the landing below, that, during the exciting and difficult hour which followed, it was impossible to remove the body till it was too late to give it anything but the burial which, after all, a soldier should most desire, on or near the battle-field.

"A letter from the Adjutant-General of the division, received this morning, says of Colonel Rodman, 'His own men, and all those who ever knew or saw him, lament him.'

"No one of those who have fallen during the siege thus far stood higher in the estimation of the commanding generals, and over no one have I heard so general and unfeigned regret.

"To the regiment his loss will be irreparable. Its excellent reputation for discipline and morals was due chiefly to him and his just and determined efforts to reward and bring forward merit, no matter where it was to be found. Every man under him knew him to be really just and kind; and every man held him in respect unusual amidst 'democratic volunteers,' and in esteem and affection of which any man might be proud.

"It was my own good fortune to be more immediately associated with him than any other officer in the regiment; and his noble bearing, his scorn of all that was mean or low, his high-minded sense of honor, his genial talent, and his kind heart attached me to him more than I had known till the news came that he was killed; and then I learned how sad a thing it is to say, 'I 've lost a friend.' His noble reputation and the kindly memory he will leave to all those who knew him will be some sad consolation to you in your grief. He fell nobly and in a noble cause. May all these sacrifices be rewarded. May God temper your sorrow to you.

"With deep respect,

"Your obedient servant,

"FRANK W. LORING.

"MR. RODMAN."

Most of those whom this book commemorates were very young men, who had no life-long habits to surmount, no settled pursuits to abandon, and to whom the new duty of military service came as the first grand interest and joy of their existence. Of the maturer men there were many whose lives were already full of active employment, more or less public in its usefulness, so that even their army service hardly implied a wholly new direction to their activities. Here, however, was one whose life had enjoyed almost too much repose, and whose mind almost too much leisure; and whose bonds were the set habits of unmarried life and the warm endearments of parental and sisterly love. From these he must break away; but beyond this effort, all was new life and joy and strength; the career at last open for strong manhood never yet adequately developed; the final outpouring of faculties reserved for this. Whatever might be the sacrifice to others involved in his departure from home and in his death on the battle-field, it is certain that to no one chronicled in this book did the war bring a nobler opening of a new career. His previous habits had given him self-control, uprightness, generous feelings, cultivated tastes, and the warmest affections. War called for all these and more: he gave all it asked for, and died in the giving.

The following testimony may well close the tale.

"HEAD-QUARTERS, DEFENCES OF NEW ORLEANS,
NEW ORLEANS, June 3, 1863.

"SIR, — It is with unfeigned grief that I approach the sanctuary of your household to condole with you upon the occasion of the death of your brave and noble son.

"But I have thought it my duty, not only as commander of the division to which he belonged, but as his personal friend, to say to you, that his blood relations cannot regret his loss more than do his comrades in arms.

"At the time of his death his regiment had passed temporarily from under my command, and I therefore leave the particulars of it to those who were present on the field at the time.

"From the time he took the field in Maryland up to within a day or two of the assault on Port Hudson, where I was not present, through our dreary camp in the marshes near New Orleans, and through our brilliant campaign on the Têche, he commanded his regiment with signal success, and endeared himself to every one, not only by his high military qualities, but by his strict morality and his high nobility and honor. His regiment — Thirty-eighth Massachusetts — was one of the best in the service, and, with him at the head of it, marched with the steadiness of regulars to the attack and capture of Fort Bisland. I wish I could express to you the deep sorrow I feel at his loss.

"I am, with great respect, your obedient servant,

"W. H. EMORY, *Major-General.*"

1843.

ARTHUR BUCKMINSTER FULLER.

Chaplain 16th Mass. Vols. (Infantry), August 1, 1861; discharged, on resignation, December 10, 1862; killed, as volunteer, at Fredericksburg, Va., December 11, 1862.

IN that wonderful fragment of early autobiography which Margaret Fuller Ossoli left behind her, and just before that brilliant passage in which she portrays the respective influence upon her childhood of the Greek and Roman traditions, she speaks lovingly of the household around her in those juvenile years, and of the "younger children" in whom her mother was so much absorbed. One of those younger children was Arthur, at whose funeral, long years after, James Freeman Clarke thus recalled the images of that happy group:—

"I first knew Arthur Buckminster Fuller as a little boy. Being a distant relative, I was in the habit of visiting his father's family while a student at Cambridge. They lived at that time in the old Dana House, on the bend of the road from Boston. In the large, old-fashioned parlor the family sat together in the evening; Mr. Timothy Fuller sitting by one corner of the open fire, with his stand, holding his papers and a lamp, at work preparing for his law duties of the next day, but occasionally taking part in the conversation; usually, as I remember, in moderating what he thought some too enthusiastic statement of his daughter Margaret. She sat talking with her friends as only she could talk, and the younger children studied their lessons or played together; and among them I well remember the bright eyes, and clear, open features of Arthur. Near by sat the mother at her work, serene, gentle, kind, a comfort and joy to all."

Arthur Buckminster Fuller was born in Cambridge, Massachusetts, August 10th, 1822; the son of Timothy and Margaret (Crane) Fuller. His maternal grandfather, Major Peter Crane of Canton, served in the Revolution, and was at one time the chaplain of his regiment. His paternal grandfather, the Reverend Timothy Fuller, represented Princeton in the Massachusetts Convention for the adoption of the Federal Constitution, and voted against that instrument because of the clause providing for the rendition of fugitives from service. He was descended from Thomas Fuller, who emigrated to America in 1638.

Timothy Fuller the younger was one of five brothers, all lawyers. His daughter Margaret has sketched his character with frankness and with vigor. He was often in public life, and was a Representative in Congress from 1817 to 1825, where he was Chairman of the Committee on Naval Affairs, and prominent as a defender of the Seminole Indians and as an opponent of the Missouri Compromise. He resided in Cambridge until 1834, when he removed, with his family, to a farm in Groton, where he died the following year.

The family being thus left fatherless, much of the responsibility of the care and training of the children devolved on the eldest sister. How much they owed to this extraordinary woman is indirectly made manifest in many passages of her "Memoirs" and "Writings,"—the latter having been edited, after her death, by the grateful hands of her brother Arthur. He was fitted for college, amid great obstacles, by his sister, by the teachers of Leicester Academy, and by Mrs. Ripley of Concord, Massachusetts, whose classical school had then a high reputation.

During his college course he aided in his own support by teaching school, was faithful to his duties, and graduated with creditable rank in 1843. On leaving college he instantly entered on the career of activity which he loved; investing what was left of his small patrimony, a few hundred dollars, in the purchase of an academy at Belvidere, Illinois. There he not only taught secular studies, but soon began the work of religious exhortation with a zeal which brooked no delay. A Unitarian of the more evangelical type, he yet obtained the fellowship of Methodists, Baptists, and Presbyterians. With the Methodists especially he sympathized by temperament and habits, and associated much with them during his whole life.

He wrote home about this time : —

"I go every Sabbath about eleven miles, take charge of a Sabbath school at ten, preach at eleven, have an intermission of half an hour at half past twelve, preach again a long sermon, take tea at once, and ride over the chill, bleak prairie, directly home, which I do not reach till late in the evening. On week days, besides the hours of teaching, I lecture and aid in debating-societies, and so forth, so that I can scarcely find time to write even these poor letters."

Two years he spent in labors such as these, and then returned to spend two years of study at the Divinity School of Harvard University. To revert to the pursuits of the student was, however, rather hard for one who had already lived the stirring life of a pioneer preacher ; and his zeal was constantly bursting over the cautious regulations of the Faculty, — he naturally demeaning himself as a full-fledged minister instead of a pupil. Much of his time was given, therefore, to extraneous occupation, though he graduated with his class in 1847.

This partial separation of pursuits, added to some peculiarities of temperament, and a rather marked use of evangelical phrases and methods, formed undoubtedly some slight barrier between Arthur Fuller and many of his companions, both at this time and afterwards. Having been accustomed to express his opinions with the greatest freedom and unction to Western audiences by no means his equals in education, he had not always the necessary tact in dealing with his equals, and hence was apt to elicit as much antagonism as sympathy. If he erred, however, everybody admitted that it was from excess of zeal ; but it is difficult to make such zeal attractive, especially among cultivated intellectualists, and certainly he did not always succeed. His intense earnestness had, or seemed to have, a flavor of self-assertion, and this often led his critics to do him less than justice. The recollection of this peculiarity in him, whatever may have been its source, added interest to his later career in the army ; for it is evident that the grander experiences of life smoothed away some of these roughnesses, and developed in him more comprehensiveness, more tact, and more power of adaptation.

After leaving the Divinity School he preached a few times at Albany, New York, and wrote thence: "I have been attending a course of anti-slavery lectures by Frederick Douglass, the fugitive slave, and have become greatly interested." Then he supplied the pulpit, for three months, of "Father Taylor," the celebrated Methodist sailor-preacher in Boston. He was afterwards settled as minister over the Unitarian Society in Manchester, New Hampshire, then over the New North Church in Boston, and then in Watertown, Massachusetts. In all these positions he worked for years with the zeal of a revivalist; and he also took active part in the usual collateral duties of a New England minister, rendering important services on school committees, and in temperance and anti-slavery reforms. He was also twice chaplain of different branches of the Legislature of Massachusetts.

He was twice married, — to Miss Elizabeth G. Davenport of Mendon; and, after her death, to Miss Emma L. Reeves of Wayland. The latter, with several children, survives him.

He devoted much time at this period to revising and editing, in their final form, the writings of his sister Margaret; interweaving in the work a great deal of new matter from her manuscripts. This work was admirably done, especially when we take into consideration the wide difference in temperament, habits, and aims between the sister and the brother. He thus speaks of this affectionate labor: —

"I have done my best and hardest work on this book. The labor of compiling and superintending such a publication and correcting the proof is greater than I could have conceived possible. It is done; and I thank God for giving me strength to do it. I pray that it may contribute to do justice to her merits. That is all the reward I can expect; and that reward would be so noble, so holy!"

And again: —

"This has been a labor of love, which I have joyed in, and have esteemed a privilege, and not a burden. If I only live to send forth Margaret's works from the press, as they should appear, I shall not have lived wholly in vain."

All the profits of these volumes were sacredly devoted to

repaying certain debts, contracted long before by his sister, at the time when she was the support and protector of the household. These debts were all due to very friendly creditors, yet he wrote joyfully when all was done: "Margaret's debts are all paid, every dollar. That sacred trust to us is now fulfilled."

In the midst of these pursuits came the call to arms, after the attack on Fort Sumter. Watertown, like other villages, had its war meeting, which was addressed by the Unitarian minister among others. A newspaper narrative describes his speech as follows: —

"Rev. Arthur B. Fuller protested against 'any further compromise with slavery. Thus far, and no farther.' He was in favor of the Constitution of these United States. He was in favor of a settlement; but, in the language of Honorable Charles Sumner, 'Nothing is ever settled that is not settled right.' Let us stand right ourselves, and then we can demand right from others. He urged the Republicans to stand by the election of Lincoln and Hamlin. . . . . He was opposed to compromise, — even to the admission of New Mexico, — because it would be in violation of our platform, and at variance with the opinions of such honored statesmen as Webster and Clay, and because it interdicted the spirit of the Gospel."

He at once began to visit the camps for religious exhortation; was soon elected chaplain of the Sixteenth Massachusetts Infantry, and was commissioned as such, August 1, 1861. In his letter of resignation, he thus stated to his parish his motives: —

"The moral and religious welfare of our patriotic soldiery cannot be neglected, save to the demoralization and permanent spiritual injury of those who are perilling their all in our country's cause. The regiment represents Middlesex County on the tented field, the county in which I was born, and which my honored father represented in our national Congress; and one company is from Watertown, where for nearly two years I have been a settled minister, — circumstances which give this call of duty a peculiar claim upon my mind and heart. I am willing to peril life for the welfare of our brave soldiery and in our country's cause. If God requires that sacrifice of me, it shall be offered on the altar of freedom, and in defence of all that is good in American institutions."

A parting festival was held at the pastor's house, and many presents were brought in, — every religious denomination in town being represented in the gifts. A prayer-meeting took place in the Methodist church, the services being conducted by Mr. Fuller in connection with Rev. Mr. Hempstead, minister of that church. An army officer, who was present, spoke of the dangers to which he was about to return; and the two clergymen offered prayers for him. It was noted afterwards as remarkable, that this officer finally came back to his home uninjured, while both the ministers became chaplains, and gave up their lives, within a few days of each other, at Fredericksburg.

Chaplain Fuller left Boston, with his regiment, August 17, 1861. Scarcely were they settled in camp, near Baltimore, when he entered with his wonted zeal upon his new labors. He writes as follows: —

"Our encampment is hardly settled enough yet for definite arrangements to have been fully carried out. After this week, however, the arrangements are as follows: Sunday school at nine, A. M.; attendance to be wholly voluntary. Preaching every Sabbath at five o'clock, P. M., the old hour at Camp Cameron, and the best hour of the day for the purpose. Prayer and conference meeting (when practicable) every day at about six and seven, P. M.; attendance of course voluntary. These services will be fully attended. Even now, every night there are quiet circles for prayer and praise.

"Besides these services, there are Bibles and religious volumes to be distributed to the men, and books for singing God's praise. We find the 'Army Melodies' useful among us, and were not the writer one of the editors of the volume, he would say much of the necessity and usefulness of supplying religious and patriotic music and words to every regiment and every naval vessel, in place of the ribald songs so sadly common in the army and on shipboard. No more refining or religious instrumentality than music can be used."

The position of an army chaplain is no easy one: the majority of clergymen fail in it. In a little world of the most accurate order, where every man's duties and position are absolutely prescribed, the chaplain alone has no definite position and no prescribed duties. In a sphere where everything is concentrated on one sole end, he alone finds himself of no direct use towards that end, and apparently superfluous. In this difficult position, nine men out of ten are almost useless, while the tenth achieves a wide-spread influence. Arthur Fuller seemed to be one of the latter class. The prime qualities required by his new position were moral energy and tact; he had always a superabundance of the one, and he must have developed the other, or he could not have been so successful as he evidently was.

For instance, it is the custom in some regiments for the chaplain to be the caterer for the officers' mess. The first proposition to this effect, in the Sixteenth Massachusetts, was promptly met by a Scripture text, "It is not reason that we should leave the word of God and serve tables." The Colonel was not quite pleased, it is said, with this piece of frankness; yet afterwards, at a complimentary dinner of the officers, when they had vainly implored the Chaplain to take wine with them, the Colonel finally proposed three cheers for the Chaplain, as "a man whom we all honor the more, because in public and private he is uniformly consistent with his principles."

In accordance with these views, the Chaplain was soon at work in resisting the most perilous of army vices. He writes: —

> "We celebrated the close of the year 1861 by forming in the Sixteenth Massachusetts Regiment a Division of the Sons of Temperance. At an early hour the new chapel-tent of the regiment was filled to overflowing with soldiers eager to listen to an exposition of the principles of the organization, and to unite in the movement, if it commended itself to their judgment. Over one hundred officers and soldiers were proposed for initiation. Authority had been received by the chaplain from the Grand Division of Massachusetts to organize this Division, which is to embrace not only soldiers of this regiment, but Massachusetts men connected with other regiments at or near Camp Hamilton, or with the naval vessels lying off the fortress."

He formed also an "Army Christian Association," and a "Soldiers' Teachers' Association," — thus transplanting the church and school-house of New England to the soil of Virginia. Then, by freely setting forth at home the demands of the regiment, he provided a "chapel-tent," — the first seen, probably, in our army. He thus describes its dedication : —

"Yesterday was a noteworthy day with the Sixteenth Massachusetts Regiment, for on it we dedicated our beautiful tabernacle tent. This tent was presented to us by various patriotic and benevolent citizens of Boston, who desire that religious services may not necessarily be suspended during the sultry heat of summer, or during the fall of the rain, so copious in Virginia, and that our evening prayer and temperance meetings may not necessarily be held in the open air. The subscriptions were secured by a most excellent lady, and she receives the grateful acknowledgments of our entire regiment. The day of dedication was also Forefathers' Day (December 22), which was very appropriate for a Massachusetts regiment, having their tabernacle in the wilderness, as did their fathers.

"Both army and navy chaplains participated in the exercises. The chaplains were representatives of nearly every sect, including Roman Catholic; but there was entire harmony, and a sweet blending of devout sentiment and Christian, patriotic utterance. Chaplains from North and South, East and West, were there, and from sea and shore, yet no discordant note was uttered. The tabernacle tent was trimmed with holly and live-oak wreaths and crosses, made by the soldiers with a taste which would have surprised our female friends. The ladies of the Hygeia Hospital, who were present, contributed a beautiful cross of mingled evergreen and flowers. Our regimental band played the Star-spangled Banner admirably, and the regimental choir sang the hymns written for the occasion, in a manner which elicited, as it deserved, much praise. Rev. Mr. Fuller's dedication discourse was founded on the text in Isaiah iv. 6, 'And there shall be a tabernacle, for a shadow in the daytime from the heat, and for a place of refuge, and for a covert from storm and rain.'"

Besides these varied labors in the regiment, Chaplain Fuller was an active newspaper correspondent, — writing letters to the Boston Journal, the Boston Traveller, the New York Tribune, the Christian Inquirer, and other journals. Among these letters was a narrative — perhaps the most graphic ever given — of the famous contest between the Merrimack and the Monitor, and all the exciting events which preceded and followed. These important letters are fully given in the Memoir of Chaplain Fuller, by his brother; but only the most exciting passage of the narrative can be here inserted. The date is March 15, 1862:—

"The morrow came, and with it came the inevitable battle between those strange combatants, the Merrimack and the Monitor. What a lovely Sabbath it was! how peaceful and balmy that Southern spring morning! Smiling Nature whispered only 'peace,' but fierce treason breathed out threatenings and slaughter, and would have war. . . . . At nine o'clock, A. M., the Merrimack, attended by her consorts, the war-steamers Jamestown and Yorktown, and a fleet of little tug-boats, crowded with ladies and gentlemen from Norfolk, who were desirous of seeing the Minnesota captured, and perhaps even Fortress Monroe taken,—certainly all its outlying vessels and the houses in its environs burnt.

"The little Monitor lay concealed in the shadow of the Minnesota. The Merrimack opens the conflict, and her guns shake the sea and air as they breathe out shot and flame. Sewall's Point sends from its mortars shell which burst in the air above the doomed Minnesota. The Minnesota, still aground, replies with a bold but ineffectual broadside. All promises an easy victory to the Merrimack, when lo! the little Monitor steams gently out and offers the monster Merrimack battle. How puny, how contemptible she seemed! nothing but that little round tub appearing above the water, and yet flinging down the gage of defiance to the gigantic Merrimack. It was little David challenging the giant Goliath once again,—the little one, the hope of Israel; the giant, the pride of the heathen Philistines. Truly our hopes were dim, and our hearts almost faint for the moment. The few men on the Monitor are sea and storm worn, and weary enough, and their little craft is an experiment, with only two guns with which to answer the Merrimack's many. Who can doubt the issue? who believe the Monitor can fail to be defeated? And if she is, what is to hinder the victorious and unopposed and unopposable Merrimack from opening the blockade of the coast, or shelling Washington, New York, and Boston, after first devastating our camp and destroying its soldiery? That *was the issue;* such might have been the result, smile now who will. Believe me, there were prayers offered—many and fervent—that Sabbath, along the shore and from the Fortress walls, as our regiment watched the battle; and sailors must have prayed, too, as never before.

"The Merrimack, after a few minutes of astounded silence, opened the contest. She tried to sink her puny foe at once by a broadside, and be no longer delayed from the Minnesota, whose capture she had determined upon. After the smoke of the cannonade had cleared away, we looked fearing, and the crew of the Merrimack looked hoping that the Monitor had sunk to rise no more. But she still lived. There she was, with the white wreaths of smoke crowning her tower, as if a coronet of glory. And valiantly she returned the fire, too; and for five hours such a lively cannonading as was heard, shaking earth and sea, was never heard before. Literally, I believe that never have ships carrying such heavy guns met, till that Sabbath morning. Every manœuvre was exhausted by the enemy. The Yorktown approached to mingle in the fray. One shot was enough to send her quickly back, a lame duck upon the waters, though she, too, is iron-clad. The Merrimack tried to run the Monitor down, and thus sink her; she only got fiercer shots by the opportunity she thus gave her little antagonist. And so it went on till the proud Merrimack, disabled, was glad to retire, and, making signals of distress, was towed away by her sorrowing consorts. David had conquered Goliath with his smooth stones, or wrought-iron balls, from his little sling, or shot-tower. Israel rejoiced in her deliverance, through the power of God, who had sent that little champion of his cause, in our direst extremity, to the battle. Since then the Merrimack has not shown herself; and the enemy confess her disabled, and her commander, Buchanan, — ominous name, — severely wounded, four of her crew killed, and seventeen wounded."

The regiment occupied Norfolk and Portsmouth and Suffolk for a time; then joined the Peninsular army, and had war and suffering in earnest, being attached to Hooker's division. Chaplain Fuller had just obtained a furlough, but refused to avail himself of it. Their first serious skirmish was on June 19, near the scene of the battle of Fair Oaks. When the regiment was ordered out, the Chaplain was lying in his tent, suffering with a severe sick-headache. Hearing one of the soldiers say, in passing near the tent, that he wished he had a sick-headache, the Chaplain at once rose, went to the field, and happening to get under a dangerous cross-fire, behaved with such coolness as to increase very greatly his influence among the men. Indeed, all through that campaign he seems to have shared his lot with the soldiers until his health began to fail. He wrote home from the field: —

"I am enduring much privation in the way of food, clothing, and exposure. But I do not think it manly to write particulars, as you desire; indeed, I endeavor not to think about it. Almost every day, and sometimes twice a day, I go out with the regiment in line of battle. I deem this my duty. For nine days I had no change of raiment, not even a clean shirt or handkerchief, and lived on hard crackers and sour coffee. But God blesses my labors, particularly among the sick and wounded, and I am far enough from repining. Of all places in the world, I am glad I am here now. I find no physical fear to be mine. This is a mere matter of organization, not merit. Meet me on earth, if it may be; in heaven, surely. And know that nothing will make me swerve from my fealty to God, to Christ his Son, to my family, my State, and my Country."

All the following summer he remained at home, very ill; but rejoined his regiment at Alexandria, November 4, 1862. Forbidden by the surgeon from accompanying it to the front, he devoted himself to labors in the hospitals and convalescent camps of that vicinity. He wrote: —

"I work very hard among the sick and dying soldiers. We have five large buildings and several tents crowded with more than five hundred sick men, and only two surgeons in attendance, and my services are greatly needed."

He again tried to rejoin his regiment at Manassas, and failing, was obliged to abandon all hope of field service. He wrote to his family: —

"The President of the United States promises me, through Senator Clark, a commission with full powers as chaplain in a hospital or stationary camp. The Surgeon-General gives the same assurance. But it is necessary that I should resign my present position before assuming the new. I go to the camp at Falmouth to-morrow morning, in order to resign. I do this with much regret."

He was discharged from service, on resignation, December 10, 1862. On the very next day his death occurred, under those extraordinary circumstances which made it unique in the history of the war. At least I know of no other case in this war, or in any, in which a chaplain, the day after his discharge, — still wearing his uniform, and therefore the more exposed, — bearing his discharge on his person, and therefore not liable to exchange in case of capture, — knowing that his family, should he be killed, could legally receive no pension, and therefore having the more to risk, — has volunteered, without a soldier's training, for the most perilous duty of a common soldier, and been killed in doing it.

The Army of the Potomac, under Burnside, was to cross the river at Fredericksburg. It was six o'clock, and though the pontoons were partly laid, yet the fire of the enemy's sharp-shooters was so furious that the work could not be finished. The boats could carry but a hundred at a time. A call was made for volunteers. Chaplain Fuller, who was present, took a rifle and stepped forward as one. He crossed the river safely, but fell at the entrance of the city, pierced by two bullets, and grazed by a third. He was instantly killed.

The best narrative of the incident is that given by Captain Moncena Dunn, Nineteenth Massachusetts Infantry, under whose orders the Chaplain had placed himself: —

"In answer to your inquiries, I would say, that, although I had previously intended, at the suggestion of a mutual friend, to make the acquaintance of Chaplain Fuller, I saw him for the first time in the streets of Fredericksburg, on the 11th December ultimo, at about half past three, P. M., where I was in command of twenty-five men deployed as skirmishers. We came over in the boats, and were in advance of the others who had crossed. Pursuant to orders, we marched up the street leading from the river, till we came to the third street traversing it, parallel with the river, and called Carolina Street, I think. We had been here but a few minutes when Chaplain Fuller accosted me with the usual military salute. He had a musket in his hand; and he said, 'Captain, I must do something for my country. What shall I do?' I replied, that there never was a better time than the present; and he could take his place on my left. I thought he could render valuable aid, because he was perfectly cool and collected. Had he appeared at all excited, I should have rejected his services; for coolness is of the first importance with skirmishers, and one excited man has an unfavorable influence upon the others. I have seldom seen a person on the field so calm and mild in his demeanor, — evidently not acting from impulse or martial rage.

"His position was directly in front of a grocery store. He fell in five minutes after he took it, having fired once or twice. He was killed instantly, and did not move after he fell. I saw the flash of the rifle which did the deed.

"I think the Chaplain fell from the ball which entered the hip. He might not have been aware of the wound from the ball entering his arm, as sometimes soldiers are not conscious of wounds in battle, or he may have been simultaneously hit by another rifle. We were in a very exposed position. Shortly before the Chaplain came up, one of General Burnside's aids accosted me, expressing surprise, and saying, 'What are you doing here, Captain? I replied that I had orders. He said that I must retire, if the Rebels pressed us too hard. In about half and hour I had definite orders to retire, and accordingly fell back, leaving the Chaplain and another man dead, and also a wounded man, who was unwilling to be moved. It is not usual, under such pressing circumstances, to attempt to remove the dead. In about an hour afterward, my regiment advanced in line with the Twentieth Massachusetts. They occupied the place where Chaplain Fuller fell; and they suffered very severely, it being much exposed. The Chaplain's body we found had been robbed, and the wounded man bayoneted by the Rebel Vandals, while the ground was left to them.

"I think, in addition to Chaplain Fuller's desire to aid at a critical juncture in the affairs of his country, by the influence of his example and his personal assistance, he may have been willing also to show that he had not resigned in the face of the enemy from any desire to shrink from danger."

An unusual recognition of the services and the gallant death of Chaplain Fuller took place in Congress, some time afterwards. His death had led to just that result of which he had been warned by an army officer before his death; — his family was left without a pension, as he was not technically in the service. On his widow's petition to Congress, a special law providing her a pension very promptly passed both Houses without opposition. Honorable Charles Sumner presented the petition in the Senate, remarking, that

"From the 1st day of August, 1861, Arthur B. Fuller had been a duly commissioned chaplain in the Sixteenth Massachusetts Regiment of Volunteers, and had followed its flag faithfully, patriotically, religiously, through all the perils of the Peninsula and wherever else it had been borne."

The petition having been referred to the Committee on Pensions, they reported,

"That it appears that Arthur B. Fuller was the chaplain of the Sixteenth Regiment of Massachusetts Volunteers; that his health was much impaired by the hardships and exposures of the Peninsular campaign; that after repeated efforts to renew his labors in the camp of his regiment, which were foiled by his sickness returning upon every such attempt, it was finally determined, by the advice of army surgeons, that his malady was such that he could not bear exposure in the field. He was accordingly honorably discharged, on surgeon's certificate of disability, on the 10th day of December, 1862. On the 11th day of December, on the call for volunteers to cross the Rappahannock at the battle of Fredericksburg, he volunteered, and was killed in the service soon after entering Fredericksburg.

"The committee think that, though Chaplain Fuller was technically out of the service of the United States, still he was really in the service of his country and in the line of duty while bravely leading on the soldiers, and dying on the field of battle. They therefore think the petitioner entitled to the relief for which she prays, and accordingly report a bill."

The body of the slain soldier was sent home to Massachusetts, as soon as the incidents of war permitted. A private funeral took place at the house of his brother, and a public one at the First Church on Chauncey Street, in Boston, on December 24, 1862.

"The church was crowded with the friends of the deceased, who wished some opportunity to express their sense of loss, their respect for his memory, and their estimation of his character and services. Governor Andrew and staff, General Andrews and staff, Chief Justice Bigelow, and other prominent public men, were present. The escort was performed by the Cadets.

"The coffin was placed in front of the pulpit, and was profusely covered with the most exquisite flowers. One by one the wreaths were placed upon the lid by loving hands, as the best expression of the cherished memories of the past. The following inscription was upon the plate: —

"REV. ARTHUR BUCKMINSTER FULLER,
Chaplain of the 16th Regiment of
Massachusetts Volunteers;
Killed at the Battle of Fredericksburg, Va.,
11th December, 1862,
Aged 40 years.
'*I must do something for my country.*'"

These words were his fitting epitaph; and few there are who have so well succeeded in matching a single electric word and deed together. Margaret Fuller Ossoli was an artist in words; she left behind her many a sentence of the rarest depth and beauty, — "lyric glimpses," Emerson called them, — and her glorious life in Italy joins with her tragic death to throw back upon those brilliant phrases the lustre of a corresponding self-devotion. Less gifted in intellect, less devoted to artistic culture, her brother and pupil left behind him this one utterance of self-devotion, putting to it, within that same hour, the seal of death. It may yet make his memory as lasting as her own.

1845.

PETER AUGUSTUS PORTER.

Colonel 129th New York Vols. (afterwards 8th New York Heavy Artillery), August 17, 1862; killed at Cold Harbor, Va., June 3, 1864.

IN how many of the students of Harvard does every favoring element seem to have combined — culture, purity, self-reliance, and courage — to give promise of high and noble achievement. One only boon of Fortune they lacked, — her last and most reluctant gift, — opportunity. At length that opportunity came: it was their death. A good Providence granted them to die, and in their death accorded them the achievement of every possibility life could have bestowed. Of such was Peter Augustus Porter, a graduate of Harvard of the Class of 1845. He died in the service of his country on the 3d of June, 1864, at the battle of Cold Harbor.

There was something impressive and noble in the circumstances of his death. Young, gifted, happily married, and with children growing up about him, using all his powers and opportunities with a high and noble aim, Colonel Porter had endeared himself to a large circle of friends by ties of more than ordinary strength and permanence. Favored in birth, and early master of his own career, he resolved that no external advantage of position should help him to any station he had not first merited by his own labor. We all know the results he achieved; but few have followed and appreciated the conscientious labor and study, the severely simple and unostentatious life, which preceded them. His more distinguished merit, however, and higher grace consisted in his benevolence and kindness of heart, in his large and constant, though secret charities, and in his consideration and tenderness towards the poor, the suffering, and the bereaved. However attractive he may have appeared in social life, and however valued for his eminent powers, his best intellectual gifts were ever reserved for the quiet hours spent with those whose relations with him were purely personal and domestic.

My first acquaintance with Colonel Porter was at the University of Heidelberg, where he appeared in my room, — a fair-haired, sunshiny youth, shadowed only by the loss of his aged and beloved father. An orphan, on the threshold of life, his career at Cambridge just terminated, with all that fortune could add to the most noble and generous natural endowments, he had left all behind him to enter on the labors of a student; and at an age when most men deem their culture achieved, he earnestly and humbly commenced anew the great task of self-education. "I want culture," he would say; "I want the equal development of all my faculties, the realization of the true, the good, and the beautiful; and for this I am willing to give my whole life if necessary, but I desire no results which are not based on solid and real knowledge." At a much later period, when time had chastened and tempered his qualities, he was still faithful to this ideal. When urged to choose a career among the many opportunities which presented themselves, he said: "My call has not come: I must bide my time; I can wait, but I cannot give myself, for the sake of occupation or success, to that which my heart does not tell me I am fitted for. I am conscious of the possession of all my faculties in their prime. Whatever I could have been I still could be; but I cannot choose, I must be chosen." The last time I saw him, — it was in command of his regiment at Fort McHenry, — I reminded him of this conversation. He smiled sweetly but sadly as he said: "I have done my duty as I have known it. For the two years I have been in command of my regiment, I have hardly been away from it a single day. We are thoroughly drilled for artillery and for infantry service. We are ready for duty: we are waiting for our turn."

His mind seemed singularly old-fashioned, and even in his early youth he had all the graces and courtesies of age. "I am a generation before you all," he would say: "I am the son of an old man. I reach back to the war of 1812. I was born almost in the wilderness. My father rode on horseback through the length of Ohio, to visit my mother in Kentucky, before his marriage. There was nothing but a bridle-path then."

To this adherence to the elder tradition we may trace the source of those hospitalities, generous yet unostentatious, which characterized his home; and his home for all humane purposes was wherever he himself was. Rich and poor were ever received by him with equal kindness, for his nature was alike Christian and kingly. We saw in him the scion of a stately old oak, grafted on a new and vigorous stock; a gentleman of the old school gracefully adapting himself to the duties of republican life. In accordance with this element of his character was his position, partly inherited and partly adopted, on the great question of human liberty, to which he bore his testimony in humane and generous actions, down to the last great sacrifice, when he gave to it his life.

His reading was thorough and solid, and confined to the best books. He was particularly drawn to the older English classics, whose stately and sober style found a response in his own character. His studies had always a direct reference to a future American literature; and I used to cherish the idea that he was destined to take a high rank among its pioneers. He had carefully and patiently examined, with this view, all the elements of our poetry from its commencement, and, with a correctness of taste which amounted almost to an instinct, had stored his memory with its most striking passages. His own verses were carefully written, and elevated in their thought and diction; but he was coy of expression, and has left but few poems. It was in conversation, perhaps, that his rare combination of native and acquired powers showed to the greatest advantage. Gentle and wise, with a beautiful fulness of expression and illustration, and a wit that was at once considerate and unrestrained, no one was more valued and cherished than he, wherever the best elements of culture were appreciated.

He being the third of his family, in direct descent, who had borne arms in the service of our country, each of the wars which tell its history had added to the lustre of his name. His grandfather, Dr. Joshua Porter, a physician in Salisbury, Connecticut, and a graduate of Yale College, was colonel of a regiment in the Revolutionary war, and took part in the battle of Saratoga. His father, Major-General Peter B. Porter, also born in Connecticut, an officer of great distinction in the war of 1812, bore a most important part in the military events on the Northern frontier, and at the battles of Lundy's Lane and the sortie from Fort Erie gained a name for courage and conduct which the historian of that period called upon his son, while yet an infant, to emulate. Later in life General Porter occupied the office of Secretary of War under John Quincy Adams.

Colonel Porter was born at Black Rock, near Buffalo, New York, on July 14, 1827. His mother was Letitia Grayson, daughter of John Breckenridge, of Kentucky, Attorney-General under Jefferson, and was widely known as a person of the highest principles and benevolence. He had the misfortune to lose her when he was only four years old, her place being thenceforth supplied by the tender affection of an only sister. At the age of seventeen he lost his father, and was thus early initiated into the responsibilities of life. He entered Harvard University, in the Sophomore class, in 1842, graduating in 1845. After this, he spent several years in Europe, as a student at the Universities of Heidelberg, Berlin, and Breslau. On his return, in 1852, he married (March 30th) his cousin, Miss Mary C. Breckenridge, a lady greatly respected and beloved by all who knew her, but who was taken from him by death in the short space of two years. In 1855 he returned to Europe, spending the winter at Ems and Paris. In 1859 he married Miss Josephine M. Morris of New York, — who as his widow survives him, — and had but just entered upon that happy home-life which it was his greatest pleasure to cultivate and embellish, when the call came which was to devote him to his country.*

* Colonel Porter left three children; namely, Peter Augustus, born in September, 1855; Letitia Elizabeth, born February, 1861, died October, 1864; George Morris, born July, 1863.

In 1861 he was elected a member of the Assembly of the State of New York, where he performed his duties with faithfulness and assiduity. In 1862 he tendered his services to the government, applying for authority to recruit a company of volunteers for the war. On receiving the application, Governor Morgan at once offered him the command of a regiment, if he would undertake the recruiting of it in his own senatorial district. He began immediately, and raised a fine regiment of infantry, the One Hundred and Twenty-ninth New York Volunteers, in the unprecedentedly short time of about two weeks. It was originally one thousand strong, but was subsequently changed to the Eighth New York Heavy Artillery, and its numbers increased to more than two thousand. For nearly two years he was stationed in the defences of Baltimore, the latter part of the time in command of Fort McHenry.

In May, 1864, General Grant entered upon his great campaign in Virginia. Colonel Porter had been unceasing in his applications for active service, but now seemed destined to a new disappointment, as the army moved without him. It was only in consequence of the losses of men sustained in the battles of the Wilderness that his regiment was called into the field. He had said to his officers, during the long months of waiting: "Some of us will die in garrison, some on the march, and others on the field of battle; yet all alike will be remembered as having died in defence of our country." It was on a bright Saturday afternoon, after twenty months of garrison duty, that the confidential order reached him to proceed to the front. At nine o'clock on the following morning, Sunday, May 15th, they were *en route* for Washington, and on Monday evening arrived by boat at Belle Plain. On the march thence to Spottsylvania Court-House, Colonel Porter was temporarily in command of a brigade. His regiment was then brigaded under General R. O. Tyler, and he resumed his own command. Daylight on the morning of May 18th found them in line of battle near Spottsylvania Court-House, on an eminence overlooking the field where the fighting was going on. At eight o'clock they had changed their position so as to find themselves within range of the enemy's guns, — this being for many of them their first experience under fire.

Upon the following day an attack was made by Early's corps upon their right and rear. The Eighth New York, with several other regiments, were immediately under orders, and moved at double-quick to repel the charge. After the whole force of the enemy had been pressed far back into the woods, Colonel Porter sought out his officers, anxiously inquiring if their men had behaved well; and on being assured that their conduct had been admirable, he exclaimed with satisfaction, "Now I know that the Eighth will stand fire, and will not disgrace itself on the battle-field." Every officer and private in the regiment knew that his dearest wish was that the regiment, to the drill and discipline of which he had given the best efforts of his mind, and which he had always esteemed it an honor to command, should acquit itself creditably in the first engagement with the enemy; and they had resolved he should not be disappointed. Their loss on that day was between thirty and forty. Colonel Porter escaped unhurt, though his life was repeatedly attempted by a sharpshooter in a neighboring tree, who, when wounded and captured, boasted of the fact, saying he had been his prisoner at Fort McHenry. With a look of pity Colonel Porter directed him to be taken to the rear and kindly cared for.

At midnight on the 20th of May, the movement towards Richmond commenced; the brigade to which he belonged being attached, as heretofore, to Gibbon's division of Hancock's corps. The march was laborious, a part of each night being employed in intrenching. On the evening of May 23d they reached the North Anna, near Hanover Station, and on the next day crossed the stream under a sharp artillery fire. That night they lay upon their arms without shelter, exposed to a drenching rain; and during the long and dreary hours Colonel Porter beguiled the tedium of his officers by some of his most brilliant and humorous sallies. The following evening they recrossed the North Anna, and the whole night was spent in erecting more breastworks. The night was dark, and the ground too broken to admit of moving about except on foot, and a long line of works must be erected before morning. The regiment was halted at the point where the works were to be made, when the whole line, men and officers, sank exhausted on the ground. Presently Colonel Porter came along in the dark, calling out to one of his officers, "I want you to take charge of this work, and it is to be completed before daylight." The officer, exhausted by the fatigue he had undergone, replied, "Colonel, I am sorry, but it is physically impossible for me to do it;. I am utterly prostrated." His commander came close to him, saying, "I know you are; I wonder you have stood it so long. I am nearly exhausted myself; but remain where you are, get what rest you can, and I will see that the work is done." Daylight found it finished.

On the 2d of June they reached Cold Harbor, and soon after noon occupied the front line of works. Colonel Porter had such information as led him to believe that a charge would be ordered that afternoon upon the enemy's works, situated within one hundred rods of the front. He gave his officers full instructions how he wished the duty to be performed, passing frequently along the whole line, a prominent mark for the enemy's sharpshooters. At length night came on, and with it a heavy rain. Major Willett, the senior surviving officer of the regiment, writes: —

"The Colonel was vigilant in guarding against surprise, and I do not think he slept at all that night. My position was on the extreme right of our line, at a large frame-and-brick house. Near by was a small evergreen, under which I took shelter from the rain. The Colonel was with me there about midnight, but soon returned to his own position near the centre of the line. He called upon me again before daylight; and we sat down on a log of wood to drink our coffee, and talk over the charge we expected to make at dawn. Suddenly the sharpshooters opposite, taking advantage of the first ray of light, opened fire upon us. With a smile, and in a cheerful tone, he spoke a few kind words, and was leaving me when he turned about, reached out his hand, and with a shade of anxiety and sorrow on his face, said, 'Good by, Major!' and was gone.

"In less than five minutes a staff officer came galloping up and inquired for Colonel Porter. I directed him to the Colonel's quarters, and he rode on, saying we were to charge at a given signal, — the firing of a gun from a battery in our rear. The gun was fired before he had reached the Colonel. I ordered my battalion over the works, and we formed in line in front. Standing upon the parapet I looked anxiously to the left for about a minute, when I saw Colonel Porter suddenly appear upon the top of the breastwork, near the extreme left of the regiment, and immediately after the men climbing over the work. For an instant they halted and closed ranks; then as the Colonel, a few yards in advance, waved his sword, the whole line went forward at double-quick into that terrible fire, which cost the regiment, in killed and wounded, over six hundred men and twenty-three officers, including its noble and beloved commander."

Colonel Porter fell, at the head of his column, within a few rods of the enemy's rifle-pits. He was wounded in the neck. He rose once to his feet and again to his knees, rallying his men, till, pierced by six bullets, he sank to rise no more. The last words he uttered were, "Dress upon the colors!" For several days he had had a strong presentiment of his approaching death. In a letter received by his family long after the battle, but written three days before, he had said, "I try to think and act and feel as if each day were to be my last, so as not to go unprepared to God. We must hope and pray and believe He will preserve us. But His will be done. It is selfish to wish to be saved at the expense of others."

His body lay two days under the guns of the enemy, whose works, by one of the sad chances of civil war, were commanded by his own cousin, John C. Breckenridge, doubly related to him by blood and marriage. It was recovered on the night of the second day by the steadiness and good conduct of five men of his regiment, — Sergeant Le Roy Williams, Privates Galen S. Hicks, John Duff, Walter Harwood, and Samuel Travis. When Mr. Cozzens, in reading his memorial of Colonel Porter to the Century Club in New York City, narrated this fine act of affection, — how on a rainy night the men had crawled as near the enemy's works as they dared go together, then how one had dragged himself up to the body, attached a rope to the sword-belt and drawn it out to where the survivors lay, and how they together had borne it, partly on their hands and knees, a distance of three miles to the hospital, — the Club caused medals to be struck in remembrance of the honorable deed. They are of gold, and bear this inscription, "A tribute from the Century for a rare act of heroic devotion in rescuing the body of Colonel Peter A. Porter from under the guns of the enemy." Two of them, by the chances of war, have yet to be found, to claim their memorial of gratitude. Perchance already with their beloved commander, they need no record to testify to their affection.

The family and friends of Colonel Porter owed an equal debt of gratitude to the devoted and faithful services of his attached servant, John Huney, who had been taken many years before as a child into his family, and had followed him with romantic affection into the field. It was owing to his unremitting efforts that the privilege was accorded them of uniting his remains with those of his ancestors. "If he had been my brother," he said, "I would have buried him at White House; but I promised you to bring him back, if he were wounded or dead."

The sentiment of personal attachment which these actions indicate was earnest and sincere in his regiment, and had grown out of the careful and just consideration he always showed his men, and from his observance of the golden rule, by which he consistently strove to direct his every action, — to do to others as he would, in like circumstances, have had them do to him. This was beautifully shown in his letter declining a nomination of Secretary of State for New York. "I left home," he wrote, "in command of a regiment composed mainly of the sons of friends and neighbors committed to my care. I can hardly ask for my discharge while theirs cannot be granted; and I have a strong desire, if alive, to carry back those whom the chances of time and war shall permit to be present, and to account in person for all."

In his will he left the following record of his upright and modest adherence to duty: "I, Peter Augustus Porter, being of sound mind, do declare this to be my last will and testament; feeling, to its full extent, the probability that I may not return from the path of duty on which I have entered. If it please God that it be so, I can say, with truth, that I have entered on the course of danger with no ambitious aspirations, nor with the idea that I am fitted, by nature or experience, to be of any important service to the government; but in obedience to the call of duty, demanding every citizen to contribute what he could, in means, labor, or life, to sustain the government of his country, — a sacrifice made the more willingly by me, when I consider how singularly benefited I have been by the institutions of the land, and that, up to this time, all the blessings of life have been showered upon me beyond what usually falls to the lot of man."

His body, placed in a rude coffin and enveloped in his country's flag, was buried in Oakwood Cemetery at Niagara, near the Episcopal Church which his family had built, and where, by faith and choice, he had long and lovingly worshipped. The solemn dirge of the great cataract, so dear to him in life, sounds forever above his grave. And it seems to those who knew and loved him, that he wrote his own best elegy in the beautiful lines which he composed in Europe, long years before, on hearing of the death of his classmate and friend, George Emerson.

"I met our friends upon a foreign shore,
And asked of thee; they told me thou wert dead!
My lips repeat, 'He is no more, — no more';
'T was all I said.

"Yet sank my spirit in me, and there went
A strange confusion o'er my saddened brow,
I could not pierce God's infinite intent;
I cannot now.

"I only know that He who in thy birth
Had shadowed forth Himself, though faint and dim,
Decreed how long thou shouldst remain on earth,
How long with Him.

"And now there comes that phantom of the past,
Rousing my soul with its elastic prime:
I see thee still as when I saw thee last, —
In that glad time, —

"Radiant in beauty of the form and mind,
And young renown of academic strife,
Joy lay around, a stainless life behind,
Before thee, life;

"A high-priest standing in the temple's space
Ere yet the sacrificial rites begin,
A giant waiting for the glorious race
He is to win.

"We thought eternal tablets would record
Thy name with theirs who, since the world began,
With an immortal strength, and toil and word,
Have wrought for man.

"We thought — alas! what thought we not of good,
Of all that hope or promise e'er begat;
Of all save early doom — O friend! how could
We think of that?

"We could not see the shadows close thee round;
We could not know prophetic cypress shed
Funereal perfume for the wreath that bound
'So dear a head.'

"We could not think the light that from afar
We deemed prelusive of the coming sun
Was but the parting radiance of his car,
When day is done.

"But now I know too well a light's withdrawn
That made this gloomy earth for me more fair;
A perfume's fled and gentle influence gone
That soothed my care.

"And yet not wholly gone: through life's sad vale
Thy soul — now prompting to resemble thee,
And now in sad monition when I fail —
Shall walk with me.

"With me? O yes! but not with me alone;
For in the fair companionship of youth,
Others than I have fondly felt and known
Thy love and truth;

'Have drunk at learning's fount with thee, and seen
How Doubt's dark depths and Thought's wild surge above
Thy mild-eyed faith, so pure and so serene,
Soared like a dove.

"Enough: what might have been is not; no more
Shall I return thy grasp, and seek thy glance:
Perchance we meet on heaven's eternal shore;
Alas! perchance!"

1846.

EZRA RIPLEY.

First Lieutenant 29th Mass. Vols. (Infantry), July 24, 1861; died July 28, 1863, near Helena, Ark., of disease contracted in the service.

LIEUTENANT EZRA RIPLEY was born August 10, 1826, being the son of the late Rev. Samuel Ripley of Waltham, and the grandson of the venerable Dr. Ezra Ripley of Concord, Massachusetts. His mother, Sarah (Bradford) Ripley, still lives at Concord, — a lady beloved and honored as are few persons in any community. Through her he was descended directly from the Pilgrim Governor Bradford. His grandfather, Gamaliel Bradford, was a lieutenant, and his great-grandfather, of the same name, was a colonel, in the war of the Revolution. His paternal grandmother was also the grandmother of Mr. Ralph Waldo Emerson of Concord.

He graduated at Harvard College in 1846, and was married, in May, 1853, to Miss Harriet M. Hayden of East Cambridge, who survives him. He had no children. In 1861 he had been for ten years a lawyer at East Cambridge, had been there twice appointed to honorable public offices, and was engaged in a large and increasing practice. But when the war broke out he gave up his business, and took part at once in the formation of a military company; the blood that was in him would not suffer him to doubt or linger.

And yet he was a slender, delicate, sensitive, and peculiarly unwarlike person, — often the subject of his own laughter for a timidity which he humorously exaggerated into something more than feminine. His health, too, was anything but robust. For these reasons most of his friends opposed his going to the war; but he would heed no opposition, and with steadfast enthusiasm set his face to do what seemed to him to be his duty. And from beginning to end, his patriotism had the support — constant, gentle, self-sacrificing, and inexpressibly comforting — of the person who was dearest to him.

After serving for a time as "Third Lieutenant" in the East Cambridge company in camp at home, he was nominated by General Butler, in the summer of 1861, to be First Lieutenant in what was afterwards Company B of the Twenty-ninth Massachusetts Regiment, — then a company of the old "Massachusetts Battalion," at Fortress Monroe. This company and Company I, of the same regiment, were the oldest volunteer troops in the three years' service, — having been mustered in on May 14, 1861. In the same modest but honorable place Lieutenant Ripley remained — a First Lieutenant — until the time of his death. Some reasons interfered with his promotion, which were in a high degree honorable to him, but they cannot properly be mentioned here.

Yet he was not without marked honor from his superior officers. While stationed at Fortress Monroe and at Newport News he was quite constantly employed as Judge-Advocate. Early in the year 1862 General Mansfield placed him upon his staff. This position he resigned in June of that year, when his regiment was ordered up the Peninsula, and it was made certain that his general was still to remain behind at Newport News. In Kentucky, he served on the staff of Colonel Pierce, Acting Brigadier-General; and at the time of his death he was Acting Assistant Adjutant-General to Colonel Christ, then acting as Brigadier-General near Vicksburg.

The abilities and character of Lieutenant Ripley justified the confidence of these officers, and might well have assured him a higher nominal rank. But there never was a person more modest, more eager to prefer others before himself, or more indifferent to his own prospects of advancement, when there was occasion to assert some neglected piece of justice. Had he lived a little longer, there is reason to believe that he would presently have received the nomination of colonel to one of the new colored regiments. He was not aware of this; but it is known that he would have rejoiced to belong to those troops in any capacity. For such a position he had distinguished qualifications, — skill, humanity, and a great and inherited interest in the welfare of the African race. He had a remarkably alert and penetrating intellect, a tenacious memory, strong native good sense, and a keen and cheerful wit. With a heart, also, which was full to overflowing with sympathy for everything that breathes, he knew well that secret which no school can teach, of compelling the obedience of men through sentiments of love, gratitude, and personal regard.

Lieutenant Ripley was in the hottest of the terrible seven days' fighting before Richmond. At Harrison's Landing his strength gave out, and he came home on sick-leave. In September he joined his regiment again, just before the battle of Antietam, — leaving home at a time when his physician did not think him well enough to be out in the damp of the evening, resisting the assurances of friends at Washington that he was not well enough to go on, and, when he could no longer for any money hire a conveyance in Maryland, taking his bag in his hand, sleeping at night under a haystack, and hurrying forward on foot to find his regiment, — just drawn up in line at the beginning of the Antietam fight. Bluff General Richardson told him on the spot that he was not well enough to be there; but he persisted that he was, and went bravely through the whole of the fighting. Just after the battles were over, he wrote from Sharpsburg and again from Harper's Ferry as follows. His ardent and generous lament for Colonel Barlow will be read with interest; although that brave officer, as all his countrymen now know, recovered from the severe wounds received in battle at Antietam, to fight with the same distinguished gallantry down to the end of the war.

"SHARPSBURG, Sunday Morning, September 21, 1862.

"At last I think I have time to write a letter, — at least I will run the risk of being ordered to march before ten minutes. Friday, September 12th, I left Washington in search of our regiment, and, after travelling about eighty miles and paying almost fifty dollars, reached them Monday morning, drawn up in line of battle on South Mountain, near the town of Bolivar. At this place there was a severe fight the day previous. Our regiment was not in it, but that night had marched to relieve our troops who had done the fighting. Sunday I hired a hack at Frederick City and followed the regiment to within three miles of the mountain, but, finding the carriage could go no farther, sent it back at twelve o'clock at night, sent my trunk and boxes to the Provost Marshal of Frederick City, slept under a haycock, and Monday morning set out, valise in hand, for the regiment. I have not seen my trunk, etc., since, but hope to get it soon. As I went up the mountain the sun rose, lifting the fog from all the surrounding hills, and presenting a scene I cannot describe; no one but those who have seen sunrise from mountain-tops can imagine it. I found the brigade drawn up in line in the wood, expecting an attack. The men of our company were very glad to see me, and I gladly took command of them. In about half an hour word came that the enemy were in full retreat towards the river, so our division, under General Richardson, started down the mountain at double-quick, and passed through the towns of Boonsborough and Keatysville, amid the cheers and patriotic greetings of the loyal citizens, who freely gave us bread, water, and what other eatables were at hand. A burning bridge delayed our passage a little, but we overtook the enemy about eleven o'clock at Sharpsburg. . . . .

"Here we lay two days and two nights; the opposing batteries meantime keeping up a terrific fire, which killed and wounded some of our men. At night we slept on the ground, covered only by rubber blankets. Tuesday night it rained, and it seemed very strange to be sleeping out in the rain. It woke me up; but, drawing my rubber blanket over my head, I slept soundly till morning. Tuesday night General Hooker forded Beaver Brook (a stream about as wide as Concord River, near mother's) with his forces, and opened the fight on Wednesday, A. M. On Wednesday, at nine o'clock in the morning, we formed in line, and were marched across the brook, which was about up to our knees; and after resting on the other side long enough to wring out our socks, and empty the water out of our shoes, we were marched to the field of battle. On the way we passed through a shower of bullets and shells. When within about sixty yards of the Rebels, we halted. They were right behind a hill in a cornfield, which was uneven, sloping ground. We could see the colors of many regiments before us; and we have since learned that the whole of Longstreet's division was opposed to our brigade. They kept up a terrible fire while we were forming our lines; some of our men dropped as we approached, and before we took position; but I saw no man in our regiment flinch, though at one time we were exposed to a front and flank fire. . . . .

"I shall never forget the sight of the Sixty-ninth New York, on our right. It was a small regiment when it went into the fight; and as it stood there on the hill, every shot from the enemy seemed to visibly reduce it, till at last it was a mere handful of men, clustered around their flag, with no reference to company or regimental lines, fighting to the last. The color-bearer fell, but before the flag reached the ground some one else seized and put it up again. No sooner was that done than the flag fell again, and was as soon planted again; and so this little cluster of Irishmen fought on till Caldwell's brigade came up to relieve us. They came up with a cheer and a shout, Colonel Barlow leading the way with his regiment, and took their stand some way ahead of our brigade. We then fell back a short distance, but soon came up again. We were at it, in the infantry fight, about an hour and a half.

"Right here I must speak of Colonel Barlow. Noble fellow! he is dead now, and his name is in everybody's mouth. When our brigade passed Caldwell's brigade, to which Barlow belonged, just at the ford, he was sitting on his horse at the head of his regiment, waiting to go into the fight. He had on an old linen coat and an old hat. We exchanged pleasant greetings with each other (my last with him); and when he came up leading the way to our relief, it seemed as if a fairy had transformed him. He was on foot. Instead of the linen coat, he had a splendid uniform on, which seemed to shine with newness, — pants inside high-topped boots, an army hat, and yellow regulation gloves. It seemed as if a new suit must have dropped on him from the skies. And then he rushed up the hill at the head of his little regiment, looking so handsome, facing his men to cheer them, moving with such grace and elasticity, that it seemed as if he were dancing with delight. I have seen brave men and brave officers; I saw that day colonels coolly and bravely lead on their regiments; but I never saw such a sight as Barlow's advance, and never expect to again. It was a picture, — it was poetry. The whole regiment gazed with admiration on him. I wish I could do justice to the brave fellow. His praise is now in every man's mouth. He chased the enemy from the ground, and drove them almost a mile, — he and two other regiments following him, — and then died as a soldier should. His loss affected me more than anything else that has happened here. I admired him, and enjoyed his society.

"We soon returned to the battle-field, and the rest of Wednesday and until late Friday, P. M., lay there supporting batteries. — sometimes being covered with grape and shell, so that escape seemed almost miraculous; at other times we lay in quiet, and undisturbed. So you see for five days we were constantly at work, either supporting batteries or fighting infantry.

"The horrors of the battle-field I must describe to you in another letter, as the mail-boy calls for this. I have seen sights and gone through what I hope will never be my lot again. We are now resting a little.

"HARPER'S FERRY, September, 23, 1862.

"Yesterday (Monday), A. M., we left Sharpsburg, the scene of our victories, and marched to this place, about twelve miles. We were nearly ten hours, marching quite slowly, and being some time fording the Potomac, the Rebels having burned the bridge. The spot is the most beautiful and romantic I ever was in. . . . . As we stand in our camp and look down the river, the mountains, separated by its bed, seem gradually to meet in the distance. I wish I could describe the picture. I stood and gazed with awe this morning, as the golden-tinted fog at sunrise rolled off the mountain and filled the gap. Just so beautiful too was the scenery in the region of the battle-field, — fertile fields, thickly-wooded mountains, and rolling valleys met the eye everywhere, and it seemed wicked that war should lay all this waste. I hope the North is satisfied with what the army has done, and to think too that the old Army of the Potomac should have done the chief part of the fighting! But, as usual, one thing was left undone, — the enemy were not bagged. I was on guard the night they left, and it was evident to us that they were leaving. . . . . That night on guard in the cornfield was horrid. As I went round to visit my men, I stumbled everywhere over dead men; everywhere I was met with the cry of Rebels, wounded two days before, calling for water. I could hear one who died about morning, and who proved to be a major, saying, in the pleasantest possible voice, 'Henry, Henry; bring me some water, Henry'; and another crying, 'O my God! won't somebody bring me some water?' As I passed along in the night, I was startled by a whisper which seemed to come from a heap of dead bodies. 'Sam, where 's the regiment?' I found he was a wounded sergeant from the Thirtieth North Carolina Regiment. I gave him some water, and afterwards he was taken into camp. He was very gentle and quiet, and bore his suffering bravely. I will not distress you with these details. The scenes were terrible enough to us, and will long haunt my memory. . . . . I am well, though I have slept on the ground eight nights, my only covering a rubber blanket, in rain and wind and dew, and have lived a good part of the time on raw salt pork, hard bread, and tea. I am well, and strong, and in good spirits."

Afterwards, while the Army of the Potomac was at Falmouth, Ripley was called home on recruiting service for the Second Massachusetts Cavalry. His intention of remaining with that regiment was not carried out, and in February, 1863, he returned to his regiment, which was then, or soon afterwards, placed in the Ninth Army Corps under General Burnside. In March this corps went into Kentucky. As they were moving westward, he wrote home a letter which was full of the pure inspirations that stirred him. He had been speaking of the beautiful mountain scenery along the Baltimore and Ohio Railroad, which had filled him with enthusiasm, and then he added: —

"I could not help thinking we had indeed a country worth fighting for. To think that we were in danger of losing the great and good government whose paternal care is extended so widely, and whose benign influence is felt in the remotest corner of these wild regions, — which offers freedom and equal rights to all, — whose very greatness is shown in this her struggle for existence, — made me almost frantic. If anything were needed to make me feel the necessity of working in the good cause to the last, to give the last drop to my country, this journey has convinced me. God forgive me if I hesitate or falter now. . . . . May you, too, feel this freshness of heart and soul, this renewed vigor, with which this mountain air and scenery have inspired me."

And so he went over into Kentucky, and, in June, to Vicksburg.

The manner of his death was characteristic. When the troops in July went on to the capital of Mississippi, Lieutenant Ripley, on account of an injury to his leg, was left behind, — "in the wilderness," as he said, — with one man to take care of him. After a few days he had nearly recovered, when word came back that Colonel Christ was sick. No orders came for Lieutenant Ripley, who was then his staff officer, but he said that he felt sure he must be needed, and, over-estimating his own strength, on the 16th of July he hastened forward, riding about seventy miles in an open wagon, under the blazing sun, and reaching Jackson just as the troops were turning about and coming again to their camp on the Yazoo River near Vicksburg. He came back with them, but now travelled in an ambulance. When they arrived at the camp he was quite ill; and it was now thought best, in accordance with his own wishes, that he should try to reach home.

On the 28th of July, at four o'clock in the afternoon, this poor, exhausted, faithful soldier left the sultry heats of Vicksburg for the North and his native New England. As the boat was passing the city he spoke of the many comrades who had fallen there, and sadly asked that he might be lifted up to look once more upon that fatal spot. The boat moved on up the swift river, but his life was flowing fast away, and at eleven o'clock that same evening he died. A cool night breeze had succeeded the intense heat of the day, and was blowing through the open doors of his room; he was attended, moreover, by a faithful man from his regiment, whom he himself had chosen. An hour before his death, he found strength to send a message of mingled love and exultation to his wife; nor did he forget to caution the messenger not to tell her of his death directly, but to see one of his brothers-in-law first.

His body was left at Helena in Arkansas. It was presently removed and buried among his kindred, in the beautiful cemetery at Concord, where a simple and graceful stone, erected through the care of several of his townsmen and friends, fitly marks his resting-place. Upon this stone was placed the following inscription, written by one whose regard for him was in itself an honor.

"In memory of Ezra Ripley, Lieutenant of the Twenty-ninth Regiment of Massachusetts Volunteers,—born at Waltham, August 10, 1826,—died on the Mississippi River, near Vicksburg, July 28, 1863.

"Of the best Pilgrim stock, descended from officers in the Revolutionary army, and from a long line of the ministers of Concord, he was worthy of his lineage.

"An able and successful lawyer, he gave himself with persistent zeal to the cause of the friendless and the oppressed.

"Of slender physical strength, and of a nature refined, sensitive, and delicate, he was led by patriotism and the love of freedom to leave home and friends for the toilsome labors of war, and shrank from no fatigue or danger, until, worn out in her service, he gave up his life for his country.

"Animæque magnæ
Prodigum."

Ezra Ripley was the friend of all poor and helpless persons, and risked everything to protect them. His lavish expenditure of his own time and means for others would never have suffered him to grow rich; but he has laid up treasure, which neither moth nor rust can corrupt, in the heart of many a prisoner in the jail at East Cambridge, and of many another poor man and woman to whom words of sympathy were unfamiliar; and his name is held dear by the soldiers who were under him.

MONTGOMERY RITCHIE.

Vol. A. D. C. (rank of Captain), June, 1861; (rank of Major), July, 1861; Captain and Commissary of Subsistence U. S. Vols., December, 1861; Captain 1st Mass. Cavalry, November 25, 1862; discharged, on resignation, May 6, 1864; died of disease contracted in the service, November 7, 1864.

MONTGOMERY RITCHIE was a man of marked character. He was modest, even to the degree of self-distrust; his manners were reserved, his impressions slowly received, but, when once received, ineffaceable. His nature, like that of many others, was liable to be mistaken, partly because it was veiled, partly because it was made up of various and even opposite qualities; but to those who penetrated it, it constantly tended towards transparency and harmony.

His self-distrust was a prominent trait. His standard was too high to be easily attained or easily approached, and he was not wont to think himself as near it as he actually was. He constantly scrutinized his own motives and actions, and often held himself back, when others, less self-questioning than he, would have pressed forward. His friends valued him the more for his humility. It was to many of them an example which he was quite unconscious of setting, and which is not the less persuasive now that it is set only by his memory.

He was self-distrustful, but he was also self-relying. He did not hesitate to decide when the hour for decision came, or shrink from action when it was time to act. He had some grave difficulties to meet, and he met them steadily; some serious trials to bear, and he bore them firmly. His resolution was often tested, and seldom, if ever, failed to stand the test. He was a man whose principle sustained him when those who were quicker than he to begin were also quicker than he to end their efforts. His modesty never paralyzed, never weakened him.

With all his reserve, he was full of ardor. His temper was hot, and it was one of the great successes of his life to bring it under control. He was warm-hearted, fervent in his affections, enthusiastic in cherishing the friends and pursuing the paths he preferred. He struggled, when he had to struggle, with zeal and fire, until he came off conqueror, either by achieving triumph, or by accepting failure in a spirit that turned failure into triumph.

His bravery was as perfect as any human quality can be. It was partly physical, the result of unusual bodily powers, developed in boxing, fencing, rowing, and gymnastic exercises. But it was chiefly moral, the growth of noble characteristics, — determination, earnestness, and magnanimity. The nearest companion of his boyhood says that he never struck a hasty blow, but would treat with scorn the provocations he received from such as he knew to be unable to stand up before him. The high courage of the boy ripened into the yet higher courage of the man. No one was ever readier to confess and to repair a wrong, if he had committed any; no one ever gave a fuller measure of honor to those whom he thought honorable, or of sympathy to those whom he considered as meriting it at his hands. Courage and high-mindedness met and mingled in him.

He was also remarkable for his integrity. Not only unwilling, but one may say unable to do a dishonorable action, he turned from anything like corruption or knavery, whether great or small, open or hidden, with sickness of the soul. He could not bear even the conventional irregularities of every-day affairs. Better, he thought, be unsuccessful in business, with a sense of unstained honor, than be successful at the slightest risk of dishonor. "There are not," he once wrote, "many trials of character, good and bad, which in my varied life I have not seen. It has been only from experience, gained, I fancy, very much later in life than is usual, that I have appreciated the fact that men are far less restrained by considerations of conscience than I supposed. . . . . I find, in all money transactions, that the great mass do not even pretend to honesty, or what is real honesty." Whether he was right or wrong in this opinion, he was resolved to be honest, and really honest himself, and his resolution was unbroken from first to last.

His integrity sprang from his truthfulness. He loved the truth, and the more he understood it, the better he loved it, the more unreservedly he gave himself to it. He shrank from what was false, not only in circumstances or persons of slight importance to him, but in such as were almost a part of his being. He wanted to get at the truth wherever it lay, in science, or commerce, or life, and it was often touching to see with what strong desire he labored to inform himself, wherever he was in doubt, rather than be ignorant, consciously, of that which was alone true.

Such are the mere outlines of his character. If they have been sketched with any distinctness, they show a man who would be among the first to spring to the defence of his country the moment it was assailed. No self-distrust would deter him, while his decision, his fervor, his courage, his integrity, and his truthfulness would all urge him on. Whatever his previous career, whatever his actual position, such a man as this was marked out for instant and for persevering service to the Union. Fort Sumter fired on, he went at once to Washington.

He was at that time thirty-five years old, having been born March 20, 1826. His birthplace was Boston; his parents were Andrew and Sophia Harrison Ritchie, his mother being the daughter of Harrison Gray Otis. His education was conducted by various teachers until 1839, when he went abroad with his brother under the charge of Mr. T. G. Bradford, with whom he spent between two and three years in France and Germany, acquiring the languages of those countries and carrying on his preparation for Harvard College, which he entered in 1842. After taking his degree in 1846, he began his commercial career in the counting-house of the late Samuel Austin, Jr., and there remained till 1849, when he sailed for Calcutta. His business there being transacted, he crossed to Bombay, and thence took the overland route, returning home through Europe in 1850. He continued in the East India trade at Boston till 1857, and afterwards engaged in the grain commission business at New York, from which he retired some time before the outbreak of the war.

He married, in 1857, Cornelia, the eldest daughter of the late General Wadsworth, of Geneseo, and was residing with his father-in-law when the cannon at Charleston called them both to the field. Ritchie left a wife and two young sons behind him when he entered the service.

It was some weeks before he obtained a position as Volunteer Aid on General Blenker's staff, and was engaged in active duty. Just before the battle of Bull Run, he was transferred to the staff of General Miles, whose warm commendation he received for the part he bore in the trying scenes that followed. He did not yield to the panic which overcame many of his comrades, but remained at his post with the rear-guard, and on the sad morning after the rout joined with General Wadsworth in caring for the wounded and directing the stragglers at Fairfax Court-House, which he and his father-in-law were among the last, if not themselves the last, to leave before the entrance of the enemy. Circumstances for which he was entirely irresponsible deprived him of the military appointment he had held, and he returned to Geneseo.

But it was only to labor "night and day," as he is described to have done, in recruiting for the Wadsworth Guards, the Geneseo or Hundred and Fourth New York Volunteers, of whom he was to have been Lieutenant-Colonel. Before the regiment was organized, however, in December, 1861, he received a summons to join the expedition then on the eve of departure, under the command of General Burnside; and, always eager for active service, he hastened to Fortress Monroe. A grievous disappointment befell him there, for, instead of the position to which he had looked forward, the post of Commissary of Subsistence proved to be awaiting him. Strong as the impulse must have been to decline the appointment and return to the Geneseo regiment, he decided, as generously as became him, that his duty was to go on with the expedition, and he began his work as Commissary, with the rank of Captain, on General Reno's staff. He was soon in battle, commanding a gunboat at Roanoke Island, and braving, at Reno's side, the hottest of the fire at Newbern. A little later, he was in action at Camden, and wrote with deep feeling of the dead and wounded that were left upon the field at night when our troops were ordered to retire. But his duties were chiefly at Newbern and Beaufort, N. C., where he was stationed as Commissary for several months, occupied, as he jestingly said, in the grocery business of those posts. It was a hard, a very hard service for him, and one that fretted his spirit so much as to demand all the determination of which he was capable, to hold him fast. He persevered until ill health compelled him to go home in the summer of 1862.

As soon as he regained his strength, he obtained a commission as Captain in the First Massachusetts Cavalry, to qualify himself for duty on the staff of General Augur in the expedition under General Banks to the Mississippi. Fatigue and exposure, with the added effects of the climate, brought on during that winter another illness, far more serious than the attack of the preceding summer. His physicians attempted to dissuade him from continuing in the service, but his self-devotion was stronger than their counsels, and he resumed his staff duties at New Orleans, then at Baton Rouge. A letter from this place, one of the very few of his letters which are now within reach, speaks of the experiment about to be tried in the opening campaign. "For my part," he writes, "I consider the success or failure of the negro troops the great problem of the day. We have now some thousands of blacks officered by whites. They resist the climate, keep their regiments one thousand strong, while white regiments get reduced to three or four hundred. They do all the drill, etc. Query, Will they fight? If they will, then Master South is beaten with his own weapons. It cannot be long before some ten thousand of these men will be led under fire. What momentous results centre in that event! If, as some predict, they fly like sheep, we are far from conquest, and from holding our conquests. If they stand, then, unless want of military genius is an incurable trait of our government, the South, from that day, is whipped. . . . . It will be poetic justice, should the cause of all our evils, Slavery, be turned to avenge our wrongs."

Port Hudson was the last scene of his service in the field. He took as prominent a part as one in his position could take, in the siege of that stronghold. Always untiring, always undaunted, always ready to expose and to exhaust himself, he here won largely upon the esteem of his commander and his comrades. One exploit illustrates the judgment as well as the gallantry which rendered him an efficient officer. He had been sent to station a regiment in support of a battery, and returned to report that the Colonel had lost his presence of mind, while the men were falling so fast that the regiment might break at any moment. The general told him to take any troops he could find, and carry them to the threatened position ; and off he rode, bringing up two fresh regiments just as the one he had distrusted broke and fled.

One day, after carrying a despatch over a peculiarly difficult part of the field, he was in the act of reporting to his commanding officer, when he fell by a sun-stroke, and lay insensible for nearly twenty-four hours. This time the surgeons carried the day against him, and he was sent to Baton Rouge, then to New Orleans, and then by sea to New York, where he arrived in the summer of 1863, — "almost a skeleton," as he was described, in the body, but in the spirit rounded and matured, as those who saw him that summer, and observed the development which he had reached through duty and suffering, can now take sad comfort in remembering.

Slowly rising from weakness and disease, but not restored to the health he had lost forever, he rejoined General Augur in the autumn, at Washington. There he remained through the following winter, at one time much harassed by the settlement of his accounts as Commissary, some items of which, for want of the necessary formalities, were questioned by the "executioners," as he playfully called them, "who sit upon our official papers." The needed vouchers were soon obtained, chiefly through the ready assistance of Dr. J. B. Upham, of Boston, who had been in charge of the Beaufort Hospital, for which, and for the hospital at Newbern, the Commissary had incurred the expenses considered unaccounted for at Washington. But it was a keen trial to one of such integrity, when even the shadow of a doubt fell upon his accounts, and, however swiftly the shadow was lifted, the sense of unmerited questioning must have remained.

A month or two later he felt that he ought to leave the army. "It seems to me," he wrote, "one year more, and unless victory forsakes our flag, the South, as a great force in the field, will be no more. . . . . I begin to think it time to put my worldly affairs in order, and to let younger and single men take their turn." He resigned his commission in the spring of 1864. His last sight of battle-fields was in the terrible Wilderness, where he went to recover the body of his father-in-law, after the death of that lamented general. It was a tragical close to the three years' service of the father and the son.

"I never had any adventures in the army," Ritchie was wont to say, when asked about his campaigns. If he had not, there were few who had a soldier's story to tell, and to tell with honorable satisfaction. But his modesty was strong to the last; and he ended his military career, as he began and pursued it, in self-retiring nobleness.

A few months passed, and the disease contracted in the service, and never expelled, returned with fresh violence. Week after week he lay suffering and emaciated, and no care of physician or kindred, no change of air or treatment, no remedy, no devotion, availed to prolong the life which was ripened for its close on earth. As death drew nigh, he was again in the field, his fellow-soldiers around him, the shell piercing the air, the horse pawing the ground. And so his battles ceased; his sufferings were over, and he entered into rest at Geneseo, November 7, 1864, in the thirty-ninth year of his age.

"I can lay my hand on my heart," he said when he left the army, in a confidence which it is no wrong to violate now, "and say that I have not done a thing you would be sorry to know." One who knew him all his life, and knew him heart to heart, says he was "as true a Christian gentleman as ever breathed." Be this assurance the wreath we hang most gladly and most tenderly above his grave.

1847.

EDWARD HUTCHINSON ROBBINS REVERE.

Assistant Surgeon 20th Regiment Mass. Vols. (Infantry), September 10, 1861; killed at Antietam, September 17, 1862.

A PRINTED memorial of Dr. Revere seems proper only as part of a design which has a wider and more public purpose than the memory of an individual. He is remembered without a printed or written sentence, by truthful words, kind deeds, steadfast friendships, faithful services, and manly honor, — as widely as he would wish, and in the only way he would desire. Even had his life found less completion, and had he not been permitted in its closing years to show how nobly and usefully he could plan, and how much and how well he could accomplish, he would yet have desired to be remembered only by what he had done.

Edward Hutchinson Robbins Revere, son of Joseph W. and Mary (Robbins) Revere, and grandson of Paul Revere of Revolutionary memory, was born at Boston, Massachusetts, July 23, 1827. He was a boy of active temperament and cheerful temper. He had a robust constitution, was ardently fond of the sports of the field and river, and his love of country life was almost a passion. He loved the country, and the country loved and strengthened him, and gave him vigor of frame and fulness of stature. This, however, prevented his receiving the strict course of city schooling, and he attended different rural schools, receiving his final preparation for college from Mrs. Ripley of Waltham.

He entered the undergraduate department of Harvard University in 1843, but left it to begin his professional studies in Boston, in January, 1846, and finally took his medical degree in 1849, at the Harvard Medical School.

In August of the same year he went to Paris, where he remained a year, devoting himself with his fullest energies and the most constant application to the prosecution of his medical studies. Before he returned home he visited the South of France, travelled through England, went to Dublin, and finally visited Scotland, the country which, from early boyhood, he had most wished to see. From his early years he had felt great enthusiasm for Scott's novels and verses, which in after days extended more widely over Scotch poetry. This poetry he loved to quote, and he spoke oftener of what he had seen in Scotland than in any other place.

Dr. Revere returned from abroad fully determined upon a country life, and immediately began to look for a place where he could engage in his profession. He fixed upon Greenfield, Massachusetts, where he opened an office in August, 1850. In the fall of 1851 he married Miss Laura P. Jordan of Canton, Massachusetts, who, with their only daughter, now survives him.

In Greenfield his remarkable facility in forming acquaintances soon made him a home, in which he seemed like an old resident, and was surrounded with warm friends. His skill, kindness, and tender care and nursing, gave him the confidence and attachment of his patients, and the friendship of the neighborhood. The eager solicitude with which the people of Greenfield, after his death, sought to know the least fact in regard to his last days, was just the tribute to his memory he would have desired from them.

Dr. Revere afterwards returned to the eastern part of the State to reside, and spent the two years preceding the war with and near his father's family, filling up his time with the kindest efforts and services for those about him, always engaging in whatever came to him in his profession with such zeal and sympathy as to win the affection of all who received his attentions; and even now, expressions of gratitude from one and another person, whom he in those years relieved, come often to gratify his family and friends.

The war for the union, government, and institutions of our country now broke out, and Dr. Revere, true to his descent, his education, and his principles, looked to know where he was most needed. Perhaps he felt that the time had come when he could usefully employ all his physical and mental powers upon a field such as he had long desired, but had not found. He well knew that in his profession in the army he could not look for fame, and that at best all he could reap would be the reflection that he had been useful, and the happiness always brought by duty performed.

Dr. Revere at once brought his practical mind to bear upon plans for securing to our sick and wounded soldiers the necessary medical skill and care. He saw that physicians from the smaller towns must, to a large extent, be relied on to fill the position of regimental surgeon. He felt that they, like himself, needed some special preparation for such duty. A large experience of surgical accidents they could not often have had, while their toilsome daily labor had usually left them but little time for systematic study.

It was owing to his personal efforts, in view of these facts, that the special lectures in Boston on Military Surgery, which proved at that moment so valuable, were given. Coming to the city, he spared no exertion to urge upon the medical authorities the pressing need of such teaching, and readily obtained their consent. He had been anxious to express before the Society for Medical Improvement his sense of the importance of early professional action, to insure a supply of capable regimental surgeons; but being himself unable to remain in town long enough for this purpose, he persuaded one of his friends to bring forward the subject, the result being, that several leading surgeons were appointed to approach the State government in the matter. It is well known that the members of this committee were immediately, through the wise action of the Executive, constituted the State Medical Commission, and that no medical appointment was conferred till they, after full examination, had approved the candidate. To Dr. Revere belongs exclusively the credit of originating this plan.

Dr. Revere had at first proposed entering the service as an Assistant Surgeon in the Navy, and had received a permission (waiving the objection of his age) for examination for that position, but he was offered a position as Assistant Surgeon of the Twentieth Regiment of Massachusetts Volunteers, of which regiment his brother, Paul J. Revere, was then Major, and he promptly accepted it. He was sworn into service on the 14th of September, 1861, and joined his regiment on the 17th of the same month near Poolsville in Maryland. He immediately entered upon the duties of his post, and with Dr. Nathan Hayward, the Surgeon of the regiment, and Dr. Henry Bryant, Brigade Surgeon, established a brigade hospital, where he treated with great skill and fidelity a large number of sick, the measles having become an epidemic in the brigade.

On the 20th of October, 1861, he joined a battalion ordered to Harrison's Island in the Potomac, preliminary to the battle of Ball's Bluff. When, about noon of the next day, the reconnoitring party which had crossed into Virginia on the night of the 20th, was by order of Colonel Baker reinforced, Dr. Revere accompanied a battalion of the Twentieth, under command of his brother, Major Revere, and reported for service on the Bluff, which was to be the scene of the contest.

During the first three or four hours of the final action of that day, Dr. Revere had his post a few feet in rear of the line of battle, being at all times under the fire of the enemy. The only assistance which he had was from his hospital steward, with such remedies and appliances as the hospital knapsack afforded. No other medical officer was on the field during the day.

This was Dr. Revere's first experience upon the battle-field. His cool, self-possessed deportment, his well-directed energy, and his self-forgetfulness were remarked by all who observed him. He had his post beside a narrow path which led from the Bluff to the river-side, where he gave such care to the wounded as their immediate necessities required, so that their lives could be saved; and they were then sent across the river for better attention and care. The wounded were very numerous, and Dr. Revere's duties were, of course, very arduous, immediate and rapid treatment being required to get the wounded across the river alive. They showed, however, when they came under more deliberate care, that Dr. Revere's duties had been well and tenderly done.

When, after the disastrous battle was over, Dr. Revere arrived at the river, two boats only were left for the survivors, both well and hurt. These boats soon becoming useless, he, with a few others, passed up the river to seek other means of escape. He was active in the endeavor to prepare for the transportation of the party in a small boat found near a flour-mill, about half a mile from the battle-field, but they were driven from it by a demonstration of the enemy's cavalry. This was the same boat which, after dark on the same day, was found by Captains Tremblett and Bartlett, and in which they escaped to the opposite bank of the river. He also aided in the preparation of a raft for the same purpose, which, from the water-soaked condition of the rails of which it was constructed, sank under the weight of one man.

In the course of the evening Dr. Revere and his companions were captured by the enemy's cavalry, and taken to Leesburg; from which place, at two o'clock the next morning, they began to march toward Richmond. The rain fell in torrents during the whole day. Neither Revere nor his companions had eaten anything for thirty-six hours; and they now marched twenty-seven miles, through mud and rain, without subsistence of any kind, save one ration of half-cooked bread and bacon, to Manassas Junction. On Thursday morning, at about eleven o'clock, the detachment of prisoners reached Richmond, having been three days and three nights without any substantial food.

In Richmond the officers were placed in a tobacco warehouse, there being from seventy-five to eighty officers confined in a room some sixty feet wide by seventy or eighty feet long. Dr. Revere's solicitude and care for the invalids, his uninterrupted cheerfulness and kindness, won for him the respect and love of all. Said one who was confined with him: "He was the only man who never spoke an irritable word. The Confederate officers even treated him with great respect, and gave him their confidence, on account of his gentlemanly deportment and manly bearing."

With Dr. Fletcher of Indiana, he was permitted to leave the prison on parole, to look after our sick and wounded in the various hospitals. Their services to our wounded, sick, and suffering men were most timely and valuable, — procuring for them, as these surgeons often did, from their private means, many delicate and nourishing articles, not found in the prison rations. Our men were sick, wounded, neglected, dejected, almost without hope. His courageous, cheerful kindness roused and cheered their spirits; and the promise of preparing them to be removed gave them new life. At the end of three weeks, two hundred of them were, under his superintendence, embarked from Richmond for home. These services were especially appreciated by our men, and are still well remembered.

He wrote from Richmond to his wife: "No one could believe that there could be such a change in the appearance of patients, as there was in the sick here, from merely knowing that we were Yankee doctors. The patients sick with typhoid fever showed it more than any others. Although there was no material change in the treatment, it seemed to brighten them up, and a few words of encouragement did them more good than any medicine, and I think the whole disease took a favorable turn from our first visit; for there has been only one death out of one hundred and ninety-six patients, in the last ten days, and that was a man who was wounded at Manassas."

While devoting himself to these men, Dr. Revere was enabled to be of service to other prisoners, — loyal private citizens from West Virginia. These men were, if possible, in a more miserable condition, and suffered more from neglect, than the prisoners from the North. When Dr. Revere proposed to minister to them, the Confederate officers said, "Don't mind them, they are of no consequence: they are some of our traitors." But the Doctor kept on, and did for them what he could. They, with our own men, remembered these services with gratitude; and often afterwards, while he was at home as a paroled prisoner, some poor fellow came to thank him. He sincerely reciprocated this attachment of all the prisoners.

November 23d he wrote: "Yesterday a large party of prisoners left for the South, — Alabama, I believe, — and twenty of the officers confined here went with them. One would hardly believe how hard it was to part with them: it seemed really like breaking up a family."

Dr. Revere, while in Richmond, became thoroughly convinced of what the country now knows, that there was a systematic determination among the Confederates to let our prisoners perish from neglect, and that this determination was stronger and more relentless against the loyal found among themselves than against Union prisoners.

Ten days after Dr. Revere arrived at Richmond, his brother, Major Paul J. Revere, was taken as one of the hostages for the privateersmen who were to be tried as pirates by our government. The fate of the privateersmen was to be the fate of the hostages. The order of the Confederate government in regard to them was, that they should be confined and treated in all respects like persons convicted of infamous crimes. It is difficult now to recall what was the feeling of the country then. Intelligent people could look upon these privateersmen in no other light than as pirates, and felt that, be the consequences what they might, it was beneath the dignity of our government to treat them otherwise. At this time Dr. Revere wrote home: "Paul and the other officers left us last Thursday for the jail, to await the trial of the privateersmen. There were seven in all from here, the rest of the fourteen being either in South Carolina or New Orleans. They are confined in one small cell, with two small windows. I hear from them every day, but am not allowed to see them. You can imagine our anxiety to hear what action the government will take when they hear of their imprisonment, for there is not the slightest doubt in my mind that whatever is done to the privateersmen will be meted out to our unfortunate comrades."

Yet he preserved his calm equanimity, and exhibited only the same cheerful and encouraging deportment to all about him. Said one of them, "He met it better than any of us." Yet, after his return home, he admitted that the agony of solicitude which he then endured had brought upon him a more serious tone of mind, which could never be removed.

Dr. Revere remained a prisoner in Richmond about four months, being released February 22, 1862, as a paroled prisoner of war. He returned home for a brief period, awaiting his exchange, which took place the last of the following April. He immediately set out for his regiment, and on the 2d of May reported for duty in the lines before Yorktown. He accompanied the Army of the Potomac in its advance upon Richmond, and was with his regiment at the battle of West Point, as also at the battle of Fair Oaks, May 31st and June 1st.

The casualties in this last battle were immense, five thousand seven hundred and thirty men having been killed and wounded during the two days' fight. When the battle terminated, the Twentieth Massachusetts found itself considerably in advance, surrounded by the killed and wounded of the enemy. Of the wounded were officers of high rank, among whom were General Pettigru, and Colonel Bull of Georgia. The medical labors were of course very arduous; and it was not until the middle of the night that a medical officer could be spared to take care of the wounded in and around the front line.

As soon as the wounded of his regiment, who had been left in the rear, had been attended to, Dr. Revere hastened to the front, to take care of the wounded of the enemy. Here again, as at Ball's Bluff, he was the only medical officer present; and he gave his patient labors and skill to the care of the suffering, binding up wounds, and administering opiates to those mortally injured, with unremitting attention, never leaving such a patient until everything — the arrangement of the blanket, the rough couch, the position in every particular — had been carefully attended to, so that the last moments of the dying might be as comfortable as possible. There was a cheerfulness and kindness in the performance of his duty which brought many an expression of gratitude from those in the greatest agony.

The month of June was passed in and about Fair Oaks, in weather very unfavorable to health. Diarrhœa, scurvy, and malarial diseases, induced by the weather and exposure, prostrated the whole army. During this period the sick report of the Twentieth Massachusetts one morning contained the names of two hundred and twenty-one men, — more than one half of the regiment, — who were affected by the above diseases. How arduous must have been the duties of the Assistant Surgeon during this time can well be conceived.

Toward the last of June the Army of the Potomac began its perilous march in retreat to the James River. The Second Corps, of which the Massachusetts Twentieth was a part, constituted the rear guard, and upon it devolved the task of fighting all day and marching all night. The regiment lost heavily in killed and wounded. The wounded were of course left upon the field; but Dr. Revere bestowed upon them every possible care and attention, to make them comfortable until they should be picked up by the enemy. His great physical strength here enabled him to aid many a poor fellow, not severely wounded, to get away from the enemy. More than once he was seen with one such unfortunate man at each shoulder, assisting them to a place of security. His labors and services during this march were wonderful. It is the testimony of one who was with him: "His labors and his usefulness to us, in assisting and encouraging the men, no one will ever know. About every other surgeon broke down under the duties." Said another: "After the seven days' bloody work upon the Peninsula, at the battle of Malvern Hill he worked down nearly the whole medical force of the army, and performed more amputations and other operations than any other, as my surgeon told me, who worked at the hospital with him."

The services of Dr. Revere upon the Peninsula were appreciated by the medical officers of the army. His "zeal, ability, courage, and discretion" were stated, and he was recommended to promotion to a Surgeoncy by Dr. Dougherty, formerly Brigade Surgeon, Dana's Brigade, and Senior Reserve Surgeon, Sedgwick's Division; Dr. D. W. Hand, Brigade Surgeon, Gorman's Brigade; and Dr. John A. Lidell, Surgeon and Medical Director, Second Corps.

After the army reached the James River, the malarial poisons began again to develop their effects upon the systems of the men. Dr. Revere, though himself a sufferer from disease, would not yield to its debilitating effects, but continued with the army in the zealous and faithful discharge of his duties. He accompanied the Army of the Potomac when it moved north to join the forces in front of Washington, where the Twentieth Massachusetts, toward the last of August, was present at Chantilly, the closing combat of General Pope's disastrous campaign.

After the disasters under General Pope, the regiment fell back with the army across the Potomac to Tenallytown, in order to move upon the enemy, who had crossed the Upper Potomac into Maryland.

On the 17th of September, 1862, Dr. Revere accompanied his regiment in its advance under General Sumner, to follow up the charge of General Hooker upon the enemy's troops under General Lee. The latter general had taken position for the battle on the heights in front of Sharpsburg, between that place and the Antietam River. The Twentieth Massachusetts was in the hottest of the fight, and lost very heavily. Dr. Revere, as usual, followed close to the line, being of opinion that his duty to his men required him to be as near as possible, in case of any casualty, so that they should receive immediate attention. He had said that morning, as he was marching to the field, "I mean that to-day no man in our regiment shall fall behind, and that every man shall do his duty." He attended to his surgical work, aided the wounded, and urged and encouraged the men. He was last seen alive about noon, calmly and industriously occupied in the strict line of his duty, in a spot where, part of our soldiers being faced to the rear, the bullets of both armies were flying over his head. As he raised himself from performing an operation upon a wounded man, he was pierced by a bullet, and sank and died upon the field of battle, just one year from the day he joined his regiment. His body was left on the field, but was afterwards recovered, and buried at Mount Auburn.

Dr. Revere, in all his army practice, aimed to save both life and limb. He never permitted an amputation where he thought that there was a hope that skill, care, and patience could avert that necessity. More than once since his death have his friends been touched and comforted by a soldier's holding up an arm or foot, and saying, "Dr. Revere saved that for me. I should have lost it if I had not fallen into his care." He was led to perform his duties thus faithfully from the sense of a higher responsibility than his great reserve upon the subject permitted him to reveal.

Such is the memorial of one of the many sons whom Harvard University sent out to die upon the battle-field. Not one of them held his life more lightly in such a cause. Brave and courageous Nature made him. Gentle, honorable, and faithful he aimed to make himself, and he succeeded. Fame he did not ask for, and he knew it could hardly follow, however well he might discharge the arduous and perilous duties which he assumed. If this testimonial shall give to any one a juster appreciation of the debt the country owes to the medical staff of the army, it will be a service which he would have rejoiced to be the means of procuring.

1848.

JOHN FRANKLIN GOODRICH.

Private 21st Iowa Vols. (Infantry), August 28, 1862; died at Vicksburg, Miss., June 4, 1863, of disease contracted in the service.

JOHN FRANKLIN GOODRICH was the son of Allen and Mary (Emerson) Goodrich, and was born in Mount Vernon, New Hampshire, August 13, 1826. He was fitted for college by Mrs. Ripley of Waltham, Massachusetts. In college he was not prominent as a scholar, nor very well known among his classmates; but the respect in which he was held was manifested at a class dinner, a few years after graduating, when he had gone to California, by the wish, pithily expressed in a toast, "that he might become as rich as he was good."

After graduation he was employed for one year as clerk in one of the manufacturing companies at Waltham. At the beginning of the California gold excitement he visited that region, remaining there five years, and obtaining a respectable competence by labor in the mines. Returning, he purchased a farm in Epworth, Dubuque County, Iowa. He was there married, September 12, 1857, to Miss Marion Pratt, whose family had emigrated to Iowa from Connecticut. They had three children, — two sons and a daughter, — and were living in prosperity on their farm when the war began.

In August, 1862, at the age of thirty-six, he enlisted as a private in the Twenty-first Iowa Volunteers (Infantry), Colonel Samuel Merrill. In a subsequent letter, referring to this enlistment (October 17, 1862), he says: —

"If there had been an abundance of young men in our State ready to enlist, I should undoubtedly have remained at home. But it was not so. The alternative remained for me to enlist and be removed far away from all the sweet amenities of home, incur all the risks of war in all its varied forms, — and those on the battle-field are not the greatest, — or remain at home in peace, and have my cheek mantle with eternal shame. It was a severe trial for my dear wife, but she endured it with Christian fortitude. It is the hardest trial I have to endure, to think that she may be constantly worrying about me."

In the same letter, in allusion to the death of a sister's child, he adds : —

"O how hard it would be for me to part with my dear little ones. I did not know before how closely about my heart had been woven the silken threads of their bright and happy lives."

And his letters to his sisters at the same time speak of his wife and children as "the source of his greatest earthly happiness."

The regiment was at first sent to Missouri, where, although not engaged in any great battle, it had its full share of watching, marching, and skirmishing. It was once highly complimented for performing a night march of twenty-eight miles, and fording eight streams on the way, some of these being waist-deep, and at November temperature. At Hartsville, Missouri, January 1, 1863, a battalion of the regiment, including less that three hundred, after being overwhelmingly outnumbered and flanked, held its position, under Lieutenant-Colonel Dunlap, — although all other regiments had retired, — until the enemy, numbering four thousand, had retreated under cover of the night. In all these duties, Goodrich is stated to have borne an honorable part, and seems to have been sustained through all by a strong, unaffected religious feeling. He expresses pleasure, in his letters, that even amid the vice and profanity of the camp he can enjoy the privilege of social worship ; and after being brought face to face with danger, he learns that "the more we are called on to do and suffer, the better off we are."

For more than two months after this battle, he remained at Hartsville with two others, on detail, to take charge of the wounded men, rejoining his regiment March 20, 1863. During this period he wrote as follows : —

"I seem to realize more and more, as the danger increases, how sweet a thing it is to live for my family. I sometimes tremble at the thought that I may in the lapse of time be brought to welcome a settlement of this great difficulty by some means other than those strictly honorable to our government, for the sake of peace. I have just finished reading the life of Washington by Weems, a contemporary of Washington. It was found on the field after the battle. Some Rebel had thrown it away, and I do not wonder; for he must be to the Rebels like a great avenging *Nemesis*, haunting their every footstep. I could wish for no greater punishment than for every Rebel to be obliged to read it; for if one spark of honor remained, his cheek would mantle with shame at his degeneracy and violation of all principles so inexpressibly dear to the heart of Washington.

"We hear no news here, and know nothing that is going on in the world. How we long to hear of glorious and decisive victories! O for a Washington to lead our armies, and march them on, in the name of the 'Lord of Hosts,' to a decisive issue! Have we not been sufficiently humbled as a nation before God? and will he not speedily avenge us of our adversary? Surely his anger endureth but for a moment.

"There are no social gatherings for religious purposes in this whole vicinity. It seems almost as though war and rebellion had obliterated the thought of God, the Bible, and an eternal state of existence from the heart of the community; but Christianity has to do with the individual rather than the community. It is as imperatively necessary for us to 'keep our hearts with all diligence' in the midst of a godless multitude as in the society of Christians. I pray God to keep me ever humble at the foot of the cross, that he will ever feed my soul with the bread of life, that it perish not in the wilderness of Sin. Although I have been separated during my stay here from the religious influences that ever attended our little Christian Association in camp, I have likewise escaped all contact with the wickedness and vice that prevail to such a fearful extent in an army. I tremble to think of the awful consequences that must necessarily result to thousands of the young men that are in the army 'drinking in iniquity as a flood.' I sometimes think that it is because iniquity doth so abound in our army, that God has no more prospered us in this war. I never allow myself for a moment to doubt the entire justice of our cause, nor that it must finally succeed, if we are *true* to the great work before us. 'God and the right' should be our motto. May we not constantly trust the Excellency of Heaven and Earth in this great affliction? 'If God be for us, who can be against us?' Then let us not be discouraged, but put up our earnest petitions to the Throne of Grace for a speedy deliverance from this great trouble."

During the siege of Vicksburg, the Twenty-first Iowa formed a part of the Thirteenth Army Corps. Foreseeing the fierce, decisive contest for the supremacy of the Mississippi that was to ensue, Goodrich wrote, just as he was embarking at St. Louis:—

"If my life is necessary in dealing the death-blow to this horrid Rebellion, I shall freely, willingly give it up. If I die, it will be with a conviction, as firm as eternal truth itself, that our country will be finally saved. As the blood of the martyrs is the seed of the Church, so the blood of patriots shed in this war is a guaranty of our country's salvation, future welfare, and prosperity."

"April 29, 1863.

"I feel that the prayers of my wife and sisters will be answered to the full satisfaction of your souls. Sister Mercy has great faith that I shall be returned to my family in safety. But I feel that it would be wrong to make this a requisite in our prayers. If it subserves God's purposes better that I should die away from the bosom of my family, let us school our hearts to say 'Thy will be done.' I know that all will be well, and that the Almighty will prove himself a God hearing and answering prayer. Then may we not leave all to his wisdom, knowing that in his hands all is safe? I know, from bitter personal experience, that it will be one of the bitterest trials to school yourself to submission to the will of God in these hours of danger. Yet we know that his will must be done, even if he sees fit to take my life. Let us pray that this cup may pass away; yet 'not as I will, but as Thou wilt.' I will not anticipate evil, but wait for God to develop his plans more fully, and in the mean time exercise implicit faith in his wisdom and goodness. I cannot but believe that all will be well, and that our government will yet be firmly established over all the rebellious territory.

Just before the battle at Port Gibson, he writes:—

"The enemy, without doubt, occupy a strong position. If they make a stand, (as we think they will,) we shall no doubt have a bloody contest. God only knows the issue. I pray him to cover my head in the day of battle, if it be his will; but if he has otherwise ordained, 'his will, not mine, be done.' It would be very sweet to meet my wife and children once again on earth. It is almost agonizing to the mind to think of the bare possibility that we may meet no more; but God is all-wise and good. He *doeth all things well.* When in action I trust I shall act prudently; but I pray God I may never shrink from duty, even if it leads me to the cannon's mouth. . . . .

"NEAR VICKSBURG, May 20, 1863.

"The battle has commenced. The enemy are very strongly intrenched, and hold a very strong position. We expect to storm their works to-day; and if it is in the power of man to take them, they will be taken. May God aid us, I earnestly hope and pray. The battle is not to the strong alone. May the God of battles be on our side, and inspire our men with true and unflinching courage, and give us a speedy victory, and thus bring an end to this awful carnage and desolation. On Sunday, the 17th instant, our regiment, in conjunction with the Twenty-third Iowa Infantry, made a charge upon the rifle-pits at Black River Bridge. Our company lost one man killed, H. W. Britton, my former messmate (poor fellow), and nine wounded, one or two mortally. God mercifully spared my life through this fiery trial, thanks to his name. We buried seven the day of the battle, and four or five have died at the hospital since. The issue of the coming contest lies in the hands of the Almighty. I am as clay in the hands of the potter. He has thus far shielded me from danger. Many must fall; I *may* be among the number. Go to the Throne of Grace for strength to endure, and a spirit to submit to his holy will and pleasure. I pray for submission to his will, whatever it may be, trusting that if we meet no more on earth, we shall form an unbroken family in that home that Christ has gone to prepare for those that love him. God grant me that unflinching courage that shall enable me to march through the stormy missiles of death without fear."

This was almost the last thing he wrote.

In the charge on the enemy at Black River, May 17th, Goodrich was one of the first to enter their works, and so at the assault on the outer works at Vicksburg, May 22d. Here he contracted the brain fever, of which, on the 4th of June, 1863, he died. He was taken into the tent of his Lieutenant, for more tender nursing; and recovering his consciousness for a little while before his death, his last messages were for the welfare of his children, that they might be brought up in the path of Christian duty.

Lieutenant Hill, of his company, writing after his death, says: —

"Mr. Goodrich was as brave a soldier as ever entered the field. Every fight that we have had he was in; and when the charge was made on the Black River works of the Rebels, he rushed forward, and was nearly the first man to mount the embankment, and nobly did he lead back a number of Rebels from their rifle-pits to our camp. The same is true at the charge on the outer works of Vicksburg. It may be said of him, that a good man has fallen. Mr. Goodrich has lived the life of a Christian from the time he enlisted until the day of his death. The evening before his death he assured me all was well, and his trust was in Christ alone. He repeated several times over, to tell his dear wife to train up his two sons for Christ; and very calmly passed away about four o'clock on the morning of the 4th of June."

LUCIUS MANLIUS SARGENT.

Surgeon 2d Mass. Vols. (Infantry), May 28, 1861; Captain 1st Mass. Cavalry, October 31, 1861; Major, January 2, 1864; Lieutenant-Colonel, September 30, 1864; killed near Bellfield, Va., December 9, 1864.

LUCIUS MANLIUS SARGENT, Jr., was born in Boston, September 15, 1826, — the son of Lucius Manlius and Sarah (Dunn) Sargent. He gave early evidence of much talent, and of a daring and impetuous nature. It is recorded of him as a child, that, when a friendly clergyman had taken him on his knee, and asked him what he meant to do in life, he answered, "I don't know, sir, whether to be a minister or a highwayman; but I should n't like to be anything half-way." "On another occasion, having by accident fired in an upper chamber a pistol which he was forbidden to touch, and hearing the rush of the alarmed family on the stairs, he cautiously lowered himself a few feet, and then dropped from a third-story window, as the only method of gaining an instant audience of his kind old nurse in the basement, to whom he poured out his griefs, and then manfully walked up stairs to explain the offence, and receive punishment."

He had from childhood a great love of reading, a retentive memory, and a very ready imagination. He delighted in poetry, and wrote verses with great facility. His instructors in preparation for college were Rev. W. A. Stearns, with Messrs. Charles K. Dillaway and Stephen M. Weld; and in 1844 he entered the Freshman Class of Harvard University.

In college he entered at once upon the rather perilous career which attends the class wit and satirist. In rhymes, *bon-mots*, and caricatures he had no rival; while his varied intellectual tastes, with his love of athletic exercises, and of gay society, furnished temptations to draw him away from the regular college studies. The paths of the class wit and the class first scholar rarely coincide. Yet one of the first scholars in Sargent's class volunteers the testimony, that, "under an outside of apparent frivolity, he cherished a sincere respect for whatever was manly and true, and had many generous impulses."

He did not complete his undergraduate course with the Class of 1848, but received his degree eleven years later, after establishing an honorable reputation as a physician. During the intermediate period he had interested himself in a variety of pursuits, into each of which he threw himself for a time with his accustomed energy. Music, painting, astronomy, and practical seamanship occupied him in turn, he having in the last-named vocation made a voyage to Liverpool before the mast.

He was married, when barely twenty-one, to Miss Letitia Sullivan, daughter of Jonathan Amory, Esq., of Jamaica Plain. After his marriage he fitted up a studio at his house, and passed much of his time in the study and practice of art. This led him into the medical profession, in a manner best stated by Dr. B. E. Cotting, afterwards his professional instructor.

"Art anatomy naturally led him to practical anatomy, and thence to medical science in general. Having decided to enter the profession, he made the business of preparation no half-way matter. His zeal was unbounded and his application unremitted. Nothing was too trivial to escape his rapid observation, nor too difficult to discourage his ardent enthusiasm. His progress was remarkable, and the position he attained unprecedented, — so that when he graduated he was already a man of mark, to whom the profession looked in full expectation of greater things in after days. The hospital created the office of Artist, to secure his services; and the Boston Society for Medical Improvement, at the earliest moment allowed by their constitution, elected him a member. He soon became one of the most prominent physicians of the section of the city where he was located; and a brilliant future seemed opening before him. . . . . To great physical strength he added the most delicate touch with the pencil, and the tenderest manipulation of the sick. . . . . But the chief obstacle to his medical career came from a source the last to be suspected by any one not intimately acquainted with his character, — extreme tender-heartedness. Fearless of gods and men, the plaintive weakness of a sick child appalled, and its death while under his care completely unnerved him."

His other professional teachers were Dr. Jeffries Wyman and Dr. Henry J. Bigelow. He took his degree at the Harvard Medical School in 1857, and was for a time House Surgeon at the Massachusetts General Hospital, and also Dispensary Physician. But the spirit of adventure was still strong in him, and at the outbreak of the war he was one of the first to volunteer for the post of regimental Surgeon, and was the first man commissioned in that capacity in Massachusetts. His regiment was the Second (Infantry), Colonel Gordon; he was commissioned May 28, 1861, and remained with the regiment in Virginia, in the faithful discharge of rather monotonous duty, until October 9, 1861, when he resigned, in order to accept the more congenial position of Captain in the First Massachusetts Cavalry (Colonel Robert Williams), to which he was commissioned on the last day of the same month. His elder brother, afterward Brevet Brigadier-General Horace Binney Sargent, was then Lieutenant-Colonel of the same regiment.

The regiment was stationed in the Department of the South until August 19, 1862, when eight companies, including that commanded by Captain Sargent, were ordered to the Army of the Potomac. From that time they took part in all the cavalry service in that region, and were especially engaged at Kelly's Ford, Sulphur Springs, Stephensburg, and Aldie. At the last action he was left for dead on the field, but subsequently revived and recovered. It proved that a rifle-ball had made a subcutaneous circuit of nearly one third the chest, without further penetration.

Of the varied duties of a cavalry officer, those which best suited his temperament were of course the most stirring and dangerous. He had in him a large element of excitability, — a trait which, while often impairing steady discipline, may yet impart peculiar power on special occasions. Recklessly daring, he was in some respects well suited to the branch of service he had chosen. To the strict routine of regimental business and order he was naturally less attracted. Yet he had the merit of adhering faithfully to his command, sharing the severest service and the poorest fare of his men; seeking neither promotion outside, nor staff position, nor leave of absence. And he showed in some respects — as, for instance, in the temporary discontinuance of intoxicating drinks — a self-control hardly to have been expected from one of his general temperament, and one whose brilliant social powers exposed him to peculiar trials.

He was promoted as Major of his regiment, January 2, 1864; and became its Lieutenant-Colonel, September 30, 1864, — a little more than two months before his death.

The precise circumstances of his death have been variously stated; and the following account, derived from officers of the regiment, varies in some degree from that given in the Report of the Adjutant-General of Massachusetts. The hurried and broken character of cavalry engagements often renders it difficult to secure accuracy of detail in their narration. It appears that soon after the successful raid on Stony Creek Station, Virginia, as the division to which the First Massachusetts Cavalry was attached (part of the Fifth Corps) was moving southward, the forces of the enemy were found strongly intrenched near Bellfield. The infantry had been left along the Weldon Railway, to tear up the track, while the cavalry was moving on, to distract the attention of the enemy. Lieutenant-Colonel Sargent, with his regiment, was at the head of the column, and was just approaching some *abatis* through which the highway ran. Just then General Davies, the brigader commander, rode up and detached the rear squadron of the regiment in pursuit of some supposed scouts or pickets of the enemy. Captain Teague, in command of the squadron, rode within range of the enemy's earthworks; and when the enemy opened upon them with shot and shell, he halted and formed line, seeing nothing more to pursue. At this moment Lieutenant-Colonel Sargent rode hastily up, and said, "Captain, General Davies orders that you —" and at this moment a piece of a shell struck him in the shoulder, shattering it, and throwing him from his horse. Captain Teague then drew back his men beyond reach of the fire, and sent a sergeant and four privates to bring in the wounded officer. During the transportation, he spoke a few words, but died within two hours of his fall. The event occurred on the 9th of December, 1864.

It was afterwards ascertained that General Davies, when he heard the firing, had directed Lieutenant-Colonel Sargent to recall the advancing squadron, and that the latter, instead of sending an orderly, had gone himself. General Davies afterwards described the movement as "a most gallant charge, contributing greatly to the success of the late movements." Certainly to fall thus, sword in hand and in the face of the enemy, was the very death which Sargent's impulsive and daring nature would have chosen. "Had he lived," wrote his former commander, Colonel Robert Williams, "I am sure that he would have added many additional laurels to those he had already gained."

WILLIAM OLIVER STEVENS.

Captain New York 72d Vols. (Infantry), May 30, 1861; Major, June 25, 1861; Colonel, September 8, 1862; died May 4, 1863, of wounds received at Chancellorsville, Va., May 3.

WILLIAM OLIVER STEVENS was son of William Stevens, — formerly a lawyer of Andover, Massachusetts, now Judge of the Police Court in Lawrence, — and of Eliza L. Stevens, daughter of George Watson. His paternal grandfather fought in the battle of Bunker Hill. The patriotism that kindled his blood burnt no less eagerly in that of the descendants, three of whom have fallen in the struggle that has just closed, — William; his brother Gorham, a youth of rare promise; and their cousin, the brave and lamented General I. I. Stevens, who had graduated with especial honors at West Point.

William was born in Belfast, Maine, on the 3d of February, 1828. In preparation for college he entered Phillips Academy at Andover, in 1841, where to this day is left a pleasant reminiscence of the short, thick-set, round-faced boy, quick and active in duty or play, frank in his intercourse, pleasant and genial in his manners, — the type of the man.

More grateful yet is the recollection of him in the minds of his classmates at Cambridge. With a cheery voice, a merry eye, dark hair curling closely over his head, and a countenance open as the day, — the window of a warm heart and generous disposition, — erect in his carriage, frank, unreserved, he at sight won the love of the shy, awkward squad that the first months of college life brought together.

It was an affection that deepened with fellowship; and being of boyish size, he soon became in a peculiar manner the pet of his class. Perhaps this was to his cost, in some ways. Such good company he made of himself, so overflowing was he with life and cheerfulness and all genial qualities, that his time was usurped by his friends: he was allowed but little opportunity for study, and so never aimed at collegiate honors. Indeed, his social qualities were so attractive that few then cared to measure the mental. He was quick of apprehension; and the fine tact he displayed implies the possession of good judgment of men and motives, and good common-sense.

He was one of the earliest enthusiasts in regard to boating in Cambridge, and was the cockswain of the Undine, one of the first college club-boats. He was very diminutive in stature at that time, although he afterwards attained to a manly height. It would be hard to say whether it were due more to this smallness of size, or were rather as a term of endearment, that he was universally known as "The Bud." It was a bud that needed only the development of a healthy life and the sunshine of a loving home to blossom and ripen into goodly fruit.

After graduation he studied law for eighteen months with his father, and again for a year with the Honorable Thomas Wright of Lawrence. The responsibilities of life opened to him, and he devoted himself diligently to his studies. "Resolute and determined," says Mr. Wright, "whatever he undertook he accomplished. He felt he had a duty to perform. He entered upon the practice of his profession determined to succeed, with a confidence in himself which afterwards proved not to have been unfounded."

But it was a self-confidence without a taint of arrogance. "Never distrustful of the future, he counted success as certain." The same confidence and hopefulness were later no mean accessions to his worth as an officer. In all the vicissitudes of war, he wore a steady, hopeful front, — a support to the wavering, a strength and encouragement to all.

He practised his profession for a few months at Newnansville, Florida, but left on account of the debilitating influence of the climate, going to Dunkirk, New York, where he established himself in 1852. He married, in 1855, Virginia T. Grosvenor, daughter of the Honorable Godfrey John Grosvenor, then of Geneva, New York, but originally from Maine. By this marriage he had two sons, — George Watson, seven years of age at the time of his father's death, and William Grosvenor, twenty months old, besides one daughter, who died in infancy.

Here he won the respect and affection of all classes. Among his associates at the bar, his courtesy in practice, his legal ability, his integrity, high sense of honor, and manly straightforwardness inspired marked confidence and esteem. In the resolutions adopted by the bar, after his death, special reference is made to "the scrupulous care with which he ever sought to guard and promote the dignity of his profession, and to make it the means of purifying the administration of justice."

In 1859 he was elected District Attorney of Chatauqua County. The vote was a very flattering one, — in Dunkirk being nearly double that of his party ticket. Some sturdy old farmers from the county, and others who, from his very youthful appearance, had voted against him, came to him after a few months' trial of him in office, to say, "Mr. Stevens, we voted against you; now we have to say, if you wish our votes at any time, or any aid whatever, count on us."

One of the first cases brought forward by him was an indictment for a capital offence, — an event that had not occurred before in the county for many years. Several other cases of importance followed, in all of which he acquitted himself to the great acceptance of the bench, the bar, and the public, receiving many expressions of encouragement and praise.

His letters to his father at this time show him as very busy, prosecuting his profession with great zeal, and with an earnest aim to master its principles and practice. He claims in these letters that he has the friendship of the whole bar. The respect of the presiding justices he certainly had. Graceful in delivery, clear in statement, logical in reasoning, with an ingenuousness that impressed his listeners with the honesty of his convictions, combining enthusiasm with great pertinacity of purpose, the future seemed to him bright and promising.

But it was soon to be overcast. When civil war grew imminent, anticipating that he might be called upon to serve his country in the field, he writes that no whispering of ambition could persuade him to leave his wife and child. "But if summoned," he adds, "I shall obey without faltering, conscientiously believing such to be my duty as a husband, a father, and a man."

The opportunity was at hand. For several years he had been the commander of a militia company (Company D of the Sixty-eighth Regiment New York State Militia). He had put his wonted zeal into the work of drilling and disciplining this little corps, till it had become the crack company in that part of the State; and at the inauguration of Perry's statue, where a number of such associations had been brought together, it had received marked applause. Perhaps it is not too much to say that to his labor, in this respect, was due, in good measure, the promptness with which the citizens of the town met the call for soldiers at the outbreak of the Rebellion. In January, 1861, he offered the services of the company to the Governor in case of emergency. It had just then fallen in numbers to twenty-eight, but was immediately filled to the full standard of eighty.

After the roll of Fort Sumter's guns, there was no hesitation in his mind. To the remonstrances of friends his reply was, "If I don't go now, my boy must." He at once prepared his company for active service, and on the 21st of April again offered it to the State, and received orders to report with it at Elmira on the 1st of May. Countermandatory orders and delays intervening, he went to Washington to seek the acceptance of the Sixty-eighth entire, or at least his company. In this he failed. He was, however, offered a Captaincy in the Regular Army, which he declined.

Learning from the Secretary of War that Daniel E. Sickles, Esq., was empowered to raise a brigade of volunteers, Stevens immediately applied to him; his company was accepted, and ordered to report at Staten Island. Returning home, he found that many of his men, impatient of delay, had joined other organizations, but his indomitable energy and perseverance were not to be thwarted; and on May 31st, within seven days of the date of his order, he reported at the designated rendezvous with a company completely uniformed, and one hundred and five strong. It was incorporated into a regiment commanded by Colonel Nelson Taylor, and known as the Third Excelsior Regiment, and subsequently as the Seventy-second New York Volunteer Infantry.

At the camp, he at once showed that he had in him the elements of an excellent officer, and displayed such knowledge of his duties, that he was selected by his Colonel, and, without a dissent from his brother officers, was commissioned as Major, June 25th. He proved an excellent disciplinarian and drill-master, having a clear and happy method of imparting instruction by explanation and illustration. Heart and mind were devoted to his work, which he mastered to its minutiæ. A true soldier, he became very sensitive of the reputation of his regiment, to the efficiency of which, says his Colonel, he added much.

His affable manner, his manliness and unaffected dignity, attracted and attached all who came within his sphere. Ready to adjust difficulties, though firm in discipline, — full of sympathy for all human interests, — he especially won the love of his men, — a love which in the rough proof of war when once given is poured out with no stint.

Assiduous study made up in him the want of previous military training. Active service in the face of the enemy is a stern school, but the most thorough for a soldier. So well did he improve it, that the brigade commander under whom he served his last campaign, and whose fullest confidence he won, — General Revere, a veteran in service, — describes him as "a truly splendid officer and magnificently brave."

Immediately after the battle of Bull Run the Excelsior Brigade was ordered to Washington, and put in the defences of the city. The large fort on the Eastern Branch, known as Fort Stanton, was built under the immediate supervision of Major Stevens. In October his command was ordered to Lower Maryland, and stationed for some time at Budd's Ferry, opposite Shipping Point, where Rebel batteries blocked the passage of the Potomac. During the winter of preparation and drill which followed, he gained the warm friendship of his division commander, General Hooker. With spring came the campaign of the Peninsula. The division was assigned to the Third Corps, General Heintzelman commanding. At the siege of Yorktown, busied in the construction of approaches, Stevens won the name of a meritorious and gallant officer.

The battle of Williamsburg was the first severe test of fighting qualities of his regiment. In following up the retreating enemy, Stoneman's cavalry found itself, on the afternoon of May 4th, checked at Fort Magruder, a bastioned work, with several redoubts on either side effectually covering the road. Hooker's division, which followed in support of the cavalry, bivouacked in the woods that night, and came up before the fort early in the morning of May 5th. It commenced the attack at half past seven o'clock, and for a while cleared the ground in its front; but the enemy, concentrating his forces, advanced to the attack, and again and again endeavored to turn Hooker's left. The firing became very hot, the enemy having a partial shelter in the woods, while the division was drawn out, partly in the open, partly in the felled timber, protecting itself as well as it could by the logs strewn on the ground. The brigade on the left was driven in, and soon after a heavy attack was made on the right also. Between these cross-fires the Excelsior Brigade lay, taking the brunt of the battle till after four o'clock, when the opportune arrival and gallant advance of Kearney's division allowed General Hooker to withdraw his troops, exhausted by the long day's fight. It had been a gallant struggle against superior numbers, protracted through rain and mud and hunger, until ammunition was nearly exhausted. They had suffered severely: the brigade had lost, perhaps, a third of its numbers, two hundred and eighteen having been killed and wounded from Major Stevens's regiment alone. The Major, who that day commanded the regiment, as the Colonel was in command of the brigade, was delighted with the behavior of his men. "Not one did I see waver," he said. "Of course," he adds, "it was necessary for me to be moving from point to point, and it was necessary to go *over* the logs to do so. I was hit three times, — first by a ball which ricochetted and bruised the calf of my right leg; next, by a ball which grazed my face just under the right side of my mouth; and again by one that grazed a shoulder-blade."

The phrase "of course" modestly apologizes for constant activity, not only in directing his own men, but in going to and fro to encourage the whole shattered line, — services that won the commendations of his brigade commander, and of Colonel Dwight, commanding the First Excelsior, which fought gallantly side by side with the Third. And the ball which "grazed" his face proved to be a buckshot, that inflicted a severe wound, and remained in his jaw till his death.

While the Major was thus engaged, his brother, a Second Lieutenant, — a stripling fresh from Cambridge, — escaped from the hospital, was toiling with a wounded leg after *his* regiment, also hotly engaged. Coming up to the scene of action, this boy gathered a couple of hundred stragglers, planted them by a battery, and defended it in the teeth of the enemy till Kearney and succor arrived.

Again the regiment was engaged at Fair Oaks, and through the seven days' battles, till the close of the campaign at Malvern Hill. The Major had long since won the love and respect of his men; and his conduct in the campaign led his commanding officers to describe him as possessed of courage of a high order, of coolness and equanimity that never failed, and of a clearness of judgment that under the most trying and confused circumstances remained unshaken.

As it seemed as if the Army of the Potomac was about to enjoy a rest from its labors, the Major, at the request of his Colonel, was sent to Dunkirk to recruit the depleted ranks of the regiment. When at home he was offered the command of a new regiment then forming, but declined it, preferring, at sacrifice of rank, to remain with those who, through danger and hardship shared in common, had learned mutual respect and trust. He was also unwilling to give aid to the disastrous policy of constantly sending out bodies of raw and inexperienced men to be instructed by incompetent hands in numerous and varied duties, when the same material, put into regiments already in the field, would give them new strength and vigor, and the recruits would themselves speedily become assimilated and learn one additional lesson of incalculable value to a soldier, — a pride in the history and name of their organization.

He returned, September 1st, with one hundred and twenty-eight recruits; and as Colonel Taylor had been commissioned as Brigadier-General, was promoted to the colonelcy, the commission dating from September 8th.

In November, marching across the country, he rejoined the Army of the Potomac at Warrenton Junction. At Fredericksburg his command was in the left grand division under Franklin, and was not engaged. The winter was given to the drill and discipline of his regiment, now largely increased by the addition of new men, and with such success that General Revere (now the brigade commander) describes it as a magnificent regiment of stalwart men in splendid condition.

The end of April found the Army of the Potomac again in motion. The Third Corps crossed the Rappahannock at the United States ford on Friday, May 1st, and, moving up towards Chancellorsville, bivouacked in the rear of the troops then briskly engaged with the enemy. During that night and the following day the enemy was busy in cutting a road through the woods in front of our line, and marching by it large masses of his force from the left to our extreme right, where late in the afternoon they burst like a tornado upon the astounded Eleventh Corps, breaking it and driving it before them.

The Third Corps was hurried up to check the rout and hold the enemy, who by their own impetus had then been thrown somewhat into confusion.

The most graphic sketch of the demeanor of Colonel Stevens on that day is to be found in a manuscript narrative by Chaplain J. H. Twichell of the Second Excelsior Regiment, from which the following is an extract: —

"To me there is no scene of individual soldiership to which I so frequently recur as to Colonel Stevens at the head of his regiment, leading it into fire at the battle of Chancellorsville. . . . .

"Those who were present at that time and place will never forget how suddenly, within half an hour, on the afternoon of May 2d, the whole aspect of our affairs was changed from bright to dark by a swift, unlooked-for disaster. When the attack, like a thunderbolt out of the clear sky for unexpectedness, struck the right wing useless at a blow, our corps was lying in reserve. We were instantly ordered into the breach, and being under arms, in ten minutes had turned the corner at the Chancellor House, and were hurrying out on the plank-road toward the quarter where the storm had burst. A third of a mile farther on we met the rout. It is always a trying thing for troops to stem a tide of confusion and retreat, while going into action, and that was the worst situation of the kind I ever witnessed. Thicker and faster poured back the panic-stricken rabble, nearer and nearer swept down the successful onslaught of the enemy. Plainly, no time was to be lost. Though we were still marching in column, the order to load without halting was given, and the men marched, and loaded, and cursed the fugitives, all at the same time. Then came the order to form in line of battle, and go into position. Being a non-combatant, I drew up beside the road, upon a little knoll, where several batteries of the Seventeenth Corps artillery were planted, to watch the process. It was while sitting there upon my horse, that I saw Colonel Stevens pass by, leading his command; and, as I have said, his appearance then comes first to my memory, when I call up the examples of individual soldiership that have fallen under my observation. I can neither forget nor describe it. His natural, habitual bearing was military. That I had noticed the first time I saw him, in the spring of 1861, when he was fresh from the court-room and his law, it was in such marked contrast with that of the generality of volunteers; but on this occasion all the soldier in him roused to its highest pitch: it was splendid. If a face ever reflected the *gaudium certaminis*, his did then. It was a noble, handsome face, always alive with expression, and now it shone with a light of eagerness and daring that made one forget the surroundings for a minute, to look at it. Truly it was a goodly sight to see that calm, undaunted front, amid the terror that was manifest on every hand. It relieved the depression of calamity, and seemed to afford reason for believing that the waning fortunes of the day would yet be restored.

Every little while he turned in his saddle, and cast his eye over the regiment pressing close behind, as if in that way to impart his own high spirit to his men; and that he did so was soon after fully proven."

The Excelsior Brigade was thrown out on the right of the plank-road, down which the enemy was advancing, and upon which Jackson, who had conceived and executed this brilliant move, intending to cut off and annihilate the army of the United States, was that evening so mysteriously killed. During the night the brigade threw up a line of log breastworks, strengthened by *abatis*, in preparation for the attack expected in the morning. The men were weary and hungry, but rest they had none: the constant alarms and driving in of the pickets kept them on the alert all night.

At daylight of the 3d, the enemy opened with artillery and musketry. For some hours the line was gallantly defended, until its left flank, resting on the road, was turned, and the breastworks enfiladed. Regiment by regiment the brigade broke off from the left before the column that bore down upon it. To meet its advance, Colonel Stevens immediately ordered a change of front; and while the movement was being executed, he was struck by a minié-ball, which pierced his chest. As the regiment was driven past him, he called to one of his old company, unclasped his sword, and gave it with the words, "Carry it to my wife, — remember me to my boy."

Captain Bliss and two men attempted to raise him. The officer was shot, and the yelling masses of the enemy immediately closed around him. "Several of his men," writes his brigade commander, who regarded him with "particular affection," — "several of his men and officers come to me actually crying with grief to announce his fall."

He was carried to a hospital at the house of a Mr. Chancellor, near the Wilderness Church, on the plank-road. He was tenderly cared for by our own surgeons and by the enemy, bearing his suffering with patient composure, and at times unconscious. When a wounded sergeant of his regiment came to his side and asked what he could do for him, the answer was, "Nothing, unless you close column by division." That day his thoughts seemed to dwell upon his men, his regiment, though he was too feeble to say much.

The next day he was removed into a small bed-chamber, and the ball, which had passed from left to right through his breast and shoulder, was extracted from its lodgement in the arm. He seemed relieved, talked freely for a while of home, of his wife and boys, his father, and his country, and with his wonted cheerful smile expressed the hope that he might recover. When at noon an officer came to parole such as were fit to take the oath, he took the pen and blank form in his hand, looked first at the one, then at the other, then gave them back, saying he could not write.

During the afternoon he became delirious; again his thoughts went back to the battle-field, and he called, as if to his men, "Forward, men, steady!" Then he sank quietly, and in the early evening passed away.

The chaplain of the Third North Carolina Volunteers, Rev. George Patterson, who had been struck with the appearance of the wounded officer, had procured him a bed and privacy, had washed his body, had bathed his temples, and had tenderly watched over him. "I thank God fervently," he afterwards wrote to Colonel Stevens's father, "that it was my privilege to nurse him. . . . . He was gentle and tender; the heart of a woman in the body of a warrior." And a surgeon of the opposing army told the father that so gallant and soldierly was the young man's aspect, he had called in several brother officers to look at him.

A further extract from the graphic narrative of Mr. Twichell will show the impression left among the officers of our own army.

"So far as I ever knew or heard, his military life was without reproach; and every commander he had, from old Joe Hooker down, had marked him as one of the most promising young officers in the Potomac Army. Indeed, his corps commander once told me that he had been only waiting till he should have fought one battle as

Colonel (he had lately been promoted to that rank) before recommending him for further advancement. He lacked no quality requisite to the utmost success in the profession of arms. He was rarely skilled in the science of it, had a strong natural liking for it, and possessed to a wonderful degree the power of controlling his men and inspiring them with enthusiastic confidence in him. Poor fellow! I saw them crying in the ranks as they stood presenting arms to his body when it was brought back from over the river.

"As a *man*, too, he was singularly free from faults. To his soldierly traits and accomplishments he added the rarer virtues of Christian morality. He was a steadfast example of modesty, purity, and temperance; yet at the same time his tent was one of the cheeriest places to spend an evening in that the army afforded; for he was the most genial entertainer, and knew the art of good-fellowship to perfection. His generosity and charity were of the kind that 'never faileth.' I recall an instance illustrative of this, which I was told by those who witnessed it.

"At one time a captain of his regiment, mistakenly conceiving himself injured by the Colonel in some official transaction, for several weeks cherished and expressed a bitter spirit toward him, and avoided meeting him as much as he could. Meanwhile the Colonel took no notice of the matter, but invariably spoke of and to the captain, without manifesting displeasure with his conduct, though its injustice must have deeply offended him.

"Finally, however, it was made known to the captain in some way that he had been entirely wrong in the case, and going to the Colonel in person, he acknowledged his fault and made a full apology. It was a scene not easily to be forgotten, when that same evening, at the customary meeting of the regimental officers for training in tactics, the Colonel made the reconciliation public, by taking the captain's hand before them all, and openly declaring his satisfaction in the fact that they were friends again. This same officer was also fatally wounded at Chancellorsville, and it was commonly reported after the battle that he was struck while stooping over the Colonel, having been the first to reach his side after he fell."

Chaplain Patterson took from Colonel Stevens's neck a locket of his wife's hair, and sent it to her, with his papers. The body, dressed in uniform, was wrapped in a blanket, and laid in the ground near the old Wilderness Church. It was soon after exhumed by one of our surgeons, placed in a rude coffin made from a door of the church, and delivered to the father at the ford. After resting awhile in the Governor's room in New York City, it was transported to Dunkirk, where it lay in state, under guard, till the day of the funeral.

All classes and ages assembled to do honor to him whose sympathetic nature, kindly to all, was in turn beloved by all. Resolutions of honor had been previously adopted by the officers of the Excelsior Brigade, by the Supreme Court, by the members of the bar in that county, and by the citizens of Dunkirk. And just before the burial, the grim Arsenal was the scene of a most touching ceremony. The infant son of Colonel Stevens, held over his lifeless body, was baptized with the customary forms of the Church, assigned the name of his father, and sanctified to the cause in defence of which that father had sacrificed this world's ease and successes, friends, wife, child, and the immeasurable opportunities of life.

1849.

EVERETT PEABODY.

Colonel 13th (afterwards 25th) Missouri Vols. (Infantry), September 1, 1861; killed at Pittsburg Landing, Tenn., April 6, 1862.

THE Rev. William B. O. Peabody, D. D., of Springfield, Massachusetts, was the son of Judge Oliver Peabody of Exeter, New Hampshire, and was born July 7, 1799. He married Eliza Amelia White, daughter of Major Moses White, who served in the army through the Revolution. Rev. Dr. Peabody was settled in Springfield, Massachusetts, in October, 1820, and remained with the same parish until his death, which took place in 1847. He was well known as a preacher, essayist, naturalist, and poet, and was universally respected for the pure and elevated character of his daily life. Those who remember the Springfield of forty years ago speak of Mrs. Peabody as lovely in person and manners, full of energy and public spirit, and taking a leading part in all schemes for doing good.

Their eldest son, Howard, died in infancy. The rest of the family consisted of one daughter and four sons, of whom Everett was the oldest. He was born in Springfield, June 13, 1830. There is little to be told about his childhood. He was a tall, athletic boy, fond of out-door sports, and excelling in them. He was particularly skilful as a swimmer. Once, while swimming across the Connecticut, at Springfield, he was taken with the cramp when half-way across. One of his schoolmates swam out to him with a plank, by the aid of which Everett reached the shore. It is a curious circumstance that this schoolmate (since dead) was in the Rebel army at Shiloh, and afterwards said that as he was marching into the Federal camp he saw Everett's body on the field, and recognized it at once.

Everett was remarkably quick to learn, and was regarded as

the most gifted boy of the family. He was fond of poetry, and would repeat page after page of Scott's poems, which were great favorites with the household. His father had a strong desire to send him to college, but had not the means to do so. Assistance was at last volunteered in such a manner that he could not refuse; and in 1845 Everett entered as Freshman in Burlington College, Vermont. He remained there but a year, and in 1846 entered Harvard as Sophomore.

At first his standing was very high, — so that one of his letters expresses the hope that he shall prove to be among the first eight scholars; and although he afterwards seemed to care less about his rank, he had a part at commencement when he graduated. He was fond of fun and frolic, and was rusticated, in 1847, for helping to make a bonfire on University steps. He was sent home to study with his father, and was at home when his father died, — his mother and only sister having died three years before. He finished the term of his suspension in the family of Rev. Rufus Ellis, then of Northampton.

While in college he never was a plodding student, but learned with singular ease and facility. I remember his asking me once to hear him recite a lesson of several pages, which he had been studying for half an hour; and I was surprised to hear him give the substance of page after page, having evidently fixed in his mind every point of importance in the lesson clearly and distinctly, while he troubled himself little about the precise phraseology. He had at this time acquired a good deal of facility in French and German, and had a great deal of miscellaneous information. His wit and love of fun made him a favorite companion at social entertainments; and he enjoyed such things himself, although not to excess.

During his last winter vacation, he made a visit to Philadelphia and Washington, and in the latter place gained an acquaintance who seemed to fascinate him a good deal, — Colonel Baker, then in Congress, and subsequently killed at Ball's Bluff. Colonel Baker confided to the young man a project of taking a party of fifty or a hundred men to California, for two years' service in the mines. Everett was delighted with the prospect of adventure involved in such an enterprise, and wrote home to his friends for aid and advice; but the project ultimately failed.

He graduated in 1849, and at once found employment at engineering on the Boston Water-Works, under Mr. Chesborough. Soon afterwards, he obtained a leveller's place on the Cleveland, Columbus, and Ashtabula Railroad. He thus describes his first experience of out-door life: —

"February 3, 1850.

"Thank Heaven, I can support myself now; and if it is a pittance I live on, it is at least earned by my own right arm, which does not snarl and tell me I am extravagant, whenever I ask it therefor. And so *au diable* with money matters. Well, it 's glorious, after all, going about in these old woods, with trees which seem to have borne the brunt of the tempests for a thousand years. Huge shafts, with buttress-like roots, and a flooring of Nature's own mosaic. Though our feet are wet and our hands cold, though we anticipate the sun and work like hodmen, there 's a luxury in it which I can feel, but not analyze. You might not think it poetry, but it is, — this wading through the swamps watching the clouds. We have nothing at the East to compare with these glorious clouds. We left off work last night about a mile and a half from the tavern where we now are. I started, along with about six of the party, and trudged through the swamp for a mile and a half or two miles, and then found ourselves four miles from the tavern, in a driving snow-storm, dark, and the walking not fit to be called walking. We came home very much fatigued."

This was the beginning of a Western residence of more than ten years, with but a few short visits to the home of his youth. He was successively employed on the Pacific Railroad (St. Louis), the Maysville and Lexington, Kentucky, the Maysville and Big Sandy, the Louisville and Frankfort, — always as assistant or resident engineer, but with always increasing salary and responsibilities.

At this time he was in splendid physical condition. His frame was large and powerful, his health was always good, and he was almost always very light-hearted and careless about the future. Except that he had a very strong ambition to rise in his profession, I never saw a man who troubled himself less about what the morrow might bring forth. At this time, the Hon. James Guthrie told the Hon. Edward Everett, if I remember his words correctly, that he thought Everett Peabody was "the best field engineer in the West." He was soon after appointed Chief Engineer of the Memphis and Ohio Railroad, with a salary of three thousand dollars. At a later period, — for everything connected with Western railroads was then fluctuating and uncertain, — he was employed as engineer of the Nashville and Chattanooga Railroad, and then of the Hannibal and St. Joseph's (Missouri) Railroad. Here he remained for three years.

Up to this time his letters to his brothers, which were numerous, showed simply the professional enthusiasm which might have been expected from his energetic and buoyant nature. As he grew older, however, the wearying effects of rough border life began to tell upon him, and the desire for home and for cultivated society became stronger and stronger. One of his brothers was married about this time; and his many letters to his new sister-in-law showed a tenderer side of his nature, and exhibited a plaintive longing that was almost pathetic. For a man of education and cultivated tastes to find himself at twenty-seven the permanent resident of a "boarding car" at the unfinished extremity of a new railway track, in the midst of an unbroken wilderness, in the dead of winter, was rather a dismal experience. The following letters speak for themselves.

"Boarding Cars, February 20, 1858.

"This Sunday evening, wearied out by a day of the most listless laziness, I can think of nothing to do, unless it be to write to you, my dear ——. . . . . The heading of this letter may puzzle you. As it is well to have the snow off the track before we pull the engine wide open, I will explain.

"A train of cars is kept at the end of the track, and pushed forward as the track progresses. These migratory dwellings contain cars for the accommodation of the men who work, — a car for cooking and one for eating, and at the end of the train, a blue car, with a peaked roof, contains my office, one end of which is decorated with bunks and shelves, which serve as sleeping apartments. An I were skilful, I would delineate, in a few rapid strokes of the pen, the inside hereof; but the gift of sketching is denied me, and the mere statement that it contains a drawing-table, a stove, a desk, and the aforesaid shelves, would seem to go as far as words can do in describing.

"The aforesaid cars are now on an embankment about forty feet high, and the snow stretches away to the north and south. The trees are black and dreary-looking, and the wind goes howling by. Bitter cold it is, too, outside. But I have finished my frugal repast of bread and butter, and do not purpose exposing my cherished nose to the night air again. Mr. Kirby, one of my assistants, is reading the 'Autocrat' by my side. . . . .

"What a great thing a locomotive is, — a sort of Daniel Webster reproduced in iron. I always feel like taking off my hat, when I see one come elbowing up. During the past week I have been renewing my acquaintance with the levers, and getting able to ride the beast again. It gives one a singular consciousness of power to feel the machinery, and to know that the whole thing is under your control; that you can say to it, Thus far, or, Do this, or, Do that,— and it is done.

"But after all, vague reminiscences come back to me of ancient sleigh-rides, of pretty faces snuggling close to your side, of muffs held up before faces to keep off the wind, and gentle words. A good dash across the Neck would be glorious now. It seems to me the only case where our stiff Puritanic rigidity is overcome,— possibly by the still stiffer rigidity of the weather, — and where people seem 'to let themselves out' for fun and frolic generally, in our old home-land.

"Naught of that in this Western land. The fun and frolic is almost entirely men's fun; and, heavens! how much we would give for one good romp in the old land! There is fun enough, and wit and nonsense enough, out here; but, after all, it is hard and angular, and lacks entirely the refining influence which womankind infuses into man's life. But the weird sisters weave, and Atropos sits ready. Let her sit. I mean to get back before she takes the final *suit*, and see if I can't find youth and life again in the 'auld countree.'"

"April 18, 1858.

"Why do you attack me so ferociously about a mild remark, that you Eastern people don't know how to love? You don't.

"I have no doubt you think you do. I have no doubt you think that this love — which, as you yourself say, becomes such a part of your nature that you don't show it, and, you might add (if it were not doggerel), know it — is strong passion and devotion; but it is n't. So far as it has any character, it is more habit than anything else. You lead — not you particularly, but all the Eastern people — two lives: one, the outside life of society (which is hypocrisy); the other, the life of love, family, or otherwise, which is real: and you have plenty of support for both, and very little care for either. But wait until you only have support for one, the outer, and none at all for the other, the inner. Wait till you have to treasure up memories of each little act of affection, in place of having the realities about you daily, and you knowing all the time that these very realities exist, and you can't get at them. Did you ever read of Tantalus, of Ixion, and the other reprobates? Wait till distance blinds you to the faults, and exalts the virtues, of your friends, and you love them with a love the more absorbing and complete because it finds no response in daily life, and because it is all your inner and real life. Then, my dear, you won't call me a truculent border ruffian.

"Pshaw! what nonsense for me to write this stuff for you to laugh at! I love my friends, and that you know full well, that gave me leave or (if I might correct Shakespeare) provoked me to speak of it."

"Bloomington, Mo., December 16, 1858.

"I have returned from a scouting expedition after game, cold, angry, and generally ill-humored. A 'Merry Christmas' to you all at home there.

"I send you a song which we shall sing to the tune of 'Benny Haven's, Oh!' at our Christmas supper.

'Our fires are blazing cheerily,
  Our loaded tables groan,
The wine is circling merrily
  Among us here alone.
But our thoughts are wandering sadly
  To the days of long ago, —
To the days when we so gladly
  Saw Christmas wassail flow.

'And the long years, whose passing
  Hath left its many stings;
And the young hopes, whose glassing
  Mirrored such noble things;

And the struggles we have fought through,
  The sorrows we have borne,
And the objects we have sought, too,
  All to our minds return.

'Our weary exile bearing
  Far from those loved before,
Our hearts shall still be sharing
  Their pleasures as of yore.
Then fill up bumpers, brothers;
  As Christmas takes its flight,
We drink this toast together
  To those at home to-night.'

"(A poor song, but mine own.)"

Early in 1859 Everett became partner in a firm organized for the purpose of building the Platte County Railroad, in Missouri, and he was appointed Chief Engineer, with complete control of the work and a salary of $3,000 per annum. He expected to make an independent fortune out of the contract, and would undoubtedly have done so, had he lived. His residence now became St. Joseph, Missouri. His employment involved a good deal of travelling, through a beautiful country, and an occasional attendance on the Legislature, as lobby-member, which he found less agreeable than instructive. His worldly prospects were bright. "I should not be surprised," he wrote, "if in two or three years each of us (there are three) should have an annual income of $20,000 or $25,000 from the road." His health and strength were in admirable condition; he described himself as "strong as an ox, and with vitality enough for a dozen of our young men of Boston." When, in the following summer (1860), he made his long-desired two months' visit at home, I noticed that, wherever we went, his commanding *physique* always attracted attention. He was six feet and one inch in height, and weighed two hundred and forty pounds. His motions were slow and steady, and his manners quiet and grave.

Such were his conditon and prospects at the outbreak of the Rebellion. The following letter is the first record of his views upon the subject.

"St. Joseph, March 24, 1861.

"I received yours this morning. It will always be better to direct letters here than to any place whence I may happen to write you. . . . .

"We have been fighting a gallant battle here for the Union, and have whipped our opponents at every point. We had a convention, called by the Legislature, for the purpose of carrying us out of the Union, filled with men who declared 'that the present grievances did not justify secession'; and we carried the State on that basis by a vote of sixty thousand majority. That convention has decided in favor of a national convention; and if one is held, we shall send the right kind of men, — men ready to compromise on some basis of settlement which will, in time, bring back the seceding States, and restore the Union. See that you do the same thing. If you drive the Border Slave States from you, and crush out us Union men who are fighting the battles here, there will be separation, and undoubtedly, sooner or later, war. We are satisfied here with Lincoln's Inaugural and Cabinet; but we have very little respect for a party which places him there to settle matters, and then ties his hands by passing no bills to give him the necessary power; which passes a high-tariff bill (to which we have no objections), and then provokes the violation of it by neither closing the Southern ports nor giving power to collect revenue outside of them.

"I am growing terribly bored with having nothing to do, and growing rusty. I shall have to pitch out somewhere before long. I shall probably make a trip out as far as Laramie this summer, in case nothing happens to prevent; and if I could get a good opening in any part of the world, I would wind up affairs here and start. Love to all.

"Yours, truly,

"Everett."

This letter shows that his residence of twelve years in the Border States had exerted the natural effect on his views, and that he looked on national affairs with the eyes of a Missouri Unionist, not of a New England man. The next letter shows him carried already far on by the enthusiasm of the war.

"St. Joseph, May 16, 1861.

"Dear ——, — Yours received this morning. The reason of my long silence is, that I made a trip — starting about April 10th — up to Fort Randal, a thousand miles up the Missouri River, and only returned about ten days ago.

"Everything has been in a state of excitement here, and about ten days ago was drifting toward thorough anarchy. I think the operations in St. Louis did no particular harm, and Harney's proclamation does a wondrous deal of good. He is a citizen of Missouri, and has the power to do what he says he will; and it is well known here that when he undertakes to do a thing he is apt to do it very roughly. Everybody knows him to be a pro-slavery man, and this takes, to a certain extent, the sting away from any exercise of authority he may make. Altogether an excellent appointment.

"Of course all business is dead. If I can get into the Regular service, in a high position, I shall join the army. I cannot yet tell whether I can muster influence enough to command a majority or a captaincy, but shall probably try and see what can be done.

"We apprehend, at present, no difficulty; and if we have one, it will not, I think, be lasting. I trust not.

"There is little to write about, except politics. The real issue in this State is between our damnable secession State government and old Harney; and as the Union men and Disunion men are each afraid of the other, and our State government is powerless, both from lack of money and of arms, I think that Missouri will be apt to be quiet, Harney's sword being thrown into that scale.

"I shall look to you presently, perhaps, to help me in my military views."

The following letter shows his first summons to military service. The volunteer corps here indicated was subsequently organized, and he was appointed its Major. It became the nucleus of the Thirteenth Missouri, and he was commissioned as its Colonel, to rank as such from September 1, 1861. After the capture of the regiment at Lexington, its number was given to another corps, and it was ultimately reorganized as the Twenty-fifth Missouri.

"HEAD-QUARTERS, DEPARTMENT WEST, ST. LOUIS ARSENAL, MAY 31, 1861.

"SIR, — I am directed by Brigadier-General Lyon, commanding, to request you to repair at once to Fort Leavenworth, to confer with the commanding officer there in regard to the organization and equipment of a reserve corps in your city.

"I am, sir, very respectfully,

"Your obedient servant,

"CHESTER HARDING, JR.,

A. A. G., 1st Brig. Mo. Vols.

"To E. PEABODY, Esq., St. Joseph, Missouri."

Major Champion Vaughan wrote soon after to General J. H. Lane: "There is no man in Northern Missouri so well calculated to give you all useful information as Major Everett Peabody, to whom I would urge upon you 'an attentive ear' in all matters he has to communicate. In the great crisis now upon Missouri, I believe no man is so likely to take hold of the helm with a manly resolution as Major Peabody, who combines in a happy degree those qualities which the occasion and the times demand."

Major Peabody's own letters now afford almost a continuous narrative: —

"CAMP LANDER, August 27, 1861.

"DEAR ——, — I am ordered to Kansas City, and expect roughness.

"I shall send home, in the course of a day or two, my contract with the Platte Railroad Company; and in case I go up, which is very likely, I want to have the rest of you take what I have made, and use it to the best advantage for all three.

"Good by, old fellow. I have a sort of presentiment that I shall go under. If I do, it shall be in a manner that the old family shall feel proud of it.

"Yours,

"EVERETT."

"LEXINGTON, September 24, 1861.

"DEAR ——, — Finding nothing to do at Kansas City, I moved down about eight hundred and fifty men to this place, on the 4th. On the 7th I started southward with Colonel Marshall (First Illinois Cavalry) in command, towards Warrensburg. After progressing, in his fashion, eighteen miles in two days, he returned here, leaving me in command of about nine hundred infantry and three hundred and fifty cavalry, with two six-pounders, and directed me to make a reconnoissance toward Warrensburg. I marched seventeen miles, and reached there at five in the evening.

"The rumors I had been hearing were, before twelve o'clock at night, reduced to certainty, — that the main body of the Missouri forces, under Price, Jackson, and Raines, were upon us, some twelve thousand strong. They were within five miles when I commenced my retreat, burning bridges, and delaying them as far as possible. I was none too quick; for, two hours after I arrived here, our pickets were driven in, and skirmishing began, and was continued during the night; they (mostly mounted) having made a forced march of thirty-five miles by a circuit, to cut us off.

"The next day (12th) we were attacked, first having severe skirmishing with their van, and afterwards a three and a half hours' cannonading, — we behind some hasty intrenchments; at evening they retired. We lost four killed and twenty-five wounded; they, about fifteen killed and thirty-five or forty wounded.

"From this time we worked assiduously at the trenches, which, however, were unfortunately situated, being below the top of the hill, so that the inside could be only partially protected by traverses from the cannonading and sharpshooting, and having no water inside the lines. Still we did the best we could. Colonel Mulligan, of Chicago, was in command (a good officer and a brave one), with a total of two thousand seven hundred men and about one thousand head of mules and horses; but seven hundred of our men were armed only with horse-pistols and sabres.

"On Wednesday last (18th), after constant skirmishing in the interval, the main attack commenced, and continued without intermission until five o'clock Friday evening, when Colonel Mulligan surrendered. During all that time our men had not in all a full meal of food or a pint of water to the man; of course there was no sleep. The enemy were receiving large reinforcements, and at the time of attack claimed to be thirty thousand strong, and were I think, fully twenty thousand. Still we should have held out two or three hours longer, had it not been for cowardice or treason on the part of one of the Home Guards officers, (a butcher or stage-driver, I believe,) who, after one charge had been repulsed, and just as another was coming on, put out the white flag. Colonel Mulligan supposed it to be hoisted by the opposite side, and sent to General Price to know the meaning; and *vice versa.* Meanwhile they had surrounded us in enormous quantities, and were even in our ditches. The surrender was unconditional, and as the place had been kept eight days (ample time for reinforcements), and as, owing to the exhausted state of the men, we could not have held out over night, I am not certain that we could have done better. The loss is about equal, — between forty and fifty killed. We have one hundred and five wounded.

"On the second day of the three days' fight, toward evening, I had had some hot words, about a company of mine, with an officer of the Irish Brigade, and we had drawn our sabres, but postponed it at Colonel Mulligan's request; and I went off to look after the company, which had just charged a building outside the intrenchments, occupied by their sharpshooters, and had taken it. I went through a very cross-fire from their sharpshooters, down to the building, just in time to find the building recharged by the enemy in overwhelming force. I brought up the retreat, and I tell you it was hot; but I got into the intrenchments safe, and was passing along, giving directions, when I was struck with a spent ball in the breast, which knocked me down, and seemed to deprive me of any power to move. I waited about half an hour, but did not recover, and the boys then undertook to carry me to the hospital. We had gone about ten yards when one was struck in the thigh, and dropped. Another came, and about five yards farther along I was struck by a slug, which went in behind the ankle, and passed round, lodging in the middle of the foot, about three fourths of an inch below the surface. It has been extracted, and I am doing well; although from the muscles and nerves concentrated in that place, and the lack of attention, it has proved a most painful wound.

"My men have been released, and sent home; some one hundred and thirty officers still here. If released on parole, I shall probably visit you, as I can do nothing in any way for three or four months to come.

"Frémont's proclamation has destroyed the chance of Missouri's remaining in the Union. Men are flocking in here by thousands. You will have to look to Virginia for success.

"Yours,

"EVERETT.

"The enemy had twelve or fifteen pieces of artillery; we had four. I have been highly complimented by both sides."

"ST. LOUIS, October 20, 1861.

"DEAR ——, — I am at last able to sit up and move about a little on crutches. The swelling is almost out of the foot, and the wound nearly healed up. I shall be able, in five or six weeks, to walk about freely, I think. Of course it is a great bore, but one must bear it.

"I ought to have written to you before, but I have had my room full of visitors, from the time I waked up in the morning till midnight; and as I knew others were writing, I neglected it.

"I have sent my officers up to St. Joseph, where I shall go when I have recovered sufficiently to move about. Those not on parole, and my friends in St. Joseph, are taking measures to reorganize the regiment; and there is, I believe, every prospect of my being released (or rather exchanged), being well, and being in command of fifteen hundred men in six weeks or two months, which will not be unsatisfactory. So you see the prospect is not gloomy.

"I have heard, comparatively, little of home affairs. Frank Huntington, who is here, tells me that the last time he saw you he thought you were looking quite unwell; and I have been fearful lest your infernal city life was gradually sapping your strength. I trust you are better now, and only urge care.

"As to affairs here, I place little confidence in General Frémont's catching Price. I think the object of Price's movement is to draw from St. Louis the whole strength of the Union forces, and entice them as far away as possible, so as to prevent reinforcements to the scattered squads of men at Ironton, Cape Girardeau, Bird's Point, Cairo, and Paducah.

"It is impossible to look into the future; but I augur little success here, unless Price gives Frémont battle, and that, as I have said before, I do not believe he will do. But we have been grossly and shamefully neglected. My men — four months or more in the service — have not received any clothing or pay, nothing but arms and ammunition; and my case is the rule rather than the exception.

"We are looking to Virginia now, with great anxiety and hope mingled. If a big blow is struck there shortly, it will simplify our task amazingly.

"Kindest love to all at home. Write constantly, and believe me,

"Yours, as ever."

"St. Louis, November 26, 1861.

"Dear ——, — I returned yesterday from St. Joseph, where I have been reorganizing my regiment, and received all your letters in a bunch. I cannot tell you how thankful I feel for the evidence of sympathy shown by you at home, for my poor boys, who have done more arduous service, fought better and suffered more than any other men in the service.

"Fortunately now everything is changed. We have received the only complete outfit for a regiment and for four companies of cavalry ever issued from the Western Department, and my boys are rallying back with a cordiality and kindness that make me feel proud of myself.

"The regiment was thoroughly disorganized and demoralized by the delays of the department in regard to payment. The recruiting officers flocked to St. Joseph like crows to the carrion, and induced about a hundred of my boys to join other regiments.

"About two weeks ago I went to St. Joseph, and all these boys applied to come back. The present prospect is that I shall rendezvous here. I have now about five hundred men, and we only commenced recruiting ten days ago.

. . . . .

"I am a nondescript animal, which I call a triped, as yet, but I trust in a short time to be on foot once more.

"Give my very best thanks for the presents you have sent me to the kind ladies who wrought them. Tell them that these evidences of kindness are intensely felt by those who receive them in the far West. You in Massachusetts, who see your men going off thoroughly equipped and prepared for the service, can hardly conceive the destitution and ragged condition of the Missouri volunteers in past time. If I had a whole pair of breeches in my regiment at Lexington, I don't know it; but I learned there that bravery did not depend on good clothes.

"I am sorry I have not written to you before, but I have been so busy I have not thought of it. Best love to all, and believe me,

"Yours, as ever."

"Army of West Tennessee,
12 miles southwest Savannah, and 18 from Corinth, Miss.,
March 31, 1862.

"Dear Frank, — In camp again, with a good regiment and well equipped. We are in General Prentiss's Division (twelve regiments), and I command the leading brigade. As we are the left centre division, we expect rough work. I have a fine brigade; my own regiment at the right, the Twelfth Michigan, Sixteenth Wisconsin, and Eighteenth Missouri forming the balance. We arrived here on the 28th, and have a very pleasant camp, — the boys as lively as crickets, and everything working smoothly. It is funny to be called General; but the boys are all delighted, and I think will do good service at the proper time. The enemy is supposed to be about eighteen miles from us. We have an immense army, — how large we have no means of knowing; they say, however, one hundred and twenty odd regiments, and they are arriving at the rate of two or three a day.

"As I wrote you before leaving, I have left my contract with Judge Krum of St. Louis. In case I go under, my old assistants, Kilby and John Severance, can give you all the necessary information in regard to the property involved. Say to them all at home, that if we have good luck I shall win my spurs. Love to all.

"Yours,

"Ev."

This was the last letter received from him. Shortly after the battle of Pittsburg Landing, he was reported to be severely wounded, and one of his brothers set out to go for him. He heard of Everett's death at Cairo, but went on to the battle-field to make arrangements for bringing the body home.

The newspaper narratives of the battle are very contradictory; but after careful study, the facts appear to be as follows. Everett felt that the army was in great danger of a surprise, and sent to General Prentiss on Saturday afternoon for permission to send out a scouting party. Receiving no answer, he sent it out without permission, on Sunday morning, between three and four o'clock. This party met the Rebel column advancing, and fell back skirmishing.

Everett had his brigade in line before the attack in force came; this was distinctly stated to his brother by officers of the brigade. The Twenty-fifth Missouri mustered six hundred on the day after the battle, which it certainly could not have done, unless the retreat had been made in good order.

While the brigade was forming, General Prentiss rode up to Everett, and reprimanded him as follows: "You have brought on an attack for which I am unprepared, and I shall hold you responsible." He replied, "General, you will soon see that I was not mistaken." As a reply to the reprimand, the remark seems not precisely appropriate, and appears rather intended to remind General Prentiss of some previous conversation, in which Everett had in vain endeavored to induce the General to prepare for an attack like this. Viewed in this light, the answer seems decisive, and is another proof that, if he had been in higher command, the attack would have been differently received.

The right of the division, under General Prentiss, was captured *en masse.* Colonel Peabody's brigade received an attack which it could not support; and when he found it was giving ground, he rode to the front, and exposed himself recklessly, to keep the men from retreating. His Major, an old Texan ranger, did the same, and was also killed, receiving eleven wounds; while Everett received five, namely, in the hand, thigh, neck, body, and head.

He was apparently killed about fifteen minutes after the attack struck his line. The Colonel commanding the left regiment of the brigade has since testified that an orderly came from Everett to ask him if he thought he could hold his position. He replied that he thought he could. The orderly returned to his post, but presently came back once more with the statement that Colonel Peabody was killed. He was placed in a position where a chivalrous officer was devoted to almost certain death, and he behaved just as his friends would have predicted in such an emergency.

The following letter brought the announcement of his death.

"CAMP PRENTISS, IN THE FIELD,
NEAR PITTSBURG, TENNESSEE, April 8, 1862.

"FRANK PEABODY, Boston.

"DEAR SIR, — I have but a few minutes to write, and will devote them to performing one of the most painful duties that have devolved on me during this war.

"Your brother, Everett Peabody, Acting Brigadier-General, and commanding the First Brigade of General Prentiss's division, was killed on the morning of the 6th of April, while gallantly urging forward the men of his brigade. The ball that killed him entered the upper lip, and passed out of the back of the head. A more gallant officer or truer gentleman has not laid down his life for his country.

"General Prentiss's division was the first in the fight, and it sustained severe repeated shocks during the day. The men fought with desperation, but were overpowered on the first day, and had to yield some ground to vastly superior numbers.

"Yesterday, the 7th, the enemy gave way, and General Grant, being reinforced by General Buell, has routed the enemy completely. The enemy, however, in the retreat, took all the effects of officers and soldiers. They have not left anything of the General's (E. Peabody) that I can find that I could send to you as a memento, —

his sword, pistols, saddle, everything, gone. We will bury him this evening in his own camp, and will mark the place.

"I was his aid until after he fell. In haste,

"I have the honor to be, very respectfully,

"GEORGE K. DONNELLY,
Captain Co. I, 25th Mo. Vols."

His officers buried him in a gun-box, placing at his head a board with his name, and below it the couplet:—

"A braver man ne'er died upon the field;
A warmer heart never to death did yield."

His body was afterwards carried to Boston, where the funeral arrangements were taken in charge by the Governor of Massachusetts, May 16, 1862. It was conveyed thence to Springfield, where, on the following day, in presence of a great concourse of people, it was laid beside the remains of his mother, in the beautiful cemetery which his father had designed and planned.

His strong, simple, generous, manly nature reveals itself perfectly in his letters. He died under circumstances where continued life would have been certain to bring further distinction and usefulness; and he singularly fulfilled the prediction contained in a song which he had written, years before, for an anniversary of the Boston Cadets:—

"And if the army of a foe invade our native land,
Or rank disunion gather up its lawless, faithless band,
Then the arm upon our ancient shield shall wield his blade of might,
And we 'll show our worthy brethren that gentlemen can fight."

1851.

WILLIAM DWIGHT SEDGWICK.

First Lieutenant 2d Mass. Vols. (Infantry), May 25, 1861 ; Major and A. A. G. U. S. Vols., September 16, 1861 ; died at Keedysville, Md., September 29, 1862, of a wound received at Antietam, September 17.

WILLIAM DWIGHT SEDGWICK was the only son of Charles and Elizabeth (Dwight) Sedgwick, and was born in Lenox, Massachusetts, June 27, 1831. Till the age of fourteen years he was brought up almost entirely at home, when his father sent him to Illinois to spend a summer with a farmer who was a relative, and who then lived in a log-house. Here he learned and performed every kind of farm-work of which a boy of that age is capable, and confirmed a constitution originally excellent. His father believed that, without some personal knowledge and experience of labor, he could not have a proper sympathy with laboring men. He spend one year at a French school, and one in a boys' school taught by Rev. Samuel P. Parker, in Stockbridge, Massachusetts, and finished in Lenox his studies preparatory to admission into college. After leaving college, he spent one winter in a law-office ; then went abroad and studied a portion of his profession at Heidelberg, Göttingen, and Breslau. He was abroad about seventeen months. After his return, he entered the Cambrdge Law School, where he remained a year, and then established himself as a lawyer in St. Louis, Missouri.

It was his good fortune to grow up, through all his boyhood and the greater part of his youth, under the eye of two excellent parents, both remarkably gifted. He was allowed to develop with great freedom and under the happiest influences and circumstances. The fear of disobeying and displeasing them was almost the only restraint he knew; and he was so accustomed to give his parents his full confidence, that, even as a young man and away from them, he never tried or wished to hide his faults, and always found in their forbearance and assistance the surest help to overcome them.

His happy natural tendencies were carefully cultivated and strengthened, and the truthfulness, humanity, and kindness to every living being, which were the characteristics of both parents, and which he saw daily and hourly practised in his father's house, became also his second nature. From his mother he inherited the happiest temper, great sweetness and cheerfulness, with great natural courage and firmness combined and from his father the refinement of sentiment, the keen enjoyment of wit and fun, and some portion of that pleasant humor for which his father's conversation is still remembered with delight by those who knew him. The free and extensive hospitality of his parents, and the attraction which the society of his aunt, Miss C. M. Sedgwick, added to the family circle, brought among the many guests a large number of distinguished and superior people into the house; and William Sedgwick enjoyed the opportunity, rare for a boy and young man, of seeing, in a perfectly unconstrained way, the best society, and of acquiring early that ease and quiet self-possession, and the winning manners, which marked him at once as the gentleman wherever he appeared. No wonder that his happy home seemed perfect to him, and his birthplace the loveliest spot on earth. His love for it became only strengthened by separation; and even with the grandeur of the Alps before him, even in Rome, he could sigh for the beauties of his own mountains, lakes, and valleys. He had great love for and enjoyment in nature, and had gained much skill in all rural and manly exercises and amusements, which were so peculiarly adapted to his taste and his strong, robust constitution, that afterwards in town-life and amid sedentary occupations he often painfully longed for them. While no amount of fatigue, of hardship, or privations, could subdue his spirits or disturb his good humor, he was yet liable to become depressed by the confinement of his life as a lawyer. With these decided tastes for out-door life and occupations, it seems but natural that the temptation to neglect his books and studies for the delight of following them proved sometimes too strong for an active and spirited young man; but his natural capacities and talents were such, that, had he really lost anything by these interruptions, he very easily could repair the want by a few hours' earnest study, where others had to give at least double the time.

Though originally he had no very strong preference for his profession, he had always regarded it as a noble and interesting one. With all his advantages at home and abroad, he had been carefully and excellently prepared for it, and in some respects was peculiarly fitted to become a distinguished member of the bar. He spoke as well and as clearly as he wrote, had a sound and excellent judgment, a lively imagination, great self-possession and readiness; and even a certain pertinacity — of which he often accused himself as a great fault, and which among his friends made him almost always carry his point — seemed only the better to qualify him for a lawyer. The few years in St. Louis were prosperous for him, and very promising for the future; and no doubt he would have continued in his profession, and would have done honor to it, had not, from the moment of the outbreak of the war, the destiny of his country occupied his mind so powerfully that only with difficulty could he turn his thoughts to other matters. He felt irresistibly drawn to become active in the great national struggle; and this last year and a half of his life, with all its new and most interesting, but often sad and terrible, experiences, did much to ripen and elevate his character.

He married, in 1857, at Hanover, in Germany, Louisa Frederica Tellkampf, daughter of Professor A. Tellkampf of that place. From his letters to his father-in-law at the beginning of the war we can best learn the earnest and intense interest which he took in the destiny of his people, and the motives that decided him to leave his profession and family to offer his services to the country. In reply to the warning of Professor Tellkampf, not to engage himself in the war, and before the former knew that he had joined the army already, he says: —

"Your views are perfectly natural; but the same reasons which should induce me to withdraw from the service of government would, if adopted by all those to whom they apply as well as to me, break up our armies and leave us at the mercy of Southern dictators. In one prediction I have seen already that I was quite right, — in saying to my friends, when they tried to persuade me to the contrary, that we should find there would be far from a superabundance of those ready for their country's call to arms, and that every one would be needed; even now we have barely enough to stand on the defensive. After having once taken the step, and feeling as *I* do, I know you could only despise me, should I forsake my country's cause because *you* regard it as almost hopeless. Were these views, which I believe are general, not only in Germany but in all Europe, to prevail throughout the North, and were those engaged now in their country's service to reason as foreigners do for us, we should be lost indeed; but we should deserve our fate, in such a case, and for very shame could only wish to be buried in the ruins our want of faith had involved us in. For my part, if my country is to perish, my hope is to perish with her. I could not wish to survive the downfall of what I regard as the world's hope. Should America cease to be a first-class power, and be broken up in contemptible little fragments, what would you think would become of England? How long would it be before she would lie before the feet of France? What would become of the surplus population of Europe? What chance would be left to Germany and Italy in the struggle for eventual freedom after the failure of the grandest experiment of a free government that the world has known? Utter discouragement and dejection would fall upon the friends of freedom everywhere, should the North now yield to the entreaties of those who say, 'Do not persist in this war, for you will be only shedding blood to no purpose.'"

In accordance with these principles, Mr. Sedgwick forsook his profession, and was commissioned (May 25, 1861) as First Lieutenant in the Second Massachusetts Volunteers (Colonel Gordon). He went into service with the regiment, was detailed as ordnance officer of Major-General Banks's corps, and was soon transferred to the staff of Major-General Sedgwick, his kinsman, with the rank of Major. All through his period of service he wrote constantly to his family; and the following extracts will show his habits of mind, and the spirit in which he served his country.

"St. Louis, Missouri, April 18, 1861.

". . . . The excitement increases here daily. I do not expect any outbreak to occur here for the present, but at the same time a breaking out of hostilities here at almost any moment would scarcely surprise me. Men like Mr. G—— and Mr. C——, who still profess to be thorough Union men, say that Lincoln's proclamation is sinful and outrageous; that to try and whip in the Cotton States is madly hopeless; and that when war breaks out, in consequence of the attempt, the Border States must infallibly defend their 'Southern brethren.' Mr. G—— thinks, moreover, that one Southerner is equal to two Northerners, and that the recognition of the Southern Confederacy by the European powers is so palpably certain as to leave no possible room for a contrary expectation. These are the sentiments of many who have said and *still* say, that if the government *could* put down the Rebellion and hang Jeff Davis and the other Rebel leaders, they should like to see it done. Thus you see how the matter strikes the Southern mind, among those who deplore secession and declare it unjustifiable. I am led to think this feeling will be pretty universal,—'Many men of many minds.'

"We are drilling here, under a pledge to obey any call made on us by the United States authorities, to resist attack or rebellion here. I am longing, as I never should have thought to do, to join the Massachusetts Volunteers. Perhaps I may not be able to 'hold myself in,' if matters come to the point of actual war. I 'm very sure that I would rather die in battle twenty times, than have Washington captured, or than that the North should now yield her principles to accommodate those of the South. At the same time I cannot avoid feeling grief and distress in the knowledge that so many people I esteem, and could agree with on every question of morality, except in these pro- and anti-slavery issues, are quite as capable of being aroused to enthusiasm on the side of this monstrous wrong as any of us at the North on the other side. God send us a good issue!"

"Camp near Darnestown, September 12, 1861.

". . . . How do people that you meet talk about the war? Does Northern spirit and determination seem to you unabated, and do you see many signs of an increase of the desire to see slavery abolished? I pray God that it may come to that. Not that I would have total and immediate abolition declared; but I want a policy adopted and persevered in which shall look to the speediest abolition possible."

"Camp Sacket, October 24, 1861.

". . . . My faith does not begin to be shaken yet, though, so far as I can see or learn, every 'impartial observer' abroad professes the unqualified conviction that this government cannot succeed in re-establishing its sway over the Southern States. I long for the day to come when the government shall declare the war to be one of emancipation, and be supported as now by the great mass of Northern men. . . . .

"The number of people about here, where they ought to be and probably are as well educated and intelligent as in most parts of the South, who can't read, is really astounding; and I should need to have great faith in a person's accuracy to believe what I have seen, did he relate it to me, — not having seen it myself. I asked a man to-day, — of about the mental calibre by nature of our sensible Berkshire farmers, — how it was possible that he and so many others were so ignorant, and that their children were brought up in the same way. He said they never had a chance to 'get learning,' — that there were no free schools, and they could not afford to send their children to any others. I asked if he knew many people about here who could read, and he answered, 'There a'n't many sure.' But I did not need his assurance of the fact; for though the country is not thickly settled, and I only see those who come into town by the one small road we are on, I have certainly given passes to fifty who could not read what I wrote for them; yet this is the 'sacred soil,' sacred to the memory of Washington and one or two other good men, but desecrated by the barbarous influences of this damnable institution. If slavery were to be successful in this contest, I fear I should be driven into an utter abandonment of all my faith in Providence. But if, for our own sins, we have yet a long and hard struggle before us, I am willing to accept it, so that we work our way through the darkness into light at last; and I think I could lay down my life cheerfully, if need be, could I but die in the full faith that the final result of the contest would be to plant the system our fathers founded more firmly, and purified from the canker that has corrupted it and endangered its existence."

"Head-Quarters, December 26, 1861.

"War with England seems to me not unlikely, though I have been very slow to believe in it. If it comes, we must bid good by to the hope of a speedy peace, and every man who can will have to turn soldier. Were it not for my wife and children, and for you and ——, I should require only the assurance that the North would continue in harmonious action to put forth its entire strength, to enable me to accept cheerfully the prospect of a war which, if we can keep under honest guidance, can but result in our coming out of it the strongest of all the nations of the earth; but which, if politicians and the traditional clinging to slavery-sympathies on the part of so many of our Northern people tear us asunder, will grind us to powder. If such is to be the result, we must accept it, believing that, though we cannot interpret God's designs or appreciate the tendency of the means he uses, his designs will yet be carried out, and that we, his instruments, are doing his work, whether we judge rightly or wrongly the immediate or proximate issue of our deeds. Leave me the faith I have now that we are engaged in a righteous war, and I shall never allow myself to despair; and as yet I am very far from that point."

In another letter, written to his father-in-law in January, 1862, he says: —

"There has been much reason for disappointment lately, but I am not disheartened, and let not go one jot or tittle of my faith. This lukewarmness, this dreadful, silly fear of hurting people who would never scruple at placing their feet upon our necks and grinding our heads into dust if they should get the opportunity, is a disease of the national mind. But I believe it is a curable disease and will be cured; and I shall not mourn as one having no hope, though I do chafe and fret that this obscuration of people's intellect does not clear away all at once. I am afraid government does not recognize as yet the truth that slavery *must fall*, and that by attacking the enemy in every weak point, and by stern measures of confiscation whenever practicable, the success of our cause is assured, which milder means will fail to bring about. I should be glad to have the war last ten years, if it must, so that its end may leave slavery in its death-throes. And I do not propose to abandon the cause while life and strength are spared me; for I believe it to be a holy one, and devised of God, however much unholiness mingles with it, as it mingles with everything involving the joint action of masses of men in this world."

"CAMP NEAR YORKTOWN, VIRGINIA, April 13, 1862.

". . . . For myself, I have no presentiment that I shall fall; and if I do, it will be Heaven's will. If I should lose a leg or an arm, I should not consider that I had made any too great sacrifice to the country's cause; and I hardly feel as if I should regret it. . . . .

"I am delighted, dear mother, that you do not allow yourself to feel unnecessarily anxious about me. I shall do my duty, but I shall not commit any folly of bravado, and shall survive this war unless Heaven wills otherwise; in which case we shall all be ready cheerfully to submit ourselves."

"HEAD-QUARTERS, &c., FAIR OAKS, June 11, 1862.

"DEAREST MOTHER, — I had your sweet letter, written after you had seen Mr. Laflin, day before yesterday. It gave me a lively impression of the far greater anxiety, and consequent suffering, entailed by war upon those at home than upon those who go out to fight. We, as soldiers are, or *ought* to be, proof against all uneasiness, except in certain trying moments, which come comparatively rarely, and when the occasion passes, the feeling of care passes also; but you at home, expecting constantly news of a battle fought, and having to wait long for certain intelligence of the result, after it has been fought, are worse off. I feel as if my sympathy were due to you more than yours to me. But I trust you will not fail in adhering to your habitual serene faith. Think of me, always, until you *know* to the contrary, as destined to be restored to you, safe and sound. It will be quite time enough to grieve when the occasion calls for it. War, with its deadly instruments and missiles, is far less dangerous than it seems. If one of our Fourth-of-July cannon were accidentally loaded with shell, and the shell should happen to burst near a group of persons, without injuring any, the newspapers and the town-talk would call it miraculous or providential. A hundred similar miracles at least have happened to us within the last three days; a hundred shell have exploded, or have passed screeching by without exploding, over ground covered with troops, wagons, and horses; result, one or two horses wounded, and a few darkies and camp-followers (perhaps a few soldiers) badly scared.

". . . . General Howard, who lost his arm on Sunday, is a very interesting man, — scarcely older than I am, — and the only army officer I have met who could properly be designated by the appellation of a 'consistent Christian'; brave as the bravest, honestly and unaffectedly believing that his life is in God's hands, and that it is, to speak more expressively than elegantly, none of his business whether he lives or dies, provided he is doing his duty. Army officers who swear as habitually as Howard prays speak of him with great affection and esteem."

These few extracts from his letters can only serve to show what he was as a patriot, how clear and sound and good his judgment, and how well, even in the beginning of the war, and in some of the darkest times of it, he foresaw with the eyes of his spirit the triumph of his country, which he was not destined to share. His letters, of which there remain a large number, seem to preserve to his friends a living part of him, and have the great charm of giving always a true and striking portrait of the mood and moment in which they were written. Many are overflowing with pleasantry and humor, — all with the tenderness and kindness of his heart. Some show an uncommon talent for the description of nature, as well as for the delineation of character; and his way of expressing himself is always happy, clear, and natural. In these, written to his most intimate friends, he freely gives his religious sentiments, his views of life and destiny; and all he says is pervaded by the generous and noble spirit from which it flows.

In his military career, he found a great advantage in having formerly hardened and disciplined his body by all manly exercises, so that he was better prepared for the great exposure and fatigue that broke down many delicate constitutions. Great physical courage seemed born with him, and was so natural that he never knew the nervousness and timidity of more sensitive natures; but it helped him, no doubt, to acquire that higher moral courage which acts independently of the judgment, the approval or blame of others, and which has as its aim only that which the mind has once recognized as right and duty. He thought so little what others might think or say of him, that his actions never seemed influenced by it; and he not only appeared always perfectly natural, self-possessed, and without restraint himself, but had also the happy gift to take restraint and reserve from others, and to awaken confidence, kind feelings, and good humor. He soon became therefore, popular among his fellow-officers and his inferiors, as he had been always where he lived.

His personal appearance was prepossessing, his figure tall and strongly built, and his face well expressed his character. It was at once a very manly and a very sweet face, with dark, expressive eyes, and handsome, regular features; and the refinement, the inborn nobility of his soul, and the high idea to which he devoted the end of his life, had set their stamp upon it. In his military service, his duties were always promptly and cheerfully fulfilled; and camp life, which throws men and officers so intimately together, gave him many opportunities to do kind offices to others. His firmness and gentleness made him also a desirable assistant when amputations and difficult operations among the wounded were to be performed. He had formerly, in the universities, steeled his nerves by witnessing such painful scenes, after he once found he was very weak in looking at the sufferings of others, and needed some self-discipline to acquire that perfect composure which he thought every man ought to have. How quietly and manfully he bore his pain his own words show (written in his diary), when he lay in the great agony of his mortal wound on the battle-field of Antietam.

> "While trying to rally our men, a musket-ball struck me in the small of my back, and I fell from my horse. As I write this, I have been lying here more than an hour, powerless to move my right leg. I think the wound must be mortal. I have been praying God to forgive my sins, to bless and comfort my darling wife and children, my dearest mother and sisters. As I have been lying here in very great pain, shells have been bursting close to me almost constantly. I wish my friends to know that I have fallen while doing my duty as well as was possible, which I can truly assert, and that I have not uttered a groan as yet, lying alone on the hard ground, in the sun, with no friend near."

Eight hours he remained in this same position, till found by his friends. He was carried into a farm-house, where he received the kindest treatment. His mother and sister had the consolation of being with him during his last sickness, and present at his death; not so his wife, who learned her misfortune only at the moment of her arrival from Europe. He left behind him three little girls, the youngest of whom he had never seen. He probably little thought, when he wrote, two days before the battle of Antietam, in a letter which alludes to the want of sleep he had undergone, "O, how I long for a few hours' assured rest!" how soon his eyes should close in the last deepest sleep, from which there is no more awakening. Many were the hearts that mourned his death, and many the tears that were shed at his early grave.

1852.

HENRY HILL DOWNES.

Private 124th Illinois Vols. (Infantry), August 11, 1862; died at Vicksburg, Miss., September 26, 1864, of disease contracted in the service.

HENRY HILL DOWNES was born at Boston, November 24, 1830. He was the son of Commodore John Downes, U. S. N., and Maria Gertrude (Hoffman) Downes. Not long after his birth, his parents removed to Charlestown, Massachusetts, where he resided till he graduated at Harvard. He was fitted for college at the Chauncey Hall School, in Boston, with the exception of a few months previous to his admission, which were passed under the instruction of George P. Sanger, Esq. He entered Harvard in the year 1849, joining the Class of 1852 in the second term of its Freshman year. Here those social qualities, courteous manners, and that kindly disposition, which had secured him so many friends while at school, still continued to make him popular.

After leaving college he decided to fit himself for the profession of the law, and for this purpose entered the office of Charles B. Goodrich, Esq. He was admitted to the bar of Suffolk County, and began to practise in 1855. He did not, however, long remain in Boston, but finding advancement rather slow, sought a more promising field for the exercise of his talents at Detroit, Michigan. There he remained but a year, and in 1857 removed to Grand Rapids, in the same State, where he continued to practise his profession till the winter of 1859-60, when he again changed his residence to Davenport, Iowa. He was there appointed Clerk of the Court of Common Pleas, and held this office till his removal to Quincy, Illinois, where he was living at the time of his enlistment in the Union army, August 11, 1862. He joined the One Hundred and Twenty-fourth Illinois Volunteers as a private, and continued to perform his military duties in the army of Major-General Grant till his last sickness.

He died September 26, 1864, in the United States Hospital at Vicksburg, Mississippi, of malarial fever. He had labored faithfully and fought well; and it is matter of satisfaction to his friends, as it was to himself, that he lived to see the successful result of that long and glorions campaign which ended in the freedom of the Mississippi. His patriotism was ardent and devoted, and he felt that his country deserved every sacrifice that he could offer.

SAMUEL FOSTER HAVEN.

Assistant Surgeon 15th Mass. Vols. (Infantry), August 5, 1861; Surgeon, July 21, 1862; killed at Fredericksburg, Va., December 13, 1862.

THE subject of this sketch was born in Dedham, Massachusetts, in the house of his grandfather, the Hon. Samuel Haven, May 20, 1831. His father, S. F. Haven, Esq. has been for many years librarian of the American Antiquarian Society, at Worcester. His mother was the daughter of the Rev. Freeman Sears of Natick, Massachusetts, who died early in life, after a brief settlement in that place. She died when Foster was not quite five years old.

Fortunately, at that tender age, the friend from whom his mother, an orphan, had received her intellectual and moral culture, in the most important period of her life, extended to him the same kind care, and watched over his early development with equal interest and affection. Whatever elevated and generous sentiments it is possible to cultivate in the mind of a child, she labored to implant or nurture. She kept a journal of her experiences in the process of guiding and enlightening his spontaneous mental operations, which evinces her devoted affection, and has a striking moral and metaphysical significance. The wide circle of the friends and acquaintances of this lady (Miss Elizabeth P. Peabody) will readily understand how every intellectual germ which could be nourished into a principle of devotion to duty or chivalrous self-sacrifice or heroic aspiration would receive an impulse and a direction from her hand which could never be wholly lost; and in this case the noble fruition of the life of her pupil bears ample testimony to the success of her early cultivation.

The details of the life of a child are, perhaps, applicable to a notice of his maturity only in the general way of showing the influence of early training on his more developed character and actions. And in this connection it may be appropriately remarked, that the record of Foster's child-life, as kept by his devoted friend, displays many touching incidents of tender, confiding affection, and evinces a truthfulness of spirit, an unwearied and almost systematic inquisitiveness and a power of self-absorption in an idea, very unusual in a child; all of which traits were eminently characteristic of his mature years.

The subsequent portion of his childhood, previous to his residence in Worcester, he passed in the care of his grandparents at Dedham, and at the family school of Rev. Mr. Kimball, in an adjoining town. He went to Worcester in 1839, — his father having removed thither two years before, — and received the remainder of his preparatory education in the public schools of that city.

At the age of seventeen he entered Harvard College, and graduated in the Class of 1852, — the last of four successive generations of his name and family in the Catalogue of the Alumni of that University. Soon after graduation he entered upon his medical studies as the pupil of Dr. Henry Sargent of Worcester, and subsequently became a member of the Tremont Street Medical Class in Boston. During the last year of his pupilage he held the position of house physician in the Massachusetts General Hospital. In the autumn of 1855, having taken his degree of Doctor in Medicine, he visited Europe, and spent nearly two years in assiduous devotion to his studies, giving especial attention to his favorite branch of Ophthalmology in London, Paris, Vienna, and Berlin.

Previous to going abroad he published an essay on "Intestinal Obstruction," which is still esteemed a valuable contribution to medical literature. After his return from Europe he established himself in practice in Boston, and while there read before the Suffolk District Medical Society an essay on "Cysticerci within the Eye," which was also found worthy of publication. Although in Boston but a short time, his stay was long enough to leave a grateful remembrance of his kindness and charity among the poor of his neighborhood, to which his medical successor bears cheerful testimony. Yet so reticent was he about all things that might seem to be creditable to himself, and so entirely pure-minded in his generosities, that not even his own father knew of his charitable habits, till after his death.

In the spring of 1858 he removed to Worcester, and there established himself in practice, intending to give special attention to diseases of the eye. Here he remained until he entered the army.

Although, owing to his peculiarly fastidious and retiring nature, he was not widely known in his profession, he had acquired an enviable reputation among his medical brethren, as well for his powers of investigation as for his scientific attainments; while his moral worth secured for him the respect of all who knew him, and his ingenuousness of heart attracted the warm affection of the small circle of his intimate friends.

Dr. Haven was essentially a student all his life. His mental organization and moral qualities admirably fitted him for scientific research. He was endowed with a subtlety of discrimination, a love for, and facility in, minute observation, a power of handling details, an honesty of purpose, and a rare industry, fidelity, and perseverance, that could not fail of success in this department. His thoroughness was remarkable. He seemed unable to slight anything. All his works were finished with the elaborate nicety of a Dutch painting.

With these characteristics, combined with attainments that were remarkable in his special department and very excellent in all branches of medicine, he might well look forward to distinction as a man of science, while his training, his decided mechanical ingenuity, and his coolness gave promise of eminence in the more practical walks of a surgical operator.

He entertained especially fastidious notions about the dignity of his profession, and was exceedingly careful to avoid even the appearance of those tricks and devices which are not infrequently resorted to by practitioners to draw public attention upon themselves. It was a part of his thoroughness and conscientiousness to prefer the solid success that professional ability is sure in the end to attain, above the more dazzling and ephemeral kind sometimes brought about by magnetic personal attractions or the loud praises and skilful manœuvres of active friends.

He was not merely a professional man. His culture was wide for a person of his years and labors. Besides his college acquaintance with the classics, — which he kept up to a considerable extent, — he was in a measure familiar with the literature of France and Germany, and was also, about the time he entered the army, studying Italian, that he might enjoy the poets of that language in their original tongue. In matters of art his taste was pure and classic. His power of versification was considerable; and he was not without some skill as a draughtsman, which, under cultivation, might have ripened into an ability above mediocrity.

He had a strong taste for authorship; and, after spending many months in preparation, he had carried one manuscript to an advanced stage, without the knowledge of any one save those whom he was obliged to consult, and had made a contract for its publication, just as the war broke out. His desire to see this launched was the strongest obstacle to his entering the service, though it caused no hesitation in his conduct. It was an account of printers and printing in this country prior to the Revolution, with a catalogue of publications, revised and extended from Isaiah Thomas's "History of Printing." His manuscript is now in the possession of the American Antiquarian Society, and it is hoped that it may yet be published.

How industriously he pursued his studies was never understood until an examination of his papers after his death revealed it. Among them were found copious and careful notes upon a variety of subjects, evincing a wonderful degree of assiduity and thoroughness. That this was not appreciated in his lifetime is due to his exceeding reticence and to his peculiar methods of labor. It was one of his frequent remarks, that he must work in his own way or he could do nothing, and his own way was usually an original method.

But overtopping his intellectual abilities and æsthetic

culture was a spirit of singular simplicity, gentleness, and heroism, associated, however, with a shyness of disposition and fastidiousness of taste that to some extent restrained its free action. He was almost childlike in the guilelessness of his life and the naturalness of his emotions. As he was quiet and undemonstrative in temperament, his thorough amiability and warm affection manifested themselves much more in practical acts of kindness than in noisy profession or sentimental talk. Truthful to an extreme, in word and deed, he could not bend himself to suit the tastes of others, nor easily adapt himself to varying circumstances. Sensitive in his nature, judging always by the standard of perfection, and influenced by a noticeable aversion to all shams and insincerity, he saw much in the world that shocked him, and much in those around him with which he did not care to become intimate. Yet there was nothing of the cynic in his disposition, nor did he take upon himself the duties of public or private censor. Whatever offended his taste or his sense of right seemed to pain rather than anger him, and caused him to retire sorrowfully within himself, yet with a heart ready and anxious to forgive as soon as his judgment should assent. With this temperament and these tastes, it is not strange that he shrank from rough contact with the world, and that his circle of intimate friends was not large, — nor that in that circle he was the most warm-hearted, sympathetic, and trustworthy.

But his conscientiousness was, perhaps, the most striking of his moral characteristics. With him the appreciation of a duty insured its performance, no matter what the cost or self-sacrifice involved. United with it was a certain chivalrousness of spirit, under the influence of which, shy and gentle as he was, he was ready to do and suffer anything in the defence and performance of what he deemed the right.

Though to a man thus constituted a military life could present but few attractions, Dr. Haven did not hesitate when the appeal came for troops. Duty seemed to call him, and that was enough. Appointed Assistant Surgeon of the Fifteenth Massachusetts Regiment, — the first regiment of three years' troops recruited in Worcester County, — he cheerfully departed for the seat of war in August, 1861, never again to return to the city of his residence, until, nearly eighteen months afterwards, he was borne through its hushed streets, with solemn honors, to his lowly resting-place.

Space will not permit to follow Surgeon Haven with anything like minuteness through his military career. Only a few of the many facts and incidents at hand can be used, illustrating the character of his devotion to duty.

Though in the service about a year and a half, he never asked leave of absence to revisit his home, nor, it is believed, was he ever absent from his post for a single day, except on imperative business. Much of the time while Assistant Surgeon, owing to the illness or absence of his superior medical officer, he had the sole charge of the sick and wounded of his regiment; yet his letters do not breathe one word of complaint, nor even a suggestion that his path of duty was a hard one.

He early arrived at the conviction, — eventually fatal to himself, — that it was the duty of a surgeon to follow his regiment into actual battle, so that he might be near at hand to succor the wounded. The counter-argument, that on a battle-field the life of a surgeon was much more valuable than that of any one whom he would be likely to save by this undue exposure, and the representation that the wounded might be readily brought to him in some place of comparative safety, availed nothing. His opinion was inflexible; and he ever acted upon it with an utter disregard of danger, that would have won distinguished promotion to any line officer in the service.

At Ball's Bluff, indeed, he was not with his regiment in the conflict itself; but, in his Station on Harrison's Island in the middle of the Potomac, he was by no means out of danger; for at one time, as he says in his short letter of October 24th, "the bullets poured in upon us like hailstones." Another brief extract from the same letter shows how little he regarded himself. One of the boats in which the wounded were removed had swamped. "It seemed an impossibility to get the wounded off before morning, and we were sure of being shelled out by daylight. Dr. H. [Dr. Hayward of the Twentieth Massachusetts Volunteers] and I decided to remain and be taken, and get off what men we could." This calamity was fortunately averted.

At Yorktown, the next summer, he put his principle of conduct into literal application, in coolly taking his seat on a log a few feet in the rear of his regiment, one day when it was supporting a battery, equally regardless of the shells of the enemy and the solicitations of his brother surgeons, who besought him to fall back with them but a few rods to a place of security.

At Fair Oaks he bore himself with distinguished intrepidity, attending to his surgical duties in the very midst of the conflict, while wounded and unwounded men, with whom he was conversing, were shot dead at his feet. His personal experiences on that eventful day, did space permit the detailing of them, would be highly interesting, though in his letter to his father he says, with characteristic shyness, they "concern nobody but you and me."

From Harrison's Landing, under date of July 13, 1862, he writes: —

"I am surprised to hear from you, that my name has been mentioned in connection with the Thirty-fourth [a new regiment then forming]. I am obliged to my friends that may have suggested it; but I really do not wish to leave the Fifteenth. There is already evidence of too much desire on the part of officers to get leave of absence for the sake of procuring higher appointments in new regiments."

He was soon after rewarded for his constancy by being promoted to the surgeonship of his own regiment, on the resignation of Dr. Bates.

His personal adventures at Antietam cannot be made more interesting than in his own words, under date of September 24, 1862: —

"As our brigade advanced in line of battle, under fire from the Rebel batteries, General Gorman (why I know not) ordered me to the left of the line, thus bringing me with the Thirty-fourth New York Regiment. This regiment became first engaged with the enemy, and partly from the deadly fire, and partly from the breaking of the regiment on its left (of another brigade), the Thirty-fourth gave way itself. With other officers, I did my best to rally the men, and only with partial success. General Sedgwick, who was at this part of the line, had his horse shot, and was wounded in two places. I looked at his wounds, and advised him to go to the rear; but he would not, and I then offered him my horse, but his wrist was broken, and he could not well ride. . . . .

"During this time the rest of the brigade had become separated, and were far to the right. I rode hither and thither all over the field, trying in vain to find the Fifteenth. At last I stumbled upon all that was left, — about one hundred and seventy-five men. [They went into battle with five hundred and eighty-three men, and lost three hundred and twenty-one killed and wounded, and twenty-four missing.]

". . . . The Colonel desired me to try and get the body of Captain Simonds, which had been brought part way back. Taking an ambulance, I found it, and while putting it in was called some way to the front to see Colonel Wristar of the California Regiment. . . . . While hastily dressing their wounds, word was brought that the Rebel skirmishers were close upon us. Colonel Wristar thought he could walk, but while helping him out he fainted, and I had just brought him to, when his own surgeon appeared.

". . . . The fight was expected to be renewed the next morning, but both sides rested on their arms. A lot of our killed and wounded lay beyond our lines, and within those of the Rebels. I made several vain efforts to get at them, and particularly to find Tom Spurr, riding even beyond our own pickets, and within half-gunshot distance of the Rebel pickets, who were in plain sight. Towards night I went, with Colonel Lee of the Twentieth, and a flag of truce, over to the Rebels to get permission to bury our dead and carry off the wounded. We parleyed some time with several staff officers, and finally with General Fitz-Hugh Lee himself; but permission would not be given, unless an arrangement had been made between the commanders of the two forces themselves.

"During the night the enemy retreated, and early in the morning we went over and found our dead and wounded, — an awful sight. The Rebels, however, had been kind to our wounded, and got them in and around a barn with large haystacks."

Surgeon Haven's last hasty note (from Falmouth, opposite Fredericksburg) bears date December 9th. At the close of it, he thus refers to the preparatory orders for the disastrous battle of the 13th: —

"We have this moment received orders to have to-morrow morning, right after breakfast, three days' rations issued to officers and men, and sixty rounds of ammunition to each man. This looks like moving, and it remains to be seen what will be done."

What *was* done can be read, not only in his own epitaph, but in the broken hearts and desolate homes of, alas! how many. A portion of the sad story can best be told in the words of his superior officer, Surgeon Sherman. After speaking of his "sacrifices to duty," and "utter disregard of danger," he says: —

"Witnessing his self-exposure at the battle of Antietam, I had, as Medical Director of the Second Division, detailed your son, in a written order, in the event of a battle, to repair to the Division Hospital, and give his services there instead of in the field with his regiment. When I communicated this order to your son, he evidently felt disappointed. He expressed a strong choice to go wherever his regiment went; and when the column to which the Fifteenth Massachusetts was attached was about to pass over the bridge in front of Fredericksburg, he was expostulated with, and reminded of the previous order; but he asked as a special favor to be allowed to go with his regiment, and said that as soon as the fight was done, he would return to the hospital and remain there."

Only a short time after, while marching through the streets of the city by the side of his regiment, toward the position assigned it in that day's battle, he was struck in the leg by a casual shell from the enemy's batteries. Taken back to the nearest hospital, it was for a time hoped that an amputation might save his life; but he never rallied from the shock. And so, cheerful in his agony, upheld by the consciousness of duty performed, in that shattered building, even then rent by an occasional shell, adding fresh confusion and horror to the scene, — surrounded by the dying and dead, amid the groans of those to assuage whose early pangs he had ventured and suffered all, — the patriot passed away; and his gentle spirit, answering to the roll-call of the mighty cannonade, took its place in the great army which that night encamped in the heavenly fields.

The following verses, inscribed to the memory of Dr. Haven, appeared in the Worcester Spy, of December 30, 1862, and were understood to have been written by Rev. D. A. Wasson: —

"With skilful touch he turned away
Death's wishful hand from wounded men;
But when was done that doleful day,
The living laid him with the slain.

"Thy hurt to heal, O native land!
What mortal might he did and dared;
And when all service of his hand
Seemed not enough, his heart he bared,

"And laid his life upon thy hurt,
By losing all, to make thee whole;
But could not lose his high desert
And place on Memory's record-roll.

"And when that sacred roll she calls,
The word, perchance, will reach his ear,
And he shall from the eternal halls,
Among God's angels, answer, 'Here!'

"We will not deem his life was brief,
For noble death is length of days;
The sun that ripens autumn's sheaf
Has poured a summer's wealth of rays."

WILLIAM STURGIS HOOPER.

Vol. A. D. C. (rank of Captain), Major-General Banks's Staff, December 4, 1862; died at Boston, September 24, 1863, of disease contracted in the service.

WILLIAM STURGIS HOOPER was born in Boston, March 3, 1833. The name of his father, Samuel Hooper, has been for many years as familiar in the commercial world as it is now in the affairs of the nation. His mother was Anne, daughter of William Sturgis, whose early career, as one of the pioneers of our commerce in the Pacific, and whose later prominence among Boston merchants, are well known in the community. Both by his father's and mother's line the subject of this sketch was allied to a race of merchants; and the taste and faculty for business which his manhood developed had been born in him, and had grown with his growth.

In his early school-days there was little of interest, and of those days he afterwards had no cheerful recollection. Not of robust constitution, possessing little rude childish energy, never "a boy among boys," he shrank from all the roughness of school life with the same sensitiveness which later, as a man in contact with men, he strove faithfully and successfully to conquer. Still he was never effeminate, and he very early manifested the fondness for field sports and all sorts of out-of-door life which he always retained. His summers in the country, or on the sea-shore, where he was his father's companion in walking and fishing, and his mother's pupil in books, and in many things not taught from books, were the pleasantest portions of this period of his life. As a child, he was ardent in whatever he undertook, but with an underlying sweetness and patience, and had an older and more serious air than his years would warrant.

Afterwards he attended the school of Mr. Francis Phelps, a well-known teacher of Boston, who bears testimony to his excellent character and mind, and to his fidelity as a student. He entered the Boston Latin School in September, 1844, at the age of eleven, and remained there until the spring of 1848, and continued his preparatory studies for the University for a few months with Mr. John B. Felton, of the Class of 1847, and finished them with his cousin, Mr. Nathaniel L. Hooper, of the Class of 1846. He entered Harvard in the autumn of 1849, at the age of sixteen, joining the Class of 1852, then commencing its Sophomore year.

His unboyish temperament had at this time developed into a rather premature manhood. He already had the air of a man of the world; and it was a common remark among his classmates that he entered college thirty years old, and grew younger every year. He remained in Cambridge until the end of the first Senior term. As a scholar he took a less prominent position than many men of far duller intellect and smaller attainments, and he perhaps felt less interest in the regular classical and mathematical curriculum, by which rank is usually obtained, than he would have taken in a more immediately practical course. Still he was faithful in his attention to the college exercises, and his standing, if not high, was respectable. Of the modern languages, and especially of German, he was very fond, and he laid up in his memory at this time a stock of German ballads which he never lost.

One rarely sees a more quiet college career than Sturgis Hooper's. Refined in his manners and tastes, singularly exempt from youthful vices, having the utmost dislike for the dissipations which Sophomores often consider manly and the vulgarities which they often think gentlemanly, joining no convivial clubs, but having his door always open to those classmates whose tastes were congenial with his own, and freely accepting their hospitalities, he went on his way, a little apart from the stir and hum around him, but never repellent or exclusive. The resolutions which the Class adopted upon his death speak of him thus: —

"Less familiarly known to most of us than almost any other of the Class, he yet commanded the esteem of all; and though, partly from the shortness of his connection with us and partly from his natural reserve, he acquired few intimacies, he was remarkably happy in never attracting a single enmity. Respected by all for his purity of life, his aversion to whatever was ignoble or degrading, his proud contempt of all evasion and indirection, his scorn of hypocrisies and shams, he at the same time won the cordial affection and friendship of those who were best enabled to know and feel the warmth of his heart, the gentleness of his courtesy, and his earnest enthusiasm for whatever was good or beautiful or true."

In social life he had the cultivation and breeding of a much older man, and his conversation was rarely trivial or uninteresting. In the society of women he was especially at ease. Faith in their purity and delicacy was one of the cardinal points of his creed. He never thought or spoke of them but with respect, and he was always impatient of any indecorous or derogatory allusion to them by others.

His favorite in-door recreation, while in college and afterwards, was chess, in which he became proficient. He was especially skilful in exercises requiring accuracy of eye and dexterity of hand, — a capital draughtsman, an expert driver, an excellent helmsman of a boat, and rarely equalled in billiard-playing or in shooting with pistol or rifle. His fondness for out-of-door pursuits — driving, riding, hunting, fishing, and boating — had now supplied the place of the athletic energy in which he was naturally deficient.

Hooper obtained from the Faculty leave of absence for the last term of the Senior year, for the purpose of making a voyage in a new ship which his father was about to despatch to California and China, and sailed from Boston in January, 1852. He was accompanied, at his invitation, by the classmate who now presents this memorial of his life. Seldom has the world been circumnavigated under pleasanter circumstances. It was as if college rooms had been carried on shipboard. College pursuits were intermingled with the ordinary sea-life of a passenger, — half sailor play and half the *dolce far niente.* The young men took their books with them, and perhaps did as much hard study and reading under the fresh trade-winds as they had ever done within the walls of Alma Mater. History, navigation, mercantile law, and book-keeping took their turns with modern languages, poetry, light literature, and chess. Hooper kept up his rifle and pistol practice and his drawing, and also spent a good deal of time in studying and devising models for boats and ships. He applied himself, moreover, to practical seamanship, and, as usual with him, was not satisfied until he had proved to himself that he could do with his own hands the work of which he understood the theory. So, after spending a month very pleasantly in California, partly at San Francisco and partly in the mining regions, he shipped regularly as third mate of the Courser for her voyage across the Pacific. The experiment was successful; and after satisfying himself that he could hold on to the yard-arm in a typhoon, he was willing to return to his passenger-life for the homeward trip from China. He reached home by the end of 1852, spent the rest of the winter in Boston, took a trip in the spring to the Southern States and Cuba (a journey which he had taken once before, while in college), attended the Law School in Cambridge during May and June, and went to Europe with his family in July, 1853. He made the tour of Great Britain and the Continent, saw everything and admired what he saw, but found nothing to overturn his love for America. "Those fellows," he writes, "who come home full of Europe, and abusing America, are entirely wrong. I am getting more certain of it every day." And again, to a friend who had rallied him on his ebullitions of patriotism, "What do you suppose there is here to cool one's patriotism? I am ten times more proud of my country than I ever was before."

His studies abroad were principally in the modern languages and in drawing. The winter of 1853–54, spent in Rome, was especially valuable in developing the artistic taste which he had always shown. His skill in drawing was something better than a mere mechanical accomplishment; and his love and talent for art were in later years a source of much pleasure and recreation amid the graver cares of business.

In the autumn of 1854 his family returned home, while he remained in Paris. Here he was attacked by a severe disease of the intestines, which rendered a surgical operation necessary. From the effects of this disease he never recovered. It left him with a chronic weakness, and implanted in his system the seeds of the consumption which finally caused his death. But this severe experience, which so enfeebled his body, left him in all else ripened and strengthened. He had passed from boyhood into manhood.

Hooper came home in the spring of 1855, and employed the following eighteen months in a partially successful attempt to restore his health by hunting, yachting, and like recreations. In the autumn of 1856 he found himself well enough to go into business, and formed, with his cousin, John H. Reed, the firm of Reed and Hooper, for the management and agency of the Bay State Iron Company, a connection which lasted until his death. For mercantile life he was admirably adapted by character, by habit, and by inherited taste and ability. He soon became most favorably known among business men, and was on the high road to success. In October, 1857, he married Alice, the youngest daughter of Jonathan Mason, Esq. Their only child, Isabella Weyman, was born in January, 1859. A happier domestic life would be hard to find. Had it not been for the bodily disease which was constantly throwing its cloud over him, it would seem as if fortune had now left him nothing to desire.

From the very commencement of the Rebellion, he had been anxious to bear his part in the war, but his feeble health and urgent business were obstacles hard to surmount. The responsibilities of this business were rendered more pressing than ever before, by the fact that the time and thoughts of his senior partner were now much engrossed by the duties of the office of Quartermaster-General of Massachusetts, to which he had been appointed. The possibility of deserting his counting-room being thus for the time out of the question, Hooper accepted the situation as patiently as he could. In April, 1861, he writes: "Thus far I sit at my desk quietly, and have nothing more to do with the war than reading the news in the papers. I am very well contented that it is so, for the present; but if this is to be such a war as it now promises to be, I do not mean to do office-work forever. I suppose every one has a strong desire to hear how shot that are sent in earnest whistle."

So, for the first eighteen months of the struggle, Hooper still remained at home, occupied with labors which had now become distasteful, and rather chafing at the restraint. At last the opportunity to go arose from the very condition of health, which his friends had considered so grave an objection to his entering the service. In the autumn of 1862 his physicians said that he must avoid the New England winter, and seek a warmer climate and a more open-air life than he could have at home. They advised him to go abroad; but he knew a better way of leaving New England than that. He at once offered himself, and was accepted, as a Volunteer Aid to General Banks, whose expedition was under orders for the South. He obtained from Governor Andrew an appointment as Assistant Adjutant-General of Massachusetts, for the purpose of getting the rank necessary to qualify him for the position he sought, and joined General Banks's staff, with the rank of Captain. The expedition sailed from New York on the 4th, and arrived at New Orleans on the 16th of December, 1862.

Captain Hooper's letters to his family are of great interest, and give a clearer and more vivid picture of the state of society and of feeling in the newly reconquered State, of the difficulties that lay in the way of reconstruction, and of the means by which General Banks was attempting to overcome them, than can easily be found elsewhere. In their personal relation, these letters, full of love for home and wife and child, are tinged with no regret that he had left them. Conscious of the great work of the hour, he is fully content at being at last engaged in it. Yet, with his characteristic modesty and tendency to disparage his own impulses, he is unwilling to claim the credit of patriotism. The fact that it was the necessity of leaving

New England on account of his health which finally gave him the long-sought opportunity of entering the service, seems always present to his mind. Thus, just after sailing, he writes : —

"I never claimed the praise of going to the war from a sense of duty; and yet when I see, as I do here, men who are really leaving all that home has pleasant for them from a real sense of duty, it makes me ashamed almost of the motives which prompted me to come, and at the same time gives me some satisfaction in thinking that, if I am not acting from the same high motives that some others are, I am at least doing the same thing, just as much as if my motives were less personal."

Hooper and another officer were at first left at Ship Island, to inspect and forward the ships and troops of the expedition as they arrived. Probably no one ever found that dreary sand-bank a comfortable place of abode, and at this time it afforded little to eat except bread and potatoes. Still he writes : —

"I am having a pleasant time, the climate seems very healthy, and the weather is superb. Of course I want to get off as soon as possible, but I am quite contented to take things as they come."

They however remained at Ship Island only about ten days, and were then transferred to New Orleans, where Captain Hooper was assigned to duties in more immediate connection with head-quarters. On December 28th he writes : —

"On Christmas day I received an order appointing me to fill the vacancy caused by the resignation of Major Bell, the President of the Sequestration Commission, (who went home with General Butler,) which separates me at once from the Adjutant-General's office, and gives me an office of my own, and the partial control of an interesting and to me wonderful institution. . . . . It is far from being an unimportant thing in this vicinity, and I find my hands as full of business, and my thinking powers taxed quite as much as I care to have them. In fact, my only anxiety now is lest I should not prove equal to the task assigned me; but the best I can I shall do, and I trust the General will be satisfied. The General tells me this shall certainly not prevent my accompanying him if he takes the field, which I feared until to-night it might."

In a letter written at midnight of December 31st he says : —

"Before going to bed I just picked up Tennyson, which was lying on my table, and opening it at random, the first lines which caught my eye were in In Memoriam: —

'Ring out, wild bells, to the wild sky,
The flying cloud, the frosty light,
The year is dying in the night,
Ring out, wild bells, and let him die.'

"They brought to my mind, what I had before forgotten, that this is the last night of 1862, and this the last chance to write to you in the old year; so, though I ought to go to bed, I will sit up a little while to cross, in imagination, the hundreds of miles of water, or of land worse than water, which separate me from all I love most, who are now, most likely, under a wilder sky than the clear, soft evening air shows here. A year does not go by without bringing much change to all of us. Certainly 1862 has brought change enough for you and me, and for many another beside; and 1863, which begins to-morrow, what has he in store for us? I suppose my little Bel, if she is not too sound asleep, is dreaming now of all the presents which 1863 will bring her to-morrow; and though I don't expect any presents, I know that 1863 will have much for you and me, too, of joy or sorrow, which we shall think as important to us as Bel's presents are to her. Thank God, we do not know what it will be. Perhaps in his eyes it is of no more consequence than Bel's presents seem to us. One thing gives me a pleasure which I hardly expected old 1862 to leave for me, and that is the belief that I am likely to be of some use here. I have not been in the Sequestration Commission long enough to feel sure; but I think now the chances are that I may do some good there, and it is a place where a man of real ability could at this time do an immense good. I think I would give anything to be able to talk with father for an hour, but perhaps it is as well that I should be obliged to rely entirely on my own ideas. However, 1863 will have other duties for me, before he is very old, than the Sequestration Commission, and I trust that he will 'ring in the thousand years of peace' before next New-Year's day, and bring us all together in happiness again. But we will take things cheerfully, however they come, and thank God for what he leaves us, if he does take the blessings of peace away."

His time during this winter was almost wholly spent in his duties on the Sequestration Commission, of which, though nominally and by rank the junior member, he performed most of the work, and the organization of which, under its new system, was principally based upon a report made by him soon after his arrival. To the ability, fidelity, and success with which he performed these duties we have the testimony of General Banks, who writes: —

"Among many patriotic officers to whose labors I have been indebted, I recall with gratitude the memory of Captain William Sturgis Hooper of Massachusetts. He entered the service of the government in 1862 as a volunteer, without compensation, bearing himself all expenses attending his career. . . . . The thorough mercantile education of Captain Hooper, and his extensive commercial experience, enabled him to render important services to the government in affairs connected with the civil administration of the department. The general direction of the business of the Commission for the management of sequestrated property, of which he was a member, was intrusted, among other interests, to his care. Important questions of international as well as military law, and of the commercial customs regulating trade in the staple products of the country, were involved in these transactions. All his duties were discharged with signal ability. His courteous deportment, sound judgment, and unimpeachable integrity disarmed the opposition of interested parties, and secured for his decisions the respect of all persons."

These duties, however, debarred him from the life in the open air for which he longed, and to which he had looked forward as the means of restoring his health. Shut up in an office, surrounded by swarms of men and women, loyal and disloyal, with complaints and demands and suggestions of every description and degree of annoyance, writing and talking and thinking from morning till night, he was constantly failing in health and strength. Still he was cheerful and hopeful, always flattering himself that his cough was a little better and his other physical disorders certainly no worse.

The modesty with which, in his letters, he always disparages his own share in the work which was going on is very remarkable, when compared with the real importance of his labors and responsibilities, as shown not merely by the facts themselves which he narrates, but by the evidence of his superiors and associates. When inclined to be discontented, he consoles himself thus: —

"Sometimes when I go from our dirty, carpetless rooms up to the handsome offices at head-quarters, and find the other aids finishing up their business for the day at two o'clock, or before, I feel rather like grumbling and calling myself a mere commissary's clerk; but when I think of the matter more seriously, I feel differently. The Sequestration Commission has been, until General Banks's arrival, an institution of almost unlimited power. When I first came here, every one looked upon it and all its officers with a species of awe, as having the fate of nearly all the property within our lines at its disposal; but now the Commission has cut its own claws and reduced itself, or rather the General has reduced it, to a comparatively harmless monster, with little power except to undo, so far as it may see fit or be able, the work which it had done before; so as fortune and the General have put me there, I do not think it would be right for me in any way to avoid the duties or the responsibilities which it involves. So, on the whole, I am well enough satisfied to be there, and do not seriously grumble, though I should like to get time for a ride on horseback every day; but this, I think, I shall be able to do after a little while, when things are reduced more to a system, and meanwhile I am contented, or reasonably so, and jolly."

When General Banks reached Louisiana, one of the first things demanding attention was the condition of the blacks. There were in the State probably over two hundred thousand slaves, three fourths of whom had flocked within the lines of the army. Within these lines President Lincoln's Emancipation Proclamation had, by its express terms, no operation. The situation of the negroes who clustered around the military posts was most distressing. Still slaves in law, they were no longer slaves in fact, for our officers and soldiers neither desired nor were permitted to aid in retaining them in servitude; and without the assistance of our forces, the former masters, whatever claim they might assert under the Proclamation, were powerless. The negroes were without clothes, food, shelter, or protection. To meet this state of things some vigorous action must be taken. The commanding general therefore directed the Sequestration Commission to prepare and report a proper system of labor.

A system was proposed by the Commission, embodying certain conditions demanded by a committee of the negroes themselves. The system was intended to secure to the negro liberty to go where he pleased, and to choose his employment and his employer, compensation for his labor, limitation of hours of work, exemption from corporal punishment and from separation of families, access to proper tribunals to enforce his rights, and an allotment of a small tract to cultivate for himself, as an encouragement to strive for the permanent acquisition of land. It also contained provisions for the support of the aged and infirm, the education of the young, the attendance of the sick, and the burial of the dead. The planters, after conference in public meeting, decided to accede to the "Contract," and thus, somewhat reluctantly, recognized the freedom of the very men whom the President's proclamation had excepted from that privilege.

Whatever difference of opinion there may be as to the means by which General Banks and his assistants attempted to solve the great problem of the day, there can be no doubt as to the fidelity of Captain Hooper's efforts. He believed in the General, he believed also in the march of events; and though his enthusiasm was often damped by the many failures and the imperfect successes which followed the most zealous efforts, he still worked and hoped and waited. General Banks writes: —

> "Early in the year 1863 many thousand negroes came within the lines of our army. Captain Hooper manifested a deep interest in all measures suggested for their protection and relief. The newly emancipated people had no truer or wiser friend. He gave great attention during the latter part of his life to the consideration of their interests. The free-labor system of Louisiana is his monument. He lived long enough to justify the belief that it was adapted to secure their liberty, but not long enough to witness the full success which it is destined to accomplish, nor to receive the thanks of those who were the subjects of his anxious care."

Towards the end of February Captain Hooper was sent by General Banks to Donaldsonville to inspect the working of the "Contract," and make a report upon it. He gives a most unfavorable account of the real state of feeling among the planters; and he evidently brought back very disheartening impressions with regard to the sincerity of the majority of those who pretended to have returned to or retained their allegiance to the Union.

"O for a land," he writes, "where one does not hear all the time of *this oath!* So far as I can judge, it is only considered binding by those who would do no harm any way, and yet it is poked at you all the time. I am getting a strong dislike to hearing of it."

With the difficulties which attended the carrying out of the labor system he was very disagreeably impressed. He found the planters unable or unwilling to understand the change of relation between themselves and their former slaves, laboring under the hallucination that slavery still continued, and attempting to coerce rather than persuade the negroes to continue at work.

"The nearer one gets to this negro question," he writes, "the more difficult and unpleasant it appears. I would not at all mind issuing wise orders on the subject of the negro, but Heaven help me from having to carry into execution even the wisest. The General is confident of success in this matter; and most of the reports which come in are so favorable that I can but hope that the locality which I visited was not a fair specimen."

So not discouraged, though a little disappointed, he went back to the city. His description of his return down the Mississippi — that once crowded thoroughfare, but then without sign of human life — is very graphic.

"Without any stop we hurry on, passing plantations which before the war brought to their owners yearly incomes of one hundred thousand dollars, now idle, the owners, perhaps, in the Rebel army, or, if still on their plantations, unable or afraid to raise a crop in the uncertainty of who will gather it. As we passed some noble places, one I remember in particular, with a superb avenue of live-oaks from the levee to the house, — a really fine old mansion-house, —

and not far off the huts of the slaves, almost a town by themselves, all deserted by its Rebel owner, — I thought of stories I had read of explorers descending great rivers in savage lands, and finding on the banks the relics of a civilization which had passed away into oblivion. Is this, perhaps, the very process which is going on here under our eyes? I do not think it is, and yet on the river I could well imagine it."

On his return he plunged again into the details of his office business, and toiled on at a task which, so far as the planters were concerned, was at least a thankless one. Through all difficulties and perplexities, he saw the great end at hand.

"The men," he writes, "who carried Louisiana out of the Union have much to answer for, I believe; and yet I hope and trust that they and others who brought on this war will prove in the end to have been the unconscious instruments of Providence for doing away with what I regard as the greatest social evil of the age. I do not doubt that slavery is gone here. No power on earth can make regular, permanent slaves of these people again, I think. The planters do not know it, but they seem to me about as crazy still as when they let Louisiana be drawn out of the Union."

And now the end of his service was approaching. He had exhausted, in the confinement of his office, the small stock of strength which he had brought from home. The shattered health, which he had hoped to restore by bodily exercise, had sunk irretrievably beneath the constant wear of mental labor and anxiety. When the opportunity to take the field came, it was too late. He accompanied our military and naval forces when they went, March 8, 1863, to make a demonstration against Port Hudson, and was present at the first reconnoissance and bombardment of the fortifications there. He performed his duties on the General's staff until about the 20th of the month, and then returned to New Orleans, convinced that he was too feeble for campaigning. Speaking of the expedition, he says: —

"I have drawn some lessons from it which I think cheaply bought at the expense of a pretty good attack of my old enemy. The most important is, that, in my present state of health, it is the height of folly for me to attempt to go into the field; in fact, an impossibility. Even the great muscles of —— would not carry him through the work, if he had to live without eating; and in my case I found that eating only pulled me down the more, by bringing on my trouble. So I do not think that you are likely to hear of my distinguishing myself at present."

Nor was this the worst. The labor which attended a subject surrounded by so many difficulties as the business of the Sequestration Commission was no less exhausting than the fatigues of a campaign, and it had now become evident to Captain Hooper that he was no longer strong enough to attend to any active duty whatever. Soon after coming back from Port Hudson, therefore, he left Louisiana for home upon sick-leave, still in the hope, never to be fulfilled, that he might yet be brought back to strength and usefulness. And thus Sturgis Hooper ended his military career, and with it all the labors of life. A soldier who never saw battle, a brave man who only lacked opportunity to show in the field how little terror death and wounds had for him, he had a part of the great work less brilliant than theirs who fell at Antietam and Gettysburg, but requiring no less manliness and moral courage, and he performed it faithfully and nobly. "His term of service," says General Banks, "was not long nor free from suffering, but there were few men of his age among the living or the dead of this great struggle who will leave a better record than his." His sacrifice of life to the cause at the desk of the Sequestration Commission was as free and as perfect as if it had been made upon the field of battle.

Of the last sad months there is little to be told. He lingered through the spring and summer, sometimes showing signs of improvement, and then again sinking the more certainly and rapidly, always hoping to live, but never fearing to die, full of patience and fortitude. His interest in the events of the day, and especially in the progress of emancipation, with which he had had so much to do, was unflagging to the last.

In the autumn the end became certain. He accepted his fate with resignation and without gloom. His religious faith was defined by no creeds, but he trusted, in death as he had done in life, to the goodness of God, and committed himself to his hands without apprehension. And so, on September 24, 1863, he passed away, at the age of thirty, "mourned by those who knew him only in the sterner relations of business, as well as by his companions in arms, and in a wide circle of those who respected him as a citizen and loved him as a friend."

Harvard College has counted her sons among the fallen on many a battle-field. Laurel-crowned they met their fate. By the grave of each we stand with swelling hearts, in pride and reverence. But almost more touching is the self-sacrifice of one who marched bravely and quietly to his doom, not to the sound of the trumpet, not amid the stir and emulation of the conflict, with no prize of fame inciting him to one grand effort, but surrounded by the prosaic details of monotonous labors, which were slowly but surely leading him to his death. Thinking only of doing his duty, of satisfying his General, of righting wrong, of helping to make his country whole again and free from taint, he kept his post through weariness, illness, and pain, so long as he found strength for each day's work. If to redress grievances and to raise up the oppressed be the office and the crown of chivalry, then no one who ever struck with sword has met his end amid more knightly service than that of William Sturgis Hooper.

PAUL JOSEPH REVERE.

Major 20th Mass. Vols. (Infantry), July 1, 1861; Lieutenant-Colonel and Assistant Inspector-General U. S. Vols., September 4, 1862; Colonel 20th Mass. Vols., April 14, 1863; died at Westminster, Md., July 4, 1863, of a wound received at Gettysburg, July 2.

PAUL JOSEPH REVERE was born in Boston, September 10, 1832, the son of Joseph W. and Mary (Robbins) Revere. His paternal grandfather was Paul Revere, of Revolutionary fame, and his maternal grandfather was Judge Edward Hutchinson Robbins of Milton. He was educated in the schools in Boston, with occasional periods of country life at school, making friends in every place, and forming warm attachments for life with many of his associates. An intimate friend writes:—

"When a boy, in that truest of all republics, the playground, his companions instinctively recognized in him a leader. There that keen sense of justice which seemed to be part and parcel of him was so conspicuous, that he was the well-known umpire in the boyish disputes of his companions, and we fondly recall the often-used expression, 'I 'll leave it to Paul.'"

In the winter of 1849 he entered Harvard University in the second term of the Freshman year, and he graduated with that class in 1852. While a Sophomore, he passed six months in the family of Rev. William Parsons Lunt, D. D., and there secured the regard of that intelligent and cultivated gentleman, with whose family Revere became connected after Dr. Lunt's death.

He left college without any taste for professional life; and in view of the necessity of following a calling, he decided on mercantile pursuits. In the summer of 1853 he went to Moosehead Lake on a hunting expedition, and travelled with an Indian guide to the source of the Saco River. He went several times to the Adirondacks, for his strong taste for active life was mingled with great love of nature and the spirit of adventure.

In 1854, at the wish of his father, he went to Lake Superior to inform himself in regard to the copper region. He had passed a month in pursuing this object, when all his mental and physical powers were taxed by an accident of no ordinary peril. He had crossed Lake Superior with two gentlemen interested in mines; and on their return, upon arriving at the lake, they found that there was a high wind, and the lake was like a disturbed sea. They were to take two boatmen to manage the boat during several hours' sail. Revere said, "This is against my judgment; let us wait." They said, "You have no experience here; we will go, and you may do as you like." Deciding to go, he took off his boots and his thick clothes, apprehending danger.

After rounding a point, the boat capsized, and all were thrown out. One of the gentlemen, Mr. Kershon, was asleep in the bottom of the boat, and was lost, as was one of the boatmen. The other, Dr. Pratt, was urged by Revere to cling with him to the bottom of the boat; but thinking that he could swim to the shore, made the attempt, and sank almost immediately. Revere diving after him, brought him to the surface, but found him dead. The others, after clinging several hours to the boat, reached the shore. Rohiscault, the old boatman, repeatedly gave up hope, and was only compelled by authority to maintain his hold; he says he owes his life to the persuasions of Mr. Revere, and relates that he held one end of the canoe, while Mr. Revere grasped the other, and, throwing himself on his back, guided the frail bark with rapid and undeviating course to land, and finally dragged his companion, half unconscious, on the beach. Revere, then discovering his overcoat still attached to the boat, took from the pocket his flask of brandy, and, having administered it, rolled the boatman on the warm sand until he was recovered sufficiently to show the way to a logger's hut.

The following year he undertook the care of an extensive wharf in Boston, and there exerted himself for the benefit of laborers and exposed women and children, until the neighboring police continually came to him as a friend to aid and protect the unfortunate about him.

In 1859 he married Lucretia Watson Lunt, daughter of Rev. W. P. Lunt, D. D., who, with two children, survives him. He had made a home near his aged father, thinking *his* comfort the highest duty; but the country's call was still higher, and that father's patriotic spirit aided him to engage in the cause. To the representations of a near and dear friend, who placed before him some family objections to a separation from home, he replied, "I have weighed it all, and there is something higher still. The institutions of this country — indeed free institutions throughout the world — hang on this moment."

To his mother he said, "I shall feel humbled to stay at home." The reply was, "Do as you think right."

With these convictions of personal and public duty, soon after the insurgent attack on Fort Sumter he offered his military services to the Chief Magistrate and Commander-in-chief of Massachusetts; and immediately entered as a pupil in the Military Club of Monsieur Salignac in Boston. On the 1st of July, 1861, Revere was commissioned Major of the Twentieth Regiment of Massachusetts Volunteers (Infantry), and soon after joined his regiment, then in camp at Readville. His devotion to his new duties was consistent with the high moral principle which had made him a soldier of the Republic. The regiment to which he was attached had in it elements which required strong and judicious government; the personal material which constituted its nucleus having been principally drawn from a disbanded and mutinous organization, and being thus demoralized. To bring these men to military subordination required the exercise of high moral power, and a strong will, which fortunately was found in Major Revere and most of his brother officers. Their efforts to establish and maintain order and good discipline were rewarded with success, the fruits of which were exhibited in the annals of the regiment from Ball's Bluff to the surrender of the insurgent army under General Lee.

Early in September the regiment was ordered to Washington, and from thence, after a few days' halt, to Poolesville, Maryland, where it reported to Brigadier-General C. P. Stone, in command of the corps of observation. Until October 20th the regiment was in the performance of picket and outpost duty, along the Potomac River, Major Revere taking his proper share of the service. On Sunday, October 20th, a battalion of the regiment was ordered to the river-bank, from which, during the night of that day, it crossed to Harrison's Island. This was preliminary to the battle of Ball's Bluff. On the morning of the 21st, at an early hour, two companies were sent into Virginia as the covering force of a reconnoitring party which had preceded them. Major Revere, who had accompanied the battalion from camp in Maryland, was left on the island in command of the force held there in reserve, and rendered a most important service in dragging round, from its east side to that opposite the Virginia bank, a scow, which added materially to the means of transportation, and was of great value in subsequent operations.

Colonel Baker, having been ordered to the command of the troops which had crossed into Virginia, and the supporting force which lay on the island and the adjacent Maryland shore, had, on assuming command, ordered the reserve of the Twentieth Regiment, among other troops, to reinforce the battalions in Virginia. Accordingly, about noon, Major Revere crossed the river. The battle of Ball's Bluff followed. The aggregate Union force present during the battle — not including the Nineteenth Massachusetts Infantry, which remained on the island and was not engaged — was, exclusive of officers, sixteen hundred and three men. Major Revere bore an honorable part in this bloody and disastrous conflict, earning a high character for cool and disciplined courage. He was slightly wounded in the leg, while endeavoring to run into the river two mountain-howitzers which had become disabled, the cannoneers having been all killed or wounded; and he was among the last to leave the field when it was irretrievably lost. The means of transportation were very limited, and escape by the boats, in the rush and confusion which prevailed, appeared very uncertain. He therefore, with some brother officers and a few men, among them his brother, Surgeon Revere, passed up the river to seek other means of crossing to the Maryland side. A boat was found and secured, but coming under the observation of the enemy, the fugitives were compelled to abandon it, and pursue their way up the river. After it became dark, an attempt was made to construct a raft of fence-rails, but the rails were water-soaked, and the raft would not float. Revere was a practised swimmer, and could easily have reached the opposite bank; he, however, with that generous self-sacrifice which entered so largely into his character, refused to leave his commander, who was somewhat advanced in years and unskilled in swimming. About half past eight at night, a scouting party of the enemy's cavalry discovered the fugitives, who had no alternative but to surrender.

The prisoners were taken to Leesburg, where the Rebel commander received them and tendered them a parole, which was declined, its terms being ambiguous. On the following morning, at two o'clock, the column of prisoners, five hundred and twenty-nine men, including fifteen officers, commenced its long and weary march to Richmond. It rained in torrents, the mud was ankle deep, and the men had been long without food; while one small wagon, without cover or seats, was the only transportation provided for the sick and wounded.

Major Revere had said nothing about his wound, and now marched on uncomplainingly, refusing to take his turn in the wagon. It was six, P. M., when the column reached the stone house historically connected with the Bull Run battle-field, — its halting-place for the night. A ration of half-cooked corn bread and bacon was here served at ten, P. M. The next morning early the column was again in motion, and at ten o'clock arrived at Manassas, where it rested till six, P. M., when the prisoners were transferred to the cars for Richmond. While at Manassas, the officers were confined in a barn, closely guarded; they had many visitors of both sexes, some of whom indulged in remarks and reflections little in keeping with their claims of chivalrous breeding. A scanty ration was furnished in the afternoon to the now almost famished prisoners, who were also drenched to the skin by the heavy rain of the previous day, so that their condition was miserable indeed. But the demeanor of Major Revere, under these trials of temper and body, was most dignified and patient; he expressed to the officer of the guard a hope that the men would be properly cared for, but asked nothing for himself.

On the morning of the 24th the train arrived in Richmond; and the prisoners, amid the jeers, taunts, and sometimes threats of a dense crowd, were marched to the tobacco warehouse assigned as their prison. The kind hospitality of fellow-prisoners, whom they found there, supplied their immediate wants; but days elapsed before they were established in any reasonable degree of comfort. Two ladies, true to their womanly instincts, — one of them, Miss E. A. Van Lew, moved also by her loyal attachment to the Union, — sought out and relieved the new-comers. Mrs. Randolph, wife of the Confederate General Randolph, and Miss Van Lew, were the ministering angels of this unlooked-for and grateful kindness, which is here recorded as a tribute to their generous and timely beneficence. Prison life in the Richmond warehouse was one of annoying discomforts: the petty tyranny of officials, — Wirz, of Andersonville notoriety, being first-sergeant of the prison guard, — the vulgar obtrusiveness of civilian visitors, and a densely crowded apartment, constituted a condition of existence which taxed its subjects almost beyond endurance. Major Revere bore these trials with manly fortitude. His deportment was dignified, but affable, in his intercourse with fellow-prisoners. The kindly traits of his disposition seemed warmed into a more lively exercise; and while he did not join in the amusements most common in a community of such varied sympathies and habits, yet he had a cheerful word and look for all. Mindful of his religious duties, he daily sought counsel of THE FATHER, in prayer and in the Scriptures.

We now pass to a period in the prison life at Richmond which was full of gloomy anxieties.

On the 10th of November, General I. H. Winder published

an order of the insurgent Secretary of War, directing him to select hostages, to be confined in the cells allotted to persons charged with infamous crimes, to answer with their lives for the safety of the Rebel privateersmen, held by the United States government, under a charge of piracy on the high seas. In closing his order Secretary Benjamin said :—

"As these measures are intended to repress the infamous attempt now made by the enemy to commit judicial murder on prisoners of war, you will execute them strictly, as the mode best calculated to prevent the commission of so heinous a crime."

Major Revere was one of the hostages selected under this order, and he entered upon the ordeal with the equanimity of a brave soldier, who stood for his country, with its honor in his keeping. On the following Thursday, the hostages, seven in number, were transferred to Henrico County Prison, and placed in charge of its warden. The cell in which they were confined, and in which, for a considerable period of time, they were required to perform every function of life, was of most contracted dimensions, — eleven feet by seventeen in area, — faintly lighted and filthy with tormenting vermin. The situation was one almost too horrible and disgusting to contemplate. The hostages did not utter one word of complaint or remonstrance, although they felt that life could not long sustain itself in an atmosphere so foul. After a while General Winder modified this barbarous treatment, allowing a half-hour each day to prisoners for a visit to the prison yard; this half-hour being often extended into an hour by the commiserating turnkey, Thomas.

In this experience, dreadful as it was, Revere evinced the same patient manliness which had always distinguished his conduct. In a single instance only did he permit his indignation to master the habitual control which he exercised over his feelings. The circumstances of this were as follows. The prison in which the hostages were confined was surrounded by a high wall, which hid from their sight every outward object except the sky and distant house-tops. On the second Saturday of their confinement, while engaged in the simple pursuits of prison life, the hostages were suddenly startled by the sharp sound of a lash and an accompanying shriek of agony. It was "whipping-day," and the negroes were receiving their allotted lashes for violations of law and decorum. The cry of agony and the pitiful moans which followed, as blow after blow in quick succession gradually reduced the sufferer to a condition of comparative insensibility, came from a woman. Revere absolutely started to his feet, the hot blood coursing its quick way through every vein. It seemed to him a personal affront, a contrived indignity to Northern "prejudice"; he learned afterward, however, that Saturday was "whipping-day," and the court-house yard the place of punishment. A brother officer, who lay by his side, has said, that, during the night which followed the incident just described, Revere trembled with rage when alluding to it. He never forgot that "whipping-day," with its cry of agony. That moaning woman was to his heart the representative of an oppressed race. He did not turn a deaf ear to the appeal for mercy and protection.

Writing from Fortress Monroe the day of his arrival there, a paroled prisoner from Richmond, after speaking of the ill-treatment of the hostages by the Rebel government, he continues: —

"However, it does not matter much now, and they never for a moment, with all their outrages, made us forget our position as gentlemen."

It is certain that he never did forget what was due to his position as a gentleman, if manly fortitude and Christian bearing be typical of that character. A prison companion, writing to a member of his family after the fatal day of Gettysburg, spoke of his deportment, while confined as a hostage, in terms which will be understood and appreciated by all who were familiar with his characteristics: —

"In the cell of Henrico County Prison, with its horrible experiences and painful suspense, there was a moral grandeur in his conduct of which I can give no idea. All were strangers except Revere and myself. How much depended, how much of ordinary comfort even rested, upon decorum and self-respect in act and speech ; how strongly yet delicately Revere restrained undue license in each ! "

But Revere was reserved for future services to his country, and for a more glorious death than that of a constructive criminal. The government of the United States released the privateersmen as pirates, changing their *status* to that of prisoners of war ; and on February 22, 1862, after four months' confinement, Major Revere returned on parole to the home from which he had been separated under such painful circumstances.

Observation and reflection, while a prisoner, had confirmed his original conviction, that the war of the Rebellion was a war for the supremacy or extermination of human slavery. He clearly saw that the institution of slavery was the salient point of the Rebellion, and that the success of the Union arms, even if it demanded "the last man and the last dollar," was an imperative duty. To a friend and brother officer who largely enjoyed his confidence, and shared with him the hardships of Richmond and accommodations of camp life, he often and earnestly spoke of this obligation, as due both to God and country. It was a conviction which had its birth in his soul.

With recruited health and strength came the desire for active service, but he was still under the military restraints of his parole, and the policy of the United States government did not seem, at that time, to encourage hope of speedy exchange. It was determined, however, to make an effort to obtain one, by personal application to Secretary Stanton. Accordingly, having selected Major McAlexander of Alabama, a prisoner of war confined at Fort Warren, and having arranged with him a plan of proceeding, Major Revere applied to the War Department at Washington for a leave of absence for Major McAlexander, permitting him to visit Richmond, on condition that he should return to Fort Warren within fifteen days, or should transmit to General Wool, commanding at Fortress Monroe, an order of the Confederate authorities, exchanging him for Revere. Secretary Stanton granted the application, expressing, however, strong doubts whether the Rebel officer or the exchange would ever be heard of again. But Major McAlexander was a gentleman of personal honor; and he successfully accomplished his mission. On May 1st Major Revere was *en route* to rejoin his regiment, then in the lines before Yorktown, Virginia. He reported for duty on May 2d, in season to move with the general advance of the army which followed the Rebel evacuation of Yorktown.

On May 7th he was present with his regiment at West Point, when the Rebel General W. H. C. Whiting made his unsuccessful attempt to force the position occupied by Franklin's division and Dana's brigade. The army was greatly hindered in its advance by the condition of the roads; and it was not till towards the last of May that General McClellan found himself within striking distance of Richmond, the objective point of the campaign. On the march up the Peninsula, Major Revere had greatly distinguished himself while in command of the skirmish line of a brigade, and intrusted with the duty of scouring the north bank of the Chickahominy, — thereby winning honorable mention from his corps commander, General Sumner.

The last days of May found the army massed on both sides of the Chickahominy, the communications between its wings being mostly maintained by temporary bridges, constructed by the troops. A sudden and violent rain, during the day and night of May 30th, had swollen the river to an unprecedented height, and greatly endangered the bridges. The Rebel general, acting upon the belief that the bridges would be swept away and the Union army divided, resolved to make a sudden and overwhelming attack upon Keyes's division, which lay at Fair Oaks, on the south side of the river, somewhat in advance of the supporting corps. In execution of this design, General Johnston concentrated, on the morning of May 31st, a heavy column under Hill, Longstreet, Smith, and Huger, intending to fall upon Keyes by early dawn; but the rain had proved unfriendly to his movements, as well as to those of the Union army. Smith and Huger were long behind the designated time in reaching their respective positions. At noon they had not appeared, and Hill and Longstreet moved to the attack of Keyes, without waiting for their expected diversion. The attack was sudden, vigorous, and overwhelming. Keyes was forced to retire, abandoning his camp, and losing many guns. The enemy pressed forward, encountering and overcoming a brigade of Couch's division, which sought to arrest the Rebel advance. Affairs looked very discouraging; a fresh column of the enemy was now moving against the right; and along the railroad, a heavy force, which had been held in reserve, was directing its march upon Fair Oaks.

In this critical condition of affairs, General Sumner was ordered to march rapidly to the scene of conflict; his corps lay on the opposite or north side of the Chickahominy, there being two hastily-constructed bridges for communication between the two portions of the army. The swift and swollen stream had swept away one of these bridges, that opposite the First Division; and the other, opposite the Second (Sedgwick's), was trembling and vibrating in its struggle for life. The division succeeded, however, in crossing, and pressed onward, for the unceasing cannonade in front still told of sharply-contested battle. The deep and miry morass, which formed the intervale of the river, had swamped all the artillery of the division, except five guns, beyond extrication; and two infantry regiments — the Nineteenth Massachusetts and Forty-second New York — were detached to protect them and guard the river. As the column approached the field of battle, it was halted to load. "We are in luck to-day," said Major Revere; "we are not left in the rear to guard the river." This was not said thoughtlessly, or with levity, for no man felt more profoundly the solemnity of battle.

The division, weakened by the causes above mentioned, hastened forward, and late in the afternoon arrived upon the field near Fair Oaks. The column of the enemy which had advanced along the railroad was deployed in front of Sedgwick's division, when the latter came into line of battle. The safety of the army depended in a measure upon its ability to stem the tide of Rebel victory, to restore the lost battle. That it did so, after a sanguinary conflict, which terminated in the repulse and disorderly flight of the Rebel troops, is historical. To Major Revere the victory had an unusual charm; he had suffered, as a consequence of defeat on a previous occasion, cruel hardships, and while in Richmond as a prisoner had been often offended by the Virginia boasts of superior courage. He had now seen the backs of this vaunting chivalry, who, throwing away their arms and leaving their wounded behind, sought safety in flight. During the night, these wounded, who lay in great numbers on the field, in the vicinity of the position occupied by the division, (for the charge which broke the Rebel line and completed the victory had carried it forward some distance,) were carefully collected, and made as comfortable as circumstances permitted. Officers and men cheerfully surrendered overcoats and blankets to protect the poor sufferers from the cold night-air, and water-carriers were detailed to supply the ever-craving cry of "Water! water!"

Major Revere was most active in this work of mercy. The maimed and dying men, whose moans and cries so painfully rose upon the ear, were no longer public enemies, they were his suffering fellow-creatures. Many times during the night he visited that long line of recumbent wounded, to be sure that no faint cry for water should be uttered unheard or unheeded; and at earliest dawn he personally went in search of a surgeon, — for the medical officers of the Twentieth had been left in the rear to care for their own wounded.

The enemy having drawn heavy reinforcements from Richmond during the night, sought, on the morning of June 1st, to retrieve their fortunes in renewed attack; but failing to penetrate the Union line, after a fierce and long struggle, they returned discomfited to their defensive works. The month of June was passed in the usual manner, of an investing army, watching and waiting for the moment of assault. Major Revere shared with his regiment during this period the arduous labors of an advanced line, — being half the time within range of the enemy's sharpshooters, who inflicted some loss on the regiment.

On June 25th, the Rebel general moved in force against the Union right, which he succeeded in turning. A result of his success was to cut off McClellan's base of supplies at the White House, forcing him to fall back on James River. On the 29th, at an early hour, the Second Corps, which, with the Third and a division of the Sixth, constituted the rear-guard in this memorable movement, silently marched out of their intrenched camp at or near Fair Oaks. Major Revere had been detached during the night of the 27th, in command of a small battalion of the Twentieth, on special duty connected with the Ordnance Department, and was absent from his regiment when the retrograde movement of the Second Corps commenced. Sedgwick's division was halted, and fronted the enemy in line of battle at Peach Orchard, a mile or more from Fair Oaks, where it had a sharp skirmish, checking the Rebel advance.

Again in the afternoon at Savage Station, where Major Revere rejoined his regiment, the division was sent into action to arrest the enemy's advance, which had now become serious and threatening. It was late in the evening before the regiments were withdrawn from the ground they had held against the Rebel troops. About nine, P. M., the Second Corps entered upon its march through White-Oak Swamp. The night was dark and wet, and the narrow road, lighted only by the glare of a few lanterns, was most dismal and gloomy; but the *morale* of the troops was wonderfully good. Encouraged by the example and voice of their officers, the men trudged along cheerfully and steadily, preserving excellent order and discipline.

Early in the morning of June 30th the column debouched from the swamp on the high ground which borders its southern side, and halted to get a few hours of repose. Major Revere, during this severe and trying night-march, exhibited the true and solid qualities of a soldier. His admonitions to "close up," and his cheerful words of encouragement, were judiciously bestowed from time to time, avoiding the unprofitable annoyance of what the men significantly call *worrying*.

The troops, after two or three hours of such rest as could

be obtained in wet clothes on the wet ground, without shelter, were summoned to continue their march. An hour or two brought them to Nelson's farm, where they were halted to cover the Quaker road, the main line of communication with James River. Franklin's division had been left at White-Oak Swamp to protect the rear, and about noon had become engaged with the enemy. Two brigades, Dana's and Gorman's of Sedgwick's division, were hastily marched to Franklin's support, but upon a fierce and successful attack of the enemy made in the afternoon upon McCall's division of Pennsylvania Reserves, which occupied the position of Glendale, in front of the Quaker road, were sent back at double-quick to aid in recovering the position. It was an oppressively hot day, and the leading brigade, Dana's, was immediately hurried into action on its arrival from the swamp, for the exigency was most imminent. The men were panting with exhaustion; many of them had fallen out of the ranks, some senseless from sunstroke, and the regiments coming up separately went forward into the copse of wood known as Glendale, without much concert of movement. Major Revere exerted himself actively as an extemporized staff officer to remedy the last-named difficulty, and by his personal efforts partially succeeded in bringing the regiments as a united brigade in front of the enemy. Reinforcements were soon sent forward, and the ground was held by the Union troops; the loss in killed and wounded, however, had been very heavy. Major Revere, in the course of the operations in and around Glendale, had his horse killed under him, and was thrown violently to the ground, fortunately without injury. It will be undoubtedly in accordance with the general opinion of his brother officers to award to him, for his conduct on this occasion, a high degree of honor.

With night came the order to march again; and the morning of July 1st found the army occupying Malvern Hill, to make its last stand against the now desperate foe. The conflict was long and obstinate, but in the end successful, and the Army of the Potomac on the next day made its way unmolested to the new base of operations on James River. The new position of the army was not free from causes of anxiety; the enemy clustered around it on both sides of the river, keeping up a constant and annoying fire of artillery, and the poisonous malaria of the bottom-land began to develop its debilitating influence upon the health of the troops. The robust constitution of Revere seemed for a time proof against this insidious enemy, but about the middle of July disease began to manifest itself in painful neuralgic affections; he did not, however, report himself sick until the early part of August, when, being utterly prostrated and unfit for duty, he was compelled to seek restored health in the more salubrious air of his Northern home.

With the last days of August came the discouraging intelligence of Pope's disastrous campaign in front of Washington; and Revere, scarcely recovered from sickness, hastened to his post of duty. He had, during his absence from the army, been appointed Inspector-General of the Second Corps, with the rank of Lieutenant-Colonel, and now reported at the headquarters of General Sumner in his new position. The Maryland campaign followed within the next two weeks, terminating with the battle of Antietam and the consequent retreat of the insurgent army into Virginia.

Lieutenant-Colonel Revere was wounded at Antietam, while endeavoring to rally and re-form some broken and flying regiments; but he nevertheless kept the field, aiding materially in bringing up and guiding into action the rear divisions of the corps. His wound forced him again to seek the repose and care of home, leaving, without knowing it, his brother dead on the field. There he remained till the following spring, a confirmed and suffering invalid.

In the mean time General Sumner had died, and as a consequence Lieutenant-Colonel Revere was mustered out of the service as Inspector-General of the Second Corps. He was now appointed Colonel of his old regiment, the Twentieth Massachusetts, and in May, 1863, reported at Falmouth, Virginia, on the north bank of the Rappahannock, as commander of the regiment. In June following, Lee led his army down the Valley of the Shenandoah, to repeat his exploit of the previous year, — an invasion of Maryland and Pennsylvania. The Army of the Potomac therefore broke camp, and moved north also, keeping the Blue Ridge between it and the enemy. Lee, by rapid marches, had reached the Upper Potomac, and crossed that river into Maryland, almost before General Hooker had penetrated his design, or felt safe to uncover the gaps, through which the Rebel troops could advance upon Washington. As soon as all doubts on this point were removed by the appearance of Lee's main army in Maryland, the Union columns were pressed rapidly forward. The Twentieth Massachusetts crossed the river near the old field of Ball's Bluff, its first battle experience. By June 30th the whole army was in Maryland, moving upon Lee, who had a week before occupied Hagerstown in force, with his advanced parties in front of York in Pennsylvania, threatening both Baltimore and Philadelphia. Major-General George G. Meade had only within a day or two relieved General Hooker, in the command of the army, and on July 1st had not arrived at the front. At this time the advanced corps (First and Eleventh) of the Union army were in the vicinity of Gettysburg, Pennsylvania, and while on the march were attacked and driven back, through that town, to a strong position on its south side, where they waited for the main body of the army to come up. During the night General Meade arrived at the front, and before morning, on July 2d, the whole army was once more in the presence of its old foe, the Army of Northern Virginia. Preparations for battle were at once made. Quietly and quickly the artillery and infantry took up their assigned positions; the men lying down in that solemn silence which precedes expected battle. Colonel Revere was here again, and for the last time, to renew his covenant with Union and Freedom. The offering of his life was to consummate the sacrifice.

The day of July 2d was passing away. The artillery on both sides had unceasingly hurled a destructive fire of solid shell and canister shot into opposing ranks, and the intermitting, rattling fire of musketry, which ever and anon reached the ear from the right, told rather of watchful observation than general battle. On the left, however, Sickles, who held a somewhat advanced position, had been fiercely attacked by Longstreet and forced to fall back more within supporting distance of the main line, after sustaining a heavy loss. But the Union army made no aggressive movement; for it was the design of General Meade to act defensively, to receive an attack from the Rebel commander in the strong position occupied by his troops.

About six, P. M., a canister shot burst a short distance above Colonel Revere, a bullet from which struck him, penetrating the vital parts, and inflicting a mortal injury, of which he died on the 4th of July following. He lived long enough to know that the Union arms were triumphant, that the enemy, after obstinate and vain efforts to force Meade's lines, had been repulsed.

In contemplating the character of Colonel Revere, we are at once and strongly impressed with the harmony of its moral proportions. The religious sentiment was marked and prominent; he habitually referred every question of personal conduct to the tribunal of conscience, able to abide the decision with unwavering trust. He believed that conscience was the light of God. Deliberate in his method of reasoning, and gifted with unusual powers of discernment, his conclusions did not suffer in comparison with the lessons of experience. A resolute will, too, enforced his convictions of duty against all obstacles of self-interest. What he thought to be right, he did. With all the sterner and rigid attributes of human nature, so necessary to overcome the rough places in the path of life, his heart was a deep and ever-welling spring of warm affection. Distress never called to him in vain for needed relief. Amid the din of battle he would kneel by a dying comrade to receive his whispered and choking accents of parting love to dear ones at home.

The remains of Colonel Revere were removed to Massachusetts and interred at Mount Auburn, amidst the verdant beauties of that Nature whose loveliness he never failed, even amid the stern scenes of war, to notice and enjoy.

ROBERT WARE.

Surgeon 44th Mass. Vols. (Infantry), August 29, 1862; died at Washington, N. C., April 10, 1863, of disease contracted in the service.

ROBERT WARE was born on the 2d of September, 1833, in Boston, being the youngest son of the late Dr. John Ware, Professor of the Theory and Practice of Medicine in Harvard University, and of Helen (Lincoln) Ware. He was prepared for college at the Boston Latin School, and entered the Freshman class at Cambridge in 1848, being its youngest member. He graduated with honor in 1852, having made a host of friends by the sweetness of his temper, his kindly wit, his manliness, and his excellent parts. He began the study of medicine in Boston, and spent the year 1855 abroad, enjoying the advantages of the hospitals of Paris, with the great benefit of his father's wisdom and presence to direct his studies. His application, with this thorough preparation, had gained him unusual qualifications for the practice of his profession, when he took his degree of M. D. in 1856.

As a young physician, he found that his first patients were the poor, and seldom have the poor the benefit of so ripe a judgment and such conscientious care. No thought of ease or pleasure could draw him from the bedside of his most wretched patient. Those physicians who succeeded him in his very large dispensary practice know how hearty were the gratitude and affection of those who had experienced his skill and forethought. Though too hard a worker to have much leisure for writing, he found time to prepare a report on small-pox during an epidemic in 1860, which gained him no little credit, and was published for distribution by vote of the Legislature of Massachusetts. His culture, however, was by no means limited to his profession. Foreign travel, and a high appreciation of art and literature, lent polish and elegance in no ordinary degree to a solid and discriminating mind.

Although so young, he had been for some years noticed by his professional seniors as giving the highest promise of success; his quickness of intellect, his patient industry and powers of observation, had marked him for a high position. The outbreak of the war found him with a growing practice, a sound reputation, and a mind deeply stirred by the rush of events. His remarkable modesty, and a feeling that his education had fitted him specially for a physician's work, made him shy of undertaking the duties of a military surgeon. When, however, he was called to a surgeon's post, it was found that cleverness as an operator was added to the list of his professional excellences.

He embraced his first opportunity of usefulness in the war by entering the service of the Sanitary Commission, in the latter part of 1861, as Inspector. Out of the few extracts from his letters which our space permits, the reader can gather somewhat of his spirit; but his keen wit, his prompt denunciation of abuses, and shrewd estimate of character, must be lost to all but his correspondents.

"NEWPORT NEWS, December 10, 1861.

". . . . Where do you suppose the name of Old Point Comfort came from? The place is certainly old, and there is no question as to its being a point, but as to comfort, *allons donc!* . . . . We used to ride out on horseback, and visit about two regiments a day. The word 'riding' reminds me of the condition to which three or four days of this business reduced me. You probably supposed, in the innocence of your heart, that the old and abominable rack of the Inquisition had been abolished, and no longer existed out of the Tower or such places. Pray divest your mind of such an error; it still lives and is active, it has been placed on four legs, endowed with a skin and hair together with a tail, and is called a quartermaster's horse. Upon this instrument of torture have I been jolted about for some days. The result must be felt to be appreciated."

"ROCKVILLE, MARYLAND, December 17.

". . . . I have been sent up here to do General Stone's division. Saturday I reached Washington from Fortress Monroe, devoted Sunday to writing a report of my doings at that place of dulness and darkies; was sent yesterday to Relay House to visit a Maine regiment, and started this noon for Poolesville. Winkle never eyed that noble quadruped, the horse, with half the murderous feeling which fills my heart, after I have been for an hour or so on the back of a quartermaster's horse. The animal furnished me to-day is a small, stumpy, coarse-haired, thick-eared, yellowish-gray beast, with the stupidity of a penguin and the hide of an alligator. I tried in vain before I left to buy a pair of spurs, but could find none that would go over my leather leggings. Tired with continuous and unavailing castigation, I resorted to the use of a stout pin. The pin doubled up, but did n't even rouse him. He was left to his own devices and the prospect of supper; one or the other finally brought him here. . . . . With me and the horse came a rubber bag containing much Sanitary knowledge, and the means of asking thirty-six hundred questions, that being the extent to which (as you will ascertain by a very simple process of arithmetic, if you assume the command to contain twenty thousand men, and the number of questions to each regiment to be one hundred and eighty) my inquisitive powers are to be exerted."

"FORTRESS MONROE, January 26, 1862.

". . . . Do you know that I am so far removed from anything approaching civilized society, and am so much in the daily habit of talking about dirt and bad air to all whom I meet, that when it comes to sitting down and talking to a person who is n't dirty and does n't breathe bad air, I hardly know what to say? . . . . I was sorry not to get over to Hampton to see the ruins of what every one speaks of as a most picturesque old town; but the day on which I intended to go was much occupied in waiting to find Captain L., who had just come from Hatteras, that I might learn whether or not I could go back with him, and I did not feel justified in taking the day for a mere excursion. That, by the way, is a great evil in selling yourself for a fixed salary; you feel perpetually as if all the time not given directly to the business in hand was so much money obtained on false pretences, and that you were nothing if not Sanitary at all times and places."

"CHESAPEAKE HOSPITAL, FORTRESS MONROE, April 1.

". . . . When I wrote the other day that I was rapidly forgetting how to practise medicine, I did not think that I should so soon be immersed in an extensive practice, and that too under the most disagreeable circumstances. Though this hospital was not half ready, and no proper means were provided for attending a single very sick man, nearly one hundred patients have been sent in here, and we have been compelled to do the best that we could. If the matter were not so serious, and the results, in the way of discomfort and perhaps death, to the soldiers, so melancholy, it would make one laugh to see the absurd inadequacy of the supplies sent here. . . . . And then the apothecary's shop! any druggist of even moderate ideas and expectations would go stark mad, and drown his woes in his own assafœtida, did he find he was expected to dispense drugs under such circumstances.

"My medical work here is so consuming of time that I have not been outside the house for three or four days, and can do nothing in the Sanitary line, and feel as if I were neglecting my own proper business, though the demand is so absorbing that I must keep on. The house is not well adapted for a hospital. This army will need nearly a thousand beds here, and yet no measures have been taken to put up temporary buildings as adjuncts to this one."

"April 10.

"My hospital labors have continued with no intermission, except for three days when I went up to Newport News, to see a large number of sick who had been sent in and were in a sad plight. . . . . We have many very sick here in this house, — four or five died yesterday. It 's a most painful thing to see men die so, away from home and friends, surrounded by people who care nothing for them. One soon learns what a little thing is a man's life. One poor fellow died yesterday of typhoid fever, and the nurse brought me down his diary, which he had kept since joining the regiment. In it often occurred, 'wrote to mother,' 'got a letter from mother,' or 'father.' The record ceased abruptly two days before his entry into the hospital, and the blank seemed to tell so sad a story of no kind friend near to tell his mother of her son, that I filled up the record with a few words about his sickness and death.

"To this hospital have now been sent the munificent provision of two hundred linen sheets, so new and stiff that one might as well ensconce himself between two panes of glass; fifty towels, fifty or sixty hospital shirts, thirty-four hospital dressing-gowns, and other articles in the same proportion. No, I am wrong; the supply of horse-radish graters is complete and ample, — there is a dozen of them, enough for a whole town; but as an offset to such prodigality, there are not more than a dozen teaspoons in the house. The nurses have laid violent hands upon all these, and carry them in their pockets to dispense medicine in. The supply of vials has been so small that the nurses have come down to the office, had the medicine put in a mug, gone up and turned the dose into the patient, and returned for another mess for another man. When castor-oil, salts, and quinine follow each other in rapid succession, you can see that the impression made on the sense of taste in the last victim must be more startling than pleasant. With the exception of the blankets and bed-sacks, every article of bedding in use has come from the people of the country, through the agency of the Sanitary Commission. Without them, the bulk of those now in bed must have lain on the slats of the bedstead, like St. Lawrence on the gridiron. The only thing that has been sent without stint by the authorities is the patients; and these, which should be the last thing to come to a hospital, were the first here."

The disastrous Peninsular campaign had now begun. What part Dr. Ware performed in caring for the sick and wounded that poured in ghastly streams from the front to the transports would hardly be gathered from his own story in his letters. Fortunately we have ample means of knowing from his associates how he toiled, and with what benefit to those who experienced his care.

"Hospital Ship Ocean Queen,
Off Yorktown, Wednesday, May 7.

". . . . This ship was put into the hands of the Commission on Monday. To-day she sailed with over eight hundred sick men."

"May 26.

"We are having busy times here with the sick, and are expecting still busier when the wounded come from the anticipated battle. To-day we sent off the steamer Spaulding with three hundred and twenty-five sick men. Perhaps I have not written enough of our method of procedure here for you to know how we manage. The Commission has had several steamers placed in its charge by government, which it has agreed to fit up with beds, &c., and to provide with surgeons for the transportation of the sick. Want of hospital room either here or at Yorktown forces men to be carried to the hospitals at Washington, and they being now full, even farther North; and in this work we are engaged. Mr. Olmsted, with some others who have been long attached to the Commission, including myself, constitute a sort of permanent staff, and see to the selecting of patients, the fitting up of the steamers, &c. With us are engaged several New York ladies, who are most useful and efficient. . . . . I should not have supposed that women of their breeding and habits could go through with so much and such fearfully disagreeable work, but they are untiring, always cheerful, ready, and uncomplaining; and by their very presence, apart from the actual assistance in nursing, soften the treatment which, at the hands of the best-intentioned men, is somewhat rough and harsh. They are charming company, and I am rapidly learning to eat with my fork — when I can get one. We take our quinine regularly in a jovial company, and laugh at each other's wry faces over the bitterness."

"June 8.

". . . . The battle has been fought, and we have had fearfully hard work with the wounded at this point. . . . . The results of the fight in the shape of wounded men began to appear on Monday, and since then every train has brought in varying numbers. Nearly four thousand have been sent away from here. . . . . I have the charge of a sort of hospital, with kitchen, &c., which has been established at the terminus of the railway, for the reception of the sick and wounded as they come down. The general hospital to which patients are sent from the front is about a third of a mile distant from the railway; and as most of the trains arrive here in the night, it would be difficult to move them to the hospital as they arrive, and they would be obliged to remain in the cars all night. At Mr. Olmsted's suggestion, therefore, about sixty tents were pitched at the side of the railway, capable of containing about four hundred men; and the kitchen, and the care of these tents, and the men in them, has been made over to me by Mr. Olmsted. Some nights we have cared for over two hundred sick or wounded men; and I wish you could be here some night to see the moving. There are many lanterns. A bright fire behind our cook-tent brings out in full relief the moving figures of the men carrying stretchers, and of the limping wounded. As soon as we can get it ready, food is sent up to the tents, and you would smile to see how grateful the men are for a piece of soft bread. The only bread at the front is the hard ship-biscuit; and many of the men, whose gums are sore from scurvy, find difficulty in eating it. Sometimes we get to bed at twelve, sometimes at three, sometimes not at all; and I am free to say that I regard sunrise as a greater humbug than ever. When the wounded first began to come down, there was immense enthusiasm on the part of the various hangers-on at the post, and men swarmed around with offers of assistance. If the cars came in pretty early, there were plenty of hands to carry them to the boats;

but if they came in late, or the task of carrying them was extended over a long time, it was amazing hard work to find people who would assist. Make what representations we would, it was impossible to get men detailed for the especial duty; and we had to rely on such help as could be got."

No better comments on his own modest story can be made than those of his fellow-workers. In the little book entitled "Hospital Transports" we read:—

"As soon as the whistle is heard, Dr. Ware is on hand (he has all the hard work of this kind to do). . . . . Dr. Ware sees them all, and knows that they have blankets, attendants, and stimulants for the night. When the morning comes, ambulances are generally sent for them from the shore hospital, but occasionally they are left on the Commission's hands for three days at a time. They would fare badly but for the sleepless devotion of Dr. Ware, who night after night works among them, often not leaving them till two or three o'clock in the morning."

Another writes:—

"He had a *passion* for usefulness. How many days and nights have I not seen him, staggering with fatigue, dropping asleep for minutes here and there, where they could be snatched, but working on, cheerful, quiet, observant and careful for others, never for one instant thinking of himself. I have never known modesty like his. I have often thought it was his one defect."

In the last of July he reached home, and wrote as follows:—

"Various and sundry reasons urged me to leave the James River. I was n't well; I had been bothered with diarrhœa for the last three weeks of our stay in the Pamunkey, and was rapidly getting no better at Harrison's Landing: I 'm not entirely over it yet. Then the government has taken in hand the business of transporting the sick; and that part of the occupation of the Commission was, so to speak, gone. And I concluded that I should be of more service in some other capacity than inspector. My lack of surgical practice stands in my way of becoming a regimental surgeon. . . . . However, I shall wait till I feel really well before I start away again. . . . . The Class Supper was quite a successful affair, so far as numbers and brilliancy went, but somehow it went against my grain. I could n't help thinking of the misery and horrors I had left down on the James, and it seemed as if we were a collection of Neros, fiddling while Rome burned."

"September 11.

"I wrote thus far last month, when the demon of laziness made a prey and a spoil of me; and then I was sent by Surgeon-General Dale to the assistance of the Second Massachusetts Regiment, which had come to great grief at Culpeper. . . . . Everything there was quiet and comfortable, till suddenly there came an order for the regiment to strike its camp and move to the rear. I was summoned into the town, where I was worked by the Medical Director for twenty-four hours in getting off the sick and wounded on the cars to Washington; all in the town were thus sent, except about eighty, who could not have borne the journey. We personally finally evacuated about four, P. M., 19th August, and made our way in the rear of the army, which had been advancing towards Washington from the Rapidan in a steady stream for about twenty-four hours. Instead of being sent to Washington on one of the trains, as I had expected, I was told to rejoin the regiment, which I found on the northern side of the Rappahannock. . . . . Having thus rejoined the regiment, when there was every prospect of immediate shindy, I could not of course leave them, and have been with them through all the marching of the two weeks' campaign, which has ended in Pope's sudden and by no means dignified exit from Virginia. We did all sorts of things except fight; we marched and counter-marched, we guarded baggage, we went hungry and thirsty, we spread our blankets on the ground with no other cover than the canopy of heaven; in short, the experience was more severe than any the regiment have ever been through, and was harder than that of the Army of the Potomac when it removed from before Richmond to Harrison's Landing. . . . . They want me to go as Surgeon of the Forty-fourth Massachusetts, and I am undecided whether I shall do right in accepting or not; if I don't go with them, I shall probably go back to the Sanitary, which also requested my services."

We now come to his last and fatal service of government, as Surgeon of the Forty-fourth. No man ever left his home from a sterner and purer sense of duty than Dr. Ware. Military life was repugnant to all his tastes; and something more than a foreboding seems to have filled his heart on the eve of his sailing for the South. He was not the man to talk about it, and perhaps not more than one or two knew that it existed. But the belief that he never should return did not hold him back one instant. The duty nearest his hand he took up, and performed cheerfully and steadily to the end.

"NEWBERN, NORTH CAROLINA, November 21, 1862.

". . . . The men, except one company, are already in barracks, and I have been at work since we returned to what we now call home in trying to get them ventilated. The men begin to appreciate the savage discipline which cut all sorts of holes in their houses at Readville, and was instrumental in causing them to lie on bare boards; for here no straw is to be obtained even for the hospital, and it has proved an advantage that the men learned to do without it while at home. The blankets of the regiment, which were stored when we started from Washington, North Carolina, have not yet appeared.

"We left Washington, North Carolina, on Sunday, and had a very hot and toilsome march, through a wholly uninteresting country, till just before sunset, when there was a sort of prophetic halt, and word came back from the Colonel that two of our companies had been detached, and he thought that some of the stretcher-men had better be sent with them. . . . . Pretty soon cannon opened on one side, and continued for a time; then there was a pause, and we heard the rattle of musketry, and the hum of the balls as they whizzed over us. Only two or three volleys were fired, at least so far as I know; for I was soon engaged in attending to the wounded, two or three of whom were brought back on the stretchers. Our donkey-cart (containing medicines, instruments, and stretchers) was drawn up on one side of the road, the lanterns were lighted, — for it had become very dark, — and we established our first hospitals among some pines. By word from Dr. Green, this was changed to a small cottage of two rooms, nearer the creek. Such bedding as the mansion afforded was laid out in one of the rooms, and the men we brought were laid upon it. The house was small, and the only light outside came from an occasional lantern. One of our men lay dead at one end of the porch. He had been instantly killed by a shot through the head. . . . . Pretty soon word came that our column had passed the creek, but that the enemy had some earthworks farther up the road. Then De Peyster was brought in, very badly wounded in the arm. After a consultation, it was decided that the arm must be removed. . . . . In the mean time the movement of troops continued. . . . . The chaplain came in, asking for some assistance to get the body of one of our men up from the creek, who was shot through the head, and that of a man belonging to the artillery. Some of Captain Lombard's men had dug a grave for their comrade in among some pines, opposite the house we occupied; and these two other men were buried there. It was a strange scene. The moon shone bright and peacefully; but there was a scent of powder in the air, and my hands were bloody from assisting in amputating De Peyster's arm. While we heard the rumble of wheels, and the voices of men from the troops passing in the road, the three bodies were laid in one grave; the chaplain said a short prayer, and then we turned from the first grave of the Forty-fourth Regiment. Just then came the rattle of musketry from some little distance up the road."

"NEWBERN, NORTH CAROLINA, December 22.

". . . . We reached Kinston on the return march [from Goldsborough bridge] Friday morning, and I left the column to go down to the boat with some of our men severely wounded, who I was anxious should be spared the journey over the road to Newbern in those infernal ambulances. I got down to the boat, which was a miserable concern, with little or no cover, and was in season to put the two worst cases in the cabin on a mattress which I took from a house near the landing. I had them comfortably settled, and left provisions, and a nurse to look after them, when the Medical Director appeared, and told me to go on board, and report to the surgeon in charge, and go down with the wounded. I sent my horse back to the regiment, and went on board. Soon men began to arrive in numbers, and the boat, which ought to have held fifty, was laden with upwards of one hundred and fifty. They were packed everywhere. We opened bundles of hay, which had been brought as a protection from the rifles of the Secesh, and spread it over the decks. A large scow, which had been laden with provisions, was cleared as far as possible, and the men laid in that. While we were at work, one of my men died, as I had expected, and I said nothing, because I thought we might get his body down to Newbern, where it could be obtained by his friends; but it became evident I was doing wrong in thus using space required for the living, and I finally had a grave dug under a splendid pine at the landing. The body was removed just in season to give room for one of our drummer-boys, who had a severe shell-wound of the thigh, and who, I feared, had gone down in the ambulance over the road. I was glad to have a bed for him."

"NEWBERN, January 10, 1863.

". . . . We are having our first experience of severe sickness here in the shape of congestive fever, of which three men have died within ten days, several others being very sick. One man died in twelve hours from the time of attack. It is more savage than anything I ever saw, except some cases of scarlet fever in children."

"January 27.

". . . . The W. H. Fry has arrived, and now the barracks will be filled with all sorts of mouldy trash in the shape of pies and decayed puddings, semi-putrescent sausages, and unwholesome litter generally; and on Sunday inspection I shall rouse the wrath of the men by having a considerable amount of it emptied into the swill-barrels. Then there are various packages for the hospital, and the donors will have to be written to and told separately that they have selected just the article we needed."

"WASHINGTON, NORTH CAROLINA, March 16.

"On the 14th, at evening, orders come to start at once from Newbern for this place. We were off in about two hours, and are now nearly arrived. It was feared that Pettigru, who made the attack on the fort on Saturday, being foiled in that, may join with Pryor, who is up here somewhere, and attack this place, which has about twelve hundred men in it; we being five hundred (only eight companies)."

"April 2.

"The face of events has greatly changed since last I wrote, and at present we are regularly besieged; cut off from the world outside, and surrounded more or less by batteries, which boom away at intervals, to keep us constantly aware of their existence. . . . . Everything remained quiet till Monday, though warnings had come in various shapes that an attack was to be made. General Foster arrived in the morning, much to our surprise and delight. Two companies were sent across the river on a reconnoissance. We soon heard a few cannon-shots, then musketry, and pretty soon a man ran to the river, and told the gunboat whose guns are trained up the road to open fire. One party soon appeared, and came back over the bridge, bringing with them Captain Richardson, wounded, who withdrew his men, as it was evident that the force there was pretty large. . . . . We had an anxious and uncomfortable night; for there was no knowing at what hour an attack might be made. Just about daylight we heard musketry down the river; and I learned that a company had gone down on a flat-boat, and fire was opened on them from the bank. . . . . The next day firing began again down below. I got up and went to the point below the town, where, from the way in which the shot whistled, it was evident that something lively was in progress. The Commodore Hull was close down at Rodman's Point, fighting the battery there. . . . . Several houses in town were struck; the enemy fired Whitworth shot, and banged away as if they had plenty of ammunition. . . . . We are obliged to pull down houses for fuel; but whether we shall get as far as short rations or not, I don't know."

"April 3.

"The enemy opened two new batteries this morning; one nearly opposite the market, and the other somewhere up the road from the bridge. Their shot were mainly thrown at the boats. The gun opposite the market was soon dismounted; and when the enemy came up with horses to take it off, a well-directed shell from the Louisiana pitched horses and men into the air. . . . . The other battery and the gunboat fired for some time; but after about three hours, the battery stopped. . . . . About two, a fleet of six gunboats made their welcome appearance below, and engaged the battery for about three quarters of an hour. . . . . Now the great question is, whether or not the boats will attempt to pass up or not to-night; a boat was to go down to-day to buoy out the channel, so that perhaps they will come up. Shot and shell are as plenty as blackberries; and I pity the unfortunate townspeople, whose houses now and then get holes knocked in them, and whose women are frightened. Many of them have taken refuge in their cellars. One family had a Whitworth shot through their house yesterday; and this morning, just as they were getting up from the table, another shot landed plump upon it. The streets are empty and still, the shops all shut, and it seems like a perpetual Sunday."

These were the last lines he wrote before his illness. He and Dr. Fisher, in whom he found a most congenial coadjutor, appreciated very highly the extraordinary opportunities for surgical and anatomical study that the condition of things afforded, and spent night after night, till the small hours, studying special topics,—the great mortality among the blacks affording large material. It was this, and his practice in the black camps, quite as much as his regimental duties, that pulled him down. On the 5th he was seized with typhoid pneumonia, the disease which, as he had told a medical friend, he feared he should not escape in the spring. "For several days he wandered in his mind, talking about the experiments he and Dr. Fisher had in hand, or imagining himself on the battle-field. The day that he died was the critical one. . . . . A violent cannonade from the Rebel batteries, nearer and more continuous than any that had preceded, excited him to wildness. It was with difficulty he could be kept to his pillow, and the slender thread that bound him to us was rudely broken." On the 10th he died "perfectly tranquil, with an inspired, happy look in his eyes." They buried him privately in the afternoon of the following day, at Washington, North Carolina ; General Foster and his staff, and the officers of the two regiments, attending. The body remained at that place till the siege was raised. It was then disinterred for removal to the North ; and as it passed through Newbern, funeral services were held there at the request of the regiment. The final interment took place at Mount Auburn on the 1st of May following.

His assistant, Dr. Fisher, wrote : —

"I cannot but think that the anxiety and fatigue of his assiduous and unremitting labors for the regiment, which he had previously borne so well, by a cumulative process predisposed him for the fatal attack. For the first three weeks at Washington, he was the senior medical officer at the post ; and after, the Rebel investment added to this responsibility the fatigue of frequent alarms and much professional labor. He performed several capital operations among the wounded negroes, all of whom I found on my arrival doing well, and bearing evidence of his kindness and foresight in their after treatment. . . . . His anxiety for the safety of the regiment occupied his last thoughts. I cannot conceive a nobler death, nor one I should more envy. It was entirely consonant with what I know of his life, which seemed guided at every moment by honor and duty. Courageous on the field of battle, he was equally so in the insidious dangers of the camp and hospital."

From the mass of testimonials to Dr. Ware's memory, the resolutions of his classmates, the votes of social and scientific organizations to which he belonged, and letters of personal friends, I select the following from a letter of Rev. Edward H. Hall, then Chaplain of the Forty-fourth: —

"You could hardly tell whether to admire most his remarkable skill or his wonderful fidelity. His professional skill was acknowledged on all sides in the department; but we, who saw him every day, were even more struck by the readiness and cheerfulness with which he answered every call. A surgeon's office, at best, to a conscientious man, is the most laborious in the regiment. Yet I never saw the time, during the hardest marches or at the most untimely hours, when Robert hesitated for a second to go to those who needed him, and give them all the time that was required. If you knew the prevailing standard of official duty in the army, you would understand how striking such single-minded fidelity must be.

"But the feeling of the men towards Robert is still more touching and even more honorable to him than that of the officers. . . . . He certainly never sought popularity; he exacted stoutly the respect that was due to his office, and was most unsparing in unmasking the shams by which a surgeon is sure to be beset. Yet in spite of all this, his real kindness, his tenderness and sympathy, impressed them so deeply, and revealed his true nature so plainly, that they could not help feeling more attracted to him than to any other officer. They feel his loss deeply and speak of it sadly. So true a man always finds himself appreciated by simply acting out the promptings of his nature."

"We who remain," says another friend, "and have been in the way of looking forward to his future, and imagining what he would some day become, find with some surprise that he was already all we had ever looked for. He had not to wait for added years to fill a place, and to perform work, which, being done, makes his life already one of the finished lives."

SIDNEY WILLARD.

Captain 35th Mass. Vols. (Infantry), August 13, 1862; Major, August 27, 1862; died December 14, 1862, of a wound received at Fredericksburg, December 13.

SIDNEY WILLARD, the eldest son of Joseph and Susanna Hickling (Lewis) Willard, was born February 3, 1831, at Lancaster, Massachusetts, where, nearly two hundred years before, Major Simon Willard, the earliest New England ancestor of the family, leading a hardy band of Puritans, had planted the little town upon the frontier. Sidney Willard was but an infant when his parents removed to Boston, and his boyhood and manhood were wholly passed in the city.

At an early age he showed a love for out-door activity, in marked contrast with a certain quiet and reserve of nature, and an aptitude (but imperfectly perceived by himself) for the sober pursuits of a scholar. To him, as to every lad whom the watchful care and gentle influences of home surround, a knowledge of himself and ready use of his own powers came but slowly. Shy and yet self-possessed, respectful to age and authority by nature and education, yet singularly fearless and independent, and with a frame of whose boyish awkwardness he was conscious, knowing not that it was the sign of great coming strength, he was slower to develop the natural points of his character than most of the companions of his early years. But through all this somewhat tardy growth there worked a steady and ripening purpose of self-development, which seemed almost to have been born in him, and which gradually brought order out of the chaos of his boyish nature.

He became a pupil of the Latin School of Boston at the age of ten. The good influences upon his nature here were twofold. The admirable drill which gives this school a fair rivalry in exact scholarship with Eton or Harrow, taught him by degrees to know his own powers of study; and though he did not attain eminence in mere rank, yet he learned those habits of thoroughness which it is the pride of the school to convey. It was good seed in good ground. But his ambition went beyond this; and while he gradually gained in scholarship, his conscientious and singularly systematic habits made the wide general reading in which he indulged an education in itself. His moral and physical development, moreover, were steadily pursued. Naturally quick-tempered, he held this impulse under the curb, until, even in extreme provocation, no sign of anger could be detected, save a passing flush, which testified to the struggle and the victory; and he conformed to the precept which he wrote in a Greek book daily used by him in school, "He that ruleth himself is better than he that taketh a city." Out-door sports attracted his companions, and gave them health rather than strength; but Willard, even at this early age, trained his powers at the gymnasium with the method and success of a Greek athlete.

While the school thus did its office in promoting the growth of his character, and his admirable home influences produced their due effect, he was, after all, to an unusual extent, his own teacher. Inborn and growing as he grew, his controlling moral sense made the duty of the moment the law of his action, and his guiding motive of conduct to find in what shape that duty lay. His judgment was too sound ever to allow his sense of duty to become morbid; and he held with admirable moderation and singularly clear perception the balance even between the opposite requirements of his nature. His purity of mind was remarkable. He was incapable of vicious companionship, not more from a conscious repugnance to depraved natures than from the unconscious rebuke which such natures felt in his presence. He was not phlegmatic or hard. The sensitive, shy, proud nature which underlay his calm exterior, but seldom suspected to exist except by those who knew him well, became very noticeable by its contrast with the outer man, and gave an added charm from that contrast. He was indeed

"To the soul that loved him sweet as summer."

Yet he was very slow to form friendships or impart confidences, and with all his self-reliance came a certain self-distrust, from his inability to give and receive that ready show of outside friendliness which is the every-day coin of social intercourse; and this produced a certain coldness of manner, as of one not open to every comer. He rarely asked for sympathy or aid in the accomplishment of a task, even though intruding doubts of his powers made the effort of achievement almost heroic. Still less did he seek applause for his performance. In all his self-culture, his labor of preparation was quiet and unnoticed, and the effort was never suspected until it became achievement. His culture and accomplishments were as sure and reliable as if hewn out of rock. He acquired considerable skill — for he had excellent taste — as a musician; and his nice touch as a draughtsman still has enduring shape in many a graceful figure or vigorous sketch in the portfolios or on the walls of his friends.

In 1848, at the age of seventeen, he entered Harvard College. He brought to the training of the college a vigorous physical frame, exact and methodical habits of study, and a keen sense of duty; but with these a certain solitariness of nature that held him much aloof from his Class, and tastes that the college course did not satisfy. He was no negligent loiterer; he was neither unable to acquire, nor unaware of the golden time for progress which he was enjoying. Life meant duty to him, and duty and its performance were the law of his existence; but he must needs make his progress mainly in his own way. Perhaps it is not too much to say, that, at the time of his graduation, he was the equal in general culture of any one in his Class, and had laid the foundations of his knowledge deep and broad.

Of that subtle discipline which the democracy of a college enforces on its members, he felt much. A perfect Nazarite in the law of the body, hardly knowing vice even in thought, he was far removed in ordinary companionship from the idle or the luxurious; yet his character won the respect and confidence even of those with whom he could not readily associate;

and those who did not appreciate his finer qualities could yet perceive his solid steadiness of purpose, or admire the regularity of his physical life, and the perfection of his athletic strength. The ordinary opportunities in college life for vigorous exercise are many, and Willard made the most of them. He became a tough and expert rower; he was the best walker, leaper, and vaulter of his Class, or perhaps of the college during his day; and in fencing and boxing, his coolness and perfect self-control, his untiring muscular strength, his supple frame, and great length of limb, made him a most formidable antagonist.

These were qualities sure of appreciation in college; but this always a little annoyed him. He could not but feel the unthinking injustice done to higher qualities by the exclusive applause bestowed upon humbler ones; and it was not his aim, in the education of his body, to be praised as a gymnast. In his last year at Harvard the boating contests between Harvard and Yale began, and in the first — on Lake Winnipiseogee — he was selected to pull the heaviest oar. The victory gave a great stimulus to boating at Cambridge, and to that hardy culture which formed a school for the war, and sent forth many of those who had contended manfully together for the prize of endurance and strength, to fight and die side by side on the battle-field.

He graduated in 1852, in the same class with Paul Revere and Foster Haven, the former a companion at the Latin School, the latter an old acquaintance before college days, and a friend almost as it were by inheritance. Endeared by many ties, and often familiarly associated, Willard and Haven met their end on the same bloody field of battle, and almost at the same moment.

After graduation, Willard entered the Law School at Cambridge, coming to the study of the law in pursuance of long-settled plans. He was eminently fitted for this career. His judgment was cool, and he inspired all who dealt with him with confidence. He was able to meet every emergency that might arise, — not by immediate preparation, but from acquirements gained long before; for every study in which he had engaged had been undertaken, not from passing fancy, or to gratify a pride of knowledge, but to develop fully each faculty in harmony with, and aid of, every other. He had great patience in acquiring information, always seeking, in conversation, rather to receive than to impart, and to possess himself of all that any source offered to him. Hence his completeness of information made his knowledge always equal to the moment, and left him master of himself and of the occasion.

He remained at the Law School for eight months, and then entered the office of the Hon. Edmund Cushing, in Charlestown, New Hampshire. His life here was uneventful in enterprise or adventure; but in the undeviating pursuit of self-culture, and the busy toil of an active mind preparing for its work, it was crowded with effort. His letters to his family, in his absence from home, were graphic, with characteristic sketches with pen and pencil, — for he drew as readily as he wrote, — and a quiet sense of humor caught, without fail, the grotesque side of country life. In his stay of more than a year, he left upon the people whom he met an enduring impression of his strength and purity of character, which found warm and affectionate expression when his death brought sharply to remembrance the qualities they had prized.

Willard left Charlestown in 1854, and, returning to Boston, entered the law office of the Hon. Charles G. Loring. He studied here until his admission to the bar in 1856, when, feeling the necessity of a wider experience of men before committing himself to any locality for life, he went to St. Paul, Minnesota, with a view to establish himself in business there, if it seemed advisable. But the West did not attract him. He had not the ready gift of adaptation to new and uncongenial men and manners, and was slow to forego his fixed habits of thought and work for immediate success. He therefore wisely gave up all thought of seeking his fortune elsewhere than in New England, and came back to practise in Boston. Success surely awaited him here, and success in his own way, and in a community peculiarly congenial to his temper and training;

but it came slowly, and not without many doubts and misgivings on his part.

At last came the reward of toil. One by one clients appeared and friends were made; and professional labor, carefully and successfully performed, gradually gave him a recognized position at the bar. He was not a fluent speaker, but his words were always well chosen and appropriate, and his reasoning compact and cogent. The hearers unconsciously accompanied the speaker's clear statement; and, disarmed by its apparent simplicity, adopted it as their own, mentally adding to it, and convinced by what they seemed to have suggested to themselves.

But he did not allow professional duties or studies, however attractive, to withdraw him from physical exercise. He never permitted any acquirement to gather rust from disuse, and steadily kept up his athletic skill. He had carefully constructed under his personal supervision, and according to a model of his own, a wherry, fitted perfectly for secure voyaging on the open sea as well as for speed on smoother water. In this he set out in August, 1860, to row from Boston to Mount Desert Island, there to meet a party of friends. It was the first ocean voyage in one of these slender skiffs which had then been attempted, and required no little hardihood to undertake. His own graphic account of it, written, by request, for the Atlantic Monthly Magazine, is the best evidence at once of his skill with the oar and with the pen. The voyage proceeded very successfully until the rocky headlands of Cape Ann were passed, when the steady easterly wind drove in the fog and storm shorewards, obscuring everything, and night fell upon the adventurous voyager, who was at sea in his frail boat, in a locality beyond exact conjecture. Carefully calculating the possibility of drifting on the treacherous shore before morning, and concluding against it, he very coolly drew about him his oil-skin outer shelter, and slept lulled by the impatient plash of the waves against his little craft. Morning broke and showed him close under the rocky islets of The Shoals, and but half-way to his intended goal; and as the easterly storm showed no signs of abating, he abandoned further progress, and rowed home. Many shorter trips in this beloved boat were from time to time successfully carried out, and he had projected a long excursion for that summer which saw him depart from his home forever for the sterner scenes of war.

In 1861, the alarum of war found Willard well established in business, engaged to be married, and surrounded by friends whose number was constantly increasing. He had found his position in life, which it was not probable any change would unfix. His home satisfied his tastes, but imposed upon him active duties and a life of energetic effort.

At an early period of his life he had been interested in military affairs. In his boyhood the battles and sieges of Froissart engrossed his attention with far more than the ordinary boy's interest in scenes of enterprise and exciting adventure. Later, he followed up this study, as he did all his studies, to a thorough and exact acquaintance with various details of military science. To his expertness in the use of the sword he had added great skill as a shot. Overcoming an early strong dislike to mathematics, he had in maturer years, with iron perseverance, made himself thoroughly versed in the higher branches, and trained to exact calculation of distances as a draughtsman. Study soon made him well informed in the theory, as experiment gave him great skill in the actual practice, of projectiles. He had joined the organization of the Boston Cadets in 1858, believing in the great value of some militia system, faulty as he felt the existing one to be. He had projected long before this time the scheme of a company where vigorous and rigid drill, and a uniform sufficient to promote discipline, but admitting the freest use of the limbs and the most active exercise, should be combined with constant practice in the use of arms, and the routine of the camp should be learned by actual trial; but he had not found time to put his plan in operation before the critical hour came.

Immediately after the passage of the ordinance of secession by South Carolina in December, 1860, and before the first note of war had sounded, he began drilling a club formed chiefly of younger members of the bar, and continued with them for several months. With the first call for volunteers arose in his mind a most painful conflict. His military tastes and competency seemed to summon him to put in practice, in a cause dearer to him than life, the physical capabilities and theoretic skill in which he had perfected himself so thoroughly. Far more than this, his strong anti-slavery convictions prompted him to enlist in a war begun by the South in defence of slavery, but which put in our hands the power forever to destroy that baneful seed of evil. But with Willard the conviction of duty was always the result of cool deliberation, never of mere enthusiastic sentiment. He was now past the age when want of fixed position in life, mere youth and absence of responsibilities, make war a source of fascinating attraction, like hunting or adventure, only far more potent than these from its realities, its perils, and its glory. Nor did this first call for volunteers awaken any general sense of the magnitude of the impending contest, of whose favorable issue no one then doubted; and to one who appreciated as Willard did the efficiency of thorough organization, it seemed an easy task for the government to use its vast powers, and create an army able to sweep unresisted from the Potomac to the Gulf of Mexico. He knew his own fitness for the administration of military affairs, — perhaps no more accomplished soldier ever entered the army from civil life, — and every man whom he trained for the war increased his sensitiveness as to his self-suggested duty to take up arms in person. But he felt equally well the reality of duties at home, that he himself was even better fitted for peace than for war, and that in enlisting he must abandon much which he had long educated himself to be able to perform, — an ability which the growing recognition of the community had fully indorsed. He could not, therefore, close his ears to the voice of duty which bade him stay. But he gave his time lavishly to complete the general preparation of the community for whatever might come. Several hundred men in different organizations received his instruction in drilling, and he was unsurpassed as a drill-master; and many also who came to him singly were taught the military knowledge requisite for the positions they sought or had obtained.

Thus passed the year 1861. The dawning spring of 1862 brought new triumphs to our cause, and it appeared that the beginning of the end was nigh. All that spring, the progress of our arms seemed certain; but it did not diminish Willard's activity in his labor of drilling, nor did it lessen his regret in bearing no share in a task to which he found himself so well suited.

Then came the long summer days, bringing first doubt, darkening our long-cherished hopes, then despair, as all the great enterprise on which we had built dwindled to shameful defeat. Sidney Willard's decision was made, and with the same quietness with which he had suppressed all suggestion of desire to take part in the war, when that desire could not be followed by performance, he now announced his purpose, and immediately set about its execution. In three days after his application for a commission, he had raised the requisite number of men, and was appointed Captain in the Thirty-fifth Regiment, then in process of formation, on the 13th of August. On the 21st, the day before his departure for the war, he was married to Miss Sarah R. Fiske, daughter of Augustus H. Fiske, Esq., an eminent lawyer, at the latter's country residence in Weston.

On the 22d of August the regiment left for the war. There was no more noticeable man in its ranks than Captain Willard, marching with stately figure through the eager, crowded streets, to enter upon a mode of life that had little in it to attract him, his face sobered by the duty which separated him from all he loved, but set with a resolution that never looked back; an untried commander, with men even more untried, hastening to the field when the country's peril was greatest.

He received his commission as Major of the regiment September 2d, while encamped at Arlington Heights. From this point his own letters tell the story. He thus writes: —

"Near Washington, August 25, 1862.

"We camped in the open field all night. . . . . It is just like camping out in the middle of Brighton road when it is hottest and dustiest. I am well and jolly, except when I think of you all; and then the thought that I am trying to do my duty is consolation ample."

A few days later, under date of

"ARLINGTON HEIGHTS, August 28.

"Our men are just getting a notion of loading and firing. We have had rumors of the defeat of Pope, Sigel, &c., but nothing authentic. We can tell literally nothing here about the movements of the armies. Regiments come and go: their tents whiten the hill-side one day, and are gone the next. . . . . I hope that the Thirty-fifth will soon prove itself an excellent regiment."

In a letter to his sister, dated Arlington Heights, September 2d, he writes: —

"I shall ever love you as I have done, not in very demonstrative mode, perchance, but yet better than you think; and, while I live you know that you have somebody to depend on, to help and assist you. I hope, God willing, after this accursed Rebellion is put down, to return to old Massachusetts; and, a better and more energetic man, to make my way, so that I can aid in other ways than mere words. . . . . I have had the appointment of Major to the regiment. . . . . Pray, who, if any one, made representations to the Governor? If you know, please let me know. The promotion is rapid enough to satisfy the most exacting; and I shall try to fill the post thoroughly, and hope to."

Shortly afterwards, his regiment, with others, moved, in support of McClellan, towards Harper's Ferry as far as Brookville, when the Major was sent back to Washington on detached service, while his regiment was hurried into action, and took part in two severe battles when it had been raised barely five weeks and could not execute a single battalion manœuvre. On the first report of the likelihood of an encounter, he hastened to the front.

"WASHINGTON, September 18.

"I sent the detachment off Tuesday evening to rejoin the regiment, and must follow just as soon as I can. . . . . My regiment is perhaps seventy miles distant, — a long way in this *bebothered* State. The great thing which I regret in staying here in Washington on regimental business is, that my regiment may have been engaged in the fighting, and I not there, — a source of great trouble and regret to me. I shall go to them just as soon as I can."

He was met half-way by tidings of loss.

"BOONSBOROUGH, MARYLAND, Monday night, September 22.

". . . . I have to-day, while on my way from Frederick hither (sixteen miles), learned the fate of my regiment. We have lost, in two battles, nearly every commissioned officer, killed or wounded. The Colonel's left arm is gone at the shoulder, and the Lieutenant-Colonel is shot through the neck. Captain Bartlett is killed, and Captains Andrews and Lathrop are the only ones fit for duty in the regiment. I believe my men (I shall, till the Lieutenant-Colonel recovers, be in command of the regiment) are not more than ten miles distant; and I hope to reach them to-morrow.

"But you can tell how sad a thing this loss of officers and men (fifty-two killed, two hundred and five wounded) is; one quarter part of the regiment gone, taking out the sick, and necessary attendants. The thousand that marched up State Street, little more than four weeks since, now number hardly more than six hundred; and I almost dread seeing the diminished ranks."

He found himself just in time to assume the command.

"September 28.

"I am working with all my might on the regiment; and hope, in the course of the week, to get things agoing systematically. You can hardly conceive what up-hill work it is. There are but three captains in the regiment, and everything has to be organized. Morning reports, accounts of the sick and wounded; bothers innumerable about forage, commissary stores, subsistence, &c.; servants' attendance, regiment's wash-sinks, guards, funds, sutlers, discipline, drill, details for different duties, postage, losses in battle, and everything else conceivable. . . . . I did not think, when I left Boston and walked over to Lynnfield, that I should be in command of the remainder of the regiment in less than five weeks."

He was a strict disciplinarian, and gave the regiment a character it never lost. Naturally he enforced those particulars wherein he never failed himself. He writes, October 2d: —

"I have intense satisfaction in my position as commander for two reasons, — it enables me to enforce cleanliness, and prohibit swearing; which last I have checked to a considerable extent, to a degree which I never thought I should be able to."

He had never been a horseman, and this requirement of his new position was not at all agreeable. The horse he had purchased at Washington, before rejoining his regiment, was a fertile source for his half-serious, half-joking abuse.

"I wish," he says, "Uncle Sam would allow his majors to walk. The horse has passed the largest part of his valuable existence, since I became his unwilling owner, tied to a stake back of my tent, where I can distinctly hear every sneeze and cough, every motion of the quadruped. . . . . Nature never intended me for a horseman. I hate the beasts."

On the 9th of October, the regiment was moved to Pleasant Valley. On October 24th he writes: —

"For five weeks our men 'have fought, marched, dug, slept, ate, and camped out in the same clothes,' having but one suit." He then describes his great relief since the return of the Lieutenant-Colonel. He is willing to bear his own share, and more; "but it is hard to do three men's work, and get blown up for six, and to tread with the greatest caution, lest you come upon the military gouty toes of some precise old tactician, who roars in wrath at the slightest error in your course of proceeding. . . . . If I live to come back, it won't be for want of all sorts of training that I am not evenly developed, body and mind."

The army under General Burnside now moved southward in a line parallel to that pursued by the retiring army of Lee down the Shenandoah Valley.

On the 10th of November, near Jefferson he writes: —

"We have been marching incessantly since November 1st; had snow-storms; slept tentless about the whole time; had salt pork, raw; hard bread, and coffee sugarless, where we could get it, and thankful for it. O, it 's jolly campaigning in the winter; turning into a potato-field, in a driving snow-storm, to sleep. . . . . I think that we shall see a fight soon. The Rebels are close to us; and, while I write, the cannonading is incessant. I shall try to do my duty like a man, when the time comes."

On November 13th he was again (and the third time) put in

command of the regiment, much against his will; "the Lieutenant-Colonel, together with the Adjutant, having been taken prisoner while eating dinner across the river at White Sulphur Springs." After leaving camp on August 22d, he was in command about half the time; and he remained in command till he fell.

November 15th, Saturday, he was, for the first time, under fire; and says, November 16th: —

"I don't think I either showed or felt the least fear. The Rebels shelled us; and I had to march my regiment back under the fire of our battery over our heads, and of the Rebels from a hill opposite directly into us. A fragment of shell (so the men said, I thought it was dirt) struck the road, and bounced right over my cap, about two feet above my head; and shot and shell struck and whizzed about in all directions. The Lieutenant of the battery was killed, and an artilleryman had his arm torn to pieces, besides wounded men in other regiments than ours. We had one man badly wounded in the leg. I was reading your letter during the shelling, while my regiment was lying under cover, and when that bit of dirt or iron, I don't know which, bounced over my head. . . . . Home-matters are what I care for in home-letters; they are indescribably pleasant."

At length the army reached the front of Fredericksburg. On November 24th he writes: —

"We have marched south along the base of the Blue Ridge; then turned to the left, and marched here. We have been on the move for three weeks and two days quite steadily. We left Pleasant Valley; marched along the Potomac to Berlin; crossed, camped; then south through Lovettsville, &c., to Amesville, Jefferson, White Sulphur Springs, Fayetteville, Warrenton Junction; then straight here, — to wit, a mile from Falmouth, and near Fredericksburg. We have zigzagged over the country (particularly in our marches near the Blue Ridge) beyond all description; but now we are promised a two days' halt.

". . . . I wish you, dear ——, the pleasantest Thanksgiving you have ever had. I shall, God willing, remember you all most lovingly on that day; and I know you will not forget me. . . . . Burnside means to push for Richmond; in what way, I am sure I can't tell or conjecture: but we shall have some very hard fighting, I expect, within the next four weeks."

"CAMP OFF FREDERICKSBURG, November 28.

"We had a quiet Thanksgiving, without any extra dinner except an old goose and four very diminutively small chickens. I thought of home as I sat at the head of the mess-table (made, by the way, of cracker-boxes, and clothless), and wished that I could fill my place, for a short time at least, at home. But I have the consolation of knowing that, as I came *because I ought, that same 'ought' will keep me up fairly to the mark.*"

He writes to his father under date of December 2d, same camp: —

"I hardly think I can make you a fitting return for all your affectionate and Christian care of me, or all your patient and loving waiting during my slow struggle to work my way in life and gain a place among men. I hope, if my life is spared to return, and with increased knowledge of men, with an experience in rough, practical life of the greatest value to me, and habit of prompt decision, with the attrition of a life as open and public as my former one was secluded and fastidious, to make my fortunes more rapidly than earlier years foreboded."

"OPPOSITE THE LOWER SUBURBS OF FREDERICKSBURG, December 7.

"Night; quiet till one, A. M.; then I stump over the crusty snow in company with the officer of the day, whose duties also cover the night, unless the Rebels cross and stir up my camp. . . . . It is freezing in true New England style, and the weather is as genuine an importation from Massachusetts as is our regiment. . . . . My tramp to-night is to visit my pickets and guards. I have guards stationed at each of the guns, which peer watchfully through the embrasures of the half-moon in which they are placed. A cold time the sentinels have of it, and the greatest vigilance is needful; for a rat-tail file and a tap with a hammer would render useless in a moment a superb piece of ordnance. I don't object to the trip a bit, though it will take me nearly two hours; but for my shoes, which are in sympathy with the shoes of more than two thirds of the regiment."

His last letter, a very hurried and brief one in pencil, written on Friday, December 12th, was affectionate as usual. Amongst other things, he says: —

"We shelled and half burnt Fredericksburg yesterday. My regiment and brigade was ordered to be in readiness, and was marched and countermarched, as I will tell at some future time, when I have pen, ink, and opportunity. . . . . The whole of Franklin's grand corps is passing in the rear of our camp, crossing the river on the left, — artillery, infantry, and cavalry, by the thousands. My men are pretty much used up by want of shoes, and consequent colds. I had, by actual count, yesterday, a force of only three hundred and fifty-three men and seventeen officers with which to go into battle. I hope to write in a few days more fully."

This was either the last letter he wrote, or else the next to the last. It bears the same date with the last letter to his wife. On Saturday, before he fell, his thought must have been upon the impending battle.

The sad duty remains of speaking of the last hours of the Christian soldier; of the man (as truly and tersely described by a friend) "who never raised his arm or his voice in anger or pride; the self-controlled, highly moral, and exemplary man, whom even the follies of youth never seemed to touch."

On Sunday evening, December 14th, a telegram was received from Falmouth, Virginia, without date, saying that "Major Willard died this afternoon, at half past one"; and soon after, in the same evening, a second telegram was received, also without date, that "Major Willard lies in Fredericksburg, wounded, shot through the body," and containing a request to his wife "to come immediately." Nothing further was heard until Monday evening, December 15th. Meanwhile the family had been in an agony of suspense, buoyed up with hope against hope. In the confusion of the day, there might have been a mistake in the first telegram received; the son, husband, and brother might be, and perhaps was, living. Several plausible theories were suggested; but Monday evening (when several members of the family, who had left Boston in the morning, were on their way to Washington) brought with it a confirmation of the intelligence.

The regiment left the city of Fredericksburg at half past eleven o'clock on Saturday morning, and was advancing against the Rebels; the Major being in front of Color-company B, when he led the regiment to the charge. Captain Lathrop was in the rear, acting as Major. Efforts were made to persuade the Major to order the charge and take his station in the rear, but without success. Waving his sword, and leading on the charge, he was seen to fall; and the cry went forth, "The Major is down!" A lad in the regiment, by the name of Krill, seems to have been the first to go to his assistance, having seen him at the moment he was shot; but he was not strong enough to lift him. Private Estes then started to his support, and was helping him through the lines to the rear, when Captain Lathrop came up on the other side, and the two attempted to take him from the field. They had proceeded but a rod or two, when he said, "You must let me lie down: I can't go any farther."

They laid him down, put him in a blanket, and endeavored to place him out of the range of the fire; but the Rebels enfilading the road, they removed him just below the bank. Here there was a shelter from the front fire; and by a little bend in the road, from the cross-fire also. Captain Lathrop lay down by his side. Here, with the consciousness of death upon him, after sending the tenderest message to the loved ones at home, and in submission saying, "But God's will be done," he added, "Tell them I tried to do my duty to my country and to the regiment"; and also expressed his desire to be buried at Mount Auburn.

Within a half-hour or an hour two soldiers appeared with a stretcher, and bore him upon it to the hospital of a Connecticut regiment. He was in pain, but never moaned nor exclaimed.

Towards night the surgeon gave him whiskey and morphine; but he doubted whether to take it, saying that he had never drunk whiskey. However, he was induced to consent, and soon became easier. He was thirsty, and wanted water, which was brought; but from self-control, says the Captain, he would not drink, but only rinsed his mouth.

About nine o'clock on Sunday morning, Captain Lathrop was obliged to be absent to attend to the regiment, now reduced to less than one third of its original number. He left the Major calm, quiet, and apparently comfortable, and did not apprehend any early change in his condition. Estes and another private remained in attendance, and the former was absent some fifteen minutes, between one and two o'clock, to take some food. Major Willard had been induced to go to sleep; and he was asleep, lying on his left side, when Estes returned. A motion of the right shoulder was noticed; presently his lips were seen to move; his eyes were open, and cast upward. Estes felt his pulse, and found none; he felt his hands, they were cold. He called the surgeon, who confirmed his fears that all was over. Sidney Willard had entered into his rest.

As he lay in the repose of death in the home of his youth, his expression was natural and life-like, as of one who had returned wearied with conflict, and had sunk into a calm but thoughtful and semi-conscious slumber.

On the 17th of December the mortal remains of Major Willard were brought home, with loving care, to the city he had left but four short months before, in the pride of manly beauty and the fulness of his strength. On Saturday, December 20th, in accordance with his almost last uttered wish, he was laid to rest in Mount Auburn, where a simple cross of granite marks the spot.

1853.

WILDER DWIGHT.

Major 2d Mass. Vols. (Infantry), May 24, 1861; Lieutenant-Colonel, June 13, 1862; died September 19, 1862, of wounds received at Antietam, September 17.

WILDER DWIGHT, second son of William and Elizabeth Amelia (White) Dwight, was born in Springfield, Massachusetts, on the 23d of April, 1833. His paternal ancestor was John Dwight of Oxfordshire, England, who settled in Dedham, Massachusetts, in 1636. His mother was descended from William White of Norfolk County, England, who settled in Ipswich, Massachusetts, in 1635. His family has belonged to New England for more than two centuries, and during that whole period has been identified with its history, its industry, its enterprises, and its institutions.

In childhood he gave promise of all that he afterwards became, — manly, courageous, self-possessed, acute, original, frank, affectionate, generous, reliable; — he was, in boyhood, not less than in manhood, one in whom to "place an absolute trust." Yet, in less vital points, he was no pattern boy. He had a quick and irritable temper, which was a source of trouble to himself and to his friends in early life, and which, early and late in life, it was his effort to control. Full of fun, and ever ready with comical suggestions, his drollery was irresistible. Many a reproof did he ward off by it in childhood; many a dark hour did he brighten by it in after years. When not six years old, it was said of him: "He has a sincere love of right, and aversion to wrong, though he does not desire to hear preaching on the subject." Before he was seven, he was pronounced uncommonly clear-headed and strong in intellect. At the age of seven and a half he began to study industriously; and from that time he was a faithful student.

At the age of thirteen he left home for the first time, to fit for college at Phillips Exeter Academy. "There," says the preceptor, "from the beginning to the end of his course, he was a pattern pupil."

The following extract from his diary kept at this time shows the character of the boy: —

"*December* 31, 1846. — To-day is the last day of the old year; and, in commencing the new, I wish to lay out some rules in relation to myself, which I will *try* to observe. In the first place, I will exercise every morning after breakfast, until school time; and, after school, at night, until supper time. Secondly, I will study after dinner until school time; and I will go to my room after supper and busy myself in studying or in reading a *useful* book until bedtime. Thirdly, while in school, I will try to busy myself about my lessons; and, at any rate, behave in an orderly manner. And I will observe strictly these rules, except when it is right for me not to do so, that is, at such times as I may think it right, though I may err in that opinion. And may I also try to correct my defects of temper. May I watch every word that comes from my mouth; and may I let my yea be yea, and my nay be nay; and may I not merely write these things down and think no more of them, but may I always keep them in my mind, and remember them most of all when I am angry, as that is the time to control myself."

At the end of two years, he was fitted for college; but not wishing to enter so early, he passed six months at the Private Military School of L. J. D. Kinsley at West Point, in order to secure the advantage of the military drill; while, at the same time, he continued his classical studies, and received instruction in French and mathematics. In May, 1849, preparatory to entering college, he returned to Exeter for a review of his studies. In the following July, he writes in his diary: —

"On Monday, July 16th, I was examined for entrance to the Freshman class, and, after due trepidation and effort, on Tuesday, at about four, P. M., I received my 'admittatur,' overjoyed at finding it an unconditional one."

He took high rank as a scholar, and maintained it throughout his college course. The following extract from his diary shows by what means he accomplished this result.

"*March*, 1850. — . . . . I am somewhat of 'a dig,' I suppose;

and though the character is rather an ignominious one in college, it is in so good repute elsewhere and among wiser persons than Freshmen or even Sophomores, that I shall endeavor always to deserve the title. Natural geniuses, that is, lazy good scholars, are few and far between. I shall, therefore, estimate myself as a very common sort of a person; and as I desire to excel, I shall choose the way which seems to promise success."

Among the privileges which he enjoyed in college, that which he valued most highly was the instruction received, in lectures and recitations, on the Evidences of Natural and Revealed Religion, from the Rev. Dr. Walker. Not less did he value the pulpit ministrations of this distinguished preacher. His diary at this period, and while he was in the Law School, is filled with abstracts of the sermons to which it was his privilege to listen. The following extract from his journal indicates the influence which these teachings exerted upon his character: —

"*Sunday, January* 4, 1852. — Heard Dr. Walker preach from the text, Ecclesiastes viii. 11, 'Because sentence against an evil work is not executed speedily, therefore the heart of the sons of men is fully set on them to do evil.'"

After a long abstract of the sermon, he writes: —

". . . . This is the sermon on which I may well found the first resolutions and actions of the opening year. All my life has been a series of violations of law, though I have ever had a theoretic veneration of it. Memory runs back over a sad list, and time passes on swift wings. To-morrow is to-day ere it is spoken, and yesterday was lost in irresolution and weakness. Now, now, now! God, God, God! Eternity, eternity, eternity! Action in the one, mercy and justice in the second! Pain or pleasure, joy or grief, in the last! Let me remember, then, that 'though a sinner do evil an hundred times, and his days be prolonged, yet surely I know that it shall be well with them that fear God, which fear before him'; that no man knoweth the ways of God, they are past finding out. Then I will trust in the goodness which is inscrutable but inexhaustible. I will apply my heart to know, to search, and to seek out wisdom, and to know the wickedness of folly. And may these thoughts glow in my mind, may they rouse my energies till I seek to embody them in my actions, and make their spirit felt in my life; and may not these aspirations be transient and shadowy."

On leaving college he entered the Law School at Cambridge, with ardent enthusiasm for the profession. There too he took a prominent position, receiving the first prize in 1855. On leaving the Law School, he passed fourteen months in foreign travel. He sometimes spoke with regret of this interruption to his studies, because it placed him further from the attainment of the main purpose of his life. He resumed his studies immediately on his return, and completed them in the offices of Hon. Caleb Cushing, the Attorney-General of the United States, Hon. E. R. Hoar, and Horace Gray, Jr., Esq., of Boston.

He was admitted to the bar in 1856, and commenced practice in 1857. Of what he was as a lawyer Judge Abbott says:—

"I can say, in reference to my appreciation of him, what I know will be appreciated as the highest evidence, in my judgment, of his qualifications as a lawyer, that I have come up before the tribunal which I respect above human tribunals, depending entirely upon briefs furnished by my associate, this young man. I have trusted, beginning with the first cause he ever had occasion to try after being admitted to the bar,—trusted, what I should rarely do, the entire preparation of causes to him, and sat down to the trial of them without any personal attention to them myself."

He soon became the partner of Horace Gray, Jr., Esq., in whose office he had formerly been a student. Judge Gray says of him:—

"I think I may say that I have never known any young man who combined, in such just and equal proportions, the theory to be learned from the books, with a readiness of practical application to the facts of cases as they came up."

Of his position and prospects at the time of the breaking out of the war, his friend, Francis E. Parker, Esq., speaks as follows:—

"He had everything which a man of high ambition most desires: he had youth and health, fortune and friends, a profession in which he delighted, the practical talents which smooth the way in it, and the confidence in himself which made labor light. But when the trouble of our country came, he thought that all advantages and successes which did not aid her were to be trampled under foot. He gave up to his country, without a moment's hesitation, all that he had gained and all that he was."

The first gun fired on Sumter was his summons to arms. When the awful tidings came, he closed his law books, never again to return to his beloved profession. While a school-boy at West Point, as the term drew near its close, he had playfully written home: "I shall, 'to the right about face,' and 'forward, quick march,' when the term is over, and I shall never evince any desire hereafter to shoulder a musket or wear a sword." Even now, his taste was unchanged. Truly did Mr. Parker say of him: "He looked the dangers of his new profession in the face, not fascinated by its glitter nor drawn from weightier thoughts by the sound of martial music, but deliberately, for the defence of the law and the support of a cause which he solemnly considered to be just."

The Hon. Richard H. Dana, Jr., said of him, after his death: —

"He had that combination of qualities which led to success in whatever he undertook. . . . . His love was for that kind of intelligent labor which looks to specific results. . . . . He had an intuitive knowledge of himself, and instinctive knowledge of other men. He adapted his means to his ends. He knew what he was suited to do, and he had a power of will, a faculty of concentration, and patience, perseverance, and confidence, which insure success. . . . . When the war broke out, he determined to become a soldier. His friends knew he would make himself one. He determined to offer the first regiment of three years' men to the army, and he did so. He went to Washington to obtain advantages and opportunities most difficult to secure; but we felt that he would succeed, and he did succeed."

Every step he took towards the prosecution of his work illustrates the truth of Mr. Dana's words, — "He had determined to become a soldier." "Adapting his means to his ends," he began by associating himself with two gentlemen of West Point education and acknowledged military ability and experience. He was no less faithful as a student under them, in military tactics, than he had been, under other teachers, in more congenial pursuits. He determined to raise a regiment for the war; consulting daily with Messrs. Gordon and Andrews, formerly of the United States Army, the future Colonel and Lieutenant-Colonel of the regiment, he made it sure that no want of military experience on his part should prove a hindrance to the perfect accomplishment of his work. He suffered not a day to pass, after the news from Sumter, before opening a subscription paper, to guarantee the expenses which would be incurred in the enterprise. His cheerful presence met a warm welcome from all whom he approached, and he had but to present his claim to meet a cordial response. The money thus raised enabled him and his associates to prosecute their enterprise without delay. The practical difficulty in their way was, that there was no law, at that time, either of the United States or the Commonwealth, under which it could be carried into operation. It was necessary to obtain from the Secretary of War special authority for the enlistment and control of the proposed regiment. For this purpose, on the 25th of April, 1861, while the excitement which followed the Baltimore riot was at its height, and the usual communication with the seat of government was cut off, Mr. Dwight and Mr. Andrews left Boston, and went by the way of Annapolis to Washington. They reached there on the evening of the 27th, at which time he wrote to his father a brief account of this eventful journey through hostile country, saying that he was to have an interview with the Secretary of War that evening.

After submitting his plan to the Secretary in conversation, he addressed to him a written statement of the same. On the next day the following letter was received from the War Department: —

"WASHINGTON CITY, April 28, 1861.

"To Messrs. WILDER DWIGHT and GEORGE L. ANDREWS.

"The plan which you communicated for raising a regiment in Massachusetts for service during the war meets my approval.

Such a regiment shall be immediately enlisted in the service of the government, as one of those which are to be called for immediately. The regiment shall be ordered to Fort Independence or some other station in Boston Harbor, for purposes of training, equipment, and drill, and shall be kept there two months, unless an emergency compels their presence elsewhere.

"I am, gentlemen, very respectfully,

"SIMON CAMERON,

Secretary of War."

From this time Wilder Dwight seemed to have but one interest in life. To see the Massachusetts Second become, in organization and in discipline, a perfect regiment, and to do, in connection with it, all that such a power could do, towards suppressing the Rebellion, — this was the aim which bounded his horizon. He was appointed, by Colonel Gordon's recommendation, Major of the regiment, which position he held until June 13, 1862, when he was promoted by Governor Andrew as its Lieutenant-Colonel. During what remained to him of life, the history of the regiment is his history. "All I want," he once wrote, "is the success of the regiment itself, — nothing more or less; and there is room enough for distinction for any one who does his share in any regiment to make it a good one." To no service assigned him by his superior officers was he ever found unequal. And as at the very entrance upon the practice of the law he had the confidence of one who had spent his life in courts, so now, a beginner in military duty, he was relied upon by his superiors in command. The spirit which he carried into his new profession is best illustrated by extracts from his own letters. On the 15th of July, 1861, just one week from the day the regiment left Boston, while "in bivouac at Bunker Hill," he writes: —

"We have just received our orders for an advance upon Winchester; a very good place is assigned us. . . . . I hope for a big, worthy battle, one that means something, and decides something; and I hope to have strength, courage, and wisdom to do my duty in it. I never felt happier or more earnest than for the last few days, and I never realized more fully the best significance of life. I have always had a dream and theory about the virtues that were called out by war. I have nothing to say of the *supply* which I can furnish, but I am vividly impressed by the *demand.* The calling needs a whole man, and it exacts very much of him. Self gets thrown into the background. It straggles out of the column, and is picked up, if at all, very late, by the rear-guard."

This letter closes with the words, "If anything happens to me, remember I meant to do my duty."

A month later, after giving a schedule of a day in camp, he says: —

"One day treads closely on another, and variety is always at hand. Here I give you the prose of it, the treadmill without the song. But there is poetry in it, too. There is a sentiment which gives the impulse to this duty and hallows the effort. I have been to Washington, and I return with a sort of desperate, teeth-set determination to do all I can in the sphere of my duty. It seems to me that the country wants active, busy, self-forgetting endeavor."

After writing earnestly of the need of improvement in discipline and organization, throughout the army, he says: —

"But out of this nettle I pluck one flower, namely, that I can be of service; and it cheers me to hope, that, by active and constant endeavor, I may, perhaps, do my small mite towards organization and efficiency. I wish I could do more. To will is present with me."

Judge Gray, in the remarks from which we have already quoted, says of him: —

"To those who really knew him, his warmth of feeling was not less remarkable than his purity of principle and strength of character. None but his intimate friends knew how much of his time was taken up in acts of kindness and charity. From the time he became a soldier, he was devoted to the care of his men, both as a matter of military judgment and of right feeling; in this, as in other things, showing how his intellect and his heart worked together."

Did these limits permit, there could be furnished from his letters many illustrations of the interest he took in everything which could promote the comfort of the men. A few extracts must suffice. On August 3d, "in bivouac on Maryland

Heights," he writes: "I am giving personal attention to every detail of food and clothing, and expect to get the system so organized that it must always work right." Again, he says: —

"The event of yesterday was the arrival of the coffee-mills. Colonel Gordon reports that the men are in ecstasies with them. I am only a witness by his report, for I was ordered off on this duty just as the coffee-mills arrived. I know how badly they were needed, and I hear how admirably they work. Night before last accumulated the evidence from reports of Captains and Quartermaster about the want of tea, hard bread, salt pork, &c. I went up to General Banks's head-quarters and had a long talk with him, urging the remedies which have occurred to my mind. The General promises to change all this, and to accomplish the regular and constant issue of the ration to the soldier, in the form and at the moment required by law."

Again, he writes: —

"I wish you to buy and forward, by express, a large coffee-roaster, which will roast thirty or forty pounds of coffee at a time. It would be of immense advantage to us."

On its arrival he writes: —

"The coffee-roaster is lovely, and wins golden opinions. At last, also, we have tea; and, indeed, we have waked up our Commissary to something like activity."

At one time he writes: —

"We had a visit from General Banks yesterday. The General visited our kitchens, and tasted, with apparent approval, my doughnuts. I say *mine*, because I regard as perhaps the most successful endeavor of my military life the general introduction of doughnuts into the regiment. If you could have seen the helplessness in which the flour ration had left us, and the stupidity of the men in its use, you would hail as the dawn the busy frying of doughnuts which goes on here now. Two barrels are a small allowance for a company. They are good to carry in the haversack, and 'stick by a fellow on the march'; and when the men have not time to build an oven, as often they have not, the idea is invaluable. Pots of beans baked in holes in the ground, with a pan of brown bread on top, is also a recent achievement, worthy of Sunday morning at an old Exeter boarding-house. The band produced that agreeable *concord* yesterday, and contributed from their success to my breakfast. Our triumphs just now are chiefly culinary; but an achievement of that kind is not to be despised. 'A soldier's courage lies in his stomach,' says Frederick the Great; and I mean that the Commissary of our division, and the Commissary of our regiment, and the captains and the cooks, shall accept the doctrine, and apply its lessons, if I can make them."

Much as he enjoys the success of these achievements, he soon complains that no opportunity is offered them for "teaching the men to take care of themselves on the march and in active duty." At one time he writes: "It is idle to disguise the fact, that it is a heaviness to the natural and unregenerate heart to see no prospect of achievement, no opportunity of action." And again: "I must say, I think the tonic of victory would be of most happy and invigorating influence. Give me a little of the ecstasy of strife; bother this constant rehearsal." After rejoicing over the victories at Roanoke, in Tennessee, and in Missouri, he exclaims: —

"Exploit, achievement, victory! and I *not there!* I may feel and express foolishness, and I think I do; but I had rather lose my life to-morrow *in a victory* than save it for fifty years without one! When I speak of myself as not there, I mean the Massachusetts Second, in whose fortunes and hopes I merge my own. I ought, perhaps, to burn this letter; but I 'll send it, I believe. In an hour or two I shall be cheerful as ever, and continue the service of standing and waiting with good heart, I hope."

He did so; yet at times his eagerness for action would express itself. Once he exclaims: —

"I presume I love life, and home, and friends as much as any one; but I should sooner give them all up to-morrow, than to have our regiment go home empty. . . . . If you have any prayers to give, give them all to the supplication that the Second Regiment of Massachusetts Volunteers may find a field whereon to write a record of itself. Do not spend your days in weakly fearing or regretting this or that life, — lives whose whole sweetness and value depend upon their opportunities, not upon their length."

A day later we find him returning to the cheerful acquiescence in events as they are, which was the principle and habit of his life. He writes: "I buried hope yesterday, had a glorious wake, and resolved to sink every other wish in the absorbing one of the success of the war, without or with the Massachusetts Second, as it may happen." Thanksgiving day occurred during the month, when, owing to the absence of his Colonel and the illness of his Lieutenant-Colonel, he was in command of the regiment. He enjoyed making the arrangements requisite to secure a happy season for the men. After a graphic and spirited account of the festivities of the day, he says: "I hope on our next Thanksgiving we may be all together; but if not, at least we can hope to be as thankful as we are now." "Our next Thanksgiving" found us standing by his grave; but these words of his were not forgotten. Many lessons of thankfulness and hope had he given us in the darkest hours of our country's trial. After the disaster of Ball's Bluff, he was asked if his heart did not sink. "Sink?" he replies, "it swims like a duck when I think of the future that some of our eyes shall see; and will not they swim, too, with intense delight, when the sight dawns upon them? For myself, even now I cannot look upon the flag which we brought away from Boston without a glow and heart-bump, which I take to be only faint symptoms of the emotion that is to come."

In December, 1861, when everything looked darkest, he writes:—

> "I can confidently wish a merry Christmas to you, and look forward to a happy New Year. We are fighting a good fight; if only we can be true to ourselves and to our cause, we have a right to indulge the brightest hopes and rely on the best promises. God is with us. Hang up every sign of Christmas,—the freshest green. Commemorate the message and the Prince of Peace. Gather the Christmas family circle, and remember the absent; for family ties are never so close as in the days of separation and trial."

As late as May 9th, the service of the regiment was still to "stand and wait." Then he writes: "Of course, this is a severe trial to me,—the severest, I think of my life,—but, equally of course, I keep a cheerful spirit, and mean to do my best to the end."

Two weeks later, the regiment saw its first action in the field, on the occasion of General Banks's retreat in May, 1862. From General Gordon's official report of his portion of the retreating forces we quote the following: —

"Major Dwight, of the Second Massachusetts, while gallantly bringing up the rear of the regiment, was missed somewhere near or in the outskirts of the town. It is hoped that this promising and brave officer, so cool upon the field, so efficient everywhere, so much beloved in his regiment, and whose gallant services on the night of the 24th instant will never be forgotten by them, may have met with no worse fate than to be held a prisoner of war."

Chaplain Quint of the Second wrote at this time: —

"Our hopes that Massachusetts will be proud of the late history of the Second Regiment are clouded by the anxiety felt by every man as to the Major's fate. . . . . You will know how nobly he commanded the little band of skirmishers on Saturday night last; when his small force was formed against cavalry and infantry, with entire success; how his clear, cool, deliberate words of command inspired the men, so that no man faltered, while, in ten minutes, one company lost one fourth of its number."

Of this command of the skirmishers, Major Dwight's journal contains the following: —

"At General Jackson's head-quarters I saw the Lieutenant-Colonel of the Fifth or Second Virginia Regiment. He asked who it was at the Run near Bartonsville. I told him I had that honor. He said that he had three companies of his regiment deployed there; and he added, that he did not care to fight us again in the dark."

Many were the tributes to his bravery at this time. Of these, none so deeply affected him as one which he received from a wounded man of the regiment, whom he was endeavoring to cheer by telling him how well he and his comrades had done in the fight. The man looked at him, with tears in his eyes, and said, "Ah, Major, I 'm afraid we should n't have done so well if it had not been for you."

Chaplain Quint wrote: —

"I hope you have heard that he fell behind the column, coming out of Winchester, by helping and encouraging along a wounded soldier."

In his journal he tells the story as follows:—

"As we went down the hill, a few of our men would turn and fire up the hill, reloading as they went on. I delayed a little to applaud their spunk. We passed down into the edge of the town. As I came along, a young soldier of Company C was wounded in the leg. I gave him my arm, but finding that he was too much wounded to go on, I took him into a house and went on. The regiment was forming in line when I reached it. Before I had time to go to the left, where Colonel Andrews was, the regiment moved off again. I followed. Just as I was near the edge of the town, one of our soldiers called out to me, 'Major, I 'm shot.' I turned to him, took him along a few steps, and then took him into a house and told the people they must take care of him. I laid him down on a bed, and opened his shirt. I then turned to go out, but the butternut soldiery was all around the house, and I quietly sat down; 'Under which king,' &c. A soldier came in and took me prisoner. I made friendly acquaintance with him. He went with me to get a surgeon for my wounded soldier, and to pick up my overcoat, which I had thrown off in the heat. . . . . In the afternoon I went upon the field with some of the prisoners from our regiment, and buried our dead. I read a portion of Scripture over their grave."

Later in the week he writes:—

"I have furnished bread and some vegetables to our prisoners at the Court-House every morning. On Wednesday I attended the funeral of Sergeant Williams, Company F. General Jackson gave permission to eight of the Second Massachusetts prisoners to go out with me, as an escort for the burial of their companion."

Thus was he occupied during the week when he was reported "missing" and mourned as dead.

The Hon. Richard H. Dana, Jr., in illustrating his talent for success, says:—

"When he was made a prisoner at Winchester, and the Rebels were taking all their prisoners to Richmond, he determined not to go to Richmond, and he did not go, but was paroled. Some of us know the sagacity and perseverance by which he gained his point."

On his arrival within the Union lines, he writes, "I cannot describe our thankfulness and heart-swell"; and on reaching his regiment, "I cannot describe their welcome; God knows I should be proud to deserve it. I have never known greater happiness or thankfulness than to-night." Of his return to the regiment, another, an eyewitness, has given the following account: —

"It was in the dusk of Monday evening, June 2d, just after evening parade, while officers and men were in or about their tents, many talking of the Major and his probable fate, that a stir was perceived among the officers. The lamented Captain Cary was heard to exclaim, 'Good heavens, the Major!' as he rushed forwards; then the Major was seen running on foot towards the regiment. The officers ran to meet him. More than one lifted him in his arms. The men ran from their tents towards the limits of the camp. They could not be restrained: they broke camp and poured down upon the Major with the wildest enthusiasm."

At this time our informant left the scene to telegraph to his family the news of his safety.

"On my return to camp," he says, "the scene of noisy excitement was changed for one of profound calm. The regiment was drawn up around the Major, who was reading to them from a paper which he held in his hand. Not a face there but was wet with tears. He gave them the names of those of their comrades who were prisoners in Winchester. He told them who were wounded and the nature of their wounds. He told them of their dead, and of the burial upon which even the Rebels of Winchester had looked with respect. Then he said: 'And now, do you want to know what the Rebels think of the Massachusetts Second? "Who was it ambuscaded us near Bartonsville?" asked a cavalry officer of me. I replied, "That was the Massachusetts Second." An officer of Rebel infantry asked me, who it was that was at the Run near Bartonsville. "That was the Massachusetts Second," said I. "Whose," asked another officer, "was the battery so splendidly served, and the line of sharpshooters behind the stone wall, who picked off every officer of ours who showed himself?" "That was the Massachusetts Second," said I. On the whole, the Rebels came to the conclusion that they had been fighting the Massachusetts Second, and that they did not care to do it again in the dark.'"

The next day he wrote from Washington : —

"I am here to see about my exchange, &c. I am sorry you had so much anxiety about me, but thankful to be able to relieve it. My reception by the regiment is reward enough. I must get back to them."

His return was long delayed; and of all the trials of his life, this was the greatest. "This is not the life for me," he said repeatedly, during the weeks when he was flattered and caressed at home. A still severer trial awaited him. On Monday, A. M., August 11th, the day on which his exchange was effected, he heard of the battle of Cedar Mountain, in which his regiment had lost so heavily. Every true soldier can appreciate the bitterness of his feeling, at hearing that his regiment had been in action without him. The loss of his friends who had fallen cut him to the heart. He suffered as he had never suffered before. Some hours were given to visiting the friends of the wounded and the killed, and to making arrangements for serving them. Then he left us, never again to return. He had repeatedly said that he did not expect to come back. Those who met him that morning saw in his face what he felt. To more than one he said in parting, "It is the last time." Yet he was not depressed by the thought. "My life is God's care, not mine," he often said; "and I am perfectly willing to leave it in his hands." Now his only desire was to rejoin the regiment, and, as he said, "help those poor fellows."

On reaching their camp, near Culpeper, he writes : —

"A sharp, sudden half-hour's work, under desperate circumstances, has crippled us sadly, as you must have heard only too well. . . . . Our five brave, honorable, beloved dead are on their way to Massachusetts. She has no spot on her soil too sacred for them, no page in her history that their names will not brighten. The regiment looks well, but oh, so gloomy! . . . . As for myself, I look *forward*."

Soon after this, a prohibition was put upon the mails, and no letter reached us from him until September 3d, when he wrote from Washington : —

"After an experience of sixteen days, here I am, humiliated, exhausted, yet well and determined. Pope's retreat, without a line and without a base, is a military novelty. We lived on the country with a witness, — green corn and green apples. Twice cut off by the enemy, everything in discomfort and confusion, forced marches, wakeful bivouacs, retreat, retreat! O, it was pitiful!"

Some days later, from "Camp near Rockville," he writes: "We want *soldiers, soldiers*, and a *general in command*. Please notice the words, all of them. For the history of the past fifteen months is the sad record of that want." On September 10th he wrote from Washington: "I am here now, two days, getting arms for our recruits. All is reported quiet beyond Rockville, and I do not return till to-morrow." This is the last he wrote us until the morning of the fatal day. From others, we have an account of the intervening days. Chaplain Quint has recorded his return to the regiment on the evening of Friday, September 12th, when "his horse bore marks of his haste to find them," the movement of the regiment during the three following days, and his last march on the evening preceding the battle of Antietam, when, "at half past ten they halted." They were roused the next morning at five, A. M., by cannonade, and their corps was speedily moved towards the front. At this time he wrote, in pencil, to his mother as follows: —

"DEAR MOTHER, — It is a misty, moisty morning. We are engaging the enemy, and are drawn up in support of Hooker, who is banging away most briskly. I write in the saddle, to send you my love, and to say that I am very well so far."

Chaplain Quint writes: —

"Colonel Dwight was as active and efficient as ever. It was not for several hours that our regiment went into action. . . . . I am told of his bravery and daring, — that after our regiment had captured a Rebel flag he galloped up and down the lines with it, amid the cheers of the men, reckless of the fire of the enemy."

His last act before receiving the mortal wound was to walk along the line of the regiment, which was drawn up under the shelter of a fence, and direct the men to keep their heads down out of reach of the enemy's fire. Colonel Andrews writes : —

"Lieutenant-Colonel Dwight was mortally wounded within three feet of me. He had just come from the left of the regiment, and was about to speak, when the ball struck him. He fell, saying, 'They have done for me.' The regiment was soon ordered to fall back, and men were ordered to carry him ; but the pain was so intense that he refused to be moved."

Here, while alone upon the field between the two armies, he took from his pocket the note which he had written in the morning, and added to it the following : —

"DEAREST MOTHER, — I am wounded so as to be helpless. Good by, if so it must be ; I think I die in victory. God defend our country. I trust in God, and love you all, to the last. Dearest love to father and all my dear brothers. Our troops have left the part of the field where I lie.

"Mother, yours,

"WILDER."

On the opposite page, in larger and firmer characters, he added these words, "All is well with those that have faith." The paper is stained with his blood, and the scarcely legible lines show with what difficulty he accomplished this last effort of a life filled with acts of fidelity and love.

Private Rupert Saddler crept out to him at great risk. He writes : —

"I saw a man with his head lying on a rail. I felt that it was the Colonel, and I hurried to him. I gave him a drink of water, and asked him where he was wounded. He said his thigh-bone was shattered. I saw his arm was bleeding. I asked, was it serious ? He said, 'It 's a pretty little wound.' I saw two of our men coming, and I called them over. The Rebels saw them, and began firing. Colonel Dwight wanted us to go back to the regiment. Said he, 'Rupert, if you live, I want you to be a good boy.' I wanted to bind up his wounds, but he said 't was no use. He gave me a paper he had been trying to write on, and the pencil ; the paper was covered with his blood. He then gave us directions how to carry him, and we lifted him carefully and carried him into a cornfield."

Magee, one of the men who helped carry him, says: "When we first came to lift him up, he said, 'Now, boys, don't think that because I'm wounded I've any less spirit than I had before. I feel just the same.'"

General Gordon writes: —

"As Wilder was brought from the fatal spot, I rode to his side. As I reined up my horse, his eye met mine, and he almost exultingly saluted me. At this moment bullets whistled over our heads, shot and shell crashed through the trees. I said, 'I must have you removed from here.' He replied, 'Never mind me, — whip them.' I ordered six men to carry him to the rear."

Chaplain Quint writes: —

"I found him in the garden of a hospital, somewhat in the rear. He was lying on a stretcher, covered by a blanket, with his eyes closed, and quite pale from loss of blood. As I kneeled down beside him, he opened his eyes, and smiled as he took my hand. 'Is that you, Chaplain?' said he. Doubtless he saw my sorrow in my face, for he said, 'Don't feel bad,' and with a firm look, and natural smile, he said, 'It's all right, — all right.' I replied, 'I thank God you feel so cheerful'; when he added, 'Now, Chaplain, I know I'm done for, but I want you to understand I don't flinch a hair. I should like to live a few days, so as to see my father and my mother. They think a good deal of me, especially my mother, — *too much*,' (this was said smilingly,) — 'but apart from that, if God calls for me this minute, I'm ready to go.'"

Colonel Andrews soon came, and, bending over him, yielded to the grief which overwhelmed him. Dwight threw his arm around his friend's neck, and, drawing him down, said, "Kiss me, dear. Don't take it so hard, dear fellow; don't take it so hard. Think how much better it is that I should be lying here than you who have wife and children at home." He then talked freely. He said: "I want it distinctly understood that I have no personal regrets in dying. My only regret is that I cannot longer serve the cause." He gave him the history of the boy Saddler, who had been in his charge before the war, and for whom he wished Colonel Andrews's sympathy and care. He also told him that he wished a soldier's burial. Turning to Chaplain Quint, he said, "I don't like display, but I think this appropriate, do not you?" The Chaplain assented; and he added, "I have lived a soldier, I die a soldier, I wish to be buried as a soldier." To another member of the regiment, a son of his clergyman, the Rev. John S. Stone, he said that he wished Dr. Stone, as his minister, to receive his last message in case he did not live to reach home and talk with him. He said: "Tell him I am ready to die. I look back upon the past with many regrets for failings and for misused opportunities, but still with the self-respect of a man who has tried to do his best. As for the future, there is but one hope, no putting forth of one's own claims, but reliance on the merits of Another: you know what I mean."

He was placed in an ambulance for the night. The men lay around it. At daybreak his wounds were dressed. He examined them in a cool, naive manner. Looking at the hole through the forearm, he said: "Now that 's a very neat little wound, a *proper* wound; but the other, pointing to the thigh, won't do so well." It was now determined to carry him to Boonesborough, where a house had been found for him. Twelve men from the new recruits were detailed for the purpose. They were divided into six parties, who relieved each other by turns. During the journey of three miles and a half, he called out the reliefs himself. On their way, they met the drum and fife corps of the regiment. He stopped them and requested them, as a last favor, to play him the Star-spangled Banner once more. He thanked them, repeating the sentiment of the song in the wish that "The star spangled banner in triumph may wave o'er the land of the free and the home of the brave." One of the men happened to ask where the rest of the regiment was. Colonel Dwight called out: "Who asked for the Second Regiment? I 'll tell you where the Second was yesterday. In the foremost front of the battle, fighting like men; and we drove them, boys, drove them." Chaplain Quint writes of him on this journey: "If water was given him, or any service rendered, his old 'Thank you' was never omitted. Indeed, the night before, in the garden, he repeatedly sent his servant and others to relieve the wounded men around him, while in pain himself."

About one, P. M., (September 18), they reached Mr. Thomas's house, where a bed was prepared for him. By following his own suggestions, they were able to place him in bed without his suffering in the process. As they lifted him, he said, "Steady and true, — steady and true." As they turned to leave the room, he roused himself and said: "Wait a minute, boys; you 've taken good care of me; I thank you very much. God bless you." They then partook of a dinner he had provided for them.

"That afternoon," says Chaplain Quint, "he suffered very much. The next morning I had no thought but that he would live several days; but *he* felt that he should not see any of his family. He spoke of it and of the time required. It was not until nearly noon that a marked change took place. I was in the kitchen, giving directions for the preparation of beef tea, when his servant came to me, saying, 'The Colonel is wanting you quick, sir.' I went in, instantly saw a change, and took his lifted hand. After looking earnestly in my face, he said, 'Chaplain, I cannot distinguish your features; what more you have to say to me, say now.' (I had, of course, remembered his dying condition, and conversed accordingly.) I said, 'Colonel, do you trust in God?' He answered, with ready firmness and cheerfulness, 'I do.' 'And in the Lord Jesus Christ, your Saviour?' 'I do.' 'Then,' said I, 'there is no need of saying more.' I said a few words of prayer over him, with a blessing, after which his own lips moved in prayer and he added audibly, 'Amen.' Then I said, 'Now what shall I say to your mother?' He answered, with his whole face lighted up: 'My mother! Tell her, *I do love my mother*' (he emphasized every word); 'tell her I do trust in God, I do trust in the Lord Jesus. Nothing else.' No more did he say then. He was soon sinking. The *last* was a few minutes later, and about fifteen minutes before he died, when he said, 'O my dear mother!' About twenty-five minutes past twelve, he died; so peacefully, that we could hardly tell the time. He died, as he had lived, a brave, gallant, noble man, a hero, and a Christian; cheerful to the last, considerate, happy."

When he breathed his last, every face, among soldiers as well as officers, was wet with tears. Colonel Andrews had sent him word of our success in the battle. "It is a glorious time to die!" was his joyful exclamation.

"So died," writes Colonel Andrews, "one of the most faithful, brave, unselfish, and devoted officers of our army. He was, I think, the officer most beloved and respected throughout the regiment by officers and men.

"His conduct as an officer and as a man was noble. On the battle-field he appeared to me to retain his self-possession most completely, and to have his soul bent upon doing his best to uphold the honor of his country's flag. He showed no consciousness of danger, although there was nothing rash in his conduct. He was uniformly kind to every one. How we all feel here in the regiment, you can perhaps imagine. It is not the same regiment.

"His friends have every consolation possible: his memory is their pride."

Mr. Justice Hoar, in his address to the Suffolk bar upon the occasion of the death of Wilder Dwight, closes with the following words: —

"Tender and loving son, firm friend, true soldier, Christian hero, — we give thee up to thy fame! For thee life has been enough.

'Goodness and greatness are not means, but ends.'

For us there is left the precious legacy of his life. Brethren, it is well that we should pause, as we are entering upon our stated and accustomed duties, to draw inspiration from such an example. For who can think of that fair and honorable life, and of the death which that young soldier died, without a new sense of what is worthiest in human pursuits, a stronger devotion to duty, a warmer ardor of patriotism, a surer faith in immortality."

1854.

RICHARD CHAPMAN GOODWIN.

Captain 2d Mass. Vols. (Infantry), May 24, 1861; killed at Cedar Mountain, Va., August 9, 1862.

RICHARD CHAPMAN, the eldest child of Ozias and Lucy (Chapman) Goodwin, was born in Boston, October 11, 1833. After the necessary preparation he entered the Latin School, whence, at the end of four years, he entered Harvard College, graduating in the Class of 1854. On leaving college, he was in a mercantile house in Boston for more than a year, when he left this country for India. Here he passed a few months, and afterwards travelled through the Holy Land, made an extensive tour through Europe, and returned to his home after an absence of nearly two years.

On the breaking out of the Rebellion, prompted wholly by the movings of his own mind, he decided to unite himself with the Second Massachusetts Regiment, under Colonel George H. Gordon, with several of his personal friends. The Second Regiment left Boston in July, 1861, and its career is well known. The connection of Captain Goodwin with it is described so truthfully by Dr. Bartol, his friend as well as pastor, in a sermon preached in the West Church the Sunday after the funeral, that an extract from it is given, rather than the words of his friends.

"The Captain of Company K, in that Second Regiment of Massachusetts Volunteers which will fill a shining page in our history, at the motion of his own will, obedient to the pleading within him of his country's call, gathered his men, and from his situation of independence and comfort went into all the labor and hazard of the war, with the simple purpose of doing his part — as he has with unspotted honor — to solve our awful problem. The Colonel of the regiment testifies to what we learn on all hands, of the respect he won from his brother officers, and the devoted regard of those whom he led. His personal behavior rose uniformly to the highest tide-mark of noble sentiment and actual fidelity. In the unavoidable and admirably planned retreat of General Banks, before overwhelming numbers, near the Shenandoah, though so exhausted that had he fallen by the way he could not have risen again, he was faithfully in his place. All the hardships and privations of a soldier's life he bore with signal fortitude; while absence weakened no familiar tie, but only drew him more strongly in all affectionate bonds; the tenderness of his heart overflowing on occasion of a Christmas visit he was able to make to his home.

"When unusual perils had been around him, and he came out safe, he gratefully recognized the providence of God in his preservation. In one of his letters, he speaks of the brief and solemn communion he had with a comrade in the terrific perils and threats of the Rebel pursuit. Upon him, as upon so many, from the sober air of our great struggle a breath of sanctity seemed to pass. His health, not wholly strong when he left, had, by the great heat of the weather, become so much impaired that he asked for a furlough. This was not granted, on the ground that his was a case rather for resignation, — an idea he would not for a moment entertain, preferring, as he said, 'rather to die there than think of it, as he must be a great deal sicker even to ask for it.' So, as the engagement came on, which, when he intimated his need of repose, he had not anticipated, he resolved, persisting against all remonstrance, weak as he was, to take his share in it and his chance with the rest. But so extreme was his bodily weakness, that it was necessary for his servant to assist him to the field which proved fatal to them both. He toiled on and up the hill in the neighborhood, fast as possible, to the point of hazard and decision, where, so far as can be known, he was instantly killed, and, without suffering, passed away."

CHARLES RUSSELL LOWELL.

Captain 6th U. S. Cavalry, May 14, 1861; Colonel 2d Mass. Cavalry, April 15, 1863; Brigadier-General of Volunteers, October 19, 1864; died at Middletown, Va., October 20, 1864, of wounds received at Cedar Creek, October 19.

CHARLES RUSSELL LOWELL, Jr., was born at Boston, January 2, 1835. He was the eldest son of Charles Russell and Anna Cabot (Jackson) Lowell, and was the grandson of the Rev. Charles Lowell, D. D., and of Patrick Tracy Jackson. From infancy he showed a rich variety and freedom of nature. He entered with eager relish into the games of boyhood, and surpassed all his companions in invention and daring; in study he displayed an equal alertness of faculty. "Those who knew him in his first ten years can recall a sturdy little figure, active but not restless, a pair of bright, soft, dark eyes, and rosy cheeks curling all over with enjoyment. He finds everything good; but the eyes are often withdrawn from the charms of life and nature, and rest with a far-away upward look on something unseen beyond."

When only thirteen, he had finished the studies of the Boston Latin School; and the next two years were spent at the English High School.

In 1850 he entered college. He was one of the youngest members of his Class; but he immediately took the first rank in scholarship, and maintained it to the end. During the four years of college life, he gradually unfolded to the vision of his friends the great and brilliant attributes — the deep, quick, and independent intellect, the vigor of will, the self-reliance, the power over men, the originality and force of moral faculty, the jubilance of spirit, itself in him amounting to a moral excellence, the earnest tenseness and life of the whole nature — which continued to distinguish him in all the phases of his career.

"When he entered college," says a classmate and near friend, "he was unusually boyish in appearance, with a ruddy countenance overflowing with health and animal spirits, and a manner somewhat brusque. He did not win popularity at once; but as his powers and character developed, and toned down the rather boisterous life and manner of the body, he came to be proudly acknowledged, without a dissenting voice, as the foremost man of the Class."

His scholarship, which was equally distinguished in all branches of study, seemed in no sense as forced product, but the natural resultant of the action of a remarkable variety of powers. His thought was at once fluent, accurate, and transcendental. He learned with such rapidity that it was commonly believed he did not study. His memory, both lively and tenacious, needed to take only one impression of an object, and then it was daguerreotyped. But deeper than his gift of memory lay an extraordinary power of concentration, and a genius for detecting in principles the key to facts. "He made as much mental effort in a minute as many people in an hour; perhaps as much of his life went to each effort."

His intellectual sympathies were without limit. He read extensively and systematically; and he talked, out of a full understanding and a fresh, free spirit, on literature, science, and philosophy. He threw himself with glad and vigorous activity into the current of college life. He was a constant participant in its sports and exercises, and a leader in its public affairs; and with all his overflowing energy of motion, he had within a deep repose of nature, delighting in nothing more than in *contemplation*, — with him no aimless and luxurious revery, but a powerful action of the reason and the spirit, to which, in later as in earlier days, his mind constantly returned, as to its congenial employment and for the renewal and purifying of its strength.

His chief interest was in philosophy. Yet he cared little for ordinary disputation; because he regarded the principles of morality and truth as lying deeper than the questions which such disputation is wont to touch. In his higher speculation he moved with a straightforward audacity which scorned conventionality of feeling or opinion. Sometimes, indeed, he would indulge himself in working off his superfluous activity by the defence of extravagant theses; but his sincere views were as profound as they were original. The full counsel of his mind he never opened probably to any one; but it can be said with certainty that his philosophy united elements which to a dry reasoner seem hardly capable of combination. Plato was his constant study and his most valued authority; he also often referred to Lucretius, whose writings he read carefully in college; and he was familiar with the thought of the English and American transcendentalists. He loved mysticism. His religious conceptions were far removed from those of the received theology; but they were the conceptions of one who, with personal insight, beholds the world of divine reality. The root of his life was in his spiritual consciousness; and in that consciousness he waited for the coming of a higher future with great-souled faith, which he was able to communicate to others by the contact of his mind.

> "Thrice in a life he flashed upon our sense.
> Time disappeared; its griefs and cares were dumb;
> Its joys mere bubbles on our sea of bliss."

His face, in its rapt moments, might have been taken for the type of intensity combined with depth of thought, — nay, rather of an ideal power exercising itself intensely and deeply.

Even at this period Lowell evinced his natural power of command by the influence he exercised throughout a large circle of friends. He drew their wills to him, as a loadstone attracts iron. He was highly valued as an adviser; for he had great soundness of judgment and unusual power of understanding matters from another's point of view. He was reserved in the expression of feeling, so that casual acquaintances sometimes supposed him wanting in it; and few of his friends fully knew (what his letters, if they could be completely published, would reveal) that it was an exquisite and manly tenderness that gave his character its tone.

The spirit in which Lowell approached his entrance into practical life was expressed in his Valedictory Oration on "The Reverence due from Old Men to Young"; a subject peculiarly illustrative of his earnestness and originality, and not likely to appear unmeaning to the reader of this book.

"When a young man is burning to do the world great service, it is a falsehood to tell him that faithful labor is the best gift the world expects from him. If young men bring mankind nothing but their strength and their spirit, the world may well spare them; but they do bring it something better, — they bring it a gift which they alone can bestow; they bring it their fresher and purer ideals. . . . . It is not true that good comes often of evil; good comes only of good, and of evil comes only evil. . . . . Each generation stands in a new position, it gets new views of past faults and failures, with new glimpses of future possibilities. . . . . This is not all, however. While mankind is constantly rising to higher ideals, there is always danger that the man may sink to lower ones. Labor has been blessed as the Lethe of the past and the present; it may well be cursed as the Lethe of the highest future. . . . . Therefore the old men, the men of the last generation, *can* not teach us of the present what *should* be, for that we know as well as they, or better; they *should* not teach us what *can* be, for the world always advances by impossibilities achieved; and if life has taught them what can *not* be, such knowledge in the world's march is only *impedimenta;* in short, though men are never too old to learn, they are often too young to be taught.

"If beauty, then, which has been called the promise of function, causes youth to be loved, the function, which already brings the world its life and its growth, should cause it to be reverenced. A nation that feels this reverence has its golden age before it; it cannot be wholly undone by unprincipled governments or evil institutions. Where this is not felt, though the course may seem rapid and prosperous, a swift undercurrent is sweeping it surely to destruction. . . . . Mere action is no proof of progress; we make it our boast *how much* we do, and thus grow blind to *what* we do. Action here is the Minotaur which claims and devours our youths. Athens bewailed the seven who yearly left her shore; with us scarce seven remain, and we urge the victims to their fate.

"Apollonius of Tyana tells us in his Travels that he saw 'a youth, one of the blackest of the Indians, who had between his eyebrows a shining moon. Another youth named Memnon, the pupil of Herodes the Sophist, had this moon when he was young; but as he approached to man's estate, its light grew fainter and fainter, and finally vanished.' The world should see with reverence on each youth's brow, as a shining moon, his fresh ideal. It should remember that he is already in the hands of a sophist more dangerous than Herodes, for that sophist is himself. It should watch, lest from too early and exclusive action, the moon on his brow, growing fainter and fainter, should finally vanish, and, sadder than all, should leave in vanishing no sense of loss."

This oration is not to be read as a mere literary exercise; it is a sincere expression of the spirit in which Lowell made his choice of a profession. "Nor was this spirit a youthful enthusiasm; it shaped his life up to its last fatal hour." On taking his degree, he was strongly urged to devote himself to letters or science. But in spite of his force of intellect and of his Platonism in philosophy, his energetic nature demanded, as a necessity, continual contact with men and things. Yet he was resolved to maintain in full vigor his life of thought and feeling; and, above all, both at this time and always, he heartily abhorred the apathy of an educated man who, after having gained a great power to benefit the world, makes his own enjoyment the purpose of his life.

He had already meditated plans for raising the condition and character of the working classes; and he now chose his course of life with reference to this object, being also determined in the same direction by the partial consciousness of that capacity of ruling men, which was perhaps, on the whole, the most remarkable of his gifts. He desired to select a profession which would afford him, not only a field of practical usefulness, but the opportunity of becoming a master in some department of science. His mind at last settled on the working of metals as the occupation best suited to his views; and he entered the iron-mill of the Ames Company at Chicopee, Massachusetts, in the spring of 1855. Here he remained half a year as a common workman. He interested himself in his fellow-workmen, and often met with them to talk on branches of science connected with their work.

"CHICOPEE, April 1, 1855.

"If you could in any way get hold of a tenth part of the letters which I enjoy myself writing to you after I get to bed, you would, though an '*infinite* shoeblack,' be satisfied with our correspondence; but through the post-office,—why, the very thought of sitting down and patching together a letter is insufferable to me. 'Silence is golden and speech is silver'; but pens, ink, and paper are mere rags, galls, and goosequills. . . . . Laughing and talking on paper may do very well for ——, but by Plato! for me it is too absurd."

"June 24.

"Your last letter was really delightful, by far the balmiest I have got since I came here. I only wish you could find time to write oftener. I *am* glad to hear that the pantaloons are finished, not however because, as you hint, I think it 'necessary to exclude work' to make life 'gracious as roses.' There is, of course, a poetry in pantaloons, as well as in woman and youth; but the point I insist on is that you are not yet able to enjoy it. For our family, work is absolutely necessary; but by Plato! our lives need not for that cease to be poems. Roses work; there is a good deal of force-pumping to be gone through before a rose can get itself fairly opened; and force-pumping, your ears will tell you this evening, is rather hard on the muscles. But you mistake, I think, in not choosing more judiciously the sort of work. Roses never think of forcing their red juice into their roots. If they did, their poetry would soon vanish; but beets don't find this work at all prosaic. On a fine day like this I can fully understand that the joy of swelling and swelling should make it highly poetic. You feel the necessity of a choice in great things,—such as settling my profession,—but in small things, I am afraid, you are inclined to overlook it. Sweep rooms,—that you can do poetically; but don't make any more pantaloons at present. Even George Herbert's Elixir can make that but poor prose for you. The pleasure of sewing at an open window I fully enter into. The happiest afternoon I ever knew (and I use the word *happiest* in its highest sense) was passed at an open window, the first of the season, filing away on cast iron. I am thinking that you did not understand my meaning, when I endeavored to convince you that the need of work is a disease; I mean that the 'divine men' have no such need. However, I will not go into that discussion again. The 'Heroes' of the world have certainly needed work, and had it, and done it well; and it is *Heroes* that *we* must try to be."

Then, after a long passage about his plans: "Don't think that I am growing uneasy, for I never was better situated, and don't be afraid that I shall grow unsettled; —

'To give room for wandering is it
That the world was made so wide.'

By the way, I have been reading 'Walt and Vult' yet again, and with renewed delight. Jean Paul enjoyed the poetry of common life better than any one that has ever written. He made the world he lived in. So did Sir T. Browne; and it is for this, among many other things, that I am so fond of him."

"August 19.

"Of this you may be sure, that, if ever I am worth knowing, you will know me as well as if I had been close under your wing. Homer says, 'The gods know one another, even though they dwell far apart.' It is equally true of men, i. e. men as *are* men."

Early in the autumn of 1855 Lowell accepted a situation of great trust and great promise in the rolling-mill of the Trenton Iron Company, New Jersey, and felt that he had now really entered on his permanent work. But at this very moment came upon him the great trial of his life. From the beginning of his establisment at Trenton, we cannot but mark in his letters, exceedingly infrequent during his whole stay there, the growing shadow of disease.

In November a friend went over from New York to see him, and found him in his room, bleeding at the lungs and seriously changed. It was necessary that he should withdraw himself immediately from the injurious atmosphere of the iron-mill, and he returned to Cambridge, — an invalid and without occupation. His disease continued through the winter obstinate and alarming; and his physician directed him to give up all work and try the effect of travel and more favoring skies.

A great fabric of noble ambitions fell before this word. In the year of discussion and change through which he had passed, his views of life had gradually cleared, and, at the same time, the beauty of his character had been revealing itself with new distinctness to his nearer friends. The first contact with affairs, so far from extinguishing his higher aspirations, had strengthened his faith in the possibility of his ideal life. He viewed the actual order of things with a generous discontent, of which Mr. Emerson said, "I hope he will never get rid of it"; — a discontent commonly censured by acting men, but in Lowell the mark of a great spirit, because it was founded on high and thoroughly considered principles, and also accompanied with a resolve to labor with sober patience for the remedy of abuses. His experiment at Chicopee had increased his confidence in his plans for elevating the condition of the workmen. He had given much thought to the leading questions connected with his occupation; and he looked forward both to the introduction of improvements in the practical organization of a mill, and to the development of higher scientific principles in metallic work as affording him a field for important original activity. In short, his profession had now fully opened to his mind as a *career*.

But it was not in Lowell's nature to remain conquered by disappointment, still less to give any outward indication of depression of feeling. In his letters he speaks of himself constantly as "the fool of fortune," a favorite of "the lady with the wheel."

"I do not entirely understand what you mean by 'preternatural fears,'" he writes from Gibraltar in May, 1856. "I have been fussy and fidgetty, and have perhaps been unnecessarily careful about exposure; but as to fear about myself, why, as Emerson somewhere says, 'I sail with God the seas.' My only fear now is that which drove the tyrant of Samos to throw his ring into the sea. I am frightened and oppressed by the terrible good fortune which has always attended me, by the kindnesses which I have done nothing to earn and which I can never repay. . . . . For Heaven's sake, don't feel anxious about my enjoying myself. I am in an agony of enjoyment all the time now."

In February, 1856, Lowell left home. First making a short visit at Havana, he then passed through the cotton States of the Union to New Orleans, and, on the 8th of April, sailed from that city in a ship bound for the Mediterranean, landing at Gibraltar near the end of May. He spent a little more than two years abroad. He journeyed much on horseback for the sake of his health, and acquired an equestrian skill which in

Algiers excited the admiration of the Arabs. At Algiers, too, he took lessons in the use of a sword, and watched the movements of the French troops as he had already studied the Austrian military system in Italy. He was thus, in several ways, unconsciously preparing himself for his army life. He also became thoroughly proficient in the principal European languages, and applied himself, with his usual intellectual activity, to the study of the great monuments of art and history, drinking in, with a thirsty mind, the culture of the Old World.

During the whole two years, he was battling with his cruel disease. Yet at no time of his life, it would seem, was Lowell more captivating. Everywhere he made new friends, who were apt to think, such was the modesty of his demeanor, that they had achieved an original discovery in becoming aware of his splendid qualities.

When Lowell returned from abroad, in June, 1858, he was still too unwell to think of resuming his former trying occupation, or of living in the climate of the Atlantic coast; and he took the office of local treasurer on the Burlington (Iowa) and Missouri River Railroad. This place did not offer the kind of work he most enjoyed, and he entered on it with great self-distrust; but his success was so decided that, in the opinion of a competent authority, "he might, before he left, have been at the head of any railroad in the West that needed a manager." He remained at Burlington two years, in which time his health became gradually established, and he began to feel once more a happy confidence that he had a share in the life of this world. But though he had subdued his disease, he never ceased to be conscious of his weakness, as one feels the aching of an old wound.

In the autumn of 1860 Lowell was requested to take charge of the Mt. Savage Iron Works, an important establishment at Cumberland, Maryland. He had come to regard himself as settled at Burlington, and had grown really attached to his mode of life. But he did not hesitate to accept this opportunity of returning to his former plans. In November we find him at Mt. Savage, in a position of great responsibility, at the head of a small city of workmen; and once again his chosen work seemed to lie before him. But going now into a Border State at the moment of the great election of 1860, and remaining there during the following five months, Lowell could not fail to find himself brought into more positive relations than ever before to political affairs, and his long-cherished plans of professional activity thrown into abeyance by the urgent anxieties and excitements of that disturbed winter. He had, for years, been a decided enemy to slavery and to the system by which it was supported. He had, at times, been strongly excited by public events. It is said that the argument of his Commencement Oration "derives the passion of a personal feeling from his indignation at the then recent surrender of Anthony Burns." But his opinions, though radical, were not generally violent, and, even in some of his last letters, it is evident that his mind dwelt above the range of the ordinary thought of any political party.

In December he visited New Orleans on business connected with the mill, and he wrote to his mother on his return: —

"MT. SAVAGE, December 28, 1860.

"I suppose you fancied me burned, or at least-barrelled; but after all, I suppose I ran less risk than friend —— exposed himself to in panic-stricken Boston. Perhaps I did not merit martyrdom so richly, however, and certainly I should not have enjoyed it so keenly. I must say I have no sympathy with those John-Brownists, nor do I believe they will make much out of the 'Free-Speech' cry. It was a piece of rowdyism to break up their meeting, but was at the same time a proof the more how free speech is in Massachusetts. Fancy a parcel of Union-savers breaking up a fanatical Southern-rights meeting in New Orleans, and you have an exact parallel. But in New Orleans a Union-lover dare not speak under his breath. Beyond 'co-operation' no man's courage hath yet ventured. This to be sure means 'time'; and 'time' means 'submission'; but even co-operation finds few and feeble advocates, though I believe the *vote* of New Orleans city will show a large majority for Union. I was present at that great historical act, the unfurling of the 'Pelican Flag,' when news was received of South Carolina's secession. It was an instructive spectacle. I wonder whether the signers of our Declaration of Independence looked as silly as those fellows."

On the 20th of April, 1861, hearing of the attack made the preceding day in Baltimore on the Sixth Massachusetts Regiment, Lowell instantly abandoned his position and set out for Washington. In what manner he made the journey is not clearly known; but he reached the capital on Monday, April 22d, one of the first-comers from the North since public communication had been broken. He thus announced his action to his mother (April 24th): "I was fortunate enough to be in Baltimore last Sunday, and to be here at present. How Jim and Henry will envy me! . . . . I shall come to see you, if I find there is nothing to be done here. So have the blue room ready."

He put himself at once at the disposal of the government, and applied for the commission of Second Lieutenant of Artillery in the Regular Army. While awaiting the result of his application, Lowell sought to be of service as a civilian. As soon as the railway was opened, he went to Annapolis, and exerted himself there for the Massachusetts troops; first, in a private capacity, as the representative of several Boston gentlemen, and afterwards as a semi-official agent of the State. It is believed that he was also at this time employed by the government as a scout, and that in this perilous service he found opportunities of indulging his dashing spirit, and obtained valuable information concerning the condition and movements of the enemy.

"WASHINGTON, May 13, 1861.

"I feel confident I am all right for a commission in the first batch of civilians; since my application none have been given except to the graduating class of West Point. When I am fairly appointed, I shall want you to send me a copy of 'Oakfield,' with your love and fondest wishes; — in exchange *perhaps* I will send my photograph. Although I did not consult you, dear, in coming here, I was very glad indeed to have your letter and father's approving. I think, too, you will agree that I am right in trying to enter the *Regular* Army. . . . . I have thought from the first that . . it will fall mainly on the regular organization to keep the armies in the field and keep them moving. Military science I have absolutely none, military talent I am too ignorant yet to recognize; but my education and experience in business and in the working of men may, if wanted, be made available at once in the regular army. . . . . Of course I am too old to be tickled with a uniform, and too apathetic to get up such a feeling against the worst traitor among them as to desire personally to slay him; but like every young soldier, I am anxious for one battle as an experience; after that, I shall be content to bide my time, working where I can do most service, and learning all I can from observation and from books. I believe no one is more anxious to see the government 'go through' than I am. I want to see the Baltimore traitors put on trial at once and armed rebellion everywhere crushed out; but I cannot help feeling that the task is a long one, and of uncertain issue; and whether we are to have a long war and subdue them, or a short war and a separation, it is evident that the army is to assume a new position among us. It will again become a profession. Hence my anxiety to get into the Artillery; if the change is to come, I want to be in position to take the best advantage of it. . . . . The government troops parade here, and crowds stare at them. In Alexandria (six miles off, I was down there last week) the Virginia troops parade, and crowds gape at *them*. As to fancying any hostile relation between them, it is almost impossible. . . . . My room-mate, S——, was at Richmond last Friday, drove all about the town and visited the camps in the neighborhood; he reports them to be in quite large force and very anxious for a fight, thoroughly convinced that they were fighting the battles of freedom!"

"May 25.

"After the movement yesterday across the river, all passing to and fro was forbidden; but Mr. Dalton and myself, by going up to Georgetown and making interest with the Irishmen of the Sixty-ninth, who have a rather Milesian idea of sentry's duty, succeeded in getting into Virginia. We visited the earthworks and many of the camps and dined at Arlington House on corn-pone and milk. There were no troops yesterday within two miles of Arlington, and the place was just in the prime of its spring beauty. I have seen no place like it in this country for position and for well-improved natural advantages. I suppose to-day it is occupied; and in spite of its importance and of its owner's treason, I cannot think of it with much pleasure. . . . . If I have been of any use to the Massachusetts troops, I am very glad of it. I wish our people would not feel so very anxious about their *comfort.* Their health and *morale* is excellent, and they are as efficient as any troops here. I am sure you do not worry so much about my comfort, and I do not see why other mothers should. The greatest kindness to our troops now is to teach them to use what they have."

"June 7.

[*To C. E. Perkins, Esq., Burlington.*] "I cannot say I take any great *pleasure* in the contemplation of the future. I fancy you feel much as I do about the profitableness of a soldier's life, and would not think of trying it, were it not for a muddled and twisted idea that somehow or other this fight was going to be one in which decent men ought to engage for the sake of *humanity*, — I use the word in its ordinary sense. It seems to me that within a year the slavery question will again take a prominent place, and that many cases will arise in which we may get fearfully in the wrong if we put our cause wholly in the hands of fighting men and foreign legions."

About the middle of June, Lowell received his commission (dated May 14, 1861), as Captain in the Third (afterwards numbered Sixth) Regiment of United States Cavalry; and he was engaged, during the summer, in recruiting in different parts of the country.

"WARREN, OHIO, August 5.

"You seem to feel worse about the Bull Run defeat than I do. To me the most discouraging part of the whole is the way in which company officers have too many of them behaved *since* the affair, — skulking about Washington, at Willard's or elsewhere, letting their names go home in the lists of killed or missing, eating and sleeping, and entirely ignoring the commands of their superiors and the moral and physical needs of their men. I regard it as a proof of something worse than loose discipline, — as a proof that these officers at least have no sense of the situation and no sentiment for their cause. If there are to be many such, we are whipped from the outset. Fancy Jim or Willy behaving so! I know that my Southern classmates in the Rebel ranks would never have treated their companies of poor white trash so contemptuously. They respect them too much as means for a great end."

During the following autumn and winter, Lowell's regiment was occupied in drilling and preparing for the field. He gave himself wholly to his new work, employing his time of leisure in making himself a master of cavalry tactics and in studying also the higher principles of military science. His talent and assiduity attracted the admiration of every officer of his regiment; and, even before he had had the opportunity of showing his sagacity and courage in action, his colonel had come to look on him as "the best officer appointed from civil life he had ever known," and honored him with the command of a squadron.

The regiment moved in March, 1862, with the Army of the Potomac, and was engaged, as a part of General Stoneman's command, in the Peninsular campaign of the ensuing season. During the whole of Lowell's career as a soldier, with the self-contained dignity of character for which he was conspicuous in all periods of his life, and which was now re-enforced by a severe principle of military propriety, he kept in his letters, and (unless pressed by questions) in his speech, a perfect silence concerning his performances, — drew no battle-pieces, seldom even mentioned having been in battle, never so much as dropped a hint of any act of wit or bravery of his own, and professed continually that he could find nothing to "narrate." We are therefore forced to rest for most of the facts which created his brilliant reputation on the memory of his companions in arms; and we may, in some instances, have failed to recover or even have misapprehended important details.

In the advance of the army towards Richmond, and especially after the evacuation of Yorktown, Lowell was constantly in action, and his gallantry was everywhere conspicuous. "For distinguished services at Williamsburg and Slatersville," he was nominated for the brevet of Major.

"I heard yesterday of a narrow escape which Charley had," writes Lieutenant James Lowell, on the 29th of May, referring to the affair at Slatersville. "He was charging, and came upon a man who aimed a double-barrelled carbine at him. C—— called out to him, '*Drop that!*' and he lowered it enough to blow to pieces C——'s coat, which was strapped on his horse behind him."

Captain Lowell further distinguished himself in a reconnoissance on the 15th of May, and in the battle of Hanover Court-

House on the 27th. On the memorable 27th of June the whole of Stoneman's command was cut off from the main army and obliged to retire down the Peninsula to Fortress Monroe. In the severe battles of the following week Lowell was therefore not engaged. But they cost him the life of his tenderly loved brother, James, who was wounded at Glendale on the 30th of June, and died in the hands of the enemy at a neighboring farm-house on the 4th of July.

On the 10th of July Captain Lowell was detailed for duty as an aid to General McClellan. He remained in this position till November, winning the esteem of his chief by efficient conduct at the second battle of Malvern Hill (August 5), and rendering energetic service in the brilliant and arduous Maryland campaign. At South Mountain (September 14), in bearing orders to General Reno, he showed a bravery which excited universal admiration. But at Antietam (September 17) he revealed the high order of his military capacity more fully than on any other occasion during the first period of the war. He went, early in the day, with orders to General Sedgwick's division, of General Sumner's corps. He met it retreating in confusion, under a hot fire. Lowell put forth all his vigor to meet the occasion. He rode rapidly from point to point of the line, driving back and rallying the men; and such was the magnetism of his presence and his voice that whole companies which a moment before had seemed uncontrollable started forward with alacrity at his word. Through the re-enforcement given to discipline by his energetic behavior, a rout which threatened disaster to the whole right of our line was checked. "I shall never forget the effect of his appearance," says an officer who saw him for a single instant, while he was engaged in this work. "He seemed a part of his horse, and instinct with a perfect animal life. At the same time his eyes glistened and his face literally shone with the spirit and intelligence of which he was the embodiment. He was the ideal of the *preux chevalier*. After I was wounded, one of my first anxieties was to know what had become of him; for it seemed to me that no mounted man could have lived through the storm of bullets that swept the wood just after I saw him enter it." He was with Sedgwick when that general was wounded; and at the same time his own horse was shot under him, while a bullet passed through his coat, and another broke the scabbard of his sabre. In recognition of his gallantry in this battle, General McClellan bestowed on Lowell the office of presenting to the President the trophies of the campaign; and he accordingly visited Washington, the bearer of thirty-nine colors taken from the enemy. This was a high honor, and by the customs of the service equivalent to a recommendation for promotion. In the midst of the excitement caused by this important victory, Lowell writes to his mother, on the 19th of September, a few pencilled lines on an official blank, in which he begins, "We had a severe fight day before yesterday"; then mentions some casualties among officers known in Massachusetts; and after a brief statement of the general results of the battle, closes without one syllable of the brilliant part he has himself played in it.

From time to time, in the course of this summer, the project of a new volunteer regiment of horse, to be commanded by Captain Lowell, had engaged the attention of the authorities of Massachusetts. In August he writes: "As to a regiment, I have given up all idea of it very willingly. . . . . Your scheme of a regiment of gentlemen, even if practicable, would not suit me at all. What do you mean by 'gentlemen'? 'Drivers of gigs'?"

In November, however, he was ordered to report to Governor Andrew, for the purpose of organizing the Second Massachusetts Cavalry, of which he was appointed Colonel. This work kept him in the neighborhood of Boston through the winter and spring of 1862–63.

During this winter, the first regiment of negroes raised in the North was projected by the government of Massachusetts. Colonel Lowell was strongly interested in the success of this movement, and he aided it with his counsel and his influence. He was heartily pleased with the selection of Colonel Shaw as its leader. "It is very important," he writes (February 9), "that the regiment should be started soberly, and not spoilt by too much fanaticism. Shaw is not a fanatic."

While Colonel Lowell was engaged in organizing the Second Cavalry a serious mutiny broke out, on the 9th of April, at barracks under the recruiting-office in Boston, where one company of the regiment was quartered. The men rushed on their officers with drawn swords. Colonel Lowell went to the barracks, and by his force of character and resolute coolness succeeded in restoring discipline; but he was obliged to shoot the ringleader in the revolt, whom he saw in the act of striking at a lieutenant with his sabre.

This tragic incident affected Lowell deeply; but he acted from a well-considered principle, put into practice with the quick decision of a fearless mind. His conduct was universally applauded. In the street-crowd that gathered on the first rumor of the occurrence, a young man was heard to say, "I was with Lowell at the High School; and if he did it, I know it is right."

He is said to have reported what he had done to Governor Andrew in the following manner. Entering his Excellency's room, he made a military salute and said, "I have to report to you, sir, that in the discharge of my duty I have shot a man"; then saluted again and immediately withdrew. "I need nothing more," said the Governor to a bystander; "Colonel Lowell is as humane as he is brave." His action was approved by the United States authorities and by those of Massachusetts, and it exerted a wholesome influence throughout the service.

In May he left Boston with his regiment, and was soon placed in command of the cavalry of the Department of Washington, with head-quarters at Vienna, Virginia. For many months he was occupied in resisting the incursions of Mosby. This was a post of danger, and one in which he rendered important service to the country. But he constantly desired an opportunity of acting on a larger and more glorious field. "I have often said," writes General Mosby, "that, of all the Federal commanders opposed to me, I had the highest respect for Colonel Lowell, both as an officer and a gentleman."

In the spring of 1863 Colonel Lowell became engaged to Josephine, daughter of Francis G. Shaw, Esq., of Staten Island, and sister to Colonel Shaw. To her most of his later letters are addressed.

"June, 1863.

"Your Capri and Sorrento have brought back my Campagna and my Jungfrau and my Pæstum, and again the season is *la gioventù dell' anno*, and I think of breezy Veii and sunny Pisa and the stone-pines of the Villa Pamfili Doria. Of course it is right to wish that some time we may go there. Of course the remembrance of such places and the hope of revisiting them makes one take 'the all in the day's work' more bravely. It is a homesickness which is healthy for the soul; but we do not *own* ourselves, and have no right to even *wish* ourselves out of harness. I don't believe you wish there was no harness, nor yet to be out of harness by reason of a break-down. Collars are our proper 'wear,' I am afraid, and we ought to enjoy going well up to them. . . . .

"A man is meant to act and to undertake, to try to succeed in his undertakings, to take all means which he thinks necessary to success; but he must not let his undertakings look too large and make a slave of him. Still less must he let the means. He must keep free and grow *integrally*. . . . .

"You know I believe Heaven is here, everywhere, if we only see God; and that, as a future state, it is not to be much dwelt upon, — only enough to make one content with death as a change not infinitely different from sleep; — that this world, and all that is in it, being created for the glory of God, (and for what other end can such a fearful and wonderful 'nature' be designed,) we especially ought to glorify him by being thankful and seeing his glory everywhere. Just how we are to show our thankfulness is a more searching question: I think not by depreciating this world to exalt another; perhaps by *bene vivere*, perhaps by 'loving well both man and bird and beast'; — probably by one person in one way, by another in another. . . . .

"I wonder whether my theories about self-culture, &c., would ever have been modified so much, whether I should ever have seen what a necessary failure they lead to, had it not been for this war. *Now* I feel every day, more and more, that a man has no right to himself at all; that, indeed, he can do nothing useful unless he recognizes this clearly. We were counting over the 'satisfactory' people of our acquaintance the other day, and very few they were. It seems to me that this change in public affairs has entirely changed my standard, and that men whom, ten years ago, I should have almost accepted as satisfactory now show lamentably deficient. Men do not yet seem to have risen with the occasion; and the perpetual perception of this is uncomfortable. It is painful here to see how sadly personal motives interfere with most of our officers' usefulness. *After* the war how much there will be to do, and how little opportunity a fellow in the field has to prepare himself for the sort of doing that will be required. It makes me quite sad sometimes; but then I reflect that the great secret of *doing*, after all, is in seeing what *is* to be done. I wish I could feel as sure of doing my duty elsewhere as I am of doing it on the field of battle; that is so little part of an officer's and patriot's duty now."

"July 3.

"Wars are bad, but there are many things far worse. . . . . Anything immediately comfortable in our affairs I don't see; but comfortable times are not the ones that make a nation great. See what too much comfort has reduced the Philadelphians to. Honestly, I dare scarcely wish that the war should end speedily."

"July 5.

"I am vexed at having to remain here, when there is so much going on close by. I almost wish I was back a Captain in the Sixth. However, I have done all I dare to get away. . . . . You must n't be disappointed. I suppose there *will* come a time when the regiment will have a chance."

"July 9.

"What glorious news about Vicksburg; and I am particularly glad to have that and Gettysburg come so near the 4th of July. A year ago on that day Jimmy died, in a farm-house on the battle-field of Glendale; the little fellow was very happy; he thought the war would soon be over, that everything was going right, and that everybody was as high-minded and courageous as himself. He was a good son and a pure and wise lover of his country. With mother and father I shall never fill his place, nor in the Commonwealth either I fear."

"July 24.

"Many nations fail, that one may become great; ours will fail, unless we gird up our loins and do honest and humble *days' work*, without trying to do the thing by the job or to get a great nation made by any patent process. It is not safe to say that we shall not have victories till we are ready for them. We shall have victories, and whether or no we are ready for them depends upon ourselves; if we are not ready, we shall fail, — *voilà tout.* If you ask what if we do fail, I have nothing to say; I should n't cry over a nation or two, more or less, *gone under!* . . . .

"I don't at all like the duty here, serving against bushwhackers; it brings me in contact with too many *citizens*, and sometimes with mothers and children. The other night a fine-looking young fellow stumbled against our pickets and was captured. It proved that he had been out to visit his mother. She came to bid him good-by the next morning, a Quaker-like looking old lady, very neat and quiet. She did n't appeal to us at all. She shed a few tears over the son, repacked his bundle carefully, slipped a roll of greenbacks into his hand, and then kissed him farewell. I was very much touched by her. Yesterday we took a little fellow only sixteen years old. He had joined one of these gangs to avoid the conscription, which is very sweeping. He told us all he knew about the company to which he belonged; but he was such a babe that it seemed to me *mean* to question him."

In July the assault on Fort Wagner took place, in which the heroic leader of the Fifty-fourth Massachusetts fell at the head of his men.

"July 26.

"—— has just sent me the report about dear Rob, and it does not seem to me possible it should be true. Was he not pre-eminently what every man-at-arms should wish to be? The manliness and patriotism and high courage of such a man *never* die with him, they live in his comrades; it should be the same with the gentleness and thoughtfulness which made him so lovable a son and brother and friend. We have been talking over the good fellows who have gone before in this war, — fellows whom Rob loved so much, many of them. There is none who has been so widely and so dearly loved as he. If 'life is but a sum of love,' Rob had had his share and done his share. It is pleasant to feel sure, without knowing any particulars, that his regiment has done well; we all feel perfectly sure of it. I hope he knew it too."

"July 26.

[*To his mother.*] "He was to me one of the most attractive men I ever knew, — he had such a single and loyal and kindly heart; I don't believe he ever did an unkind or thoughtless act without trying to make up for it afterwards. In that he was like Jimmy. It *cannot* be so hard for such a man to die: it *is* not so hard for his friends to lose him. . . . . Tell —— not to feel anxious, and don't *you* feel anxious, dear, about *anybody*. It is not our business."

"August 1.

"Everything that comes about Rob shows his death to have been more and more completely that which every soldier and every man would long to die; but it is given to very few, for very few do their duty as Rob did. I am thankful they buried him 'with his niggers.' They were brave men, and they were *his* men."

Colonel Lowell married on the 31st of October, 1863. He has left a daughter, Carlotta Russell Lowell, born after his death.

The season of 1863 – 64 was one of great tranquillity. Mrs. Lowell was able to accompany her husband to the army, and to remain at Vienna for several months; and though Colonel Lowell was constantly employed in the distasteful service to which he had been assigned, it was not till midsummer that he found again the opportunity of distinguishing himself in the open field.

In July, 1864, he took a conspicuous part in resisting General Early, who in that month made a demonstration upon Washington. On the 14th of July, going on a reconnoissance, with his own regiment and an additional battalion, he sent a part of his command forward, and himself followed with the remainder. A little beyond Rockville, the advance column was suddenly overwhelmed by a greatly superior force of the enemy, and took up a rapid retreat. Just as Colonel Lowell had reached the middle of the town, the flying battalion came charging down upon him. He had not even time to turn his men. There was a violent collision; and then the whole brigade went whirling in mad confusion towards Washington. The enemy were at their heels. With brilliant audacity, Lowell shouted the order, "Dismount!" Seizing their carbines, the men sprang from their saddles at the word of their dauntless commander. In another instant, they were in line. On came the assailants; but, as they drew near, such a deadly volley was poured into their ranks that both horses and riders recoiled before it. Lowell saw the enemy waver, advanced, and turned the fortune of the day. With his little force, just now routed and in full retreat, but unable, even in a moment of panic, to forget its discipline, he held his ground against two brigades of the enemy's best cavalry. Colonel Lowell's control over his men on this occasion has been compared by his officers, not inaptly, to Sheridan's famous rally of his army at the battle of Cedar Creek.

On the 26th of July, Colonel Lowell was put in command of a new "Provisional Brigade," and was ordered to report to General Hunter, then at the head of the Army of the Shenandoah. This brigade, which numbered nineteen hundred men, contained, besides the Second Massachusetts, representatives of every cavalry regiment in the service; and Lowell never gave a more signal proof of his wonderful administrative power than when he brought this heterogeneous collection of men in a few days into a state of organic unity.

On the 6th of August General Sheridan took command of the Army of the Shenandoah, which, on the 10th, moved up the valley from Harper's Ferry, the Provisional Brigade taking the outside position. The next day Lowell overtook the rear-guard of the enemy, and, after a sharp skirmish, drove it pell-mell through Winchester. On the 16th, Sheridan began to retire down the valley, the cavalry protecting his rear; and for two weeks from this date Lowell's brigade was fighting every day. On the 21st, the army was again encamped near the Ferry. Colonel Lowell's business was now to watch the movements of the enemy. It was in the discharge of this duty that his soldiership made its first deep impression on the commanding general; and day by day from this moment, as he was tried in new service, his reputation rose to a higher and higher point at head-quarters and throughout the army. On the 26th of August, he led an attack on the advance of the enemy. To succeed, it must be made with great rapidity. "Charging up to a rail-fence behind which were the enemy, and which he could not leap, he actually whacked their muskets with his sabre. In tearing down the fence, men were clubbed with muskets, and two killed in this way; but over they went, —

nothing could resist them. The Second Massachusetts captured seventy-four men, a lieutenant-colonel, three captains, and several lieutenants. This was the first time that Colonel Lowell's men ever really measured him. Such a noble scorn of death and danger they never saw before, and it inspired them with a courage that quailed at nothing."

On the 3d of September the army was again in motion; and on the 8th, Colonel Lowell was appointed to the command of the "Reserve Brigade," which was made to consist of three regiments of regular cavalry, one of artillery, and his own volunteer regiment, and was considered the best cavalry brigade in the service. This appointment was the more honorable to Lowell, as he owed it in no degree to personal favor or influence. He had been utterly unknown to General Sheridan at the beginning of the campaign, and the high estimation he now enjoyed had flowed from his own merits only.

In the superb charge at Winchester (19th September), when our cavalry rode over a whole division of the enemy and drove their army flying through the town and for miles up the turnpike, till night ended the pursuit, Lowell achieved new distinction. "At one moment," says an officer of his regiment, "he found himself, with one captain and four men, face to face with a Rebel gun. The piece was discharged, killing both the horses and tearing off the captain's arm. The Colonel quietly mounted the first horse that came up; and the gun was his." "A little more spunk," said Lowell, never satisfied that enough had been done, to a member of Sheridan's staff, "and we should have had all their colors." "A little more go," was the answer, "and you would have been in Richmond."

The 9th of October was the date of a hardly less brilliant fight, called by our men, in allusion to the complete rout of the Confederates, the "Woodstock Races." Here the cavalry of Sheridan's army tried its strength against that of the enemy, which was commanded by General Rosser, the long-expected "savior of the valley." Colonel Lowell held the Strasburg turnpike, and it fell to him to lead the attack that day. "It almost rained lead; and the men crouched behind rocks, trees, fences. It seemed as if they could not go on. The Colonel rode up among them and along the line; then they *must* advance. The enemy opened two guns at short range, shotted with grape and canister; — but on, still on. Our first line was half destroyed, and the reserve was ordered up; but the Colonel rode all the while in advance of every man in his command. Remembering Winchester, the enemy grew tremulous; and our bugles sounded the charge. The recall was not heard nor the pace abated till our men were seventeen miles away, beyond Edinburgh." In this battle, in the words of General Sheridan, "everything on wheels was captured."

These are only shining points in a campaign which gave every day new proofs of Lowell's quality. "He was perfectly brave," says one who saw him constantly in the valley. Thirteen horses were shot under him in the course of as many weeks; and as he went ruddy and buoyant into the storm of death, he seemed to know that he was protected from its fury by some decree of fate. But he was not a soldier of dashing courage only. He was distinguished by self-devotion and sleepless vigilance, by coolness, sound judgment, and military knowledge, by rapidity and sureness of eye, and skill in turning peril into an opportunity of victory, by persistency undiscouraged, by absolute promptness, by self-reliance and self-possession, by a discipline, temperate and just, but unflinching, and by an inborn spirit of command. "In whatever position Lowell was placed," remarks one who knew him well through life, "it always seemed to those around him that he was made for just that work." His men, some of them dissatisfied at first to be led by a commander who appeared even more youthful than he was, never shrank from following him into any danger after they had seen him in one battle. "His officers loved him, and wished for nothing so much as to show him what they dared to do; and he would watch them with tears in his eyes." In the midst of this laborious campaign, he found time to read several books of serious thought, — a few such books he always carried in his baggage, — and he liked to engage his officers in discussions suggested by his reading. In his views of public affairs "he was always an enthusiast, never a fanatic," says one who talked with him intimately at different periods of the war. Honorably ambitious of advancement, he ever earnestly maintained the principle that promotions should be neither made nor sought on any ground but that of military merit. "He was free, eminently free, from the finesse of the politician."

"Those who knew him at any period in life know how wonderfully he united the aspirations of immortal youth with an instinctive knowledge of the world, patience with persistent energy, freedom from illusions with nobleness of aim."

"I know none like him left, so sparkling, so rapid in his eye, so true, so sound, so noble. I will not say he had no faults; but, in my long intercourse with him, I never saw them as faults that jarred. The worst and only complaint I have ever had was that he would not tell me of himself. He had *the impersonality of genius.*"

"From the time he entered the army he was happy. He had found all he asked, — an object worthy of his efforts. The vague desire to do something for his fellow-men became a settled resolve to do all he could, whether much or little, for his country. Though quick to perceive shortcomings, and to feel their discouraging influence, he never lost his faith. He was inflexible in duty; for he believed that through fidelity in trifles only could the great whole be gained. Especially was every good and noble growth quickened during the last two years."

"September 5, 1864.

"I like Sheridan immensely. Whether he succeeds or fails, he is the first general I have seen who puts as much heart and time and thought into his work as if he were doing it for his own exclusive profit. He works like a mill-owner or an iron-master; not like a soldier. Never sleeps, never worries, is never cross, but is n't afraid to come down on a man who deserves it."

"September 10.

[*To a disabled officer.*] "I hope that you are going to live like a plain republican, mindful of the beauty and of the duty of simplicity. Nothing fancy now, sir, if you please; it 's disreputable to spend money when the government is so hard up, and when there are so many poor officers. I hope that you have outgrown all foolish ambitions, and are now content to become a 'useful citizen.' . . . . *Don't* grow rich; if you once begin, you will find it much more difficult to be a useful citizen. Don't seek office, but don't 'disremember' that the 'useful citizen' always holds his time, his trouble, his money, and his life ready at the *hint* of his country. The useful citizen is a mighty unpretending hero; but we are not going to have any country very long, unless such heroism is developed. There! what a stale sermon I 'm preaching! But being a soldier, it does seem to me that I should like nothing so well as being a useful citizen. Well, trying to be one, I mean. I shall stay in the service, of course, till the war is over, or till I 'm disabled; but then I look forward to a pleasanter career. . . .

"I believe I have lost *all* my ambitions. . . . . I don't think I would turn my hand to be a distinguished chemist or a famous mathematician. *All* I now care about is to be a useful citizen, with money enough to buy bread and firewood, and to teach my children to ride on horseback, and look strangers in the face, especially Southern strangers."

"October 5.

"The new moon looked very strangely calm and peaceful and almost reproachful in the west last night, with the whole north and east, far and near, lighted up by burning barns and houses. . . . . I would *cheerfully* assist in making this whole valley a desert, from Staunton northward; for that would have, I am sure, an important effect on the campaign of the spring; but in *partial* burnings I see less justice and less propriety. I was sorry enough the other day that my brigade should have had a part in the hanging and shooting of some of Mosby's men."

"October 10.

"I don't think I now care at all about being a Brigadier-General. I am *perfectly* satisfied to be a Colonel, if I can always have a brigade to command. That 's modest, is n't it?"

"October 17.

[*To J. M. Forbes, Esq.*] "I am very glad that we have not a 'handy' writer among us. The reputation of regiments is made and is known in the army; the comparative merits are *well* known there. Such a notice as I saw of the —— —— makes a regiment ridiculous, besides giving the public false history."

"October 17.

[*To his mother.*] "If I 'm ever taken prisoner, you 'll find one fellow who won't think he 's badly treated, and won't come home and make the friends of all prisoners sick with his twaddle. . . . . People must be patient: we are going quite fast enough."

On the 15th of October, General Sheridan left the army, then strongly intrenched near Cedar Creek, for the purpose of visiting Front Royal and other points in the valley. The story of the 19th is well known. It will be remembered how, in the dawn of that day, the enemy succeeded in accomplishing a surprise; how the whole left of our line, suddenly exposed to a deadly fire poured into them from the rear, were driven from their position and rushed headlong down the valley, while the only hope that seemed to remain was that of saving the army from total destruction; and how, at midday, into that routed and huddled mass Sheridan came galloping from Winchester, with a speed that left most of his escort far in the rear, and, received by the troops with wild cheers and a spontaneous resolution to renew the battle, how he turned ruin into victory.

Late in the evening of the 18th Colonel Lowell had orders to make a reconnoissance, as soon as the fog broke the next morning, in front of the position occupied by the cavalry, on the right of the line. He caused *reveille* to be sounded at four o'clock, and at half past four his brigade was in motion. Crossing the creek, he encountered the enemy in force. A sharp skirmish ensued, — the beginning of the battle. Lowell held his position till half past seven, when he was relieved by infantry, and withdrew. His punctuality in making his advance had saved the right wing of the army from a disaster, possibly as great as that which befell the other end of the line.

Soon after eight o'clock the whole cavalry corps passed from the right of the field to the left, a distance of three miles, with the object of obtaining an advantageous position for covering the retreat of the army. The Reserve Brigade took the lead in this movement. Passing along the fast-retiring line of battle, between the infantry front and the skirmish line, they had an excellent view of the state of affairs, and were exposed sometimes to a heavy fire. "We met everywhere flying men and officers," said a member of the brigade. "We asked the officers why they went to the rear. 'They had no command.' We asked the men. 'They had no officers.'" "They moved past me, that splendid cavalry!" wrote shortly after a distinguished general. "If they reached the pike, I felt secure. Lowell got by me before I could speak, but I looked after him for a long distance. Exquisitely mounted, the picture of a soldier, — erect, confident, defiant, — he moved at the head of the finest brigade of cavalry that at this day scorns the earth it treads."

Striking the turnpike just north of Middletown, which was already occupied by the enemy, Lowell at once established his position at the extreme left of the line; and he maintained it almost unchanged, against great superiority of numbers, till the final advance in which he received his mortal wound. He attended in person to the disposition of his men, riding backwards and forwards along the line of skirmishers, a conspicuous mark for the sharpshooters on the roofs of the village. His horse was shot under him early in the day. In a charge at one o'clock, he was himself struck in the side of the right breast by a spent ball, which, without breaking the skin, imbedded itself in the muscle and deprived him of voice and strength. "It is only my *poor* lung," he said faintly to the officers who urged him to go to the rear. "You would not have me leave the field without having shed blood!" The force of the blow was sufficient to collapse the lung and cause internal hemorrhage, and it would probably have been fatal if he had had no other hurt.

For an hour and a half he lay on the ground under a temporary shelter. Presently an order came for a general advance along the line at three o'clock, — the advance which was destined to give us victory. "I feel well *now*," said he, though too weak to mount to his saddle without assistance. He sat his horse firm and erect as ever. The color had come back to his cheeks. But he could not speak above a whisper. He gave his orders through a member of his staff; and his brigade was, as usual, the first ready. Just as they were in the thickest of the fire that was poured on them from the town, a cry arose, "The Colonel is hit!" He fell from his horse into the arms of his aids, and was carried forward, in the track of his rapidly advancing brigade, to a house within the village.

The ball had severed his spine at the neck; and his body was completely paralyzed below the wound. He gave no signs of suffering; his mind was perfectly clear; and he rested calm and cheerful, though he knew from the beginning that he had no chance of life. He dictated some private messages of affection. Then, from time to time through the night, as his waning strength would allow, he gave complete directions about all the details of his command. Not the smallest thing was forgotten; no one was left in doubt. In the intervals he remained silent, with his eyes closed. Twice he directed his surgeon to leave him and look to the injuries of other officers and of some wounded prisoners whose voices he heard without. He expressed pleasure at the triumphant issue of the fight, and at Colonel Gansevoort's victory over Mosby, news of which was brought in that day. As dawn approached, it was evident that his spirit was gradually freeing itself from its vesture of decay. He had finished his "day's work"; and he lay tranquil, his mind withdrawn, it seemed, into that chamber of still thought, known so imperfectly to the nearest of his friends, wherein was the seat of his deepest life. Even in his last hour he was fully conscious, and seemed to retain his strength. But he spoke less and less often; and as day rose into full morning, he ceased to breathe the air of earth.

A letter, from one whose official position under government gives his opinion authority, says, "I do not think there was any officer in all the army so much beloved as Lowell." "We all shed tears," said Custer, "when we knew we had lost him. It is the greatest loss the cavalry corps has ever suffered." "I do not think there was a quality," said Sheridan, "which I could have added to Lowell. He was the perfection of a man and a soldier." His commission as Brigadier-General of Volunteers, "determined on days before," was signed on the 19th of October, too late for him to wear the honor he had earned so well.

The funeral of General Lowell took place on Friday, the 28th of October, at the College Chapel at Cambridge. It was fit that Harvard should pay the last honors to this son of hers, than whom none nobler ever left her lap. In an address, spoken in the presence of a dense assemblage, the Rev. George Putnam drew a vivid picture of the departed hero, and consecrated the occasion, with fine felicity, not to Lowell only, but also to those many dear friends of his to whom he had been as a leader, yet who before him had fallen and nearly all still rested where they fell. Then the relics of this high-minded, gallant, and gifted soldier were restored to the earth at Mount Auburn, with the honors befitting his military rank.

> "Not on the vulgar mass
> Called 'work' must sentence pass,
> Things done, that took the eye and had the price;
> O'er which, from level stand,
> The low world laid its hand,
> Found straightway to its mind, could value in a trice:
>
> "Thoughts hardly to be packed
> Into a narrow act,
> Fancies that broke through language and escaped;
> All I could never be,
> All men ignored in me,
> This I was worth to God, whose wheel the pitcher shaped."

JAMES SAVAGE.

Captain 2d Mass. Vols. (Infantry), May 24, 1861; Major, June 23, 1862; Lieutenant-Colonel, September 17, 1862; died at Charlottesville, Va., October 22, 1862, of wounds received at Cedar Mountain, August 9.

JAMES SAVAGE, Jr., the subject of this memoir, was the only son of the Hon. James Savage of Boston, well known for his historical researches connected with the early settlers of New England, and of Elizabeth Otis (Stillman) Savage.

Major Thomas Savage, the founder of the family in America, came to this country in 1635, settled in Boston, and rendered valuable service to the Colony as commander of the Massachusetts forces in King Philip's war. His son inherited the martial instincts of the father, and was the "noble, heroic youth" spoken of by the old chronicler of that war, who holding the rank of Ensign in Captain Moseley's company, was twice wounded. These words might be aptly quoted to describe James Savage, Jr.

Born in Boston, April 21, 1832, he inherited a sensitive, earnest, and joyous nature, united with a physical constitution not equal to the enterprises which his adventurous spirit craved. His love of out-door play was inexhaustible; and the city streets among which his childhood was spent, while depriving him of the freedom of the country, gave him equal opportunity for adventure in a different way. A favorite enjoyment was to lead a band of playmates to some distant part of the city, by cross-routes known only to boys and cats, scaling sheds and walls, climbing the leads of houses, and dropping from eaves, at imminent risk of their necks. One of his comrades says: "We knew no barrier too high nor place too difficult to enter. We were not mischievous or ill-disposed. Neither man nor animal suffered from our games; but the delight of starting at Brattle Square and going to Boylston Street 'across lots,' never entering a public street except to cross it, can never be known to those who have not, as I have, chased Jim Savage in *coram* and *hie-spy*. The boy who took to the street for security or success lost caste at once." The same companion says: "I have not seen Savage for years, but I remember him as yesterday, full of fun and courage, with his 'hockey' in hand, ready to plunge into any *mêlée* to get a blow at the ball. He was thin, and light in weight, and in a severe hustle would get pushed to the outside by mere want of weight, but he was sure to go in again and again. His side at football would win if he could make it, for in rush or race it took a good player to compete with him; and yet withal he was such a gentle and noble fellow that everybody loved him, and felt that he would never do a mean thing. He was one that never complained or made a fuss if the game was not arranged to suit him; all he wanted was fair play."

In those days, twenty years ago, Boston boys were often called into sterner encounters; there were frequently severe battles between the sons of more wealthy parents and the Irish boys. Beside these contests there were long-standing feuds between Northenders and Southenders, between Boston and Roxbury boys. Temple Place, James's home, was nearly middle ground, and those who lived in that neighborhood were ever in danger of a blow. James Savage never engaged in a quarrel if he could avoid it, but when one was forced upon him he never thought of dodging. If a friend was in trouble, or an insult offered to those who could not defend themselves, James was ready to strike; and when he did strike, it was with all his might. Many of his companions have said, in later days, that he was unconquerable as long as his strength lasted. Careless of pain, his only thought was to reduce his opponent to submission.

But the boy's life was not all play; for, though not distinguished as a scholar, he was exceedingly fond of reading, particularly those books of history which treat of the wars of Greece and Rome and the Middle Ages. He never wearied of the feats of knight-errantry, and read and re-read Irving's Conquest of Granada until he had it by heart. In the winter evenings, when a very little boy, he would sit at the table and fight the battles of the Moors and Spaniards, using spools to represent the contending knights and squadrons. Of the early display of this martial spirit and other manifestations of character a picture is given in the following letter from his teacher, Mr. George Fowle, whose kindly sympathy James ever remembered with gratitude.

"You could not have made me a more pleasing gift than that of the likeness of our loved and loving James. . . . . He was always prompt and ready for all our school doings, whether of frolic or labor, picnic or exhibition. He showed his military turn at an early age. At one time when English history had warmed up the boys into a military ardor, they divided themselves into Saxons and Normans, and James was chosen commander of the latter. Our old Scotch carpenter, whom you may remember, Mr. Troup, was called upon to furnish us with wooden swords and shields, and I was laboriously engaged in making devices and mottoes to be placed upon the shields. I had the shield of James in my possession till I lost it on my removal to my present rooms. The device was a bull in wild career and the motto,

'When I wave my sword on high,
See the Saxon porkers fly.'

We had been reading 'Ivanhoe' at the time, as illustrative of the reign of Richard Cœur-de-Lion, and James hit upon Front-de-Bœuf as his pattern."

His relish for the heroic made him delight in the poetry which recounts the deeds of valor in stirring verse; and he seemed never weary, even when he became a man, of reading Macaulay's Lays, Aytoun's Border Minstrelsy, and Scott's Poems. On the eve of actual battle, James was heard quoting from "Henry of Navarre." Being so full of romantic feeling, it was to be expected that he would have a vivid perception of beauty, and so, indeed, he had; it was to him the manifestation of God in the world. He had a fine ear, and his musical taste was apparent when so small that he had to climb upon the music-stool before the piano, and twine his legs around its stem to keep from falling off. Thus perched, he would study out simple tunes, and then practise them until they were perfectly familiar. As he grew older, his pleasure in this art increased, and led him to an excellence rarely attained by amateurs, especially in the delicacy of touch and feeling with which he played. Possessed of a good voice and ear, he sang with ease; and when he had no instrument at hand, he found in song an expression for his feelings, whether sad or joyous, often helping others to beguile a weary hour in city and camp by singing.

Added to his love of music was a love of nature, which he seemed to have inherited from his mother, who, through her life, was keenly alive to all that reminded her of the fields and flowers, the forests and mountains, of her native State.

We have seen in him the adventurous boy, the eager playmate; yet there was a side to his character in singular contrast to this, and not less conspicuous to the ordinary observer. He was extremely shy and diffident, although free from the false pride which, centring in self-esteem, renders so many unable to do their best from dread of failure and ridicule. At school he was a fair scholar, doing his duty and getting his lessons without needing either bridle or spur, and yet, when suddenly called upon to show what he knew, he would hesitate and forget, and be often unable to say a word. In after years this diffidence did not altogether leave him, but was a cause of disappointment to him on many occasions.

It would seem that this boy, living so much in the open air, would have been rugged and sturdy, with a constitution capable of defying all ordinary ills. But the kindly influences of air and exercise were not sufficient to secure his perfect health, and in his thirteenth year he was sent to school in Lunenburg, Worcester County, that he might have the benefit of pure country air and simple food. In spite of this, however, he ultimately became a sufferer from dyspepsia, which not only prostrated his body, but reacted on his mind, causing frequent despondency, and making it more difficult to conquer the diffidence so natural to him.

In the summer of 1849 he entered Harvard University, having finished his preparation at the Boston Latin School;

but he did not enter without "conditions," obliging him to make up during the first term for his seemingly defective preparation in certain studies. When he came up to be examined, his constitutional diffidence so possessed him that he was unable to give proof of attainment commensurate with his actual knowledge, or with the requirements of a free admission, and thus he started on his college career oppressed by the weight of these added tasks as well as dispirited by ill health. In the midst of these difficulties, he found his spirits cheered and his mind sustained by his piano, which at the same time drew many friends around him. The musically inclined in his Class soon found him out, but until his Senior year he did not become truly known to his classmates. Though much inclined to be alone at times, few men were more dependent on the love of friends and the pleasures of social intercourse.

During the three previous years he had lost his mother and two lovely sisters, whose deaths followed each other at short intervals, the passing bell of one prolonging its sad tone into that of the next. Yearning for sympathy, the quiet, unchanging love which his home afforded had sustained him; and when these blows fell upon him, he was bowed by a sadness which only such deep and tender natures feel. He loved his friends with great earnestness, and yet was so little demonstrative that some whom he loved the best were often unaware of the depth of his affection, until sorrow or danger threatened, when the warmth of his attachment showed itself in untiring devotion.

Although not a disciple of any special religious creed, he was in the truest sense a religious man, penetrated by a clear faith and loving trust in God, whose presence he seemed to feel ever around him. Long after, and almost at the end of his earthly career, he expressed to a friend his firm conviction that God was ever near to comfort and sustain his trusting creatures; adding, that he felt "as if God's hand was always under him." The friend asked him how he had attained this earnest faith? He replied, "*By contemplation.*"

This religious consciousness showed itself in the atmosphere of moral purity which encircled him. He was so pure-minded and fervent, that impurity shrank from contact with him, and the conversation in which he participated, however careless and free, had no tinge of coarseness. For vulgar men and things he had an instinctive repugnance. A classmate says : "No man, however coarse, indulged in vulgar or sensual talk before him ; somehow it did not seem to agree with the atmosphere in which he lived."

It could not be expected that a young man of his temperament should attain to college honors. Though eager in the acquisition of knowledge, he was by nature devoid of the ambition of distinction which is an incentive to study ; and even had this motive been added, it could not have overcome the diffidence which also stood in the way of his success. A classmate who sat next him for four years says : "It was impossible for him to recite. He would go into the class as well prepared as any one, and on being called upon, stand up, and sometimes be unable to say a word. A mist seemed to rise before him, and he could not recall anything that he was expected to answer." But his college life was by no means unprofitable in book learning. He studied botany and the natural sciences with eagerness, and read all books within his reach which treated of theoretical and practical agriculture and landscape gardening. Long before graduating he had determined to pursue agriculture in some form as a profession.

The pleasure of his last college days and anticipated travels was clouded by the loss of another dearly loved sister in the summer of 1854 ; but James's tone of mind and body had become more elastic during the last few months of a happier life, and though he suffered, he yielded less to sorrow than before. In all his trials he turned for solace to nature and music. Seldom giving expression to his feelings, his silence showed that those suffer most whose wounds bleed inwardly. The open manifestation of sorrow, however real, is the healing process by which nature throws off anguish and opens the mind to healthy action. Yet it would be wrong to convey the impression that James was generally despondent. His fervor and enthusiasm never abandoned him; but he could not resist occasional attacks of melancholy.

In the autumn of 1854 he sailed for Europe, accompanied by two classmates and intimate friends, — Horace Furness and Atherton Blight. It was James's especial plan to study agricultural chemistry as a preparation for his chosen profession; and with this view he attended the lectures of Professor Liebig at Munich and Professor Rose at Berlin. On his way to the former city, he stopped to examine the famous agricultural school of Hohenheim; and he afterwards spent a winter of study in Munich. His friend Horace Furness wrote to James's sister, after his death: —

"What was always so peculiarly charming to me in Jim's character was, that with his great physical strength and love of out-door life and athletic exercises, wherein he always showed to such manly advantage, he united the most refined tastes and an almost feminine delicacy. I remember so vividly how once in Munich, on a very warm, enervating spring day, he walked between five and six miles to gather a handful of little blue gentians, and when he brought them home to our rooms, he hung over them with the keenest delight. He used to drink in the beauty of a summer landscape with more rapture than any man I ever met. I shall never forget the almost crazy joy with which he greeted the first sight in our lives of that exquisite little pink-fringed bellflower that grows almost in the very ice of the glaciers, — I think it is *Soldanella glacialis;* and how appreciative he was in poetry and music. Indeed, his was a most rare combination of the manly and tender; and I do not think that there ever lived a more pure-minded young man. His character was as stainless as a saint's."

In the spring and summer the friends made a tour embracing the Tyrol, of which the following letter gives some glimpses.

"WEIMAR, June 3, 1855.

"MY DEAR SISTER L——, — I am writing to you from classic Weimar, which, you know, belongs to Goethe and Schiller, Herder and Wieland. I saw in my walk this morning the Stadtkirche where Herder lies buried, and his house opposite the church. In the burial-ground of St. James's Church I saw the graves of Lucas

Cranach (it seems as if half the pictures I had seen lately at Nuremberg and other places were by him and Musæus); in the new churchyard, the tombs of Goethe and Schiller.

"And now, you see, I have at length torn myself away from Munich. Have n't you sometimes had misgivings that I intended to cut you all at home, and had married and settled down in Munich for life? No, I have left, and, what 's more, I have seen Nuremberg! I don't think I can make an attempt at description. It has given me more pleasure than *all* that I had seen before.

"It is all old; it is all rich; it is all history; it is all carving, — carving in brown stone of every pattern and figure. No fish, flesh, or fowl that is not carved there. And then those old fellows, who, so to speak, left their lives everywhere about their dear old city, — Albert Dürer, Adam Kraft, Veit Stoss, and Peter Vischer too. And yet the Bavarian court resides at Munich, a city on a perfect flat, no beauty in the houses, and the worst climate in the world."

It had been his intention to spend another studious winter in Berlin; but the damp and chilly climate proved so unfavorable to his health, that he was compelled to retreat to Italy, where he enjoyed himself to the utmost. "In no city have I enjoyed so much as in Rome," he writes April 1, 1856, "and the parting will be a sad one." After a short stay in France and England, he returned home that summer.

He passed the remaining season of fine weather in vain search for a farm where he might carry out his plans and use the knowledge of agriculture he had long been acquiring. The decided wish of his father, however, induced him to devote himself to the study of the law during the following winter, attending the lectures at Cambridge and reading at home. But his constitution was wholly unfit for a sedentary life; and his taste leading him otherwise, it was without regret on his own account that he relinquished his studies, though it pained him to disappoint his friends. In the following letter, after speaking of the uncertainty from which he had suffered before deciding, he says: —

"I gave up the study of the law last week, and have returned the ponderous volumes to the library at Cambridge, and have settled with the steward. I have been studying hard at Kent and Greenleaf ever since I left you, and making myself generally miserable thereby. I have not the health for such study, if I had the taste, which is also wanting. As you may guess, I have taken to farming. The last two weeks have been spent in looking for a farm near Boston. I have not yet fully decided on the spot; and to-morrow I have a farm to visit in Weston and one in Concord, but the situation I like best of those I have seen is one on the Blue Hill."

The spot at length selected was in Ashland, Massachusetts. In his eagerness to become a farmer he attached no importance to the absence of congenial companions. Perhaps his thoughts turned to the solitude of nature with the anticipation of freedom and relief from the painful pressure of social forms. He selected the place he thought best adapted to farming, and began his new enterprise with earnestness. He liked work, and took no exception to its quality. He was ready for whatever was to be done, and found a continual and varied pleasure in preparing and planting his land and harvesting his crops. He engaged a worthy man and his wife to work the farm with him and to keep his house. The following letter gives a picture of his farming life.

"ASHLAND, August 20.

"MY DEAR SISTER, — What with starting a new yoke of oxen, 'shee-a-baack!' and ditching my pasture-ground, I have had no time to write before. The oxen are doing finely, and are universally admired; they work very steadily and are up to anything. I have sold five bushels of potatoes, many of which show some signs of the rot which I prophesy will be very prevalent this fall; there never was, I suppose, such a wet summer since the flood. We have had this week new potatoes for the table, corn and beans, and a few tomatoes are ripening. My flowers are doing finely; my heliotrope is magnificent, and portulaccas begin to make a show. I have a gentleman from Cork now living under my roof, who is engaged in draining the pasture; and the monotony was enlivened the other night by an Italian with images to sell, who spent the night in my barn and refreshed the Ashland air with the classic accents of Tuscany. His home was Florence.

"*Adé*, from your affectionate brother."

During the first years he did not suffer from the isolation of his life, but by degrees it preyed upon his spirits and his health. In the long evenings his fireside was lonely. Although his walls were hung with pictures and mementos of home and travel, and his shelves filled with his favorite authors, their silent voices failed to give him the companionship he craved. If he had been married, the daily labors of the farm would have been cheered by hopes that reached beyond the harvest of the fields, and his loneliness relieved by objects of deeper interest. He finally wrote to a friend: —

> "Of all disappointments, I have learned that no young man who has not firm health and a wife can go into our farming country and give himself up to the pursuits of agriculture. My farm is for sale. Of the requisites mentioned above, I have neither the first nor second. I have only failed because my health was not improved as I expected, and because I was not made to live deprived of all society. In our country life I find that, if one has not the last-mentioned article (a wife) in his own home, he must be content to live pretty much in solitude. Of love and enjoyment of the occupation and the delightful freedom of country life, no one can have more than I."

The autumn of 1859 at length arrived. The country was generally depressed. A gloomy uncertainty prevailed at the North, and the progress of events was watched with painful anxiety. In his early manhood James had given little thought to the political strifes, or even to the general movement of public affairs. But later he had become aroused by the teachings of Theodore Parker, and his attention was strongly drawn to the condition of the Southern States. When he saw plainly the outrages of the system of slavery, he hesitated no longer, but from that moment gave his earnest heart to the work, feeling that all he could give and all he could do towards the freedom of the slave he was bound by his duty to God and humanity to offer.

Clear and strong as were these convictions, and sympathizing as he did with the high motives and heroism of Captain John Brown (though not approving of his course of action), he attended the meeting in commemoration of his death, held in

Boston, in 1860, where he remained through the day, despite the insults of an excited mob, and showed then and on subsequent like occasions his determination at all personal risks to protect freedom of discussion, and, as he said, to "give truth fair play."

In the ensuing winter he joined the Salignac Drill-Club in Boston, where he soon became a sergeant. One of his brother officers writes of this club as follows: —

"I found a new class then forming. The first day we were drilled by a sergeant who did not seem to have a power of imparting instruction. The second day by another sergeant, whose name I did not know, but with whom all things went smoothly. I was very much impressed with his simple and earnest manner. He was dressed in the blue uniform of the school, with its red binding, and seemed very much interested in his work. For several days he attended as instructor with others, and we all hailed his appearance with satisfaction. About a week after joining the class, I mentioned to one of the old members whom I knew, that I wanted very much to take some part in organizing a negro force. He said to me, 'Why don't you talk to Savage about it; he is one of your kind.' I asked him to point Savage out. He did so, and to my delight he proved to be the favorite sergeant. He seemed much interested, but said he had promised to take hold of Gordon's regiment, and proposed to me to go into it. I took his advice."

In the spring of 1861 it had become clear that war was the only alternative. A friend, who gave a dinner to a number of classmates at that time, says: —

"Savage was one of the company. Of course we were all excited, and all talked more or less about the state of the country and the war; and, although all but myself have since then served in the army, Savage was the only one that day who had decided to go into the service; and it was singular to see how simple a matter it seemed to him. There was no excitement or enthusiasm; it was to him an obvious duty, to be done as a matter of course."

A lady who was with him very often at a bowling club, during the winter of 1859–60, describes James as

"One of the men whom women instinctively trust; there was such a reserved force and gentleness pervading all his simplest actions, that one could not doubt for a moment that he might be relied upon in any emergency. On the afternoon when the news of the fall of Fort Sumter came, the young men got to the club late, and all were talking over the news very excitedly; but Mr. Savage was calm and quiet, and seemed the least affected of any, yet he was the first to apply for a commission."

In conjunction with his friends, Wilder Dwight (who after wards fell at the battle of Antietam) and Greeley S. Curtis (eventually Colonel of the First Massachusetts Cavalry), a plan was formed to organize a regiment of infantry to be offered to the United States. It was anxiously discussed at his home in Temple Place. In order to give it a high military character, two graduates of West Point, Messrs. Gordon and Andrews, who had formerly resigned their commissions in the army, were induced to take the highest appointments. Mr. Dwight undertook to get permission to raise the regiment as well as to secure funds for arming and equipping the men; while Curtis and Savage were to carry forward the organization and recruiting. Their efforts resulted in the formation of the Second Regiment of Massachusetts Volunteers, in which Dwight was commissioned as Major, and Curtis and Savage were Captains. It will be admitted by all that this regiment has been unsurpassed for discipline, for efficiency, and probably for its fearful losses of officers and men on the battle-field.

From the beginning of the enterprise James manifested a new impulse of life. The romantic feelings of his childhood had been absorbed by the military histories of former times, and the interest that bound his thoughts with never-wearied attention to the old battle-fields of England and Spain was now gathered in living power to the real strife, the actual war of his own people in a cause worthy of all sacrifice. His health improved, and, however much he suffered from indigestion, his old enemy, dyspepsia, never prostrated him. Camp life agreed with him, and he learned to laugh over the impunity with which he dined on hard bread and salt pork, — a dinner which formerly would have been to him impossible of digestion. From the day he received his appointment as Captain he worked diligently to recruit and drill his men. His company was one of the first to complete its number. He went, in company with his Lieutenant, Henry Lee Higginson (afterwards Major, First Massachusetts Cavalry), to the neighborhood of Fitchburg, where he obtained recruits of the first quality. The whole company felt James's personal influence, and, although not better drilled than some others, it was always distinguished for good behavior.

More than two months were passed in drilling and preparation at Camp Andrew, formerly Brook Farm, ten miles from Boston. On the 8th of July the regiment entered the city to take its departure for the seat of war. During the rest of that summer it remained at Harper's Ferry and Maryland Heights. There was little to do besides guard duty and drilling; but James was never at a loss for occupation and amusement in the woods and fields, and his tent was the frequent resort of those officers especially whose tendencies of thought were progressive rather than conservative, while one of those who disagreed with his opinions wrote home at this time that he never left Savage's tent without wishing to be a better man. In the autumn the regiment moved from place to place along the Potomac; as described in the following letter.

"ON PICKET ON THE POTOMAC, October 30, 1861.

"MY DEAREST ——, — Your eagerly expected letter of the 27th has just been sent me from camp. I am away on two days' picket duty with my company, about a mile and a half from our camp. We are stationed along the canal and river-bank, guarding about two miles of the shore, — a company of the Massachusetts Twelfth being on like duty above, and one of the New York Twenty-eighth below us. My company during the daytime occupies six or seven stations along the river-bank, a sergeant or corporal and eight or ten men remaining at each. At night the company is drawn in from the stations, and, divided into three reliefs, patrols the tow-path of the canal for two miles, the sentries meeting each other on their beats and being within hailing distance. By stations are meant prominent positions on the river, where is thrown up a brush hut, and a screen is formed of bushes, to prevent our fires from being observed from the other side of the river.

". . . . At nine in the evening [October 21st] we started, and walking all night reached Conrad's Ferry at half past six the next morning, in a heavy rain, the roads full of mud. We crossed the canal at that point on a canal-boat, connected with the shore by a single plank, over which the regiment had to pass, a man at a time.

"All that dismal day (the 22d) we stood ankle-deep in the mud, supporting nature by a few cold, hard beans obtained from a hospital tent. We managed to keep some fires agoing, thanks to dry rail-fences, and the men cooked their rations and stood it splendidly.

"We saw on the Virginia bank a dozen poor fellows, the remnant of the massacre [at Ball's Bluff], and with a little skiff, which would carry but one besides the man with the paddle, they were brought away safely after five or six hours' labor.

"I should have said that all the way through Poolesville and along the road we heard rumors of the catastrophe from stragglers of the Fifteenth, who had swum the river and told sad tales of the regiments cut off. At Conrad's Ferry we learned further particulars, and in the only house there I saw several wounded men brought in for shelter from the storm, — one poor fellow who had been struck in the left eye by a rifle-ball, and whose face was swollen beyond recognition. The attendant told me the ball was still in his cheek. This was my first experience of war. There were others wounded, and one lieutenant of the California regiment brought in dead out of the river.

". . . . The next day we marched back, but found that the camp had been moved in our absence two miles farther up; and so we 'toted' on and got in before dark, and again got into dry shoes and stockings (this time borrowed). We had been in not above an hour when orders came for the regiment to march for Edward's Ferry. Again started on a muddy, rutted road, and, struggling on for four or five hours, reached the general's head-quarters. Up to this point we had been kept up by the hope that we were to cross the river and meet the enemy, but we found we were not expected; some order had miscarried, or had not been sent, and we were ordered to countermarch and return to camp. The distance was about eight miles; but this was the third night that three of our companies had been on their feet, to say nothing of the days. Our Colonel told us not to compel our men to keep the ranks, and if it had been ordered, obedience could not have been enforced. We were footsore, wet, and discouraged. Some halted where they were.

Most of the officers turned in to different camps as they came to them on the road or bivouacked by the fences. Henry reached camp with difficulty, and I came in with one man alongside and two just in front. Perhaps there might have been a dozen of my company who slept in their tents that night."

The first time his company and himself were under fire was when deployed as skirmishers in the advance of the army under Banks up the Shenandoah Valley. After describing the position of his men, he says: —

"Then the shelling would be splendid for a minute or two, till the enemy retired. It was the first experience of our men under fire; and a grand display it was, like a terrible thunder-storm, only more exciting. . . . . Yesterday I picked the first flower I have seen, — a hepatica. I passed it running, for I had my company deployed as skirmishers, and was chasing away six or eight Rebel cavalry, who had the impertinence to approach our camp and fire on a squad going for water. It was getting dark; but as I ran through the wood, the flower attracted my attention, all alone as it stood up above the dry oak leaves, and I made a dash at it and captured it, though I believe the Rebels got off in safety, unless a bullet or two went with them."

He had steadily declined proffered promotion, which would remove him from his loved Second Regiment, saying that he would never leave it save for a colored regiment. But his ardent desire to aid the slave in securing his freedom was stronger than even his affection for his regiment. Major Copeland describes an interview with James when the question of raising such a colored regiment was discussed. The matter had been talked over between Major Copeland and Lieutenant Shaw, before mentioning it to James. He says: —

"Savage came to my tent, back of head-quarters at Strasburg. The tent was pitched on a delicious bit of greensward, — a rare sight in these days; and for a few moments we lay on the grass, enjoying the sky, the air, and the fragrance. Presently I began to describe our plan for a colored regiment, and our belief that through it we could insert a wedge which would not only sever the connection between master and slave, but which would aid the race in its own regeneration. At length I said, 'Now, Jim, we want you to go with us, will you?' Jim was lying down, resting on his elbow; he sprang up instantly, seized my hand, and, giving it a hearty shake, said, 'Yes, I 'll go with you, if it is only as sergeant.' No one was more disappointed at the failure of the plan, and no one would have been more proud than he to have seen his dearly loved 'Bob' leading his determined and well-drilled command into the field of action."

The following letter merits insertion as indicating his feeling on the same general subject.

"About four miles south of Strasburg, Virginia,
Sunday, March 30, 1862.

"My dearest ——, ... The march was quiet and through the most lovely country, approaching the Shenandoah range and river. The next day, Sunday, we were to have gone as far as Goose Creek, wherever that may be; but the hastily constructed bridge over the river broke down early in the day, and two mules out of a mule team became fractious and were drowned, which must have been a relief to them. So we waited all day for the bridge to be mended, and were entertained by the contrabands from the neighboring country, who flocked to see the 'sogers,' and told us strange stories that they had learned from their masters about us Yankees. How that they said that if the d—d Yankees got hold of them, they would cut their right hands and feet off, so that they could no longer be of service to their masters; and they thought that their masters had gained all the battles in the war, and had whipped us terribly, and nothing was ever said to them of the Union victories, and how sorry they were that we were not victorious at Bull Run. And then they told us of the effect that the attack of 'old Mr. Brown,' as he is here called by the blacks, had on them and their masters; how they thought he must have had some hundreds of men with him; and how all the blacks about there knew he was their friend and the terror of their white rulers. One man (almost as white as I, quite as light as Captain R——), the son of his master, and the father of nine children, two of whom he had with him, interested me very much. His boys were very handsome little fellows, about eight and ten years, and looked like Neapolitans, perhaps a little fairer. His gratitude to God, when he told us how his wife and children had all been left to him, while so many of his neighbors had lost theirs by having them sold, was very touching. He did n't know how he could ever have borne it;

they might as well, he said, have taken his heart right out of his body at once and trampled on it, and with the words came the expressive gesture.

"We talked with him and his dear little boys for near two hours, and that was my Sunday's sermon. If you had been with me you could have learned no better lesson."

One of his intimate companions said:—

"No one ever saw James so earnest and noble as when he heard the tale of suffering and outrage, and saw before him the way to right the wrongs of the suffering race, if not by his personal arm, at least by the grand sword-arm of his country."

He was promoted to be Major of the Regiment on June 13, 1862 (Lieut.-Colonel, Sept. 17); and it is the testimony of all that the period immediately after this was almost the happiest of his life. His health was good, his gayety overflowing, all diffidence and despondency disappeared, the country in which they were encamped was beautiful, and his daily rides, in the society of his favorite companions (Shaw, Russell, Copeland, and Dr. Stone), were a constant delight. The latter writes:—

"I think James was never more happy since the time he joined the army than in the short time he acted as Major after receiving his commission. The fatigue of marching was not to be compared with what he had to bear while in the line. It was only his strong determination to keep up and do his duty that prevented him many times while in the line from going in an ambulance, as I often tried to persuade him to do. At Little Washington he enjoyed himself exceedingly. The country was wonderfully beautiful, and the weather lovely; and he rode a great deal, all about the roads along the foot of the Blue Ridge, often early in the morning, coming back to breakfast all fresh and radiant, his only exclamation, 'O Doctor, I had *such* a ride!'"

We are now near the end of his career. For many years his sky had been often overcast, but gleams of joyous sunlight had illuminated the clouds; and as the sun rose higher, its fervors dispelled the mists and shadows, revealing a beautiful and noble landscape. At last the clouds were almost gone, and men saw clearly that which they had always believed was present, but hidden. But he had done his work, and shown how an earnest and pure heart could overcome both constitutional weakness and the disappointments which come to all enthusiastic men ; and now he was to meet in battle the end he had long looked forward to with earnest readiness.

In the following letter from Lieutenant Miller, formerly one of James's sergeants, we may read the story of his wounds and capture.

"The 9th of August, 1862, was a very hot, sultry day. Our brigade marched from Culpeper to within about one mile of Cedar Mountain, where we halted in a piece of woods. Our artillery was already slightly engaged with the Rebels. At about five o'clock, P. M., a brigade of our *corps d'armée* advanced and attacked the Rebels. They were soon repulsed, and *our* brigade was ordered forward. We advanced through a piece of woods, my company (A) being thrown forward as skirmishers. My company advanced to within one hundred yards of the Rebels, and we maintained our position while the regiment formed in line of battle in our rear.

"My Captain (Abbott) had just given the order to fall back on the regiment, when I was struck and fell insensible. When I recovered my senses, I attempted to walk back to the regiment, but was taken prisoner, and led about two miles to the rear of the enemy's lines, where they laid me on the ground with about one hundred and fifty more wounded. About midnight the surgeon dressed my wound, and told me that Major Savage, of my regiment, was also wounded and a prisoner. In the morning I got one of the nurses to lead me to the Major, when I laid down beside him, and we talked and chatted together to pass the time during the day. The Major was very cheerful, though in considerable pain. About nine o'clock that night the Major was put in an ambulance and taken away. The next morning I, too, was sent to the rear. . . . . Major Savage received three wounds. First, a bullet broke his right arm near the shoulder, the ball lodging in the flesh; second, another ball broke his right leg just above the ankle ; while he was falling he received a severe contusion on the left hip from a spent ball. About a week after our capture, the surgeons decided to remove the ball in his arm by cutting it out. They accordingly gave him ether. Large quantities were administered without any effect, when the Major sat up in bed, and in a few minutes the ball was removed. Three weeks from the day of our capture, Professor Davis and several other surgeons decided, in consultation, that the Major's leg would never heal, and should be amputated. Upon the Major being informed of the decision, he merely remarked, 'The sooner the better.' The same afternoon he was taken out of the ward to the tent where all amputations were performed. . . . . In about an hour and a half the Major was brought back. The leg was taken off about six inches below the knee. . . . . The next day the stump began to bleed, and it was only by great skill and promptitude that the surgeons saved him from bleeding to death. This was the first time I had any serious doubts about his ultimate recovery. But on the second day it bled again. The bleeding was stopped by applying iodine. It bled a third time, when they were obliged to open the flaps and re-tie the artery. The Major was now so low that the surgeons decided he could not possibly survive twelve hours. They gave him large quantities of brandy. Thinking he would not live till morning, and as he seemed sensible of his condition, I asked him if he would like to see and converse with a chaplain, or if he had any message to send to any of his friends. But to all these questions he answered, 'No.' His mind seemed to be at peace."

The terrible news of Cedar Mountain battle, which was to cast a gloom over many households, came almost too fast to the anxious and waiting hearts. In all cases where the enemy remain in possession of the battle-field there must he uncertainty as to the fate of many of the missing. For some days there were very confused accounts of James's fate, though the general opinion seemed to be that he was severely though not fatally wounded. The only comfort to be had was the assurance that his loved Harry (Captain Russell) had stayed to cheer and aid him, though he must in consequence become a prisoner. Captain Shaw, then serving as Aid to General Gordon, used every effort to learn his fate. He wrote thus to James's father: —

"NEAR CULPEPER COURT-HOUSE, August 12, 1862.

"DEAR SIR, — Major Savage was wounded and taken prisoner in the late engagement, as was telegraphed you. Since that message was sent we have learned that his wounds were not considered serious, and that he is in a house within the enemy's lines. Lieutenant Abbott sent him twenty dollars by a Rebel officer, and I have no doubt it will reach him safely. Captain Russell, who was taken with him, stayed, I think, to take care of him. I feel the deepest sympathy with you all, and the greatest anxiety to get near Jim.

"In great haste, very respectfully yours,

"ROBERT G. SHAW."

Again on the following day he wrote, but without having obtained further information. Uncertainty was at last removed by the receipt of a letter from the Surgeon dated August 18th, giving an account of his case and its chances, with a note also from Mr. T. J. Randolph to his friend Professor Rogers, the brother-in-law of Major Savage, saying that he would endeavor to communicate once a week with his friends of his condition. The last words written by dear James came at the bottom of the surgeon's letter, feebly traced by his left hand, to his brother, Professor Rogers.

"MY DEAREST WILLIAM, — Your friends here leave nothing to be desired. I am pretty much broken up, but am sure of the best treatment. Best love to all.

"From your Major."

Then there came a short message from his beloved friend, Captain H. S. Russell, from the Libby Prison in Richmond: —

"I was taken while tying a handkerchief round Jim Savage's leg. Write to his father that he was wounded in the arm and leg, and taken. I have not seen him since I left Culpeper, as he was not well enough to march."

After some weeks, during which occasional letters were received from the surgeon and other friends, giving rise to alternate hopes and fears, a letter came, bearing on its envelope the words, "Announcing the death of a prisoner of war." It was from Dr. J. S. Davis, stating that James had died of exhaustion, on the 22d of October, without acute suffering. His mind had been perfectly clear till within a few hours of death, after which "the circumstances which surrounded him faded from his view, and he thought himself at home."

So passed away the noble and earnest soldier, who had been the truest and most unselfish of sons, brothers, and friends, and whose sole question in the hour of doubt was, "What is it right for me to do?" When conscience answered, he hesitated not, but braced his soul to the work. The sweet steadfastness and patience with which he bore his sorrows endeared him to his enemies, and when overborne by the agonies of the surgical operations, he strangled the utterances of his pain.

This memoir has purposely omitted a reference to the loving relations of home, which are so beautifully suggested in the letters which have furnished much of this short sketch. To those who knew him well, he was inexpressibly dear, and we have seen how his comrades felt in his death the loss not merely of a friend, but something of that holier and more delicate affection which marks the love and friendship between man and woman. This extended to the men under his command, as the following letter well illustrates. It was written by one of his men while in hospital.

"CAPTAIN JAMES SAVAGE: —

"Dear and honored Sir, — Permit me, with the first returning of my strength, to pay my grateful acknowledgments to you, my duly appreciated and always beloved Captain. I think you yourself feel that none of your company, though all loving you so fully, understood the *reason* for that love as myself. O, never-to-be-forgotten days, when Captain Savage deigned a smile of approbation on the proud color-company drilling under his most gentle, yet most complete, command. How many of your men have I heard say, 'How sweet it were to die defending Captain Savage!'"

One of the agents of the Sanitary Commission, the Rev. Francis Tiffany of Springfield, while pursuing his duties in this connection, accidentally fell into conversation with a soldier. "Well," said the man, "of all the officers ever I saw, *Major Savage* was the noblest Christian gentleman."

A brother officer thus sums up his character: —

"To an almost feminine gentleness, refinement, and amiability he joined the indomitable pluck, energy, and resolution which become the man. When, before the regiment had yet been in action, officers around their camp or picket fires at night would discuss its possible behavior, there was one universal sentiment, namely, that 'Jim Savage' at least would fight, as it was once expressed, 'like Mr. Valiant-for-Truth, until his sword clove to his hand.' And this prediction he well fulfilled at Newtown, Winchester, and Cedar Mountain."

Robert Shaw wrote, after the death of his friend: —

"There is no life like the one we have been leading to show what a man is really made of; and Jim's true purity, conscientiousness, and manliness were well known to us all. The mere fact of having him among us did us all much good .... Neither shall I ever forget the three weeks I lived in the same room with him at Frederick, when I learned how truly good a man can be..... Out of his own family, there can be no more sincere mourning for his loss than in this regiment; and the best wish we can have for a friend is, that he may resemble James Savage."

1855.

GEORGE FOSTER HODGES.

Private 5th Mass. Vols. (Infantry), April 20, 1861; First Lieutenant, May 8, 1861; First Lieutenant and Adjutant 18th Mass. Vols. (Infantry), August 20, 1861; died at Hall's Hill, Va., January 31, 1862, of disease contracted in the service.

GEORGE FOSTER HODGES was born in Providence, Rhode Island, January 12, 1837. He was the son of Almond D. Hodges, Esq., now of Boston, President of the Washington Bank, and of Martha (Comstock) Hodges. He entered Harvard College in 1852, when only fifteen, as a member of the Sophomore class, and graduated with honor and the regard of his classmates in 1855. In January, 1856, he became an assistant teacher in the school of Mr. Stephen M. Weld of Jamaica Plain. This position he held for a short time only, as he sailed for Cuba during the next October. He stayed awhile at Havana, and then went into the interior as tutor in a private family. In June, 1857, he returned home, not being pleased with Cuban habits and customs. On September 14, 1857, he entered the office of Hon. Peleg W. Chandler and George O. Shattuck, Esq., in Boston, where he remained until he went to the Harvard Law School, where he joined the Middle Class in the first term of 1858–59. He finished the course, and received the degree of LL. B., and then for a while returned to Mr. Chandler's office. For the greater part of the time, until 1861 he resided in Cambridge, where he was Librarian of the Law School, and worked on the law books of Professor Parsons. He made the Index to Parsons's Maritime Law, and had a very important share in preparing Parsons's Notes and Bills, rendering valuable service in the composition of that work. He was exhaustive in his research, and, perhaps, unsurpassed in the school for thorough work. On April 20, 1861, he enlisted as a private in the

Charlestown City Guards, Captain Boyd, Fifth Regiment Massachusetts Militia, commanded by Colonel Samuel C. Lawrence, and the next morning left Boston for Washington. On May 8th he was commissioned Regimental Paymaster, with the rank of First Lieutenant, which office was abolished in the service after the return of the three months' men. He entered Alexandria, Virginia, with the Fifth, at the time when Colonel Ellsworth was killed. After the battle of Bull Run, he carried Colonel Lawrence, who had been wounded, from the field to Centreville. On July 30, 1861, he returned to Boston with his regiment; but being determined "to see the thing through," as he expressed it, he obtained a commission on August 20, 1861, as Adjutant of the Eighteenth Regiment Massachusetts Volunteers.

On January 31, 1862, at one o'clock in the morning, he died, at Hall's Hill, near Alexandria, Virginia, of typhoid fever, contracted in the discharge of his duty. He was recovering from a first attack, when a relapse came on and terminated fatally. Of him his brother writes: —

"He was so loath to speak of what he himself did at the war, that we of the family know but little of his deeds and that little was mostly learned from his comrades. By them he was always spoken of with love and respect."

Hodges was very young in college, and those of his classmates who were with him afterwards understood best his promise and sterling worth. One of them writes in the Secretary's Report of his Class for 1865: —

"I was, myself, much in company with Hodges during his residence at the Law School, at the time while I was officially connected with the college. Our old acquaintance ripened into warm friendship. His extreme youth, when we were all together, prevented his being then well known as the vigorous, noble-hearted man he in reality was, both in body and mind. He would have risen to eminence in the law; for his industry, patience, and clear perception of logical relations I have seldom known equalled. His death was to me a personal loss deeply felt. He was the more valued and appreciated, on some accounts, perhaps, because in my own profession; but his personal qualities won very much upon all who, in his maturity, had the opportunity of knowing him. To them he was loyal to the last degree. If ever man was entitled to be called a faithful friend, Hodges was that man."

All who knew him well say the same of him, and the eminent lawyers with whom he studied bear testimony to his peculiar excellence in his profession also.

"When I first heard of the death of your son," Mr. Chandler wrote to Hodges's father, "I thought I would write you a note at once. . . . . It may be some consolation to you to know how much your boy was loved and respected by others, and to feel that you have the sympathy of all who knew him. Nor is there any reason why I should not repeat, now and here, what I have often said of him while alive, that I never knew his superior in many respects. In point of ability he stood in the very first class. His great success as a lawyer appeared to be absolutely certain. More than this, he was faithful, sincere, truthful, and simple-hearted. In simplicity, manliness, and other similar qualities, I never knew his superior. He was a universal favorite in my family, and I never heard one of his college mates speak of him except in terms of praise."

And Mr. Shattuck says of him: —

"Hodges was a very diligent student, and by constant application for more than three years, had become a thorough master of the principles of the common law. Every day's acquaintance brought out more distinctly his high character and his remarkable moral and intellectual strength.

"He carefully weighed all questions of duty which were presented; and when his convictions were once formed, nothing seemed to deter him from acting in accordance with them. I well recollect the seriousness with which for several days he considered the question of entering the army. He carefully considered his duty to his family, his friends, and his country; but when the question was once decided, he seemed to have forgotten himself, and seized the first opportunity to serve his country by enlisting as a private.

"Hodges was unobtrusive, but very active in benevolent labors. While studying law, he regularly taught in the Evening School of the Warren Street Chapel. When he tried his first case, and was successful, he carried part of the fee he earned to its Treasurer, saying to him, 'This is one half of my first fee. Take it, that it may do good to others.'"

His death was too early in the war to afford opportunity for brilliant military service; but his immediate superiors, Colonel Barnes and his classmate Major Joseph Hayes, both afterwards general officers, bear testimony to his fidelity and conscientious discharge of his duty.

When Rev. William S. Mackenzie, another classmate, heard of Hodges's death, he wrote to Hodges's father as follows: —

"My acquaintance with him commenced early in the college course, and was very intimate all the way through. I never knew him to be guilty of a piece of meanness. Indeed, he always seemed to me to look on any such thing in another with surprise mingled with sadness. When others would become indignant and utter remonstrances in violent language, he was thoughtful, sad, and silent. He appeared to be incapable of understanding how anybody could descend to say or do mean things, and such as imposed on conscience. 'Foster,' I used to say, 'you are an unsophisticated fellow.' But that word did not do him justice. It was a pure noble-mindedness (is that the word?) that made him so promptly and keenly sensitive, and so averse to anything that outraged manliness.

"He was singularly affectionate, kind, and compassionate. Those qualities shone in his face, spoke in the tones of his voice, and, as I can bear witness, in many unobtrusive but significant acts. There was no selfishness apparent in anything he did or said. It did not seem to occur to him when doing a favor, however costly, that he was making any sacrifice. He loved to help any one; it cost him no effort, it was spontaneous and cheerful. There was a gush of good-will in his face, and a naturally affectionate tone in his words. I was a poor boy, with very little to help me along in college. My struggles with want were severe. Putting both hands on my shoulders, and looking into my face, Foster would frequently say, 'Mac, how are you getting along?' If reluctant to disclose the truth, in sympathetic tones of voice he would coax me to tell him. If I consented, it was sure to fill his eyes with tears. He had a tender heart; tears came quickly and easily. With a voice made husky by emotion he would often say, 'Never mind, Mac, you will get along, and come out right side up in the end.' Many a timely favor came into my hands from some unknown source in the Class. It was very evident to my mind that he was often very intimately concerned in those favors."

Colonel Lawrence, of the Fifth Massachusetts Militia, was also a classmate of Hodges, and gives the following account of the way in which Hodges enlisted, and afterwards saved his Colonel's life at the first battle of Bull Run: —

"When my regiment was called out, and we were about to start for Washington, I met Hodges on Court Street. Said he, 'Colonel, I want to go with you. Have you a place for one man more in your regiment?' I replied, 'Hodges, are you willing to go as a private?' 'Yes,' said he, 'I mean to go any how, for I can't stay at home in this war.' So we went down to Faneuil Hall, and I put him into the Charlestown City Guards as a private, and so he went to Washington. I there detailed him to write for me at head-quarters, and procured his appointment as paymaster of the regiment. While he served in the ranks, and afterwards, I never knew a more energetic, active, attentive, devoted soldier. He always went to drill, though his duty did not require it of him; but he was eager to learn, and became very thorough in his knowledge of tactics, through his desire to fit himself to become an Adjutant. He often rode with me, and was very fearless. When we went on the Bull Run campaign, my regiment, the Fifth Massachusetts Volunteer Militia, had the advance of Heintzelman's column; and, as I went at the head of the regiment through the thick woods, often in advance of the line of skirmishers, Hodges was always with me. When we came under fire, Hodges was left with the wagons, where it was proper for him to stay. But at a time when the fire was very heavy, whom should I see but Hodges, quietly walking up through it all. 'Hodges,' I exclaimed, 'are you here?' 'Yes,' he replied very quietly, 'I thought I could be of some help to you.' He then stayed with me, acting as Aid, to carry orders through the regiment, as the noise made it impossible for my voice to be heard.

"Just at the close of the battle I was wounded, while near the right of the regiment. Hodges came up and ordered the men to carry me to the rear. He had me put into an ambulance, which is the last thing I remember then, for I became insensible. Four or five men, I believe, accompanied the ambulance a short distance. In the confusion of the general retreat, the others, supposing me almost dead, and that it was impossible for me to survive, all left me; but not so Hodges. He took me out of the ambulance, which the driver had left, and, bearing me over a fence into a wood, supported me against a tree. He told me that all had gone, and I should probably be soon taken a prisoner, but that he would stay with me and be taken too. I told him to go, as it was bad enough for one to be taken prisoner. 'No,' said he, 'I shall stay, for it is not right to leave you, our Colonel, helpless here alone; and besides, I want you to understand I will not desert a classmate.' And so he stayed until assistance came. By Hodges's means I escaped captivity at that time, and probably death. He was a noble fellow, and none could wish a better friend."

Hodges died too soon for the fame which follows success, whether in arms or a professional career. He was the only member of the class of 1855 who died in the war, — a fact rather singular, since twenty-seven out of its eighty-three members served in the army. But if fidelity, in its broadest sense, — fidelity to country, friends, and duty, — is the noblest element of manly character, it can be truly said that no nobler man gave up life in his country's service than Foster Hodges.

1856.

CHARLES BROOKS BROWN.

Private 3d Mass. Vols. (Infantry), April 17–July 22, 1861; Private 19th Mass. Vols. (Infantry), August 23, 1861; Sergeant; re-enlisted December 20, 1863; died at Spottsylvania Court-House, Va., May 13, 1864, of a wound received in action May 12.

CHARLES BROOKS BROWN was son of Major Wallace and Mary (Brooks) Brown, and was born in Cambridge, Massachusetts, September 29, 1835. He was the sixth in a family of eleven children. He received his early education in the public schools of Cambridge, and at the age of eleven years entered the High School. He was a pupil of that school at the time when it was put under the charge of Mr. Elbridge Smith, who infused new life into the institution, and soon caused it to rank among the foremost schools of the country. Brown, like many others, caught a new spirit under the new administration. He had always exhibited quickness of mind and eagerness to do as well as others whatever interested him. But he had cherished no thought of ever receiving more than a common-school education, and had expected erelong to engage in the business of his father, — that of soap-making. The size of his family and the humbleness of his father's means seemed to forbid his receiving further advantages. As he himself once remarked, it had been one of his earliest pleasures as a boy to go to the College buildings on Commencement days and take a look at the mysterious alcoves of the Library, and watch the College processions, without suspecting that he himself would ever become a participant in similar scenes. But while at the High School the desire to go to college suddenly took possession of him.

Up to this time his tastes had led him to take more interest in the natural sciences and in mathematics than in the classics, and he had many deficiencies in the latter to supply, within a short time, in order to enter college with those of his class in school who had that destination. He had been particularly interested in chemistry, a knowledge of which he thought would be useful to him in what was to be his future pursuit. As he appeared to his schoolmates at this time, his chief characteristics were such as are generally expressed by the term "rough and ready." He was a favorite of the boys at their games, being strong of muscle and of an active temperament, and putting his whole spirit into anything in which he participated. He was below the average in stature, and for some time bore among his schoolmates the nickname of "Stubby," which was often changed to "Stuffy," to express his tenacity. In general, he was at this time recognized by his schoolmates as a boy of great pluck, quick mind, and good capacities, but with a relish for out-door sports, and for the every-day activities of life, rather than for persevering study.

But upon making up his mind to gain a college education, he directed all his vigor and persistency to fitting himself for admission, and with such success as to enter the Freshman class at Harvard in the year 1852, after passing a good examination in all studies except Ancient Geography.

During his college course he was very studious, and devoted himself to his prescribed duties with great assiduity. His tastes at college, as at school, were for the natural sciences and metaphysics, though he was not a poor scholar in the classics. He received a "Detur," and had parts at the Junior and Senior Exhibitions; his part at the May Exhibition of 1855 being in a Greek Dialogue. He graduated in the Class of 1856, with the rank of twentieth in a class of ninety-two members. His Commencement part was a Disquisition on "Sir William Hamilton." The mingling in him of blunt and hardy qualities with the finer traits of character so impressed his classmates, that the part given to him in the mock programme for the Junior Exhibition of October 17, 1854, was, "A Mineralogical Essay, — 'Rough Diamonds,' — by C. B. Brown."

He was obliged to depend chiefly upon himself for the means with which to meet the college expenses, and he pursued his studies and maintained his rank in the Class, subject to the interruptions caused by pecuniary necessities. He met his expenses by keeping school during the winter, and with the aid furnished by the college monitorships, and, moreover, by the use of his pen. He was quite averse to having his friends know of his habit of relying on his pen, and was himself inclined to forget, so far as he could, his efforts in that respect. For his writings comprised a strange variety of subjects. Sometimes he wrote a sermon or a theological discussion for a religious newspaper, — for he had quite a taste for theological subjects, and had a familiar knowledge of the Bible; again, it would be a novelette for a weekly paper; and then, again, it might be a conundrum sent in competition for some prize offered. His surprise one day at receiving such a prize for a conundrum which he had devised while going to recitation, and which he had sent to a New York paper, and his joy at the unexpected windfall, led to his informing one of his friends of his habit of writing for the press, which he had before kept a profound secret.

A leading quality in Brown's character as he appeared to his college classmates was persistency. When he set himself to a work, he clung to it with almost dogged obstinacy. There was also in his nature, perhaps, a natural love of contest. This showed itself in social converse in his readiness to take sides upon any subject in question, and in his enjoyment of a vigorous defence of his opinions. He was always quick and frank to announce his views, and earnest in supporting them. In work or study, a spirit of competition was easily awakened in him. In sports, too, he enjoyed the excitement of contest, and particularly enjoyed out-door exercises requiring muscular strength, because of his sturdiness of body. He had also a great liking for all games requiring thought and patience. In the game of checkers, the homely associations of which were to him pleasing, he particularly excelled; and there were few amusements he enjoyed more than coming in as a stranger upon a party of proficient players of that game at a country inn, or elsewhere, and putting to shame the champion of the village.

After graduation he selected the profession of the law, and in April, 1857, entered the law office of Messrs. Griffin and Boardman in Charlestown, Massachusetts. He was admitted to the Suffolk Bar in Boston, January 28, 1858, and soon afterwards went to the West to practise his profession. While looking for an opening, he visited Springfield, Illinois, where he made the acqaintance of Abraham Lincoln, and of his law-partner, Mr. Herndon; and after visits to St. Louis and elsewhere, he, at their suggestion, returned to Springfield and commenced practice in an office adjacent to theirs.

He took part in the political contest of 1858 between Lincoln and Douglas, making various public speeches during the campaign on the side of the former, whom he ardently admired. Upon his return to the East, he was surprised to find how little Mr. Lincoln was known in New England; and it was his delight to talk with every one on this theme. He brought home with him two good photographs of Mr. Lincoln, one of which he kept in his own room, and the other of which he hung up in the room of a friend whom he frequently visited, and where he never tired of discoursing about his hero. His enthusiasm for a man who was then little known at the East led some of his friends to smile at what they thought his extravagance of earnestness. Subsequently, upon the nomination of Mr. Lincoln for the Presidency, he felt proud to have the opportunity of lending one of his much-derided likenesses to be copied, and to see copies of it circulated in public among the first pictures of Mr. Lincoln that were seen in New England.

While he was in Springfield, Mr. Lincoln was about to send his oldest son to some Eastern college. Brown, on finding that Harvard was not regarded with so much favor at the West as some other colleges, advocated in frequent conversations with Mr. Lincoln, and with his usual ardor, the merits and advantages of his own college. He claimed that the very conservatism charged upon Cambridge was salutary to a Western boy; and that the practical tendencies and vigor of Western life would react favorably upon Cambridge. The result was, that Mr. Lincoln decided in favor of Harvard for his son.

Brown remained at the West about a year and a half, when he returned to New England and opened an office in Charlestown, Massachusetts, removing, however, afterwards to Boston. On November 14, 1860, he delivered an Oration in the City Hall, Cambridge, before the Cambridge High School Association, having been appointed orator for the occasion of its annual reunion.

He rejoiced in the election of Mr. Lincoln to the Presidency, and in the ascendency of the political principles represented by him. Thus it happened that at the outbreak of the Rebellion, in the following spring, not only was his general love of country ardent, but his special opinions and sympathies were such as to be easily touched by events. The attack on Fort Sumter aroused his inmost nature.

On the 17th of April, 1861, he left his home in Cambridge, in the morning, to go to his office in Boston, but learning that a Cambridge company of volunteers, which had been forming, was to be equipped and to leave for the seat of war immediately, he went and joined them, and that night was on board a steamer bound for Fortress Monroe, as a private in Company C, Third Regiment Massachusetts Volunteer Militia. He served with his company at Fortress Monroe and vicinity during the three months' campaign, and received his discharge July 22, 1861.

But on his return home, and after the news of the battle of Bull Run, he could not keep quiet, and without waiting to consider how he could with most ease and honor to himself serve his country, he looked around to see what regiment would be likely to leave soon for the field; and on the 23d of August, 1861, enlisted as a private in Company G, Nineteenth Regiment Massachusetts Volunteers; and five days afterwards was marching with his regiment, in which he soon became a sergeant. They were ordered to the vicinity of Poolesville, Maryland, where his company, with others, did duty in picketing the river. Passages like the following, from his letters at this time, show the interest he took from the very first in the reputation which the sons of Harvard should sustain in the war.

He writes, October 10, 1861 : —

"There is a slight prospect of our being ordered to Missouri or Kentucky. I want to go anywhere, providing I can see active service ; and if ever C. B. gets into a battle, rest assured that he will never disgrace the Class of '56 or the old Cambridge High School."

After the battle of Ball's Bluff, October 21, 1861, his company was engaged all night in removing the wounded from Harrison's Island. He writes : —

"About four o'clock in the morning, Caspar Crowninshield, of boat-club renown, turned up in shirt and drawers, with a blanket over his shoulders, after a cold swim across the river. All unite in praising his gallant conduct on the field of battle, and old Harvard has good reason to be proud of the courage and ability shown by her representatives."

Some of his vacations at school and college he had spent among the farmers of New Hampshire, where with his readiness to learn anything that was practical, he had become familiar with many of the duties of hard-working men. The following extract shows how he could turn this practical knowledge to account. He writes, December 19, 1861 : —

"Here I am, on the banks of the Potomac, still on picket duty. I have constructed a log-house, twelve feet by ten, with ridge-pole, &c., and it is large enough for my guard and myself. I have the best house on the tow-path of the canal. My practice in New Hampshire comes in play, for I always do my share. My house is bullet-proof, or very nearly so, with loopholes on three sides, and stands in a good position as regards the river ; so if the Rebels should attempt to cross, even with my small force of four men I could give them a warm reception."

In March, 1862, the regiment was transferred to the Peninsula, to participate in the campaign against Richmond. He shared in the labors before Yorktown and in the seven days' fighting before Richmond ; and throughout the whole campaign his letters show, in the gloomiest periods, no signs of despondency on his part. He writes, June 6, 1862, from camp at Fair Oaks Station: —

"I have not seen my knapsack since a week ago yesterday. Since then we have been constantly on duty, and I have not had my cartridge-box or roundabout off for eight days, except for a few moments. . . . . I enjoy first-rate health, notwithstanding the hardships of the campaign, and cannot give up my belief in the final capture of Richmond."

He writes, June 12th, of his experience in advancing pickets; and, in speaking of an order given him to send a man forward and then have the rest follow, says: —

"It looked dubious, but as I never would send a man in where I was unwilling to go myself, when the order came, on I went myself."

At the battle of Fair Oaks in June, 1862, he was wounded by a minié-ball passing through the left leg a little above the ankle. He persisted in firing his gun several times after he was wounded, and then with its aid as a crutch hobbled off the field. He was sent to the United States General Hospital at David's Island, New York.

While in the hospital he had the opportunity of receiving his discharge from the service, and some of his friends urged his procuring it. His wound seemed to him to be healing too slowly, and for a few days he was despondent, and wrote: —

"I am in doubt whether to take my discharge or not. Should I tell the doctor how I am, the discharge would be given without a shadow of doubt; but again it would look like backing out, — that I don't like."

He resolved to remain in the service, and soon had the satisfaction of finding his wound improving, so that by October 15th he left the hospital, and in November, 1862, rejoined his regiment near Warrenton, Virginia. About a month after his return the battle of Fredericksburg took place.

The following extract from the correspondence of the Boston Journal describes his conduct at the battle of Fredericksburg, December 13, 1862: —

"This regiment (Nineteenth Massachusetts) was presented with a new stand of colors, to replace those sent home stripped and torn by Rebel bullets. In the action of the 13th, the new colors had fourteen holes in them; and we are informed that they were carried by eleven different men, nine of whom were killed or wounded within one hour. Sergeant Charles Brown was the seventh man. He received a wound in the head, which stunned and for a time confused him. Lieutenant Hume, thinking his wound mortal, told him to give up the colors; but he refused, saying, 'I will not give them to any man.' Finding he was fast becoming weak, he rushed out in advance of the line, staggered and fell, driving the color-lance into the earth; and there he lay, dizzy and bleeding, still grasping the lance with both hands, until Lieutenant Hume caught them up."

Referring in his letters to the scenes of that day, he writes: —

"The color-sergeants had been shot, and no one seemed willing to take the colors, when I made the offer, and to the front I went. When I took the colors I bade farewell to life; but God saved me. . . . . The Boston Journal gave your humble servant a good 'puff,' in consequence, as I suppose, of a nearly accurate account of the affair as related by Lieutenant Hume to some correspondent of that paper. Give yourself no uneasiness, however, in regard to the wound I received. It would have felled a bullock; but the effect was temporary. I stayed with the regiment all the time, and the next day was all right, though my head was a little sore. As regards the remark of the correspondent, that 'such sergeants should be commissioned,' that will come right, if I live, unless something happens not now thought of."

After the battle of Fredericksburg followed the winter-quarters at Falmouth. The following illustrates his *esprit de corps*. Writing January 13, 1863, he says: —

"I am looking forward with somewhat gloomy anticipations to another battle. I do not fear it. Anybody who was ever with me in battle knows that I am not a man to run; but what I fear is this: the three regiments of our brigade, who always do about all the fighting of the brigade, are almost dismayed.. We have six regiments, yet the Twentieth Massachusetts, the Seventh Michigan, and our regiment know as well beforehand as afterwards, that if there is any risky job to do, we shall have to do it; and it makes the boys a little down-hearted. I have command of my company about half of the time; the Lieutenant being sick. In my company I have but twelve privates on duty; so that the boys feel, in a fight, as if their time had come. All I feel afraid of is, that the regiment may some time get into a fight, and not behave well, and lose some of their reputation. I would rather be shot half a dozen times than see the old Nineteenth run."

In spite of his hardy constitution, and although he had a year before written that he was "as tough as a knot, and could stand being wet all day, lie down in wet blankets, and wake up in the morning and not feel the effects of it," the exposures of the service began now to tell upon him; and April 24, 1863, he writes that he is "in full enjoyment of the blessings of fever and ague, and rheumatism."

While he was suffering with these sicknesses the second battle of Fredericksburg (Chancellorsville) took place. When at midnight of May 2, 1863, his regiment was marched to the river-bank preparatory to crossing, the Surgeon of the regiment advised him to remain behind on account of his sickness. But as he afterwards wrote, "Notwithstanding any unfavorable effect it might have upon me, it was my duty to try and go." The enemy prevented the laying of the pontoon bridges, and twenty-five volunteers from each regiment were called for to cross in boats. Sergeant Brown volunteered to go, but was not allowed to go, on account of being needed in his position of Acting First Sergeant. After a crossing was effected, he participated with his regiment in the fighting and labors of the 3d and 4th of May, and on the 5th recrossed.

"On reaching this side," he writes, "the excitement and nerve that had sustained me through the entire affair left me, and I was entirely exhausted, and was ordered to fall out and have my things carried, and told to take my own time to reach the camp. I have been unable to do anything since I returned."

When in June, 1863, the army moved, under Hooker towards Maryland, he was sent, against his own will and protestations, to the hospital at Chestnut Hill, Philadelphia, being almost entirely disabled with fever and ague, and rheumatism. From here he writes: —

"Sometimes I feel very hopeful, and feel that the time will be short before I return once more to active service; then perhaps the very next day I feel discouraged, and fear that I shall never again face the foe. . . . . It is the first time I have been sick to amount to anything since I was in the army; but now the old wound in my leg bothers me considerably (the one I had in the head never gave me any trouble), but I do not expect it will be long before I have a chance to get back to the front again. I hate to be away from the regiment."

He writes again, congratulating a brother upon not being drafted, since he thought their family in sending three sons to the war was doing its share, and says:—

"Don't think I am tired of the war or a disbeliever in maintaining it. I am in for carrying it on until the South will get so badly whipped that they will not *dream* of rebellion again for a century. But one family should not be called upon to make all the sacrifices; and this is why I would not have you go."

He writes from hospital at Chestnut Hill, Philadelphia:—

"I am sorry you think I have done my share in putting down the Rebellion. I do not. My experience up to this time has only served to make me anxious to conclude the war and to be in at the death. Do not imagine that I admire military service, or am at all fond of martial pomp. Far from it. But my entire sympathies are enlisted in putting down this Rebellion. It is the old conflict, — the Roundheads and the Cavaliers; and one or the other must succumb."

At length, much to his joy, he was able to leave hospital, and he rejoined his regiment November 23, 1863. On account of the absence of the commissioned officers from sickness, or duty elsewhere, he took command of the company upon his return, and three days afterwards was sharing in the fatigues and perils of the reconnoissance across the Rapidan.

For the first two weeks of December, 1863, he had a very serious question to reflect upon and decide, — that of re-enlisting. With the exception of a month's interval between his return from the three months' campaign and his second enlistment, he had now been in constant service since the very opening of the war, had been twice wounded, had received a severe shock to his rugged constitution from the exposures of the service, and was a soldier in a regiment which was so reliable, and had done such gallant service, that it was sure to find its place in the thickest of the fight in any future campaign. All this he had done and endured with no higher rank than that of Sergeant, while of a nature more than ordinarily ambitious, and while feeling as deeply as any one could that his abilities and education entitled him to be a commissioned officer. Ways were opened to him of procuring an officer's position elsewhere; friends were suggesting to him that he had done his share of the hard work of the war. But to his own mind there seemed but one line of conduct for him to follow. He must at all events continue in the war until the Rebellion was crushed; and remaining in the service, he must abide with his old regiment, and receive his promotion there, or not at all. So he writes to his parents entreating them to be contented and to overcome their natural disappointment until his furlough, at least; and on December 20, 1863, he deliberately re-enlisted in the ranks.

To those who knew his peculiar temperament, there was something more in this action than either patriotism on the one side or personal indifference on the other. For this resolute, hardy, self-trained young man there was a kind of pride in the very humbleness of his station, and in the thought that the rank which others sought through private favor or influence would come to him through his deserts, or not at all. Some personal opposition or discouragement which he encountered within his own regiment perhaps increased his unwillingness to leave it. He had spent most of his life in conquering obstacles, and could patiently bide his time while conquering a few more. He was far from being an unambitious man; but his was a kind of ambition which enjoyed the thought of suddenly emerging from obscurity and ascending several steps at once, or, should this fail, of going down to posterity as simple Sergeant Brown. This last is the alternative which fate chose for him, and this the laurel which after all suits his strong nature best.

After the usual month's furlough allowed on re-enlistment, he returned with his regiment to the army of the Potomac in March, 1864; and May 3, 1864, entered upon the campaign in the Wilderness, having charge of his company. Just as the campaign commenced, he received from Major-General Butler an appointment, which friends had procured for him, as First Lieutenant in that general's department, dated April 26, 1864. But without seeking for leave or orders to report under that appointment, he put the document in his pocket, and passed safely through the hard fighting of the first few days, until the morning of May 12, 1864, when, in command of his company, he shared in the glories of the charge of Hancock's corps at Spottsylvania Court-House.

The line of works had been carried, cannon and prisoners captured, and half of the regiment killed or wounded, when another advance was made. During this advance, while leading on his company, Sergeant Brown was struck by the fragments of a shell which burst close beside him. His right leg was taken almost off by the explosion, and his left leg was badly mangled.

Immediately after being wounded, he drew from his pocket his unused commission as Lieutenant, now stained with his blood, and a likeness of his betrothed, and told the comrades who came to wait upon him to send those home with the news of his death. He was obliged to lie on the battle-field an hour before he could be conveyed to an ambulance, was then carried three miles for that purpose, and then driven to the field hospital of the Second Corps. He was received into the hospital tent about ten o'clock in the morning, and so great was the vitality of his system, that he lived until half past six o'clock of the following morning.

After he was taken into the tent, he told an attendant that his fighting days were over, and he wished him not to leave him until he died, and to inform his parents that he died doing his duty. His mind would often wander, and at times he spoke as if to his mother, and at other times as if to his company on the field.

Two of his brothers, James and Henry, belonged to the same corps. James was wounded in the same battle, and died the same day with Charles; and after the battle had ended, Henry visited his wounded brothers. When he came to the hospital where Charles was lying, and had been recognized by him, Charles seemed anxious to know how the battle was going; and among his first questions he asked, "Shall we win the day?" Henry told him his brother James was mortally wounded. "It will be hard," replied Charles, "for mother to lose both of us"; and the news of his brother's condition more than his own approaching death, seemed to unnerve and prostrate him. From that moment he sank rapidly until the morning of the following day, when he died.

His betrothed, whom he had first known through a letter of religious counsel which she had written to him as a soldier, and to whom he had become engaged during his last furlough, was taken ill of rapid consumption upon receiving the news of his death, and died six months later with his name upon her lips.

DANIEL HACK.

Private 14th Mass. Battery, January 24, 1864; discharged for disability, March, 1864; enlisted as private in Connecticut (but unassigned), March, 1864; died of disease at Hartford, Conn., April 17, 1864.

DANIEL HACK was the son of Christopher Amory and Sarah (Seaver) Hack, and was born in Taunton, Massachusetts, December 21, 1834. He was the second of four children, all sons. From earliest childhood he was noted for the beauty of his countenance, the sweetness of his temper, and the quickness of his intellect. He had a high forehead, a full, deep-set eye, dark curling hair, clustering thickly upon his temples, and a frank, manly, and captivating expression. Though he was not tall, and his frame was slender and delicate, there was yet a remarkable grace in his light step and his upright carriage. He inherited from his maternal grandfather an accurate and retentive memory, a great love of reading, and an easy and copious flow of language both in speaking and writing.

At an early age he became a pupil of Bristol Academy, one of the oldest and best of the New England Academies, and was under the instruction and training, first of Samuel Ripley Townsend and afterwards of Henry Blatchford Wheelwright, by whom he was fitted for college. With these teachers he was always a favorite pupil, from his docility, his aptness to learn, his eagerness in study, and his correct and exemplary conduct. He was equally a favorite with his teacher in the Sunday school, and with his companions in sports and studies. His preparation for college was thorough, and he entered with honor in the summer of 1852. No young man had more of the confidence of friends, as to his future success.

In the winter of his Sophomore year he taught school in Taunton. In October of the Junior year he was compelled by ill health to leave college for a time and return home, and did not go back until the beginning of the spring term. The loss of so much time, and the difficulty of making up so many studies, were fatal to his hope of class distinction, and his rank at graduation in 1856 was not so high as had been predicted by those who knew his ambition and ability. His college course, however, was by no means a failure. His range of reading was wide, especially in English literature, and few young men could converse more intelligently on topics of general literary interest.

He intended to become a lawyer; and for this purpose entered his name with Hon. E. H. Bennett of Taunton, with whom he read law for a short time, but continued ill health and other causes prevented him from carrying out this plan.

From April, 1857, to March, 1858, he resided in the town of Richmond, Vermont, where he made many friends, who remember and speak of him with the deepest affection. Returning to Taunton in 1858, he connected himself with his father in the printing-office, in the duties of which he had long before become expert. It was the amusement of his school-days' leisure, and in after years he turned it to a useful account. His correct taste, and an eye for the beautiful in art, rendered him an adept in the business of Job Printing, and his judgment and skill were in demand among all the customers of the establishment.

When the war broke out in 1861, his patriotism was aroused; and if his physical condition had allowed it, he would probably have enlisted in one of the companies formed in his native town. In the year 1862, when Washington was threatened, and the President called for men for thirty days, he was still more anxious to go; and again, at the leaving of the Fourth Massachusetts Regiment, on its second service of nine months in the Department of the Gulf. In the course and conduct of the war he took the greatest interest, and was familiar with its operations, and ardent for the national cause. It was a mortification that his schoolmates and classmates were able to show their zeal and self-sacrifice, while he was compelled to stay at home. In January, 1864, against the wishes of friends, who knew his physical unfitness for military service, — and, indeed, without their knowledge, — he enlisted in the Fourteenth Massachusetts Battery, (Captain Wright,) then in camp at Readville. There he was detailed as clerk at the post headquarters. At a review of the troops by Major-General Burnside, he stood for several hours with wet feet; took a severe cold, which brought on a congestion of the lungs; went home on a three days' furlough, which was extended to three weeks on account of his continued illness, and returned to camp on the 14th of March. It was then found, on examination, that he was physically unfit for the service, and he was dropped without having been mustered in.

This new discouragement did not hinder him from trying again. He went alone to Hartford, Connecticut, and enlisted as a private there; but before being assigned to any regiment, was taken sick and died in Hartford, April 17th, 1864, aged twenty-nine years and four months. His relatives were with him in his last illness, and brought his body home for burial. The funeral services were held in his father's house, four days later. His body rests in the Mount Pleasant Cemetery in Taunton.

Not much more can be said of the uneventful life of this young man, whose military service was so short, and who, though he twice enlisted as a private soldier, never saw a battle. Those who knew him from early childhood, — and the writer of this notice is one of them, — knew him to be amiable, generous, honorable in his intentions, and without malice in his heart. Many have mourned that his early promise should have been clouded by physical disease and lost in premature death; yet it is their satisfaction to remember that he gave his life to the cause of freedom and his country.

STEPHEN GEORGE PERKINS.

Second Lieutenant 2d Mass. Vols. (Infantry), July 8, 1861; First Lieutenant July 11, 1862; killed at Cedar Mountain, Va., August 9, 1862.

I APPROACH with infinite reluctance one of the most difficult themes for biography to be embraced in these volumes. There hung around Stephen Perkins a peculiar atmosphere, not merely suggestive of admiration, not merely of affection, but of some indescribable commingling of the two, more subtile than either, which renders his most intimate friends unwilling to attempt his portraiture, and thus leaves the task for me. And I, his cousin and his teacher, can hardly overcome this same shrinking, or force myself to break that silence which his proud and fastidious nature would doubtless have preferred. For he made no claims, ran no race, won no prize, achieved no eminence but in dying; and perhaps from peculiarity of temperament, would have achieved none had he lived. Yet his friends were all among the most gifted young men of his day, and it is now observable that not one of these companions seems able to talk of him without a tinge of romance. So peculiar and subtile the impression of superiority which he made, I observe that it can be better measured by a certain lowering and trembling of the voice in those who attempt to describe him, than by any account they can give. One of them said, the other day: "I could write nothing about Stephen Perkins, because the simplest things I could say of him would seem like such absurd exaggeration. Suppose I should say that my few years' intercourse with him had done more for me than any other influence of my life, — who would believe it? Yet it would be the most commonplace truth."

He was born in Boston, Massachusetts, September 18, 1835. His father was Stephen Higginson Perkins, a well-known Boston merchant and a man of varied culture, whose life has been devoted in great measure to the study, and latterly to the practice, of art. Stephen's mother was Sarah (Sullivan) Perkins, daughter of the Hon. Richard Sullivan of Boston, and one of a family of sisters well remembered in that city for their charms of person and of mind. When Stephen was seven years old, I took charge of him and his two brothers, as their private tutor, residing in the family in Brookline for nearly two years. He was then a sweet, modest, lovable, boy, with a healthy and active mind, but without indications of the philosophic, introspective mood which he afterwards developed. And though his physical activity was great and constant, he was then short of stature, and only his large bones and very powerful muscles gave promise of that superb *physique* which he finally attained. Beloved as he was by all who came in contact with him, and becoming constantly a finer and finer type of noble and intelligent boyhood, yet I do not think that any one ever predicted of him the precise combination of traits and tendencies which his manhood showed.

He passed from my instruction to that of Dr. Charles Kraitsir, a learned Hungarian, whose theories of language were then attracting some attention; and he was afterwards successively the pupil of Messrs. T. G. Bradford and William P. Atkinson. He entered college with the Class of 1855, but was compelled to leave it by weakness of the eyes, and afterwards joined the Class of 1856. During most of his college career he was obliged by the same infirmity to study with the aid of a reader, his chief dependence in this way being Francis Channing Barlow, since Major-General of Volunteers. This drawback made the attainment of college rank impossible, but his remarkable abilities were fully recognized by his classmates and teachers. In his social relations, however, he had developed that peculiar reserve and imperturbability of manner which were his later characteristics; and everybody admitted it to be a good hit, when in the distribution of mock parts for an imaginary exhibition, that assigned to Perkins was "a Dissertation on Icebergs."

After his graduation he travelled in Europe, returning in

1857; spent a year in the Law School at Cambridge; but afterwards left that department of the University for the Scientific School, where he obtained a degree in Mathematics in 1861.

At this period the first trait which impressed a stranger on meeting him was his distinguished physical aspect. Those present at the College Regatta at Springfield, in 1855, will remember the admiration excited by the picked crew of the Harvard four-oar, the "Y. Y." composed of John and Langdon Erving, Alexander Agassiz, and Stephen Perkins. Three of these young men, including Stephen, were over six feet in height, and all were in the finest condition, according to the standard of training in those early days. Discouraged at the very first stroke pulled, by the breaking of the "stretcher" of the stroke-oar, they yet rowed a stern-race with perseverance so admirable, that they lacked but three or four seconds of victory, being then beaten only by the six-oar of their own University. To this result, as I am since told by one of the crew, the peculiar imperturbability of Perkins's temperament greatly contributed. He had an aversion to "spurts," and believed in a certain total of effort, to which it made no sort of difference whether his opponents were in sight or out of sight. This coolness of habit characterized his whole physical nature. He was not light, agile, nor adroit; but to whatever undertaking he addressed his rather indolent strength, that work was done.

And his beauty of face was as characteristic as that of his figure. The highest point attained, twenty years since, by American miniature-painting, in the judgment of many connoisseurs both in this country and in Europe, was a likeness of Stephen Perkins taken by Staigg about 1843. None who have ever seen it can forget the charm of those dark-blue eyes, that fresh complexion, and that open smile, — traits of boyish beauty which he always retained.

But the peculiar charm of this stately mien lay, after all, in something undefinable, a certain type of temperament, a sensation of tranquil strength, of indefinite resources, of reserved power. What he accomplished seemed far less than the victories he seemed to waive and scorn. There seemed a sort of Greek languor about him; not the best temperament for usefulness perhaps, nor even for happiness, but undoubtedly the most potent for personal fascination, though he would not have deigned to use it consciously for any such end. He seemed to attempt nothing; in fact it was the drawback upon his life that he did not greatly care to attempt anything; and yet his mere preferences seemed to carry more weight than the vigorous efforts of other men. Each of his associates had some anecdote to tell, showing how Stephen had at some time "conquered without the crossing of bayonets," effecting by a single quiet word or look what others had toiled and stormed in vain to accomplish. Quite democratic in his theories and sympathies, — though he never got credit for this with strangers, — and utterly despising every affectation of personal or social advantage, yet he had at his command all the haughtiness of a Venetian nobleman, and could at a moment's notice put barriers insurmountable and immeasurable between himself and any offender.

The sort of temperament which Charles Reade endeavors to describe in his Lord Ipsden in "Christie Johnstone" — but without there freeing it from a certain air of affectation — was natural and almost controlling in Stephen Perkins. Holding in his hands youth, beauty, culture, social advantages, he seemed yet to grasp them all lightly, as if for the next breeze to bear away. He dallied with his great powers, not in mere indolence, still less in conceit; but as if some hidden problem were first to be solved before these trivial faculties could become worth exercising. Meantime it was the very consciousness of this unstated problem which seemed to give him his influence. This delaying quality was the very thing that charmed. It suggested vast spaces of time and hidden resources of ability. It was not alone that thought in him lay behind action, but something else seemed to lie behind thought; as in a machine-shop the flume is behind the wheel, and the silent reservior beyond the flume. His control of those about him was not a thing won by effort, but a thing possessed in virtue of mere head-of-water.

Thus it was noticeable that his intimates seldom praised him for this or that special gift, except perhaps that of conversation, but always labored to carry their explanations back to some ultimate force, expressed or implied. And it is equally remarkable that their enthusiasm bore no reference to any expected success in any special direction. Usually the admiration and the predictions of young people go together; where they see gifts, they expect miracles. In his case they seemed to recognize a rarer quality than that which wins success, and they were content to allow him a whole eternity to grow in, demanding nothing meanwhile. They did not pretend to understand or explain or justify him; they only knew that there was but one Stephen Perkins. It was a dangerous form of admiration; a weaker person would have been spoiled by it. He only received it all with that same equanimity with which he took everything else. When his friends were pleased, they called this stoical mood philosophy; when they were a little provoked, they called it laziness; when very much provoked, they called it conceit, — and revoked the phrase in self-contrition the next day. For they knew very well that under all this motionless surface there was a nature absolutely noble, that would gladly give up all the superficial joys of life, could it but live itself out clearly and find its true career at last. And older men and women, whose society he always rather sought, found him modest, gentle and truthful, though they might miss something of that fresh enthusiasm which seems the proper birthright of youth.

It is almost needless to say, after what has been said of his temperament, that he had a choice taste in books, and knew his Emerson from beginning to end. He liked, too, to hear Theodore Parker preach, but would not acknowledge to any positive thrill of the blood from that powerful electric battery; and if moved thereby to any special act of courage or self-sacrifice, would have been sure to keep it out of sight. Habitually defending all who where attacked or criticised, he also habitually understated all emotions; and when the war came, treated it as he treated the rest of life, with only a sort of guarded and critical interest. He held it at arm's length for philosophic consideration. Of course life was nothing; but after all, might not the whole game, about which the nation was excited, prove as valueless as the particular pawn which was all he could contribute if he took part? Even when he had actually enlisted, he was very willing to let it be supposed that it was only from *ennui*, or because he was tired of being asked whether he were not going. One of his intimates told me that he only once ventured to put the question to Stephen point-blank, why he went into the army, and then he only replied, with his accustomed shrewd, meditative smile, that "it was an ancient and honorable profession." But one of his female relatives has since said that at the outbreak of the war, on her remarking to him, rather heedlessly, that the war was not likely to come home to their two lives, for instance, in any immediate way, — he answered, with an unwonted seriousness that was almost sternness, "I do not know that it will make any difference in your life, but it is likely to make a very great difference to mine." In a few days he had enlisted.

In passing to the sequel of the story, it would be easy for a stranger to conjecture that this proved one of the cases where the war gave the needed fulness and completion to a life otherwise incomplete. But I do not think it was so with Stephen Perkins. With his rare powers, and his sensitive, haughty nature, the course of development was not to be so easily rounded. On the 8th of July, 1861, he was commissioned Second Lieutenant in the Second Massachusetts (Infantry); was promoted First Lieutenant in the same month of the following year, and was killed within a month after his promotion. The intermediate period was the most tedious epoch of the war, and he was engaged in its most tedious service, in the Army of the Potomac. Danger and exertion would have seemed to him worthy the sacrifice they brought; but he chafed under a forlorn and monotonous routine, and amid a seemingly aimless waste of resources. Life, which had appeared of little value at home, seemed utterly valueless there, and the secret languor of the blood increased rather than diminished. His letters showed much of his accustomed philosophy, but no enthusiasm and little enjoyment. None of them are now accessible to quote from, and I speak of them from memory alone. He complied with forms which he detested, fulfilled a routine which he undervalued, and saw a seemingly useless campaign draw its slow length along. It will always remain uncertain what influence active service might have had in concentrating his powers of action and developing the latent enthusiasm of his nature. But it is certain that inactive service, under generals in whom his shrewd sagacity put no faith, and with noble companions whose lives he saw wasted, gave neither joy nor tonic to his nature.

The disastrous battle of Cedar Mountain, the first important engagement of the Second Massachusetts, took place on the 9th of August, 1862. The regiment was under fire but half an hour, yet of twenty-two officers who went in only eight came out unhurt; five were killed, five wounded, three others wounded and captured, and one captured while attending a wounded comrade. Of the five killed, three stand recorded in these volumes, — Abbott, Goodwin, and Perkins, — besides Savage, who died of his wounds. Of those five killed, moreover, three went into battle almost too ill to stand, of whom Stephen Perkins was one. "All our officers behaved nobly," wrote Robert Shaw after this battle, in a letter which will be found elsewhere in full. "Those who ought to have stayed away did n't. It was splendid to see those sick fellows walk straight up into the shower of bullets as if it were so much rain; men who, until this year, had lived lives of perfect ease and luxury."

In a contest so hot, individual casualties pass for a time unnoticed, and often the precise facts can never be established. Robert Shaw says: "The men were ordered to lie down until the enemy came nearer. Almost all the officers kept on their feet, though." This readily explains the fearful loss among those thus prominent. It is stated by Colonel H. S. Russell, then Captain in the Second, that when the regiment had been in position about twenty minutes, Stephen Perkins received a wound in his right hand, but refused to go to the rear, saying that a handkerchief was all he wanted, and this was given him. Ten minutes afterwards, Russell noticed him again, and in a few minutes more, when the regiment was withdrawn, he was not in his place. The body was found a little way to the rear, pierced with three bullets.

His remains were identified on the next day by General Gordon and Captain Shaw, and were, after due preparation, sent to Washington, and thence to Oakhill Cemetery, Georgetown. There took place on the 25th of September that simple and touching funeral ceremony, the narrative of whose pathetic loneliness has touched many hearts; while it was yet more consonant with the nature of Stephen Perkins than would have been any priestly or military splendor. The services were performed by Rev. John C. Smith of the Fourth Presbyterian Church in Washington, who thus describes the scene: —

"There were but four of us, — the father, Dr. Francis H. Brown, Surgeon of Judiciary Square Hospital, and a young ministerial friend, Mr. D. R. Frazier, from the Union Theological Seminary, New York. As we were about to leave the Superintendent's house, I beckoned to three wounded convalescents near by, and said to them, 'Boys, I have come here to bury a young officer; we have no guard, fall in and act for us.' They obeyed promptly, giving the usual military sign. We went to the vault and received the body; then moved in the following order, namely, Superintendent and convalescents in front, myself and the young minister; the body carried by hand; the father leaning on the arm of Dr. Brown (also a Boston man). . . . .

"Reader, if you visit the metropolis and desire to see the grave marked by the marble placed there by the father's love, go to the monument of the Russian Ambassador, M. de Bodisco, and a few yards eastwardly you will see the spot where lie the remains of the gallant young Lieutenant of the Second Massachusetts."

Thus closed the brief earthly life of one whose slow and large development would alone seem enough to guarantee immortality, in a universe where nothing runs to waste. To Stephen Perkins, with his haughty humility, the accidents of place and fame were nothing, and the most unnoticed funeral and briefest record would have appeared most fitting. And he who, with no steady hand, has woven this slight tribute to the noble promise that he loved, may now gladly let the garland drop, and leave the rest to silence.

1857.

HOWARD DWIGHT.

First Lieutenant 24th Mass. Vols. (Infantry), September 1, 1861; First Lieutenant 4th Missouri Cavalry, October 4, 1861; Captain, September 4, 1862; Captain and A. A. G. (U. S. Vols.), November 10, 1862; killed by guerillas, Bayou Bœuf, La., May 4, 1863.

HOWARD DWIGHT, fourth son of William and Elizabeth A. Dwight, and grandson, on the mother's side, of Hon. D. A. White of Salem, was born in Springfield, Massachusetts, October 29, 1837. His characteristics in boyhood were great sweetness of disposition, accompanied by a spirit which would suffer no encroachment upon his rights; great simplicity and ingenuousness, with straightforward honesty of purpose, manly resolution to persevere in whatever he undertook, and excellent mental powers. His father said of him while he was a school-boy, that it was an intellectual treat to study a lesson with him, his mind was so clear and so true in its operations. He was affectionate, but undemonstrative. Refined and gentlemanly in his bearing, he was reserved, even to those of his own household, — who were accustomed to say of him, that he spoke only when he had something to say worth saying, and when he did speak it was always to the point. In the year 1850 he entered Phillips Exeter Academy. Mr. Soule, the respected Principal of the Academy, thus writes of him: —

"I remember him as a lad of thirteen, full of health and joyous activity, frank, impulsive, and attractive to his classmates and companions. In his intercourse with his instructors he was always trustworthy and manly in his bearing. During his last term here, his habits of study improved so rapidly, and his progress was such in exact scholarship, that I regretted his leaving. His character and general deportment were unexceptionable."

He was prepared for college by Thomas G. Bradford, Esq., of Boston, for whom he always expressed great affection and esteem. That the regard was reciprocated by this teacher is apparent from the following tribute from his pen. Mr. Bradford writes: —

"I think I appreciate the character of Howard. I know his noble and endearing qualities, his warm and kind impulses; his affectionate, true, frank, generous heart; his clear, discriminating, well-balanced intellect; his energy of purpose, decision and straightforwardness in will and action; his lofty notions of right and honor, and other traits of mind and heart which made him so true a man. I can say of him, that I not only loved him, but, although he was a mere boy when I was connected with him, that I truly respected him.

He left Mr. Bradford's school to enter Harvard College in the year 1853. He had passed a brilliant examination, and gave every promise of taking high rank in his Class. It was said of him by the distinguished President of the University, Dr. Walker, that, "as easily as he could put forth his hand, he could take the highest honors of the Class, if he applied himself to that object." Although he allowed himself to be diverted from it, and failed to accomplish what had been hoped for him as to college rank, he succeeded in awakening a strong interest in his instructors; and among his Class he was an object of enthusiastic regard. After his death, besides passing the customary resolutions expressive of their sorrow at his loss, they addressed a letter to his family, of which the following is an extract: —

"His position among us was so peculiar, both in the influence which he exercised and the regard in which he was held, that it was our general desire, when we came together upon the occasion of his death, that, besides the resolutions adopted as a public tribute to his memory, a private communication should be made to his family, in which a freer expression could be given to our sentiments, and which, by its informality, should the more feelingly assure them how important we estimate the loss we have sustained."

This letter contains a just and discriminating analysis of his character as a man and as a scholar, and perhaps indicates, clearly enough, the faults which stood in the way of his taking the high rank in his Class to which his uncommon abilities seemed to entitle him. The following passage occurs in it: —

"He was a leader among us from our earliest college days, and had continued the object of our increasing pride and hope. Intellectually, it is not invidious to say he had no superior in our ranks. He combined in his mental constitution rare clearness of judgment and quickness of perception, with a tenacious memory and singular felicity of expression; and to these gifts added a remarkable eloquence of manner in public speaking. His prominent characteristics seem to us to have been energy, intrepidity, and public spirit. His cast of mind was thoroughly practical, not given to subtleties or abstruseness, but regarding what was broad, practicable, and expedient. He was earnest as a partisan, and full of the inspiration of leadership, but knew how to be courteous towards his opponents, and just to their positions; while in public and in private he set forth his own opinions and maintained his own principles, with cogent force and fearless resolution. His energy was something exhaustless, and he showed as much acuteness in the construction of his plans as he did unwearied persistency in their prosecution. If his restless vigor was sometimes difficult for himself to govern, as it was for others to withstand, it was generally subjected to prudence, while his ardent ambition was regulated by generous feeling and guided by masterly executive skill. These effective and manly qualities were the basis even of his faults; but if his forcible temperament, his unbounded vitality, and exuberant animal spirits ever led him into errors, they did not vitiate the refinement of his sensibilities nor impair the genial heartiness of his disposition. His calmer nature was sensitive and elevated, and he often betrayed in his looks or language a singular simplicity of feeling, half unsuspected to those impressed by his more salient characteristics. His ready kindness of feeling was indicated in a smile of peculiar sweetness, and a manner which he could make most winning, adapting himself with grateful skill to persons of divers characters or positions. Affable and courteous in general, among his nearer associates, he was genial and affectionate, and possessed a brilliant combination of qualities which we shall never cease to miss in our reunions. . . . . While we lament him, it is still with a just pride in the rich sacrifice we were able to make, when so valuable a life was manfully surrendered to a sacred cause. . . . . It is a still greater consolation, as we reflect upon his death, to remember that it was with a warm and intelligent personal interest that he engaged in the cause to which he has given his life. We do not forget that he was impelled, not merely by the ardor of adventure appropriate to our years, but by a manly devotion to the principles which the cause of our country represents, an earnestly cherished conviction which he had manifested long before it became necessary to support those principles by arms. That he felt their importance, and would have deemed their triumph worth his life, may assist our resolution to resign him without complaint, if not without sorrow."

Howard Dwight never ceased to cherish the scholarly and literary tastes which had been so marked in him during his college life, but from which it might have been apprehended that the activities of business and army life would have a tendency to divorce him. When he and his brothers left home for the army, it was remarked that, though they, unwilling to be drawn aside from the study of their new profession, were content to take with them only books of a purely military character, he could not be happy unless he had Shakespeare, Tennyson, and Macaulay for his daily companions. The hard-worn volumes give evidence of his constant use of them. After leaving college he repeatedly expressed himself tempted to follow the bent of his tastes, and continue his education in some foreign university; but other considerations had weight with him, and he soon turned his attention to manufacturing, "with the purpose," to use his own language, "of making himself master of its theory."

He was thus occupied until the summer of 1859, when it was proposed to him to take charge of building and running a cotton-press in Memphis, Tennessee.

Hitherto he had engaged in no pursuit that had properly tasked his energies. His life had been an easy one, admitting of leisure and self-indulgence. He eagerly welcomed the prospect of duties which, he well knew, while they offered a good field for the exercise of his abilities, would demand of him constant labor and self-denial.

He went to Memphis in September, 1859. His duties during that and the following winter were severe. He writes of rising, in midwinter, at six o'clock, so as to be at the press when the men went to work at seven; and as he was unable to leave his work at noon, to go to the hotel for dinner, he found himself, to use his own language, "obliged to be satisfied with the corn-bread and bacon which the negroes live on." He adds: "I have been running the press, too, at night, so I have only been able to let up between the hours of six and seven in the evening. You may fancy the relief brought to my somewhat overwrought body and mind by the advent of Saturday night."

This life was a good preparation for that upon which he was so soon to enter, in the army; and in the performance of his duties as a man of business in Memphis, he showed the same energy, ability, and fidelity for which, as a soldier, he was afterwards distinguished.

His life was made, as he expressed it, "one of turmoil and trouble," during the winter of 1860-61, by the beginnings of rebellion in Tennessee, the State of which, as he said, he had "become by residence, voting, and everything else that could make him so, a citizen." "I have had my eyes," he writes, "suddenly opened to the fact that we are not one people, and that I am almost certain to become a foreigner, while supposing myself at home."

He writes, on one occasion, of going about among his secession friends, crying "Liberty and Union, one and inseparable," and adds, "I don't know that I did any good; but it certainly raised agreeable emotions in my breast, if not in theirs."

One thus frank and earnest in avowing his Union sentiments could not but find himself in an uncomfortable position as a citizen of Tennessee in April, 1861. Howard Dwight was not a man to be easily intimidated, but, from the day that Sumter fell until he left Memphis, a month later, his situation was not without peril, and to his friends at home this was a season of great anxiety on his account. For weeks before he left Memphis he must have appreciated the danger. The "rag of Secession," as he called the Rebel flag, was raised, and the voice of Secession was loud about him. A man less faithful to duty might have sought his own safety, and left his post at once. Not so with him. He was careful for the safety of those in his employ; and, at an early period, he sent away a faithful Irish laborer, whom he knew to be true to the Union. But, for himself, he had charge of the property of another, and he would not leave it without permission to do so.

Meantime, communication between Massachusetts and Tennessee was interrupted. He could get no letters from home; he knew nothing of what was occurring outside of Memphis. At last, everything around him told him that liberty and even life would be endangered by remaining longer among rebels and traitors. He came away, hardly knowing if he had a country.

The first evidence he had that the cause of the Union was not so desperate as was indicated by his rebellious surroundings was in seeing the American flag waving at Cairo. His eloquent account of the emotions awakened by the sight of the stars and stripes will not be forgotten by those who heard it. It was not his wont to talk about his own feelings; but as he told us how the sight affected the passengers on the boat, that there was not a dry eye among them, and that he saw two strong men throw themselves on each other's neck and weep, we felt that he too had had a baptism of suffering, and had come out of it strong for noble action.

The Rebellion was destructive to his business prospects, but to that aspect of it he gave no heed. Pecuniary considerations at such an hour could have no weight with him. He at once applied himself to aiding his brother Wilder, then Major of the Second Regiment Massachusetts Volunteers, in procuring arms for that regiment, and turned his attention, without delay, to seeking a commission for himself in our army.

He entered the service the 1st of September, 1861, as First Lieutenant in Captain Stackpole's company in the Twenty-fourth Massachusetts Regiment. While he was recruiting for his company in Northfield, Massachusetts, he received the following letter from his brother Wilder: —

"PLEASANT HILL CAMP, NEAR DARNESTOWN,
September 6, 1861.

"DEAR HOWARD, — Advice is cheap. When lost, it goes to the moon, according to the old superstition, and does no harm. Hear mine. General Frémont is on his way to Memphis. As sure as sunrise, he will go there. Go with him. Now is the opportunity for adventure, for success. Energy and aptitude are in demand. This autumn they will bear fruit. The wheel is entitled to every man's shoulder; offer yours. In other words, pack your trunk, take a few letters of introduction and authentication from the Governor and others, go to Frémont, tell him you wish to serve in his army. . . . . You will do yourself credit, and be in the midst of some of the most brilliant achievements of the war. I have said my say after reflection, and from a near view of the field.

"Yours affectionately,

"WILDER DWIGHT.

"TO LIEUTENANT HOWARD DWIGHT."

He returned home without delay, being induced to follow the advice of his brother by the fact that he had been a citizen of Tennessee for two years previous to the breaking out of the Rebellion; and where he had faced Secession he chose to fight it.

The second day after his return from Northfield he had furnished himself with the necessary letters, had taken leave of his chosen friends and companions of the Twenty-fourth Regiment, from whom it was hard to separate himself, and was on his way to the Department of the West. On October 4, 1861, he was appointed by General Frémont a Second Lieutenant in Company C, Fourth Regiment Missouri Cavalry, Frémont Hussars.

On the 21st of March following he was commissioned by the Governor of Missouri as First Lieutenant, to rank from the 4th of October, 1861. At the battle of Pea Ridge he held a responsible position, concerning which he wrote soon after as follows: —

"On the morning of the 6th of March, when the battle may be said to have opened, I found myself in command of our camp, all my senior officers having been sent with detachments on expeditions before the enemy's advance was known, not to rejoin us until the

7th. I had somewhat over one hundred men under me, and was to have formed the rear-guard of cavalry for Sigel's and Asboth's divisions, but, owing to delay on the part of other cavalry, ordered for advance-guard, the arrangement was suddenly changed at three, A. M., we having been ordered to be ready to march at two, A. M., and I was ordered to the advance with fifty men."

He showed himself entirely equal to the duties which devolved upon him. On the 7th he made a charge upon the enemy, the effect of which was favorable to the success of our arms during that part of the engagement. From the time of his promotion to a first lieutenancy, he was doing the duty of a captain, although his promotion to a captaincy was long deferred.

On the 1st of May, 1862, his name was sent to the Governor of Missouri for promotion to a captaincy, but as late as August 5th he wrote: "You are right in continuing to address me as Lieutenant. My promotion is based on the transfer of one of our captains to a battery of which he has been in command for some time. Until this is accomplished, my title will not come."

It was not until the 4th of November, 1862, that he was appointed and commissioned, by the Governor of Missouri, as Captain, Company C, Fourth Regiment Missouri Cavalry, to rank from the 4th of September, 1862.

Captain Dwight's duties while in the Department of the West were arduous and severe. In the midst of these labors, a year from the time he left his home, he received the sad tidings of the death of his brother Wilder, who fell at Antietam. On this occasion he wrote from Helena, Arkansas, September 31, 1862, as follows: —

"I cannot think of it as real yet; the void it makes in the home that is almost constantly in my mind is so great. I had seen by telegram, in one of the papers, that Wilder was wounded, but some how had not for a moment felt it possible that he could be lost to us. To me he has ever been the most affectionate brother and truest friend when I have most needed aid.

"It is a great comfort to me, however, to reflect that his death was one which had no horrors for him, and to the possibility of which he looked forward so cheerfully; and I glory in his career as a soldier, though the end is so hard to bear. I need not assure you how fully you and father and all at home have my sympathy in this affliction, and how much I regret that I cannot be at home to be of some use or comfort to you. I feel that I can do nothing better, however, than, where I am, to imitate, as closely as I may, the bright example that Wilder has given me. I am under marching orders, and shall be more than ever glad of the change to active service."

He passed unharmed through the hardships and dangers of the Missouri campaign; and on the 10th of November, 1862, he was appointed by the President of the United States Assistant Adjutant-General of Volunteers, with the rank of Captain, and ordered to report in person to Brigadier-General George L. Andrews, United States Volunteers.

On the staff of General Andrews, Captain Dwight saw active service in the Department of the Gulf. Important duties were assigned him, which he performed ably and faithfully. He participated in all the stirring scenes of the Têche campaign, during the spring of 1863, and there distinguished himself by his gallantry as he had done on the battle-field of Pea Ridge. There, too, he escaped unharmed, though constantly exposed to the shot and shell of the enemy, and at one time having his horse shot under him. He escaped, however, only to fall two weeks later, under circumstances peculiarly distressing to his friends, who would have asked for him "a death more consonant with his ardent and heroic temper." At the time of his death, May 4, 1863, he was temporarily attached to the brigade of his brother, Brigadier-General William Dwight, Jr., to whom he was bearing despatches from General Banks. General Dwight's official report of the day's operations contains the following: —

"An event occurred to-day of a nature distressing to me, personally, and of such a character as to demand the attention of the authorities in this department, that we may know upon what terms we are waging this war. Captain Howard Dwight, Assistant Adjutant-General to Brigadier-General George L. Andrews, was murdered to-day under the following circumstances. Captain

Dwight had passed the artillery attached to this brigade in a wagon in which he was driving, when, finding his progress impeded by the army wagon train, he left his wagon, and mounted his horse to ride forward and join my advance.

"He had passed a point at which there is a turn in the Bayou Bœuf, when he was ordered to halt. He was in a place where all previous experience authorized him to suppose that he was in little or no danger. In fact, the account given by an eyewitness shows, so far was he from suspecting danger, that, on being ordered to halt, instead of putting spurs to his horse, which would probably have insured his escape, he deliberately turned, and walked his horse back to see what it meant. On reaching the edge of the Bayou, he found himself confronted by three Rebel cavalrymen, who were on the opposite side of the Bayou, at the water's edge. He asked, 'Who are you?' The reply was, 'Who are you?' and immediately the three rifles were brought to bear upon him. In this position he submitted to the necessity of the case, and surrendered himself a prisoner. One of the Rebels then said, 'He 's a damned Yankee; let 's kill him.' Captain Dwight calmly replied, 'You must not fire. I am your prisoner.' Again the Rebels said to each other, 'Kill the damned Yankee'; and immediately one of them fired. The ball passed through Captain Dwight's brain, killing him instantly. The scene was witnessed by two boys, who remained by the body until the arrival of our cavalry, who were but three minutes behind when the event occurred, and hearing the report of the rifle hastened forward. These boys bear testimony to the calm courage with which Captain Dwight met his fate, under circumstances far more trying than those generally presented amidst the excitement of the battle-field.

"He died with the same imperturbable bravery which had marked his life. His placid features, after death, retained the same expression which had been natural to him in life. They showed that, whatever are the horrors of an execution, this execution possessed no terrors to him."

The body, under the charge of his younger brother, Lieutenant Charles Dwight, was immediately taken to New Orleans and borne to his former residence, there to await the departure of a steamer which should transport it to his home in Massachusetts. A guard of men, detailed for the purpose from the Forty-seventh Massachusetts Volunteers, was placed around the house both day and night.

The brother and immediate friends of the deceased wrapped the coffin in the American flag, and covered it with flowers. These arrangements being concluded, they left the apartment and retired for the night. When, the next morning, the afflicted brother again entered the room, a scene presented itself which showed that there were others, besides the immediate friends, who sought to pay their tribute of respect to the memory of this brave son of New England.

Members of the Union Association of Colored Women had visited the room early in the morning. They had brought white linen, with which they had covered the furniture of the room, and upon which they had sewed green leaves. They had filled the room and covered the coffin with the freshest and sweetest flowers, made into wreaths and bouquets. They had made the scene one upon which the eye rested with delight. Each morning this labor of love was repeated. Each morning the faded flowers of the previous day were removed, and those of fresh beauty and fragrance took their place.

Before Lieutenant Dwight left New Orleans, he attempted to express his thanks to those who had shown such tender care for him whom he mourned. He said to one of their number, "I want to thank you, but I know not how to express my thanks." "You owe us no thanks," was the reply; "who are *your* friends if *we* are not? All we ask of you is, that when you go home, you will tell the Northern people how we feel, and say to them that we want our husbands and our sons to be allowed to fight in this war."

Captain Dwight was the object of enthusiastic regard in the Department of the Gulf, as he had been in the Army of the West. After his death, resolutions were passed by his brother officers, showing that in that relation he was hardly less valued than he was by the band of classmates who soon after met to give expression to their love and grief in terms so tender and affectionate, and so keenly appreciative of his worth, that they fell like balm upon the wounded hearts of his family.

General Banks, in a letter to the Rebel General Taylor, in relation to the murder of Captain Dwight, says of him: —

"Captain Dwight was one of the most upright and exemplary young men of his country. Never, in a single instance, in his short but brilliant career, had he failed to recognize what was due from a high-toned and brave officer. On our march to Opelousas, and while in occupation of that town, he exerted himself to the utmost to restrain lawless men from infringement upon the personal rights, or the appropriation to their own use of the property of citizens of that town, and contributed much to bring to the punishment of death men who had violated alike the laws of war and of property. His name and character were without blemish. The man does not live who can charge upon him the commission of a dishonorable act, or the omission of any duty imposed upon him by the laws of humanity or of honor. It is deeply to be regretted that such a man should lose his life under such circumstances; but it illustrates too strongly the conduct of the troops in that and other campaigns, to allow it to pass without permanent correction. And if the sacrifice of his life shall result in suppressing so flagrant an abuse of the rules of war, he will have achieved as great a good as other men accomplish in the longest life. His career will have closed with the evidence of his untiring efforts to restrain lawless men from the commission of crimes; and the sacrifice of his life will illustrate the open and flagrant disregard of these principles by the men in arms against his country."

His funeral, in New Orleans, was attended by some of the best and highest in the land. From old and young he had won affection and esteem. The church was thronged with those eager to pay him the last tribute of respect. At the request of a friend, classmate, and brother officer, his favorite hymn which he so often sang, "I would not live alway," was given a place in the funeral services. When they were concluded, a large concourse of people followed the funeral procession to the steamship which was to convey his body to the North; and as the box containing it was about to be lowered into the hold of the vessel, flowers were strewn upon it by the hands of those who knew Howard Dwight only as he would most wish to be known, as a true patriot and soldier, ready, as he had more than once declared, to give his life for his country.

JAMES AMORY PERKINS.

First Lieutenant 24th Mass. Vols. (Infantry), September 2, 1861; killed at Morris Island, S. C., August 26, 1863.

JAMES AMORY PERKINS was born in Dorchester, Massachusetts, on the 9th of July, 1836. His father was William Perkins, a merchant in Boston. His mother was Catherine Callender, daughter of John Amory, Esq., of Dorchester. Both his parents survive him.

His youth was passed in Boston. At school he is remembered as having been at first an exceedingly quiet boy, in fact almost too studious and retiring; by degrees, however, becoming more social in his ways, and developing something of the humorous disposition which afterwards became so prominently characteristic of him. He was not a strong lad, and enjoyed little of that pleasure which comes from robust and exuberant health; but his powers of endurance, as shown in walking and boating, were excellent, especially for a boy of his apparent want of strength. His force of will could control the sense of fatigue, though it could not impart power to the muscles. At school he was always a hard worker, and a faithful, diligent, and accurate student. His powers of mind were excellent, and his standing was always among the first.

At the age of sixteen he made a voyage to England for the benefit of his health. At this time, although he had been for years pursuing the study of the classics, he had given up the idea of entering college, thinking that a more active life would agree better with his constitution. Accordingly, on his return from Europe, he went into his father's counting-room, but remained there only a short time. He found that he could not be satisfied without availing himself of the advantages of a liberal education, and therefore returned to school, and finally entered college in July, 1853.

His college life was very successful in every way. He

thoroughly enjoyed it. He was active and diligent in improving the opportunities afforded him of acquiring knowledge, and his abilities enabled him easily to take a high rank in scholarship. He naturally fell in with the literary tone of Cambridge, and his reading was thorough and extensive, chiefly in historical and in critical works. With all this, he was a genuine lover of the social life within the college walls, and no one was more sought after than he for the various societies and friendly clubs which constitute such a delightful part of the student's life. At the close of his course he had risen in rank to a very high place; he had read much, and to more purpose than almost any one else, and he had participated in the social life of college as much as those who had neglected their studies and literary culture.

On leaving Cambridge he made up his mind to devote himself to business. He left at once for Calcutta, to acquaint himself with the East India trade, with which his father's house was mainly concerned. There and in Bombay he remained about a year. He returned to his country by way of Europe, after travelling in Italy, Switzerland, France, and England, and reached home in June, 1859.

He at once settled down to business in his father's counting-room in Boston, and remained there, working faithfully and zealously, as was his wont, for two years, until the commencement of the war. He was surrounded by his old friends, classmates, and others, and his society was most eagerly and constantly sought. His literary tastes were always a source of enjoyment to him, and his mind was continually being enlarged and strengthened by sound and various reading.

On the breaking out of the Rebellion, he threw himself into the service of his country with all the strength of his character. Nothing could restrain him from going into the army. His health was far from being firm, but his power of will seemed equal to overcoming even this great obstacle. He sought for and obtained a commission of First Lieutenant in the Twenty-fourth Regiment Massachusetts Volunteers, which was then being raised by the late lamented General Thomas G. Stevenson. His classmate and old friend, Captain (now Brevet Lieutenant-Colonel) J. Lewis Stackpole, commanded the company.

The Twenty-fourth Massachusetts was among the troops which constituted the force sent to North Carolina under General Burnside. The regiments destined for this command were sent at first to Annapolis in November, 1861, where they spent a short time in preparatory organization and brigade drill. The whole expedition set sail from Annapolis on the 9th of January, 1862, and arrived the next day at Fortress Monroe. After a short delay, the fleet, composed in great part of vessels by no means in a fit condition for such important service, left Old Point, and arrived off Hatteras Inlet on the morning of the 13th. Here began one of the most trying episodes of the war. The extreme danger to which the fleet, with its precious freight of eight or ten thousand men, was exposed in endeavoring to pass through Hatteras Inlet, — owing to ignorance of the channel and the too great draught of water of most of the transports, — the confusion and alarm on board the ships, the noble exertions of Burnside and Foster and other officers, and the wonderful passage of the straits at last, without serious loss, will long be remembered.

The first object attempted by the expedition was the capture of Roanoke Island, which was accomplished early in February. After some feints in the direction of Plymouth and Norfolk, General Burnside landed near the mouth of the Neuse, marched his troops within a short distance of the enemy's works, and on the 14th of March, after a short contest with musketry, in which our troops suffered more than the enemy, carried the lines by a brilliant assault, capturing many guns and prisoners. He advanced at once to Newbern, which place was evacuated, and became from this time to the close of the war the head-quarters of our forces in North Carolina.

The Twenty-fourth Massachusetts was stationed near Newbern all the summer and autumn of 1862, and saw no active service until November, when General Foster, who then commanded the department, made an expedition to Little Washington and

Plymouth. Lieutenant Perkins's health had been a good deal impaired by chills and fever; and after this march, which was wearisome, and followed by exhausting picket duty in the swamp country, he was obliged to go down to Beaufort to recruit. He had by no means, however, regained his strength when he rejoined his regiment to take part in the expedition to Kinston and Goldsborough, in December, 1862. Nothing but his indomitable pluck enabled him, in his debilitated condition, to stand the fatigues of this long march.

The Twenty-fourth left Newbern, with other portions of the Eighteenth Corps, for South Carolina, in January, 1863, when General Hunter undertook operations against Charleston in conjunction with the fleet under the late Admiral Dupont. The land forces, however, effected little, and the great naval contest of the 7th of April ended unsuccessfully for us. In June, General Gillmore relieved General Hunter, and soon afterwards he commenced the series of operations by which he captured Fort Wagner and silenced Fort Sumter. Folly Island was first seized, and then a landing effected on Morris Island, at the northern extremity of which was Fort Wagner. Some of Lieutenant Perkins's letters written at this time, besides giving an excellent picture of what was going on, show unconsciously how bravely he was bearing up against debility and sickness, and how faithfully he was doing his duty, in spite of all depressing influences.

"SEABROOK ISLAND, SOUTH CAROLINA, July 10, 1863.

"They are banging away furiously on Folly Island. About five o'clock this morning the fire commenced, and it has been very heavy down to this time, seven, A. M. Every regiment in the department, but two or three, is up there on Folly. Six companies only of the Twenty-fourth have gone. Four of us, unlucky ones, are left here in garrison by order of General Gillmore. He said they should be of the Twenty-fourth, and the Colonel, or General Stevenson, said that the four companies should be the four largest. . . . . The society I am in is very good here, but I am inexpressibly disgusted, of course. I hate to be separated from the regiment. I should like to be 'in' for anything the regiment had to do, and I do abominate this kind of duty. We run as much risk, in a certain way, as our friends on Folly. Four companies are no force to hold this island if the Rebels choose to try to take it; and our only way of keeping out of trouble is to humbug the rascals, and make them think we are all here still. The regiments all embarked and left in the night, the steamers not coming for them till after dark. When they left, they went towards the Head, and, in some cases, when the troops left here at too late an hour to land at Stono before daylight, they went all the way to the Head, landed on St. Helena, and at night embarked again, went up to Folly in the dark, and disembarked there before there was light enough for Secesh or anybody else to see them. So there is no chance of the Rebels having seen our men leave. And we keep the tents all standing, the bands playing, and drums beating at the usual hours; even the candles are lighted in the tents at dark, and put out punctually at taps. The part of our four companies consists in keeping up the old picket line, so that the Rebels may not miss us there. I am now picketing the ground which four companies used to occupy. Company C, down at the left, does the other half of the work. My pickets are nearly a mile off in some cases. They distribute themselves along the line of the old posts, show themselves at all the places where we used to have men, patrol where we have not force enough to put posts, and generally give the Secesh an impression that we are 'round.' But there are only twenty-five or thirty men out where there used to be a hundred and fifty, and the support, namely, our company, is necessarily a long distance in the rear, and the main reserve (Companies E and F) is a long distance behind us, and behind that there is no infantry force except a parcel of cripples and invalids. There is a battery of artillery in the intrenchment in front of our camp, and, better still, there is the gunboat South Carolina. It is a very magnificent game of bluff that we are playing. I felt pretty nervous for the first two days, but since they commenced fire on Folly I feel a good deal easier in my mind. The Secesh pickets act just as they used to, out in the field in front. They come down and brandish their sabres from the house nearest our lines, innocent men that they are. But we have got to be careful, and particularly prompt in getting out of the way if they advance in force."

"MORRIS ISLAND, August 11.

"At last I have another chance to write you. It happens to be decently cool at this moment, that is, one can sit still in his shirt-sleeves, with the sides of the tent all raised, and not be in a perspiration. Moreover, the tent has been made comparatively decent by the exertions of W—— and myself. Above all, I am neither on guard or fatigue, therefore I have a chance to write a little. . . . . I hope A—— is strong again, since you say he is coming out. If he feels fresh and energetic, he will be of a great deal of use. Amongst a set of exhausted persons, such as we are, a fresh man would be a great help. All the life is out of us, — out of me, at any rate.

"They work us very hard. Up every morning at half past three. Every man on duty every other day at the least. Every officer nearly as badly off. Yesterday I was on guard. Two days before that I was down at the landing for thirteen hours and a half, working for the ordnance officer, landing shot and shell, hauling guns, &c. To-morrow night we go into the trenches. . . . . The men don't gain much in strength, of course. I have got up as high as twenty-five privates for duty, with only thirty-three sick, all told. But there I have stuck for five days past. I can't go any higher. A man will go on duty, be immediately set to work, and fall sick again. So it is, only worse, in the other companies. The sun is too much for any one."

"MORRIS ISLAND, August 17.

"The fight has begun. Our batteries opened this morning about six o'clock. There had been a good deal of firing, indeed, ever since twelve, but all the guns had not opened. About the same time the Ironsides moved in with the Montauk and another monitor, the Montauk leading, and going in very close. A little later the other four followed, all but the Nantucket. She is off somewhere. There are six wooden boats in there too, half a mile or so astern of the monitors. The Ironsides was completely covered with smoke for a long time after she first went in. Her broadside of eleven-inch guns was throwing out flashes of fire and clouds of smoke almost as fast as if it was a line of muskets.

". . . . The work lately has been tremendous. Nearly all our regiment was at work last night; every man was, the day and night before; and half of them the day before that. I was on duty night before last hauling up a hundred-pounder. The tide was high and we had to drag it through the deep sand; and it took us five hours to get it up. I suppose it is pounding away now.

". . . . The men are getting better in spite of the work. I don't see how it is, but our sick-list is six less this morning than it was yesterday. We are gaining very satisfactorily. There are not more than thirty sick altogether."

"August 22.

"I had to come down at noon the day we went into the trenches. I was pretty sick then, for me, and I barely managed to walk half the distance. I found an ambulance luckily which brought me the rest of the way. It is the first time since I have been in the service that I have not been able to walk. I got into the tent, took some medicine, had the sand washed off, and felt a good deal better. So it has been ever since. I feel pretty bright at times, especially in the morning; but a chill comes over me at noon, and I am good for nothing until next day. . . . . Our men are all sick again. We are down nearly as low as we were in the worst times. It is discouraging to be losing ground so, just as we seemed to be gaining so fast. The trouble is mostly chills.

"There, I have written a very melancholy letter; but it could not be helped. The next time I write, no doubt everything will be much more cheerful."

It was the last letter the brave man ever wrote. Four days afterwards he fell at the post of duty.

"On the afternoon of the 26th of August," writes a friend and brother officer, "three hundred men of his regiment were ordered to be in line in the foremost trenches, to charge and capture the advanced rifle-pits of the enemy. At this time Lieutenant Perkins, almost conquered by fever, had been prevailed upon to abstain from work for a few days; but now nothing could induce him not to rejoin his regiment. To use the words in which Brigadier-General Stevenson wrote, 'My friend had been quite ill for two or three weeks and was off duty, but he insisted on going forward with the regiment, notwithstanding all the officers advised him to remain in camp. When the regiment was having extra ammunition issued to them before starting, I persuaded him to come to my tent and dine with me, which he did; and I begged him not to go to the front. He answered that he could not remain behind, he should be so uneasy during all the time the regiment was gone. Colonel Osborne at one time proposed to *order* him to remaim in camp, but did not, as James was so desirous of going.' The regiment charged. In a few moments they had gained the works of the enemy, captured seventy prisoners, and with their spades were throwing up a breastwork in the very front and teeth of the concentrated fire of Fort Wagner. Perkins's men were avoiding this tremendous cannonade by sometimes dodging; and the work was not so brisk as he wished it. 'It is no use to dodge,' he said, 'do as I do,' and stood upright and firm. The words had hardly left his mouth when a ball struck him in the upper part of his arm and passed through his body. He fell, and never spoke again."

His remains were brought to Boston immediately, and were buried at Mount Auburn on the 8th of September, 1863.

"Lieutenant Perkins," writes a brother officer, "was especially distinguished for his undaunted and unwearied readiness to do more than his part of whatever was to be done. This did not spring from the physical vigor and restlessness which calls for constant work to do; though constant exercise had given him strength and endurance, it had not given him a vigorous constitution. It did not spring from the buoyancy and flow of animal spirits which underrates obstacles. He was naturally despondent; disposed to see what he thought were his own shortcomings, perhaps sometimes to overrate the difficulties that lay in his way. But this tendency, though it often marred his own comfort, never interfered with the cheerful performance of any duty. . . . . And so his friends knew that they could lean on him as one to be always trusted."

Rarely do we see a more robust character than that of James Amory Perkins. Able, untiring, conscientious, he conquered every difficulty in his path, and thoroughly discharged every duty he had to perform. His military service was enlivened by little of the "pomp and circumstance of glorious war." His was not a brilliant career, where rank and reputation give excitement. He entered the army, and he left it, with modest rank, and his duties were the simple, unexciting, and laborious cares of a company officer. He exchanged for this life all that wealth and friends and home could give him, and he never murmured at the sacrifice. His nature led him at times to be morbidly despondent in seasons of trial, but his high spirit never allowed him to falter on the road. He deserves the unusual honor of having conquered his own disposition in this respect, and of maintaining, in situations where everything around him assailed a nature apt to be depressed at all times, a lofty and cheerful courage; and this, too, when he was far away from home and friends, and enfeebled by bodily suffering.

By his classmates and friends his loss will always be most

deeply felt. His memory is fresh in the minds of all. His unwearied industry, his thorough scholarship, his extensive reading, his genial spirit, his playful humor, his unselfishness, his kindness, his modesty, his true manliness, his deep conscientiousness, — all this we shall never forget; and when we remember how, in the last two years of his life, his character shone out so brightly in endurance, bravery, and devotion to his country's service, we may well feel that in him we have lost a noble and heroic man.

GEORGE WHITTEMORE, Jr.

Private 1st Co. Mass. Sharpshooters, August, 1861; Corporal; Sergeant; killed at Antietam, Md., September 17, 1862.

THIS memoir can be but a brief sketch, yet it aims to give glimpses of a character of much harmony and strength, and a career of persistent fidelity; though the one shrank from publicity, and the other was undecorated with the badges of rank.

George Whittemore, Jr., son of George and Anna Whittemore, was born in Boston, December 19, 1837. He attended the public schools of that city, graduating from the Latin School, a medal scholar, in 1853. He immediately entered Harvard College, as a member of the Class of 1857. A few years before this his parents had removed to Gloucester, Massachusetts; and there, on the sea-shore and in the woods, during his vacations, were early developed his simple tastes and the manly physical habits which added vigor to a naturally strong constitution. As a boy he was usually gentle and quiet; but the earnest spirit under his calm exterior flashed into energetic and lively action whenever he was thoroughly roused by social enjoyment, or moved by invitations to daring adventure. The force of will, (never hardening into wilfulness,) which he exhibited at a later period, was not manifested in his childhood. Under kindly domestic influence, there was little to call out the innate strength of his nature.

At Cambridge he was a close student, ranking among the first twelve of his Class. He excelled as a classical scholar. As a writer, he took several prizes for English composition, and he was noted for his clear comprehension of abstruse metaphysical questions. He taught school during the winters of his Sophomore and Junior years at Gloucester, and in the winter of his Senior year at Northampton. He was fond of athletic exercises and expert as an oarsman. His devotion to his books and his retiring manners prevented his forming many intimate acquaintances; but he was respected by all his associates and classmates for his fine intellectual and moral qualities.

On leaving college he was engaged as an assistant in the private classical school of Mr. E. S. Dixwell in Boston. Whilst occupying this position, and afterwards in the office of Messrs. J. J. Clarke and Lemuel Shaw, he studied law. He passed the usual examination and was admitted to the Suffolk Bar on the very day when he left home as a soldier. In the summer of 1860, to recruit his health, he went with a small party on an excursion which was to have been continued for several months in the Southwest. An unusual drought in that part of the country compelled him to give up the plan when only partially executed, and he returned alone on horseback, visiting the Adirondack regions on his way back.

The first years of his maturity found him a strong, well-balanced, self-contained man, able to bear and ready to help others bear all the shocks of life, with a rich, warm nature, but one expressing itself in deeds rather than in words, — full of tenderness and care for others, and quick of indignation against anything he felt to be unjust, inhuman, or wrong.

On the breaking out of the war, he joined a drill-club; but it was not until after the disastrous battle of Bull Run that he fully determined to enter the army. With him, to resolve was to act; and he enlisted as a private in the First Company of Sharpshooters from his native State, in August, 1861. He had no acquaintances in the company, and joined it against the remonstrances of his friends, who felt that he was equal to and ought to take a higher position. He was not afterwards wholly satisfied with the step he had taken; yet the considerations which decided his course were both characteristic and honorable, inasmuch as they prompted him simply to take the place in which he thought he could be the most useful. He was very near-sighted, and constantly used glasses; was an expert with the rifle, and capable of enduring fatigue; was doubtful of his military ability to act as an officer, and averse to the restraints and routine of an infantry regiment. For these reasons, he preferred at first, believing that the contest would be short, the independence and the opportunities for individual enterprise he hoped to find in an unattached command, and in the use of the telescopic rifle.

What it meant for such a man to be a soldier in this way can easily be imagined. His prospect of a peaceful future had been bright. The cherished home of his childhood and youth held him in a loving embrace; and there was one to be left upon whom he had bestowed his strongest affections. All this was to be put in mortal peril, and yet he did not hesitate. He had everything to lose, nothing to win, as men usually count losing and winning. But the risk must be taken, the privation must be endured; thus he felt and thus he acted.

He was a faithful correspondent, writing constantly to his kindred and friends, most frequently to his father; for between his parents and himself the relation was one of strong and tender mutual regard and entire confidence. His letters tell where and how he served; what he became, or rather, how perfectly he continued to be himself during the twelve months spent amid scenes so strange and so distasteful in many respects to his whole nature. The following extracts need no comment, and are therefore given in one group.

"NEAR WASHINGTON, D. C., September 9, 1861.

"You ask if I am satisfied. I am as well satisfied as when I first formed the resolution to go to the war, and the whole affair has the same aspect as then. I have only one wish, which I have had from the first, that the war may be ended as soon as possible (not by compromise), and that we may go home. Some things here are better, and some worse, than I expected. . . . . Had a delightful bath yesterday morning. The creek, though not very wide, is deep in some parts, with high banks, covered with trees except where they open on a little meadow here and there. It reminds me of the North Branch of Concord River. Imagine one swimming up the North Branch. Would n't it be the *ne plus ultra* of delightful bathing? I suppose the creek runs into the Potomac."

"DISTRICT COLUMBIA, September 10, 1861.

"The day was intensely hot, and after waiting some time for

marching orders, we went off to the shade of the woods. I was patient and comfortable, lay down, took out 'Körner,' and did not care if we stayed there all day. But we were not so fortunate."

"CAMP NEAR EDWARD'S FERRY, September 29, 1861.

"I am very well and strong, and need to be to endure the work we are doing now. Last night some of our company went out on picket. We lay out on the tow-path in our blankets and overcoats, and I slept soundly with my cartridge-box for a pillow. At two, shots were heard, and our line jumped up, thinking the enemy were crossing the river. As I did not find myself killed, nor hear that any one else was, I was disposed to lie still and wait for something more. But the alarm had been given, and every man must pack up his goods and be in marching order."

"NEAR EDWARD'S FERRY, October 22.

"I begin to realize the risks and sufferings of war. I cannot well reconcile myself to parting from all I love in the world, but those left behind suffer more. If there is any consolation in the next world, and I believe there is, I shall know it at once. However, I hope for the best, and do not think much about these things."

"NEAR EDWARD'S FERRY, October 23, 1861.

"It is dull, of course. It is not the life I should choose, even in pleasant weather, unless I was a colonel or general, in which case there might be some enjoyment in it; but as a private there is nothing to attract one who has such a home as I have. However, a man will not be miserable unless he has a very sensitive temperament, feels everything keenly, and broods over trouble. Now if I were constituted as you are, I could not endure this life a month; but as I am able to bear disagreeable things, and have a latent relish for a loafing life, I am not at all miserable."

"NEAR EDWARD'S FERRY, October 28, 1861.

"We have seen our first fighting. We went over the river on Monday. The colonel or general commanding showed us the position of the enemy, and told us 'to go there and see what we could do.' . . . . Our company have done all the fighting at this place, with the exception of some shells thrown by the artillery. Our men both on Monday and Tuesday were put up close to the enemy, quite unsupported; and this, with their being without food for twenty-four hours and doing nearly all the fighting, has, I find, gained them some credit with everybody. Even General Gorman, who calls the guns great humbugs, gives credit to the men."

"November 10.

"You thought, walking in those splendid autumn woods, it would be far preferable to die there than to die shut up in a sick-chamber with all the paraphernalia of sickness about you. Yes, I think so; but perhaps the idea as it presents itself to my mind, of a sudden, painless death in full activity, even in battle, is not so pleasant for you to think of. To me it seems the most desirable form in which to meet it."

"CAMP BENTON, November 20, 1861.

"The principal discomfort here arises from the impossibility of being neat. I was never fastidious, but cannot reconcile myself to the estate of things here and to our crowded condition. We have eleven or twelve in tents which were made to hold eight. I shall break off, for the crowd of men and clatter of voices in this smoky tabernacle of ours seem to make the letter unfit to send to you, the pattern of fastidious neatness. I wonder if any of the smoke or other odors goes in the letter to Boston. I believe it can't be helped in the present state of things."

"CAMP BENTON, December 4, 1861.

"Will —— go into the army? If he does, I should advise him to get a commission. I have come to the conclusion that a man of ability and education is not only under no obligation to go into the ranks as a private, but that he ought not to. He thereby puts it out of his power to use his advantages. He has no opportunity to do any good proportioned to his ability. By looking about, —— may find a situation suited to him. In short, 'every man in his place.' You will see I have come to this conclusion by reflecting on my own case. You must not infer from this that I am unhappy. I can wait patiently for the end of this dull life, and much of it I enjoy."

"December 13, 1861.

"Send something more to read or study as soon as you find from my accounts that the mails are tolerably reliable."

"CUMBERLAND, January 12, 1862.

"I have had more pleasure and more hard work this week than in any month in camp. This is a mountain country, as you know, — the Alleghanies and the Blue Ridge. I like the mountain travelling; and to me it is easier than any other, there is so much pleasant scenery all the way. The air is fresher and more invigorating. There is plenty of water, and the people are far more hospitable and intelligent than in the counties lower down on the river.

Climbing these mountains is not so hard as Kearsarge or Mount Washington."

"PAWPAW, March 7, 1862.

"It is one great satisfaction to me to reflect that you are not and cannot be here, or know anything of this life, and that in a few months (how long they seem!) *I* shall know it only as a thing of the past. You speak of being plentifully supplied with pure air. I think I can surpass you at your own practice. On our return from Blooming Gap we slept on the ground in a thick snow-storm, and I was surprised to find myself not very cold. A good fire at one's feet is a comfortable thing at such a time."

"NEAR YORKTOWN, April 9, 1862.

"On Monday our company was not called into play until late in the afternoon, when we came in front of the Rebel batteries in two squads, supported by two regiments. Only our squad fired, and that with only thirty or forty shots; but the Rebels answered with volleys that would have cut us up if we had not been protected by a small knoll. I posted myself behind a large tree near the top of the knoll, and received some credit for coolness, but it was the coolness of perfect safety. Some doubts arose in my mind when the first shell came. It burst over my head so near that I felt the hot air on my face and the presence of the gas in my ears, and it scattered the branches all around me; but I thought it would not happen twice in succession, and stayed where I was. The Colonel, having found out what he wished to, retired, and we with him. It was growing dark, began to rain hard, and the roads, under the tramp of so many men, were mere sloughs. We had the choice to lie down in the mud or sit up all night about the fire. I chose the latter, and with a rubber blanket and a good fire was pretty comfortable."

"CAMP NEAR YORKTOWN, April 13, 1862.

"DEAR FATHER,—I have received ten letters during the week. I cannot tell you how precious they are to me. The love and kindness in them all are enough to make one contented, if not happy, in far worse circumstances than mine. I wonder if I shall ever see you all again. I have very little fear of being killed, a great deal more of being sick; but I have not felt as though I were to die yet in either way. We are encamped, if the term may be used,—for we have no tents, and are sheltering ourselves in the cellar and outbuildings of a little farm-house, while the brigade are out in the fields and woods. Yesterday I spent the day with a dozen of our men in the outskirts of the woods, within two hundred yards of the works. We lay concealed and very quiet, so as not to draw their fire; our orders being not to fire, unless they opened with cannon upon our troops elsewhere, in which case we were to shoot the gunners. As they did not fire excepting once, when they did no harm, we did not. The day was beautiful, the woods warm and pleasant, and I could not help enjoying it. How different the woods seem from what they have in former seasons. Now the sun shines warm as ever, the tops of the pine-trees whisper in the wind, and the dry leaves and pine needles are as luxurious to lie on; but grape-shot and shells may at any moment come cutting everything to pieces. We don't sit in a social circle as in our picnics at home, but each one takes a tree to himself; and, instead of wandering round in pleasant meditations, we creep on our hands and knees, and talk in whispers."

"CAMP NEAR YORKTOWN, April 21, 1862.

"Quarter of a mile from the Rebels' first battery is a rising ground, where the ruins of a fine house stand. There is little left but three large chimneys and the brick foundations of the house. These ruins have been the scene of the sharpshooters' operations for a few days past, and I have been mostly there. So little shooting has been going on, that we have been able to make our arrangements almost as we pleased, and we established ourselves in a style of luxurious comfort quite unknown to privates. From the furniture lying around, two men took bureaus and set them up by a chimney to rest their guns on. Another found a thick tree that divided about five feet from the ground. He cut out the notch large enough for his gun, and put up a seat behind it, where he spied around very much at his ease. I took a position at the side of a chimney, with a black-walnut table in front, the leaf hanging down and making a tolerable protection from bullets, &c., at this distance; and to cover my head I set up two or three timbers, charred rafters, &c., the ends slanting up over my head, leaving a narrow port-hole for the gun. It happened to do me service. Towards night our batteries, stationed very near the chimneys, threw some shell into the works, while we kept our guns levelled at their embrasures. At last, after our cannon had sprinkled their shot and shell in various parts of the fort, an iron howitzer, on the battery nearest and just opposite to us, which not a man had approached all day, now, touched off by an unseen hand, threw a charge of grape or canister at us. It struck the ground a few yards before us, and scattered. Some of the balls struck my table, knocked down one timber from before it, and scattered the nails, charcoal, &c., over the table. One ball glanced and struck a tub behind me. My companion behind the chimney wanted to know if I was 'hit.' He seemed to think a ball that struck behind me must have gone through me. This iron howitzer is the one the negroes fired when the place became too hot for the chivalry."

"NEAR YORKTOWN, May 3, 1862.

"There has been more or less firing about us all day. Just now it is perfectly quiet, though at intervals there comes back to us the music of a band in the Rebel camp. Only the song of birds, the hum of mosquitoes, and an occasional woodpecker breaks the stillness. A gun goes off now and then, but reminds me, in the quiet, of a sportsman's fowling-piece rather than of a soldier's rifle. It is past three o'clock, and the rifle-pit in which I am writing begins to afford a little shade. Now that the days are longer and we can sit out of doors, my interest in these German books increases. I wish —— would be looking about for something more, and send it out, if the mails continue regular, in about a fortnight."

"KENT COURT-HOUSE, VIRGINIA, May 12, 1862.

"Three letters from you of different dates have just arrived. The day has been quite hot and dusty, for the passing of so many men, horses, and wagons have worn the sod away already. But how different everything looks since I received these letters! It was merely hot and dull before, now it might have been ten times hotter and duller, and these letters would have made up for all. So it would have been if they had come to me as they should, one at a time. But coming all at once, they are a greater pleasure, especially as they are all in different tones. I have finished the French books, but not 'Egmont' as yet. Have just received the 'Parasite,' and hope to be able to hold on to it until I finish it. If we have no longer marches than we have had recently, I shall have no trouble."

"FAIR OAKS, June 12, 1862.

"The Rebels continued throwing shell at intervals, and we had orders to go out and see if we could not silence the guns. Most of our available men had been sent in another direction; but we mustered a dozen or twenty, and went along the front of our picket lines for a good place to fire from. It was not easy to find, for the Rebel guns were protected by the nature of the ground; and that is perhaps the reason that they have been allowed to annoy us in this way with impunity. It seems, beside, to be the object not to bring on an engagement at present. The artillerymen say they have orders not to fire. We found a place at last within sight of the Rebel batteries, but also within easy range of their grape and canister and sharpshooters. It was at some old ruins on a ridge in a wheat-field, their cannon and sharpshooters being in the woods on the farther side, three or four hundred yards off. It was very warm out there in the sun. The stock of one of the rifles was blistered by it, and the barrels were too hot to keep one's hands on. We relieved each other by turns at the old ruins, while the rest stayed in the edge of the woods. A swamp was near by, with quantities of magnolias."

"June 15.

"I have enjoyed the day very much, most in picking magnolias for half an hour. It was a perfect delight. They grow on slim trees thirty feet high, so slender I could bend them down by my weight, climbing up a few feet. The place was full of them, and every one had five or ten buds just at the right stage for picking, being half open. Many of the flowers are withered, many are in the green hard bud, and others all the way between."

"Fair Oaks, June 19, 1862.

"Our quiet life ended with May. On the 31st, we set out from the camp two miles the other side of the Chickahominy, crossed the river and swamp in water up to our knees, and stumbled on the enemy. Before a line of battle was fairly formed, the firing began, and our company, who have no place in a line of bayonets, and in the hurry of the moment had been assigned no station, was ordered to lie down. The shower of bullets fired over the heads of the line fell all about us, but only one of our men was hit. The fight here on Saturday night lasted not over an hour, but it was well after dark before it was decided. While it lasted it was furious, not broken for an instant, and at times swelling into a louder roar, like gusts of wind in a storm, as the Rebels charged up to one or another part of our line. The battle of Sunday was in the woods, and hidden from our view; but we saw the regiments as they filed in, saw the smoke, and the wounded and prisoners as they were brought out. Our division was not engaged, occupying the battlefield of the day before."

"July 2.

"Another hard day's fight and another hard night's march yesterday. The Rebels attacked at noon, and the engagement continued till long after dark. To-day we have rain, which perhaps prevents them from following. I begin now to long for one quiet day without a battle. We have carried these rifles on our shoulders lately, and it is wearing the men down fast." [The telescopic rifles weighed from fifteen to fifty pounds.]

Whilst asleep in a barn, on one occasion, with men of his own and other companies, Whittemore's rifle was stolen from him. This happened a few days before the battle of Antietam; and at the commencement of that engagement he was unarmed, and at liberty to be a non-combatant. He was urged, if not actually ordered, to remain in the rear. This he could not do. He went coolly toward the front, looking for a weapon. An officer saw him take a gun from a fallen soldier and calmly load and fire until he was hit and instantly killed. This occurred in the woods adjoining the corn-field where Sedgwick's division met with its heavy losses. The next day, when the ground came into possession of the Federal army, his body was carefully and tenderly buried by his comrades, with a head-board inscribed, "Sergeant Whittemore." It was soon after removed to Mount Auburn. There it rests in a spot that was a favorite resort of his while in college. It is situated on the slope of Harvard Hill, — an enclosure endeared by family associations, and which he was careful to adorn and keep in order.

In view of his exceeding worth to others, and as we think of all he might have been had he remained with us longer, we cannot help feeling and saying, "George Whittemore died before his time." Yet it is only in this view, and only as we thus think, that we are allowed to deem his death premature. His life had already reached roundness and completeness; his spirit was already trained to follow in its further growth its own aspirations. The memory of that spirit remains with us still, — a reality without a shadow on its clearness. And yet, alas! there are those who will sometimes ask,

"But who shall so forecast the years,
And find in loss a gain to match?
Or reach a hand through time to catch
The far-off interest of tears?"

1858.

SAMUEL HENRY EELLS.

Hospital Steward 12th Michigan Vols. (Infantry), February 7, 1862; Assistant Surgeon February 1, 1863; died at Detroit, Mich., January 31, 1864, of disease contracted in the service.

SAMUEL HENRY EELLS was the son of Rev. James Henry and Maria Antoinette (Fletcher) Eells, and was born in Oberlin, Ohio, August 19, 1836. A few months after his birth, his father was drowned in attempting to cross the Maumee River. Ten years later the family removed to Boston, and young Eells was placed at the Brimmer Public School. Thence he was transferred to the Quincy School, where he received a Franklin medal; and thence entered the public Latin School, where he was fitted for college. In 1854 his mother died, and he came under the guardianship of his uncle, George N. Fletcher, Esq., of Detroit, Michigan.

His college life was quiet and uneventful, and most of his classmates knew him very little. Yet he always looked back with warm affection upon this period and its associations; as was shown by a very cordial letter which he wrote from Arkansas to the Class Secretary, three months before his death, in which was enclosed a liberal contribution to the Class fund.

He wrote in the "Class Book," just before graduating:—

"My plans for the future are yet somewhat undecided. I think, however, of studying medicine. There has been a great number of clergymen in the Eells family; and my relations on my father's side have been anxious that I should follow the example of my father, grandfather, great-great-grandfather, and great-great-great-grandfather, besides a number of others not in the direct line. But for myself, I have been uniformly opposed to the idea, and am still of the same opinion."

Accordingly, after graduation, he went to Detroit, Michigan, and began at once the study of medicine with Dr. C. H. Barrett of that city, residing meanwhile in the family of his guardian. He attended also the medical lectures of Michigan University, at Ann Arbor, during the winter of 1861–62; but before his course of study was completed, the war changed all his plans.

On February 7, 1862, he enlisted as Hospital Steward in the Twelfth Michigan Volunteers (Infantry), then in camp at Niles, Michigan. He took part in the battle of Shiloh, where he was made prisoner, — an experience which is graphically described in one of his letters.

"PITTSBURG LANDING, TENNESSEE, April 13, 1862.

"MY DEAR FRIENDS, — I have not heard a word from you since I left Niles. Don't you write, or do the letters fail of coming through? I presume it is the latter. At any rate, I presume you would like to hear from me, and to know that I am alive and uninjured after this great battle. Well, I am so; but I got my share of the bad luck of last Sunday, for I have been a prisoner among the Secesh until last night, and had rather a hard time of it; but have got back safe to our lines, and mighty glad I was to do so too.

"The papers will give you the details of the battle better than I could do, but I will tell you all I know about it in brief. Our pickets had been skirmishing two or three days previously; but our commanders do not seem to have known of the enemy's advance in force. We had no artillery in the front, either, nor any strong force on picket duty. On Sunday morning, about two o'clock, the attack began on our camp. The pickets had been driven in within a mile of the camp, and our men then went out to reinforce them. You must understand that the attack began along the whole line about the same time; but the camps were disposed irregularly, and ours was the first attacked at this point. The camp was not intrenched at all, and the trees in front of it not even cut down. The first that I saw of the fight was the line of our men drawn up a little way in front of the tents, and firing at the enemy, whom I could not see. The Rebels greatly outnumbered us, but we were in hopes our men could hold them at bay until reinforcements should arrive. None came, however, and our men were gradually forced back. They retired slowly, fighting as they went, and doing splendidly for green troops, until they came to the camp. Then the enemy began to come in at the sides as well as in front, — flanking is the technical term, — and our men were forced to run to escape being surrounded. All this time I was in the hospital tents, helping to dress the wounded; but I managed to run out once in a while to see the fight.

"The wounded came in pretty fast, and soon filled up the hospital, and then they were laid down on the ground outside. We were all hard at work, and only just begun at that, when the rout began. Everybody else was running off as fast as possible; but the surgeons resolved that they would not leave their wounded, and I was not going either when my services were most required. Most of the hospital attendants ran away, but some remained, and we continued our work of attending to the wounded, though the bullets began to come unpleasantly near and thick. One passed through the tent, and within three inches of my head, as I was dressing a wounded man, smashing a bottle of ammonia liniment that stood on a box beside me, and sending the fluid right into my face and eyes. Very soon the Rebels came pouring in on all sides. We, of course, made no resistance, and they did not fire upon us, though some levelled their guns at us, and we rather expected to be shot than otherwise. I know I expected every moment to get hit, for the balls were flying all around, though I do not think they were meant for the hospital or any of us there. The ground outside was covered with the wounded all around, and the yellow flag was over the tent. I did not know but what I should get frightened in the first battle; but I believe I did n't. I was too busy; and, if I had been ever so much scared, I don't think I could have run off and left our wounded crying for help. It was a pitiful sight, I can tell you. I hope never to see the like again. Such groans and cries for help, and especially for 'Water! water!' all the time. We could not attend to them half as fast as they needed, though we worked as hard as we could. Soon after the first appearance of the Rebels, General Hindman, of Arkansas, rode up, and placed a guard over us, and assured us we should not be molested, though we must consider ourselves prisoners. Two Rebel surgeons came up too, and established their hospitals right by ours, and made liberal use of our medicines and hospital stores.

"There we worked all day upon the Rebel wounded as well as our own, for there were a great number of them brought there. Towards night they commenced carrying the wounded away, and Dr. Kedgie and I were sent off with the first load that went of our men. During all the day we could hear the battle still going on between us and the river, which was about four miles off; and every now and then a shot or shell would come crashing through the trees among us, but none of us happened to get hit. Our men were slowly driven back to the river, and many of them were made prisoners; but when they got to the landing, the gunboats on the river opened fire on the Rebels, and an immense battery of over a hundred guns, it is said, on the bluff assisted, and the enemy's advance was effectually stopped. This was about sundown, and next morning General Buell arrived with fresh troops, another fight took place, and the Rebels were driven back faster than they drove us the day before. We prisoners, however, knew nothing of this; for we were marched off with many of our wounded men, some walking and some in wagons, to a Rebel hospital about five miles from here."

He remained a prisoner but a few days, there being an agreement between the surgeons on both sides that the wounded in the joint hospitals should be allowed to return to their respective camps on recovery, and their hospital attendants with them. After his exchange, he took part in the battle of the Hatchie, in the siege of Vicksburg, and in the expedition into Arkansas, under General Steele. On February 1, 1863, he was promoted to be Assistant Surgeon on the recommendation of his medical superiors, in spite of his want of a diploma. A letter written later in the season, gives some account of the wearisome and exhausting service on which he now entered.

"CAMP AT SNYDER'S BLUFF, MISSISSIPPI, July 25, 1863.

"I wrote you last from the Big Black. We have returned from that interesting country, after staying long enough to more than treble our sick-list, and are back here in the old camp, but expecting every day to leave. I understand our division is ordered to Helena, Arkansas, and will leave as soon as transportation can be furnished us. Helena is not the most eligible place in the world to go to; but we shall be glad to get away from here, for we can hardly go to a worse place, unless it should be Vicksburg. That is now the hottest, dirtiest, most unhealthy, and in every respect the most undesirable place within our lines. The regiment marched back here, but I was put in charge of over a hundred sick and convalescents belonging to our brigade, to bring them around by railroad from the Big Black to Vicksburg, and from there to this place by boat, and a nice time I had of it. The heat was intolerable, and the sand on the levee, over ankle deep, fairly scorched one s feet through boots. We had to stay there more than twenty-four hours before we could get a boat to take us on board, though there were half a dozen lying across the river, with steam up ready to go anywhere on the receipt of orders. We got off at last, however, and brought all the men safely through. Our sick-list is larger now than it has been for over a year, but there are very few serious cases. Intermittent fever is the prevailing disease; and as long as we can get quinine enough, we can manage that. We have not lost a man since we came here, which is more than any other regiment I know of can say; in fact, we have only lost one man by disease (and that was small-pox) since last November. The new regiments suffer most, as would of course be expected. . . . .

"I wish I could daguerreotype our camp for you. I have thought that very often you could have so much better an idea of our situation here than from any description. The position of the army here would be interesting too, I should think, to you folks at home. From the pictures in the papers of scenes that I know, I am satisfied they can seldom approach the truth, and are not at all trustworthy. If you could see the whole side of the high bluff covered with tents for miles, — tents now empty, for most of the soldiers that were here are out at the Big Black, or in that vicinity; the Rebel rifle-pits running all along the edge of the slope, and ours too, sometimes parallel, sometimes crossing theirs; the places for guns on every commanding summit; the Rebel ports partly grassed over now, with the charred remains of gun-carriages, shot and shell lying among the weeds and brush; the exploded magazines; the caves the Rebs lived in, dug in the side of the bluff! Then if you could go to Vicksburg, in the miles of captured works; the big guns that have killed so many of our brave soldiers, some dismounted, some still in position and guarded by blue-coats; then if you could go into the town, see almost every building torn by shot and shells, some with clean round holes through and through, some with great holes in the roof, and the interior knocked into ruins by the explosion of shell; the streets full of filth, mingled with musket-balls, grape, cannon-shot, and every species of missile; and above all, the old stars and stripes floating from the cupola of the proud old Court-House, the crown of the city, like the State-House at Boston; the gunboats in the river; the chartered transports, miles of them lying at the levee; — if you could see all these things, or if I could only give you a pen-picture of them, you would get some idea of the war, of its magnitude, and how it is conducted, how much it is costing every day."

The results of these labors and exposures soon became apparent. In August he was attacked by chills and fever, followed by camp diarrhœa, and still later by ulcerated sore throat, terminating in bronchial consumption. Early in December he obtained leave of absence, and returned to Detroit, very weak and unable to speak above a whisper, but still retaining his courage and hopeful of ultimate recovery. In the words of his guardian: "When he was told, a few hours before his death, that he could not live, he received it without a fear, and looked on death calmly as his spirit went out, even after he had ceased to move a muscle, being still conscious, seemingly to the last breath. He fully believed God would do rightly with him, and did not fear to trust him." He died on the last day of January, 1864.

He had previously written as follows, from the camp near Brownsville, Arkansas, September 5, 1863, to Dr. F. H. Brown of Boston, who was then collecting information as to the Harvard military record: —

"I enlisted as Hospital Steward in February, 1862, and in February, 1863, was promoted to Assistant Surgeon. Being with the Army of the Tennessee all the time, I have had but little opportunity to learn what was going on at the East, and particularly in Cambridge. I shall be glad to get any information with regard to my Alma Mater and the doings of her sons, especially in the war, and shall be happy to pay any sum which may be necessary for this purpose."

Before the letter could be answered, he himself had added, in his own modest and silent way, another act of sacrifice to those noble deeds of which he wrote; and the sum which he contributed was his life.

JAMES JACKSON LOWELL.

First Lieutenant 20th Mass. Vols., July 10, 1861; died at Nelson's Farm, near Richmond, July 4, 1862, of a wound received at Glendale, June 30.

JAMES JACKSON LOWELL was the younger brother of General Charles Russell Lowell, whose brillant career has been narrated earlier in this volume. He was born at Cambridge, on the 15th of October, 1837, at the house of his grandfather, the house now occupied by the raciest of American poets, his uncle. He came of the best Massachusetts stock, being descended on the father's side from John Lowell, one of the framers of the Constitution of the State, and a Judge in the United States courts, whose son, Francis Cabot, was one of the two founders of American cotton manufactures, and father of the founder of the Lowell Institute of Boston; and on the mother's side from Patrick Tracy Jackson, co-founder with Francis Cabot Lowell of the city of Lowell, and brother of Charles Jackson, Judge of the Supreme Court of Massachusetts. His lineage is referred to for no trivial purpose. Both branches of his family have been long conspicuous for public spirit and the sense and love of justice, — qualities which were peculiarly marked in James Lowell's character.

Lowell passed his early youth in Boston, and went through the course of the public Latin School. His family had taken up their residence in Cambridge before he entered college, which was in 1854. In 1858 he was graduated, first scholar as his brother had been before him. His Class contained men of excellent abilities, with whom he could be closely joined by intellectual and moral sympathies; among these were Patten and Spurr, who served with him, the one in the same regiment, the other in the same brigade, and met the same fate; *nunc ipsa pericula jungunt!* His classmates were proud of him; he was certainly one of the brightest minds that had appeared in

College for a long time. He was liked quite as much as he was admired. His exterior was very engaging, both his looks and his manners. His figure was light and agile, his face radiant with intelligence and moral sweetness. He was full of life, enjoyed keenly and pursued eagerly, and crowded every hour with work or pleasure. While he would walk a dozen or eighteen miles for wild-flowers, skate all day, and dance as long as the music would play, he found no study too dry, and would have liked to embrace all science and all literature. He was, moreover, habitually meditative, and loved to ponder deep questions of philosophy and of life. His pale, oval face, and his dark, thoughtful eyes, with their drooping lashes, gave an impression of a poetical nature, and the question was often asked in his early days whether he was a poet. But his expression was more spiritual and his bent more practical than poetical: practical in a sense opposed to imaginative, not to philosophical, for, as already indicated, his inclination to speculation was marked. He always sought to see things as a whole; and though he liked to view every subject in its great features, and in the best light consistent with truth, he loved reality and hated illusion and exaggeration.

That Lowell should have begun early to take an interest in public affairs and public men will readily be supposed from what has been said. He thought it a duty to study and act on all questions of public concern. In one of his books he had written down these words of Marcus Antoninus: "Every action of yours which has not a near or remote relation to the public good as its end, destroys the harmony and uniformity of life." It is true that boys often copy out these fine things in a glow of feeling, but nothing was more unlike Lowell than superficial enthusiasm. In an oration on "Loyalty," delivered at the College Exhibition of October, 1857, he expressed his idea of the true relation of a free citizen to the state in words which no one can read lightly who knows how they were followed up. After describing the inferior forms of devotion manifested among nations who considered that the citizen existed only for his country, he said:—

"But among those who feel the blood of the Teutons running in their veins, there is a loftier feeling even than this. Each feels himself a whole, an individual, a being whose chief end is to live independently for himself. He is willing and glad to die for his country, but he must have his individual rights acknowledged. He thinks that government the best which governs least: the state exists for him, and not he for the state. . . . .

"The distinction between fidelity and loyalty lies here: in the latter the agent must be *free*, but even a slave may be faithful. Loyalty is the feeling of one who is independent and self-relying; but a dog may show fidelity. . . . .

"Where is there a more touching example of devotion to freedom and to truth than that of Körner, the warrior-bard? In 1813 he writes to his father: 'Germany rises: the Prussian eagle by the beating of her mighty wings awakes in all true hearts the great hope of German freedom.' He then declares his intention to go forth, and adds: 'That I simply offer my life is of little import: but that I offer it crowned as it is with all the flowery wreaths of love, of friendship, and of joy; that I cast away the sweet sensations which lived in the anticipation that I should never cause you inquietude or anguish, — this is indeed a sacrifice which can only be opposed to such a prize, — our country's freedom.'

"Let us especially cultivate it, for it belongs to youth, to the heroic age: let us not prove recreants. Like the world in its youth, let us be strong in loyalty: but while it was loyal to persons, let us be loyal to principles. One man is but a narrow limit, but a principle is broad as the earth and high as heaven, and with the enlargement of our ideas and views, the field of loyalty also is enlarged. This is the loyalty of to-day and of the future, and we should be leaders in extending it. 'There needs not a great soul to make a hero: there needs a God-created soul which will be true to its origin': therefore let us be foremost in proclaiming our loyalty to our intuitions. . . . . For is not a liberal education a sham and a deception, if it does not clear our intuitions, and expand our minds in every direction? But the heroes will be, not those who recite best here, or those who know the most, but those whose knowledge best clears their perceptions. Yet clear-sightedness alone will not suffice: firmness and perseverance, true grit, must be added, and then we have the man who is needed now, the man who is loyal to the highest principles, with whom matters of personal interest yield to the state, the state to conscience."

While Lowell was in college, one of his classmates says, he liked all studies, and had arguments for and against all professions, but inclined most to the law. When the time came to decide, he wisely chose the law. His impartial and philosophical mind fitted him peculiarly for the science of jurisprudence, and he would have made an admirable judge. After some study of the introductory books at home, he entered the Cambridge Law School in 1860. The events of the winter of 1860–61 occupied much of his thoughts. He regarded with warm indignation the expedients proposed to save the Union by the sacrifice of liberty, and seeing a more excellent way, began to drill diligently that he might be ready to do his part. When Sumter fell, his brother Charles went straight to Washington, and applied for a lieutenancy in an artillery regiment. James Lowell conferred with his cousin William Putnam, who was also then studying at the Law School, and in June they began enlisting men for a company of the Nineteenth Massachusetts Regiment, to be commanded by Mr. Schmitt, the German instructor in the college. When they had raised eighty-five men, and the officers were ready to be commissioned, orders were given to transfer this company to the Twentieth Regiment. Almost all the men refused to join the Twentieth, and therefore the work of recruiting had to be done over again. The time at which this regiment was raised was unfavorable for enlisting, and the consequence was, that neither in numbers nor in quality were the rank and file up to the average. It is well known that the admirable character of the officers (more than a score of whom were from Harvard College) made the Twentieth Regiment, notwithstanding its original inferiority, one of the most efficient and distinguished in the whole service.

Lowell and Putnam received their commissions as First and Second Lieutenants on the 10th of July. A nobler pair never took the field. Putnam with his fair hair, bright complexion, deep eyes, and uncontaminated countenance, was the impersonation of knightly youth. He was our Euryalus, *quo pulchrior alter non fuit Aeneadum*. The cousins were beautifully matched in person, mental accomplishments, and pure heroism of character. The regiment was ordered to the seat of war at the beginning of September. Captain Schmitt's company was the smallest of the ten. In October, Lowell writes that there are fifty vacancies, — a dispiriting state of things for both men and officers; but, though strongly condemning the practice of forming skeleton regiments to the detriment of those already in the field, he was resolved to make the best of circumstances.

After a few days at Washington, the Twentieth was ordered to Poolesville, Maryland, where it lay in camp until the 20th of October. On the 18th of that month Lowell writes to Patten: "Hitherto our life has been like a perpetual picnic; work enough, perhaps drudgery enough, but also open air enough, and in a way freedom enough. . . . . We have been here in quiet so long, that we scarcely feel as if this were war; but the bloody fight may come any day, when may we be victorious, live or die." The bloody fight came — alas! without the victory — in three days. On the 21st of October was fought the battle of Ball's Bluff, in which so many brave men were slaughtered for no military purpose. Lowell was shot in the thigh, Captain Schmitt very badly wounded, and Putnam killed. The deep gloom which followed that most unnecessary calamity will not soon be forgotten. Our only consolation was the gallant behavior of our troops in a desperate situation, and the firmer resolution which misfortune inspired in an earnest people. Patten and Ropes, two of our best, went into the Twentieth Regiment soon after this battle, — Patten in Putnam's place.

Lowell made light of his wound and wanted to stay with his regiment; but what with his fear of being an encumbrance, and his hope of returning sooner to duty, he yielded to advice and went home. He remained with his family from the middle of November to the beginning of February. He had the less trouble from his wound on account of his vigorous health. There was not a sounder man in the army; indeed, he was never off duty except while getting well of this hurt. While he was at home, some of his classmates presented him with a sword, to replace one which had been lost in the dreadful confusion of Ball's Bluff. The formal letter in which he acknowledged the gift contained a passage which, as a main object in collecting these biographies is to illustrate the spirit with which our soldiers went into the war, deserves especially to be recorded. When the Class meets in years to come, he says, and honors its statesmen and judges, its divines and doctors, let also the score who went to fight for their country be remembered, and let not those who never returned be forgotten: —

"Those who died for the cause, not of the Constitution and the laws, — a superficial cause, the Rebels have now the same, — but of civilization and law, and the self-restrained freedom which is their result. As the Greeks at Marathon and Salamis, Charles Martel and the Franks at Tours, and the Germans at the Danube, saved Europe from Asiatic barbarism, so we, at places to be famous in future times, shall have saved America from a similar tide of barbarism; and we may hope to be purified and strengthened ourselves by the struggle."

Once more with his men, he would have been fully contented if his company had not been so small. When recruits came in, free to choose, they always preferred to join the large companies. Having one day to go out to battalion drill with only five files, his spirits sunk a little, but only for a moment. This is the way he expresses himself in his letters: —

"I am quite well again, and feel ready for any march which the men could stand. Lander's famous marches must have been on harder ground than we have here: such a march would be simply impossible here on most days. But we have not so far to go to find the enemy. Whenever the work comes I shall try to do my part, and whatever my fate is then, we know that it will be for the best.

"You must not think that I fret over our small company, because I write for recruits. I thank mother for her good advice, but I rarely feel that any injustice has been done our company, and then I have only slight suspicions. I much more commonly attribute all the blame, if blame there is, to ourselves, and feel that there may have been something wrong somewhere, or that we are not in our proper places, and are not so well fitted as others for military matters. . . . .

"I determined to do what I could to get recruits; but I can do very well without them if I must."

On the 11th of March the Twentieth left the camp at Poolesville, and were transferred to the Peninsula. They reached Yorktown on the 8th of April, and remained there until the evacuation of that place on the 4th of May. The regiment took no part in the actions at Williamsburg and West Point. They went up the York and Pamunkey to White House. On the 25th, Lowell writes from Chickahominy Creek, regretting that he is not in the advance with his brother. The severe fighting at Fair Oaks occurred on Saturday, the 31st of May, and Sunday, the 1st of June. The Twentieth was engaged the first day, but was not in the worst of the fight; on Sunday they were only spectators. Lowell describes as follows what he saw of the affair of Saturday, in a letter to a young friend:—

"We have at last been engaged in a regular battle, though the Rebels have been so shy in using their big guns that shells are a rarity, and grape and canister are still unknown to us. At Ball's Bluff we had very severe firing for the space occupied. It was as if a whole regiment were firing at a wall ten feet square; the bullets within that space would be very thick. At Yorktown we saw the Rebels far off in their works, and occasionally saw and felt their bullets and shells. . . . . At West Point we were held as a reserve; and the reserves not being called into action, because the first line and the gunboats drove the Rebels back, we scarcely saw the evolutions of our own battalions and brigades on the wide plain. . . . . The scene of the fight was just hidden by a wooded hill; but our batteries were actively engaged within sight. At Fair Oaks we had a foretaste of what is coming before the forts of Richmond. . . . . On Saturday we had an inspection under the Colonel, and soon afterwards we heard firing in front, and being ordered forwards, though the firing had then ceased, we advanced by a new road through an interminable swamp, and across the Chickahominy; and then, after a pause to load our pieces, we went on again; and the cannon beginning once more, we dashed forward through a brook up to our waists and mud up to our knees, and came up into the field of battle in the midst of random shots. The right and centre of the line were already formed and engaged, and shells were flying from both sides. At the centre was a house with out-buildings; near this was a battery of ours, and the battle raged warmly. We formed into line in the rear of the centre (on the right by file into line). As we had been fairly on the run for some minutes, the companies, especially those near the left (since we were marching by the right flank), were broken, and I supposed that some of my own weaker and doubtful men had fallen out on the way. Much to my delight I found that every man was there. The line was formed and dressed, amid much confusion from contrary orders, &c., and the bullets which missed the line before us came whizzing round our heads. The man on my left, one of my corporals, was mortally wounded, and the corporal next on my right, of the next company, had a ball strike the ground directly before his left foot, and I felt it slightly myself; but I had at no time in the fight even a slight graze. . . . . We marched forward a few paces in line of battle close to the Fifteenth Massachusetts, when Tom Spurr, a classmate of mine, called out to me and waved his sword. But we were soon faced to the left, and marched round to the left of the line, re-formed our own line, with the Seventh Michigan of our brigade on our left, and marched steadily forward to fire and charge on the enemy, if they waited for us to come.

"The regiment on the right (Thirty-fourth New York, of our division, Gorman's brigade) was a little in front at first, and although the regiment had had a bad reputation at Poolesville, and since we entered Virginia, yet it went forward with great firmness, halted and delivered its fire, advanced again and fired, and would have charged, had not the fire already cleared the woods in front of all the active Rebels. We were even with them before their second fire, and advanced across a fenced road, on the opposite side of which a wood lay before our right wing, and a very deep plain (five hundred yards perhaps) before our left wing. The Seventh Michigan had another wood in front of their left wing (this wood was not very far from us, as the two regiments joined each other). There was at first a line of Rebels in front of us, and the shots came across the field, but only a scattering fire. As we approached the fence beyond the road, we were on the watch for a sudden attack from behind it, but the Rebels fled back and scattered over the field. The men opened a fire on them, thinking that orders had been given, or else the first man from impulse and the others from imitation. We at once stopped them and crossed the fences. Then a volley came from the Rebels in front of the woods on the left, at the Seventh Michigan. It was very heavy, and looked beautifully in the gloomy twilight. Then we fired with a will, and drove the Rebels back into the woods, and the fight was at an end. We stacked arms and rested where we were, without sleep throughout the night, establishing pickets, and sending out small parties for stragglers and the wounded. With cavalry, or an hour more of daylight, we could have taken a great many prisoners. We secured, as it was, men of twelve different regiments and seven different States. Though we looked for harder work the next day, the men had been so cool and brave, — not a man of E shrunk back after we formed the line, — that we felt ready for anything. Rebel arms, and here and there their owners, lay scattered about. Our regiment lost two men shot dead, and about seventeen wounded; one of Company E, at least, mortally. But no volley was fired at us directly, I think; though I may be mistaken, and there were many bullets which found their way towards us. On Sunday morning we were ready before daylight, and we saw Rebel horsemen and skirmishers in front; but our batteries had come up in force, most had been unable to get over the river and marshes in time for Saturday's fight, and the Rebs soon beat a retreat from that point. About two hours later, six, A. M., they attacked the left of our force, which was now very large, and for many hours a fearful fire was kept up at that point; but we could only see the smoke and hear the reports of the guns, and see our new troops constantly entering the woods, for the line was long, the fields wide, and the fight just within the woods. About noon the Rebels retired, unsuccessful in their attempt to drive us into the river or butcher us. All our troops moved towards the left, and in the afternoon and night an attack on us (we then occupied the centre of the field and the right of the line) was expected, as the balloon had reported very large reinforcements on their way from Richmond.

"We had many alarms, but the Rebels did not attack us, and on Monday we secured our position, buried the dead, collected the arms, &c., but got little rest. Since that time we have been on picket duty near the railroad and turnpike, and have now been unable to take off our arms or equipments for a week. We are under arms, ready for an attack, about half the time, day and night, but have had no attack yet; and I think the Rebel rank and file will scarcely be brought to attack us again, where they have been discomfited so signally. They had a partial success Saturday morning, as at Shiloh on the first day, and in part for the same reason, it is hinted; but the punishment followed more quickly on this occasion than the other, for we punished them on the same day. The Rebels did their best to drive us across the river, and laid a deep plot, but we defeated them. They had meant to make it a three days' affair rather than fail; but their disaster Sunday taught them the impossibility of success, and Monday was quiet."

The battle was followed by twelve days of extremely fatiguing duty, which very few of the regiment bore as well as Lowell. He writes thus to his classmate Hartwell:—

"Our fight of the 31st and 1st was followed by the hardest work yet put before us,—ten days of unceasing vigilance in the face of the enemy. Rain or shine, night or day, we were under arms at the slightest alarm, and remained in line for an hour or two; we did not mean to be surprised, like Casey's division. For twelve days we kept on our clothes and equipments. As knapsacks and baggage were not brought near us for nearly that length of time, we could not have changed our clothes even if we had been able to call fifteen or five minutes our own. We were washed by the rain, and then dried ourselves in the sun, or before fires, which were permitted in the daytime. For five days we have been in the rear, near enough the front line to be turned out in case of firing, but far enough back to sleep half of the nights without equipments on, and to indulge in frequent baths; also to pitch our shelter-tents and think a little of our meals. But even in this place of comparative rest, three, A. M., always finds us in line of battle, and for an hour and a half we are ready for the attack of the enemy. Six o'clock used to seem an early hour to arouse us for prayers, but our day seems nearly half gone at that time."

Lowell remained near Fair Oaks until the 28th of June. He had entire confidence in the skill of McClellan, and felt sure of his success. He knew nothing of what was preparing for the Army of the Potomac, and very little of what was going on. Like a true soldier, he was intent on doing what his hand found to do, even though he was working in the dark. He writes to Hartwell on the 26th:—

"Sunday [22d] was a quiet day with us, but we have since had skirmishes at our front, in which we were generally rumored *to be advancing*, and yet found our forces in their old position at night, the movements being merely reconnoissances on one side or the other. But to-day there has been quite heavy firing on our left, and we are at last rumored *to have advanced*, and remained forward. . . . . We think we are gaining ground upon the Rebels, not merely because we are not losing it (at first we were content with that), but because we beat them generally in the skirmishes. But it is very hard to learn the truth about these little fights; some men talk one way, some the other, and one can rarely tell which to believe. . . . .

"I don't wish to be shot in a skirmish or on picket, but in a real fight, if I am to be hit again. . . . .

"The fighting yesterday [at Oak Grove] was quite severe, and the loss quite heavy; but we still hold our advanced position. To-day our part of the lines has been quiet; but there has been very heavy cannonading, and probably a severe battle on our right in Porter's corps [Mechanicsville]. It is rumored that he has driven back Stonewall Jackson, and turned the left flank of the enemy; and all our camps have rung with cheers since dark. But the Rebel bands are playing away vigorously in front, perhaps for a reported victory; perhaps to deceive and bother us; perhaps to keep up the spirits of the Rebels; perhaps, and perhaps, and perhaps. As the truth now appears, it is our own bands, which have been dumb for a month, but are now allowed to play; but we hear the Rebel drums after. We are looking for orders to march at any moment, and I really have hopes of seeing Richmond before this month is ended. . . . .

"*June 27.* — All right, except that we are still in camp; but a brisk cannonading is going on."

This is the last letter Lowell ever wrote. The orders came, but not to march on Richmond. He was ordered to Savage's Station (being then in command of his company) to destroy ammunition, and on the 29th joined in the retreat across the Peninsula. He led his company until the afternoon of the 30th, when he received a mortal wound in the fight at Glendale. He was shot in the abdomen while the regiment was advancing over an open field. To those who came to help him when he fell he said, "Don't mind me, men, go forward." He was carried to a neighboring farm-house, which had been taken as a hospital. When told, in answer to an inquiry, that his wound was probably mortal, he said that he was as ready to die as to live, were it not for his friends. "He felt that his death was altogether right, and hoped they would think so at home." In the evening Patten was brought in wounded. Lowell asked that his comrade might be laid next him, took his hand and held it, and talked of the sudden termination of his life without a regret. When our troops moved on, and orders came for all who could to fall in, he insisted on Patten's leaving him. Patten asked if he had no messages for home. "I have written them all," he said; "tell them how it was, Pat." The officers of his regiment who went to bid him farewell tell us that the grasp of his hand was warm and firm and his countenance smiling and happy. He desired that his father might be told that he was struck while dressing the line of his men; besides this he had no message but "Good by" He expressed a wish that his sword might not fall into the enemy's hands, — a wish that was faithfully attended to by Colonel Palfrey, through whose personal care it was preserved and sent home. All who saw him testify to the perfect composure of his mind and to the beautiful expression of his face. Two of our surgeons who had been left with the wounded at the farm were much impressed by his behavior, and one of them told the Rebel officers to talk with *him*, if they wished to know how a Northern soldier thought and felt. He lingered four days, and died on the 4th of July. A private of his regiment wrapped him in a blanket and laid him to rest under a tree. The name of the place is Nelson's, or Frazier's Farm.

Lowell was among the earliest of the Harvard soldiers to fall by the hand of the enemy. Colonel Peabody preceded him about three months, having been killed at Pittsburg Landing, and Major How died on the field in the same battle in which Lowell received his mortal wound. He was also the earliest to fall of seven kinsmen, the lives of five of whom will be found in these volumes.

While the soul of this noble young soldier was passing slowly away, his sister, who had for some time been serving as volunteer nurse on a hospital steamer, was lying at Harrison's Bar, on the James River, only a few miles off. She heard of his dangerous wound, and tried every expedient to get to him, but without success. Three years after, that same sister, who had continued all this while in the hospital service, set out from Richmond to find her brother's grave. Following the line of our Army's retreat from Fair Oaks, in his very footsteps, she with some difficulty tracked out the farm-house and at last discovered the tree which marked the place of his burial. The day happened to be June 30th, the anniversary of that on which he was wounded, and the grave was found at about the same time in the afternoon when he was brought into the hospital. The remains were removed by affectionate hands in the succeeding November, and deposited in Mount Auburn beside those of his brother.

This was a short life, only a span long: but if the essential thing in life be the bringing of our wills into free co-operation with the will of God, this life of less than twenty-five years was yet complete. That harmony once achieved, and immortality so assured, it can be of little moment whether death comes sooner or later. Though the final act of sacrifice has importance in our eyes, as setting a visible seal to his integrity, we see, and we should see without surprise, that it cost Lowell no struggle. The serenity with which he received the summons of death must not be misunderstood. It did not come from blind enthusiasm, nor even from an unusual exaltation of feeling. It was also as remote as possible from apathy: it had no character of insensibility. It has already been said that his enjoyment of life was intense. No one had a keener relish for its every-day pleasures. It was crowned for him, in Körner's words, "with the flowery wreaths of love, of friendship, and of joy." No one could be less indifferent to the grief his death would cause at home; no one could have taken a deeper satisfaction in witnessing and assisting in the extension of knowledge and the improvement of the condition of mankind. The coexistence of this vivid enjoyment of the world with a readiness to relinquish all its delights and hopes at a moment's call, has been portrayed and explained by the one who knew him best, in these verses.

"Twin fountains sent forth Our Delight. From one
Came all that Nature to her darling brings

To make a lover of each looker on;
Fair gifts — not graces yet — nor rooted quite;
Fair silver vessels for the golden fruit.

"But lest the lover's soul, dizzy with joy,
Lost in a perfumed cloud should lie before
The lovely and the fair, crying, 'No more, —
I want no more,' — from the twin fountain flowed,
Deep, simple, stern, a rill of Hebrew life.
'Lord, I am thine: do with me as thou wilt;
Set thou my feet aright; they seek thy goal.'
Thus prayed this rich-fraught soul, and in his thought
Beheld himself a pilgrim weak and poor."

A minuter analysis than it is possible to go into here would show a rare symmetry in Lowell's character, the result of a religious discipline acting upon a pure and generous nature. His whole life, says one who knew it all, was "luminous with love." Even in childhood his love was not the accidental, unspiritual attachment of most boys. Though impetuous, and by no means wanting in energy of will, he was docile and modest. The eagerness with which he pursued his objects occasioned him many trials of temper, and the self-chastisement which was thus required kept him from thinking highly of himself. He never excused his faults, or used any sophistry in extenuating them, but felt them keenly and repented of them humbly. Towards himself he was rigid; but though he expected every man to do his duty, — for a sense of justice is generally recognized as his distinguished trait, — he was lenient to others. Though he was not given to the expression of religious sentiment, he lived habitually near to God, and in lowly dependence upon him. In a book of extracts, he entered, probably about the time of his leaving college, some lines of Ben Jonson as a sort of charge to himself, which may serve as an epitome both of his character and of his career.

"That by commanding first thyself thou mak'st
Thy person fit for any charge thou tak'st;
That whatsoever face thy fate puts on,
Thou shrink or start not, but be always one;
That thou think nothing great but what is good,
And from that thought strive to be understood: —
These take, and now go seek thy peace in war;
Who falls for love of God shall rise a star."

EDWARD BROMFIELD MASON.

Assistant Surgeon 14th Mass. Vols. (1st Mass. Heavy Artillery), March 1, 1862; Second Lieutenant 2d Mass. Cavalry, June 4, 1863; died September 14, 1863, at Readville, Mass., of injuries received from an accident in camp.

EDWARD BROMFIELD MASON was born July 2, 1837, in Boston. He was the son of William Powell and Hannah (Rogers) Mason, and the grandson of Jonathan Mason, who was United States Senator from Massachusetts from 1800 to 1803. As a boy, he was unusually attractive in person and character, uniting in an uncommon degree gentleness and warm affections with a spirit of daring and cool courage that helped him out of, as well as led him into, many difficulties.

After going through the usual course of studies in various schools, at fifteen years of age he accompanied his parents to Europe, and the eighteen months passed there developed and fostered a love of adventure, and an enthusiasm for the beautiful in nature and in art, which were most marked features in his character. Naturally modest, and free from any inclination for display, it was only to his most intimate and sympathetic friends that he showed himself freely. With them, his graphic descriptions of what had most interested him abroad, his vivid imagination, his lively and genial humor, and his intense enjoyment of everything that was striking and beautiful in life, imparted a singular glow and charm to his conversation.

On his return from Europe, at the close of the year 1853, he was fitted for Harvard College by Mr. Samuel Eliot, and entered the Sophomore Class in July, 1855. He graduated with his Class, and after leaving college commenced the study of medicine with Professor Wyman and Dr. Nichols at Cambridge. At this period an incident occurred, strikingly illustrating his kind feelings, his fearlessness, and his disregard of self. A fellow-student, with whom he was but slightly acquainted, was suddenly attacked with a severe form of small-pox.

Being at a distance from his relatives and friends, he suffered much from want of suitable attendance and nursing; and the nature of his disease and his limited means rendered it difficult to obtain assistance. Edward, regardless of his own exposure, pitying his helpless and friendless condition, visited and watched with him, and thought so little of these charitable acts that they never came to the knowledge of his family and friends until he himself was taken down with the varioloid in consequence.

Before the completion of his medical course, the war of the Rebellion broke out, and both he and his brother were anxious to bear their part in defending the Union. Their father, however, just slowly recovering from a long and dangerous illness, which left it uncertain how far he might regain his former state of health, felt so unable to meet the trial of parting with both of his sons at once for so dangerous a service, that they promised that one of them should certainly remain at home with him. The oldest, in November, 1861, was appointed Aid to Major-General McClellan. Edward, however, remained at home, completed his medical course of studies, and, in July, 1861, after passing a very good examination, received his diploma of M. D.

No longer occupied by a daily attendance at Cambridge, at the Medical School and the Hospital; in a high state of health, with a vigorous frame, an active imagination, and a courageous spirit; excited by the daily reports from our armies, — he felt a renewal of his original desire to enter the service. He became restless and uneasy, and expressed himself strongly as feeling that he was put in a wrong position by remaining quietly at home, while so many of his companions were in the field, or hastening thither to join our Massachusetts regiments. Under these circumstances, his parents, seriously questioning whether they were justified in taking advantage of his affection for them, and any longer opposing a desire so natural, patriotic, and honorable to him, consented to release him from his promise, with the understanding that he should apply for a commission as Assistant Surgeon, instead of a more exposed position in the line.

To this limited release, he finally, with reluctance, assented, having previously set his heart upon obtaining a second lieutenancy in a regiment in which some of his former companions were commissioned. After waiting anxiously for a length of time, he finally received a commission as Assistant Surgeon in the Fourteenth Massachusetts Volunteers, commanded by Colonel W. B. Greene, then stationed at Fort Albany; and in February, 1862, he joined the regiment.

As month after month rolled by, and while other regiments passed to the front, the Fourteenth still remained stationary to guard the capital, he became very impatient at the continued inaction; and but for the pain he knew he would give his parents, would willingly have taken any position which would bring him into more active service.

The dull routine of his duties at Fort Albany was, however, unexpectedly interrupted in August, 1862, by an order sent to Colonel Greene to join the Army of the Potomac, and advance towards the enemy. Dr. Mason wrote home in great spirits at the prospect before him.

On the 28th of the month, near Fairfax Court-House, Colonel Greene found a cavalry force of the enemy twice as large as his own before him, commanded by General Fitz-Hugh Lee. An immediate attack was expected, which was not made, however, owing to the strength of Colonel Greene's position. Unfortunately the Surgeons, Drs. Dana and Mason, while selecting a house for the accommodation of the wounded, just outside the lines of their regiment, were suddenly captured and taken to the head-quarters of General Lee. Here Dr. Mason unexpectedly met his former classmate at Cambridge, W. F. Lee, nephew of General R. E. Lee, and a Colonel in the Rebel service. He received the prisoner kindly, and presented him to the General, who after examining him very closely as to the position and numbers of our troops, released him and his companion, retaining their horses, equipments, and attendants. Dr. Mason's replies to General Lee's questions proved very satisfactory to Colonel Greene.

In a letter to Dr. Mason's father, referring to these incidents, Colonel Greene writes as follows :—

"The Doctor was very cool throughout the whole business. The principal surgeon reported that Dr. Mason wanted to fight when he was captured, and that he refused to give up his pistol until he was ordered to do so by Dr. Dana, his immediate superior, who expressed great admiration of his assistant.

"Dr. Mason told me, when he made his report, that he would apply to Governor Andrew for a position in the line, and that I would soon lose the power of ordering him to the rear. He asked me to give him a letter of recommendation, and to state in it that I thought he would do better in the line than as a surgeon. . . . . I gave him as good a letter as I knew how to write. It was certainly my opinion that he would make an excellent line officer."

Dr. Mason, on writing home, said that Colonel Greene had given him a very handsome letter of recommendation.

After an absence of about three weeks, the regiment returned to Fort Albany, much to the disappointment of Dr. Mason, which disappointment was enhanced by the resignation of Colonel Greene, which took place shortly afterwards. Early in December, however, he received an order from head-quarters to serve as medical director on the staff of Colonel Cogswell, acting Brigadier-General; but in January, 1863, Colonel Tannett, the new commander of the Fourteenth, ordered him to Maryland Heights to look after four companies of the Fourteenth, which were stationed there. He then wrote to his father: —

"I had long wished to make a change and to obtain if possible a commission in the First Massachusetts Cavalry, when my present position as medical director was offered me. I accepted it with pleasure, and desired to retain it as long as possible, hoping that something might turn up in the mean time; but now that I am compelled to return to my former position and go to Harper's Ferry, this wish of mine is strengthened, and I have decided to write an application to the Governor, desiring him to transfer me from the medical staff, and commission me as a line officer in either the First or Second Massachusetts Cavalry. I am afraid you will consider this step as rash and ill-advised. I am sorry on your and mother's account to feel compelled to take it, but I am not satisfied to remain as Assistant Surgeon in my present situation for the rest of the war, attending only to the sick, and without any opportunity of obtaining experience in the surgical part of my profession. Colonel Cogswell, who will probably be confirmed as Brigadier-General in a few weeks, has promised to take me on his staff as aide-de-camp. If you still feel opposed to my making this change, please write."

After much delay, — during which, following the wishes of his parents, he applied for a transfer as Assistant Surgeon from his present position to a regiment in the field, and found that such a transfer was against the regulations, — he accepted a commission as Second Lieutenant in the Second Massachusetts Cavalry, offered him by Colonel Lowell.

In August he sent in his resignation as Assistant Surgeon, and shortly afterwards reported himself at Readville, where a part of the regiment was recruiting. At an evening parade, his horse, an undisciplined one, reared and fell backwards upon him, inflicting a serious injury, which after a fortnight of severe suffering proved fatal to him.

The following extract from a tribute to his memory which appeared in the papers shortly after his death, from the pen of a friend in no way connected with him, will show how those estimated his character who had an opportunity of forming an unprejudiced judgment of it.

"No careful observer of his thoughtful and expressive face can have failed to see beneath that clear serenity a latent power capable of being brought into earnest action; and in the nameless slight courtesies, addressed to those who most needed them, which mark the true gentleman, no one could have hesitated to recognize the self-forgetfulness which led him to brave the peril of a fearful disease, from which the timid shrank, in order to minister to the extreme needs of a friend. All honor to the simple goodness which would have refused praise for a deed which was doubtless a necessity to his kindly nature, — a deed which won for him the respect of many who would have hesitated to follow his example.

"Endowed with all the qualities that make home lovely, — amiable, unselfish, intelligent, — with a touch, if we mistake not, of romance, which might instigate the possessor to swerve a little from the beaten track, this young man seemed born to make brighter the fortunate circumstances in which he was placed by

Providence, while a rare modesty secured the regard of all who really knew him."

The delineation of Dr. Mason's character in this extract will be accepted by all who knew him intimately as eminently just. Should those who formerly felt an interest in the subject of this memorial find that it accords with their view of his character, void as it is of any brilliant deeds or great services, they may possibly believe with the writer, that if Dr. Mason had been permitted to follow his inclination from the first, he would have borne himself as bravely in defence of his country as those noble companions of his who fell in the field; and would probably have found with them a soldier's grave.

HENRY LYMAN PATTEN.

Second Lieutenant 20th Mass. Vols. (Infantry), November 25, 1861; First Lieutenant, October 1, 1862; Captain, May 1, 1863; Major, June 20, 1864; died at Philadelphia, Pa., September 10, 1864, of a wound received at Deep Bottom, Va., August 17.

HENRY LYMAN PATTEN, of the Twentieth Massachusetts Volunteers, was born in Kingston, New Hampshire, on the 4th of April, 1836. His father, Colcord Patten, and his mother, Maria (Fletcher) Patten, were substantial New England people, whose children (Henry being the youngest) have all become worthy citizens. His early life gave bright promise of distinction. His singularly quick intelligence and love of books caused him, after the usual course of district schools, to be sent to the public Latin School of Boston. Thence, having graduated with high honors and prizes as a medal scholar, he passed into Harvard College in July, 1854.

At this time Patten was a fine specimen of the college student. In person he was short, straight, compact, well-knit, vigorous, and elastic. In later years, his shoulders so filled and broadened as to remove the idea of insignificance which his small stature gave. His face, with its regular features, was thoroughly handsome: its frank and open expression was the trustworthy index of his character, and his passport to confidence and love. His cheeks were ruddy with health, his hazel eyes full of light and meaning, his lips mobile and expressive, his forehead broad and shapely. He was almost equally proficient in all the college studies, except the modern languages, but perhaps showed most skill in the classics and metaphysics. Through several college terms he ranked third or fourth scholar in a class of nearly a hundred. Lack of money, however, (an inconvenience which vexed him for many years,) forced him to be absent through part of his course, teaching schools or private pupils. This double pressure slightly lowered his numerical rank, but did not touch his prestige among his fellow-students and professors as a brilliant and thorough scholar.

His character was, in college, a singular mixture of boyishness and maturity. He was fond of athletic and out-door sports, and passed nearly as much of his college career on the Delta as in the recitation-room. He was a quick and daring football player, and one of the best cricketers in the Class. A friend writes of him, that "his only fault as a cricket-player was that he was too rash, and was frequently put out in attempting to make runs when the ball was almost in the hand of the bowler of the opposite side." He very often neglected the Class tasks to play out a match game, or for a walk, or for skating, — or sometimes, it must be owned, for a favorite book, or agreeable company, or a friendly idle chat. Among his comrades he won a reputation for frankness, generosity, courage, quickness, intelligence, and an overflow of good-humor and animal spirits. In conversation, his address was pleasing, his words select and forcible, his utterances direct and frank. He had no reservations. There was no worse thing left in his mind to be said after the hearer's back was turned. Sometimes his emphatic style of assent or dissent was unpleasantly brusque: but his vivacity and vigor, and the general *bonhomie* of his bearing, made him an excellent conversationalist and an agreeable companion.

He was an active member, in successive years, of the Anonyma, Institute of 1770, Psi Upsilon, and Hasty Pudding Club, and of a much-prized private club. As he possessed a fine oratorical delivery, and a ringing and melodious voice, he became an effective as well as fluent debater. He was, too, an unusually good writer, as his college dissertations, exhibition parts, and his exceedingly entertaining letters attest.

If among his many noble traits frankness be pronounced the most striking, his generosity held at least the second place. He was generous to a fault, spending his money instantly on getting it, and never on himself alone. He was charitable in his judgment of others. One of the most judicious of his comrades said: —

"I do not remember ever to have heard him speak ill of any

person not present. I know no one with more liberality in judging other's actions, or more sympathy with the feelings and sufferings of others, or a more prompt and indulgent appreciation of the temptation under which a wrong or mean action might have been committed, than Patten. Nevertheless, he was wonderfully firm in sticking to his own opinions and practices, and settled in his convictions."

College days being over, and his Commencement speech pronounced, Patten turned to the law. It was the summer of 1858. A twelvemonth earlier, in vacation, he had written from Kingston to a friend: —

"My brother, though not a lawyer exactly, is the 'squire,' and has an office in which are several law books, a dozen or so, into which I now and then peep. I think you and I will never repent our choice of a profession. I never have seen a sensible fellow yet who, having studied law, did not think it the best of pursuits."

But the omnipresent question of finances again came up, and the result was a year's devotion to teaching, with the view of accumulating money enough to carry him through a year of law study. It need hardly be added that this plan took three years for its accomplishment, instead of one. After many disappointments in seeking a place, he became a tutor in the Free Academy at Utica, New York. There he kept up a correspondence with some old friends, and sighed to be in Cambridge, "studying law and reading Plautus."

His year at Utica ended, Patten obtained a situation as private tutor, through the aid of President Walker of Harvard University, who had always been his friend. His pupil, George Appleton, a youth of eighteen, was a grandson of William Appleton of Boston, and son (by a former marriage) of Mrs. Arnold, herself a daughter of George W. Lyman. Her residence was at Montgomery, Georgia, twelve miles from Savannah, on the beautiful Vernon River. Thither Patten went for a year, in the autumn of 1859. He passed much leisure time in shooting the abundant small game, his pupil being extremely fond of field sports. For a while the genial tutor also was quite enamored of this pursuit (though he got surfeited in due time) and enthusiastically wrote: "When you ride horseback or row, you are likely to be thinking about ordinary cares all the time, —*post equitem sedet atra cura*, — and perches on the oar-blade, too. But when a covey of partridges start, — whir, whir, whir! — away fly all thoughts but those of the game." In one of his admirable Savannah letters to friends, we find a scholarly criticism on Dr. Eliot's rendering of the word ἁρπαγμόν as "to be robbed," in a sermon which he discusses. Controversial theology and metaphysics had always great charms for him; and, with congenial comrades, he would speculate earnestly on these topics for hours together on long walks or before the evening fire. He was much pleased, while at Savannah, with the writings of Mansel. His letters, also, are full of earnest and candid discussions of slavery. He tells with fidelity what he sees of it. His theory is that of "necessary evil for the present." He desires its speedy end, but finds "many excuses and palliating circumstances for slaveholders," and "insurmountable difficulties at present" in its removal. Meanwhile he "can never forget the immense injustice on which the system rests." Politics he reviews quite as earnestly, it being the year of the Presidential election. His favorite candidates were Bell and Everett, but he would have voted for Mr. Seward, had he been the Republican nominee. In the spring of 1860, he attacked Blackstone again, though not very earnestly, and found "no book more interesting." But lighter reading, as of favorite novels, like "The Virginians," was better suited to the approaching summer; and out-door pleasures made him, he says, "dwindle in mind and grow fat in body." As his engagement approached an end, he sighed for "Northern air" and a more ambitious career.

In the summer of 1860, accordingly, he returned North, and accepted, in September, an assistant professorship in the Academic Department of Washington University, St. Louis, offered to him by his friend Chancellor Hoyt of that University. Here our young pedagogue passed another successful year, and thence returning, he entered the Cambridge Law School in the summer of 1861, and at the same time received a proctorship in the College. But the great war of Rebellion, which was to make, to crown, and to terminate his career on earth, had already come. Some of his old comrades were already in the field. In August, directly on returning to Kingston from the West, we find him eager to have a share in the good cause. One of his letters "believes it not immodest to say" he could fill a second lieutenancy as well as some who had been commissioned. But he was working against great obstacles. He writes to an intimate friend: "I feel with you on the military question, ... but I have no prospect of a lieutenancy. —— would not lift a finger for me, as he does not wish me to go. But if I *could* have a lieutenancy, I would accept." He adds, that the want of vigor in the war "alternately drives me frantic and depresses me"; and closes by asking, "Can you send me up a manual of tactics?"

The Twentieth Massachusetts marched away to the front in September, and a month later, at Ball's Bluff, received its baptism of blood. On hearing this news, Patten, who had chafed so long to be away, breaking loose from all hindrances, devoted himself forever to the country. The example of his intimate friend Lowell, for whom he had always great admiration and affection, — which were thoroughly reciprocated, — had greatly influenced him, as it did many other college classmates. The repulse at Leesburg ploughed grievous gaps in the ranks of the Twentieth, which many young heroes sprang forward to fill, — a score for every lad who had fallen. In Company E, Captain Schmitt and First Lieutenant J. J. Lowell were wounded, and the gallant Second Lieutenant Putnam killed. Patten instantly applied to succeed young Putnam, and, thanks to his bearing, character, and record, and the enthusiastic support of his friends, after exciting competition, succeeded. He was long on the tiptoe of expectation; but, resolved to fight in the good cause at any rate, presented himself in the regimental camp not only before a commission had been given to him, but even before he had had a nomination. A letter soon after sent to Cambridge expresses his exultation at his appointment.

"CAMP BENTON, November 15, 1861.

"DEAR A——, — Appointed at last! one of the fortunate two, out of thirty applicants. I have spent a week of anxiety, however. It was doubtful about my appointment, Colonel Palfrey being determined to select the two he considered the best. For all I know, you are the other. He sent two names to the Governor, of which mine was one. . . . . The officers of this regiment are fine fellows, and I consider myself fortunate to be among them. Will you dispose of my goods and chattels, and have cash paid? And could you talk with Mr. Lowell about the things I want? . . . . Tell the Professors why I did not see them and bid them good by. May you soon be with me!"

Henceforth the history of the Twentieth Massachusetts is Patten's history. He never was absent, till death, from any battle in that remarkable series of battles which it fought. He never was absent even from any great march or any severe duty. He had taken the resolve to cling to the regiment so long as it carried its banner or its name. His undivided soul was in the country's cause. "We are in for the war," he used to say till the fatal bullet found him, "though it lasted twenty years." Never, except when struck down on the field or prostrate from disease, did he accept even a brief furlough, and that he reluctantly consented to snatch only when no arduous labor or peril was in prospect. He always hurried back to camp, in trepidation lest something might have happened and he away. Under his eye, and in his daily round of bivouac, march, and battle, the Twentieth dwindled away to a fragment, filled again, again and again dwindled and filled, till he saw only in its unquenchable spirit the sign of what he found it in the Maryland camp.

Some of Patten's young friends joined in buying him a handsome sword, which they sent with a complimentary letter. It was a grateful present for a double reason. Till it arrived, he wore a sword which had been lent him. When it came, his letter of thanks pleasantly traced different parts of the weapon and accoutrements to individual givers, — the point, the hilt, &c., according to fanciful analogies. "The belt," he concludes, addressing the original source of the little gift, "'is yours. For all hangs upon that, and that clasps the closest. But the rest shall be undivided."

When once he had resolved to give his life to the country, Patten, as was said, went to camp on the chances of a commission; and fearing he might fail of one, even after appointment, he writes thence, "I firmly intend to go in as private rather than go home." Many weeks elapsed, during which he was without rank, sword, or uniform. One letter, in his impatient hand, says he has "expected his commission every night for the last two weeks. . . . . We are afraid of dull inactivity this winter. But, pshaw! I can't write anything till I am settled. I am feverishly impatient." His commission as Second Lieutenant of Company E bore date November 25, 1861. That winter he passed with the Twentieth, of Lander's brigade, in Camp Benton, at Poolesville, Maryland, diligently studying, — his eyes and ears wide open to his new duties, and his heart inspired with ever-increasing loyalty and devotion. His letters vividly picture these new experiences and especially the guard duties, — the guard on a beautiful night, with a huge open fire, and the camp-fires of the evening's pickets glimmering against the dark Virginia mountains. "One does not sleep much under such circumstances," wrote Lieutenant Patten; "there is a little romance in it." He soon showed himself a thorough and admirable officer; yet he of course thought otherwise. "My military education," he says, "comes on slowly. Theoretically, I do very well, and find no difficulty in managing my peaceful company. But the *grand air* is preciously wanting in your humble friend."

Towards the end of February Lieutenant Patten, who had been chafing all winter at the general inactivity, exultingly writes a hurried line: "We really expect an advance, and the thought thrills every fibre of us. An advance! and battle! — perhaps death, — surely victory and glory. The regiment is ready, — on, on to Richmond and victory." Shortly after, in March, the division, Sedgwick's, moved across the Potomac and up the Shenandoah Valley nearly to Winchester in support of Banks's movement, and then was withdrawn to Bolivar.

During this operation, our Lieutenant insisted that he had slept better in the open air than ever under any roof.

The great Peninsular campaign followed, beginning in April, 1862. At Yorktown, Lieutenant Patten got his first sight of siege and battle. Thence Sedgwick's division was despatched in the column which occupied West Point; but the Twentieth was only drawn up in support in the action there. The whole of Sumner's corps was now north of the Chickahominy, while those of Keyes and Heintzelman were south of it. By so faulty a disposition the enemy was sure to profit. When, at Fair Oaks, on the 31st of May, the left wing of the army was driven back, the danger was imminent. But Sumner, hearing the thunders of battle from the left bank of the river, and reading the necessities of the hour with the inspiration of a genuine soldier, marched *au canon*, without waiting for orders. Sedgwick's division was in advance, crossed the swaying and dangerous Chickahominy bridge, made a forced march through the deep mire all day long, and at six at night, after the greatest exertions, reached the scene of action and deployed column. It was not too soon. The enemy, driving all before him, was sweeping down upon our troops with a destructive fire. Sumner at once hurled at him the head of his gallant column, composed of Dana's and Gorman's brigades, — five excellent regiments in all. In Dana's was the Twentieth Massachusetts. The troops streamed with fixed bayonets into the woods, amid great enthusiasm, checked the enemy's course, drove him back in confusion, and saved the day at Fair Oaks. "That one act of heroic duty," says the historian of the Potomac Army, "must embalm brave old Sumner's memory in the hearts of his countrymen."

Then followed the turning of the right wing of the army at Beaver Dam Creek, and the memorable seven days' retreat to the new base on the James. In that terrible time of trial, which brought out from every soldier whatever of virtue there was in him, Patten's gallantry and manliness were so brilliant as to receive special official mention in the report of his commanding officer. In three successive battles, at Gaines's Mill,

Savage Station, and White Oak Swamp, Sumner's columns held off the exultant rush of the enemy with stubborn grip, and met each dash of Magruder with an answering blow, till the army and all its trains had safely traversed the swamp. But it was a week of hourly fighting and marching. The swamp being passed, the next day, June 30th, A. P. Hill and Longstreet, surging up against our rear, were repulsed with great loss in the battle of Glendale. Here Dana's brigade was conspicuous, and the Twentieth Massachusetts plucked fresh laurels, though with the loss of many priceless officers and men. Both officers of Company E were among the wounded, — Lieutenant Lowell mortally, Lieutenant Patten with a deep flesh wound in the leg. They were carried from the field and laid side by side in the field hospital. Anguished with pain, Patten nerved himself to go forward with his company and regiment the same night (the battle was on a Monday afternoon), and, exchanging farewells with his comrade, found rest at length for his wounded frame in the camps of the army at Harrison's Landing.

His duty done, and his anxiety for his company (thenceforward under his own charge) being set at rest, he began to feel the effects of his wound. During the battle he had refused, with characteristic endurance, to yield to it, and had led his company, after Lowell's fall and after his own hurt, till the fighting was done, and they took him away. Colonel Palfrey, his commanding officer, vividly recalling Patten's conspicuous bravery on that day, wrote thus two years after: —

"It was not till the battle of Glendale that he had an opportunity to display that singular constancy of which the harder service of his after life furnished numerous instances. His determination on that occasion, when he fought through the battle after receiving a painful wound in the leg, made a deep impression upon me; and it gave me sincere pleasure to make particular mention of him in my official report of that engagement. His subsequent conduct more than justified the reputation he then acquired."

A few weeks prior to this letter, the same officer directly addressing a letter of sympathy to Patten, then struggling with his fifth and final wound, had said: "I know your pluck and toughness are almost unequalled. After seeing you fight through Glendale with such a wound, ... I feel that you can bear anything." While, however, his praise was in the mouths of all his brother officers, and especially of his own men, who from that time idolized him, Patten seemed unconscious of having done anything worth mentioning.

As for that injury which his commander called "such a wound," he made light of it, — never would have mentioned it had it not been necessary. But, in truth, he had succumbed at Harrison's Landing, and they had sent him North among the wounded. Instantly on arriving at Annapolis he hastened to discharge a duty which had been weighing on him during the passage; and, with characteristic modesty and self-forgetfulness, wrote this letter, of which the first five words and the last two sentences seem, in the original, to have been written some time after the rest: —

"IN HOSPITAL AT ANNAPOLIS, July 5, 1862.

"DEAR ——, — I write to you sad news, for I know not how to write directly to the ——. I telegraphed to-day to Dr. Walker, but very briefly. Jimmy [Lowell] was mortally wounded, in just the same way as Putnam, only more severely, in the fight last Monday afternoon. When I came in from the field, I found the brigade surgeon and the two regimental surgeons dressing his wound. He was entirely free from pain; and, while perfectly aware of his situation, was cheerful and quite talkative. He could not be moved, and we had to leave him behind in a hospital, in charge of one of our surgeons. Of course, as we evacuated that night, the enemy has possession of the hospital. The battle was about a mile and a half, I should think, from White Oak Swamp. As Jimmy fell, knowing at once that his wound was fatal, he said to some of his men, who stopped a moment to assist him, 'Never mind me, men; go forward.' . . . . Colonel Palfrey has his sword. They would not let me take it, as it was then quite uncertain whether I could take care of it, and moreover I felt very uncertain whether I should escape the hands of the Rebels. I forgot to say that such was the nature of Jim's wound that Dr. Hayward said he could not live through the night.

"You must either tell this to the family yourself immediately, or, what perhaps would be better, get some old and intimate friend of the family to tell them.

"I hear that Charley is wounded. I suppose you know all about it. I shall be in Boston in the course of a week, having a slight wound in the calf of the leg from a smooth-bore musket. Love to all.

"HENRY."

Never, either with tongue or with pen, has he anything to say of his own exploits. His thoughts are always with others and for others. As in the present case, the fall of a comrade makes the news of the battle "sad news," no matter how glorious his own conduct, how narrow his escape, how joyful his safety and prospects. A word at the end of this letter alone explains his "slight wound," — so described as to make it appear nothing, — if he had not unthinkingly mentioned his danger of falling into the enemy's hands and his physical inability to take care of a dear companion's sword. So it was with all his wounds, even to the mortal one.

Now, therefore, the young soldier took perforce his first furlough, believing the campaign over, and seeking, before the next one, health for his exhausted frame and healing for his wounds in the bracing air of his New Hampshire home. As he limped about with his cane, his astonished friends found him already developed into a thorough soldier. They found him enthusiastic for the cause, for the Army of the Potomac, and never tired of sounding the praises of his regiment, — making up for this profuseness of eulogy by his extreme reticence and modesty with regard to himself. He was hardly at home when, unexpectedly, news came of Pope's disastrous campaign. Heedless of the remonstrance of his kind surgeon, away he went on his cane, with his wound unhealed, and, to his inexpressible satisfaction, reached his regiment before it had again encountered the enemy. The battle of Chantilly followed on the 1st of September. There the brigade fought, and then brought up and covered the rear of Pope's retreat to Washington. Without pause succeeded the great Maryland campaign, consisting of the brilliant battle of South Mountain and the terrific and decisive engagement of Antietam. At this latter battle the regiment was severely engaged, with very great loss of officers and men; and Patten was reported to be "in the thickest of the fight." These actions took place on the 14th and 17th of September, and closed up the long battle-summer. When, some months later, the fearful losses among the officers of the Twentieth gave young Patten a chance for promotion, his commission as First Lieutenant was antedated to October 1, 1862. It was a grade tolerably well earned.

Not long after, he received from certain friends the assurance that, if he would consent to it, he should have a majorship in a new regiment, and all the rest and recreation possible in a long recruiting service at home. The bait might have been tempting, considering his exhaustion, and the fact that some of his young friends were reaching colonelships and brigadier-generalships without having been through a half of his service. But it had no attraction for him. With no lack of ambition, he would yet have served always in his subordinate position, rather than have been the commanding officer of any other regiment.

Burnside's brief but bloody campaign followed. In the memorable attempt to carry the heights beyond Fredericksburg, the first thing necessary was to throw pontoon-bridges across the Rappahannock. Hall's brigade, consisting of the Nineteenth and Twentieth Massachusetts and Seventh Michigan, "volunteered," as General Couch reports, as a forlorn hope, for a perilous scheme now resolved upon. They were three of those five regiments of Sedgwick's division who had routed the enemy at Fair Oaks. This brigade was sent down the steep bank unsupported, and at its foot they sustained for fifteen or twenty minutes the enemy's cutting fire, while open boats could be prepared and pushed into the stream. In these unprotected boats the brigade, by several instalments, made the passage of the stream, under concentrated fire, till they had gained the cover of the opposite bank. "The affair," says Mr. Swinton's History, "was gallantly executed, and the army, assembled on the northern bank, spectators of this piece of heroism, paid the brave fellows the rich tribute of soldiers' cheers." But the harder half of the task remained. This was the ordeal of marching straight through the town, and driving out the picket marksmen who, having been forced back from the bank, had taken refuge in the houses. This most severe of trials was too much even for the other fine regiments of the brigade, and the Twentieth marched alone through the town, in column of companies, with the fire of unseen rifles wasting them in front, in rear, and on either flank, from every house, till the street was strewn with their dead, and nearly one hundred officers and men, being one in three, lay killed or wounded within fifty yards. Nevertheless, they carried the town and the bridge was laid. The brigade commander reported that he "cannot presume to express" what is due to "the Twentieth Regiment for its unflinching bravery and splendid discipline." Next day the regiment held the extreme right of Couch's corps, in the murderous charge up Marye's Heights; and a cross-fire of artillery and musketry ploughed lanes in the ranks of the column. The Twentieth lost sixty of about two hundred men; and many supporting regiments broke and fled from the field. In this two days' attempt on Fredericksburg, it lost one hundred and fifty-seven killed and wounded, out of the scanty three hundred and seven to which the Peninsula and Antietam had brought it down. Patten was one of the two or three officers who were in the thickest of all and escaped unhurt.

But we must, henceforth, abandon details, and hurry into lines what is worthy of volumes. The next great action for the Twentieth, and consequently for Patten, was Chancellorsville, where the division (the Second of the Second Corps) was assigned to General Sedgwick's famous column on the left, which carried Fredericksburg, stormed Marye's Heights, threatening Lee's whole army with destruction, and, when Hooker had failed like Burnside, held the line of outposts till all had recrossed the river.

Meade now succeeded, and Gettysburg was fought. In that tremendous battle the Twentieth, as usual, was under the hottest fire. It was in that division, for example, on Cemetery Ridge, which, during the battle of July 3d, received Pickett's magnificent charge with pluck as magnificent. The crest was soon covered with dead and wounded; but all who survived of the attacking column remained prisoners on the ridge. The Twentieth Massachusetts carried to Gettysburg ten officers and two hundred and eighteen men. Of these, seven officers and one hundred and one men fell in the action; three officers and one hundred and sixteen men came out unscathed, or too slightly wounded to be reported. Patten was twice wounded, but even after his second wound refused to quit the field. One wound was in the leg, the other in the hand. The middle finger of his right hand was amputated.

That his wounds might the sooner heal, Patten took a furlough. It was a twelvemonth since he had been home. He now received the rank of Captain, antedated to May 1, 1863; he had had at least the satisfaction of performing its duties on a lieutenant's rank and pay for a full year. On this visit, as always, he was full of enthusiasm for his company, his regiment, and, above all, for the immortal cause. He was loud in his praises of McClellan also, of whom he remained an unyielding champion to the end. On all these points he was never tired of talking, and they seemed to absorb the whole of his once varied and changeable thoughts. There was little now in the army to keep him away from home; but he returned, as usual, at the first moment, and went through all Meade's exhausting series of marches and manœuvres, which resulted in the battle of Bristoe, where Warren thoroughly repulsed A. P. Hill. Warren's Second Division did this work, and the Twentieth captured two of the five guns there taken. Soon after, Patten marched with the army to Mine Run; and his regiment, deployed as skirmishers, drove in the enemy's skirmishers at Robertson's Tavern with memorable rapidity.

Patten's days were now nearly numbered. He came back from Mine Run with a debilitating disease of the bowels, almost surely fastened upon him for life. One whiff of fresh Northern air was all he would allow himself. Against the remonstrances of friends, he rushed back to camp the moment he had strength to perform the smallest part of his duties. On the 24th of January, 1864, he writes: —

"MY DEAR MOTHER, — It is indeed a rare luxury to receive a letter both from mother and —— in one week. I am duly grateful. There is nothing to excite your sympathy for the poor soldier just at present, except his loneliness. The weather is fine, our camp is clean and cheery, our quarters comfortable, and our regiment in lovely condition. I am perfectly well.

"I am most sorry to hear that you and father are not well. I shall probably come home and see you by and by. But I must wait until all the rest have had their turn, on account of my visit home in November last.

"There is no news to tell you. Most of our old men have re-enlisted; but we did not want to go home as a regiment, so we took the conscripts of the Nineteenth, and let *them* go.

"We are in for the war all of us, and the Twentieth will retain its name and organization for three years more, if the war lasts so long.

"He who puts his hand to the plough must not look backward. And as for the chances of life or death, one learns that neither is welcome without honor or duty, — either is welcome in the path of honor and duty. . . . .

"Love to all, and cheery hearts.

"HENRY L. PATTEN."

In May, 1864, commenced the grand final campaign. The regiment, as always, was in the Second Division, Second Corps. Captain Patten was still suffering from weakness, was scarcely fit to be in camp, much less to do the hard work now forced upon the army. But he dashed into the two days' Wilderness battle with all his old enthusiasm. Hancock's corps was hotly engaged on both days, and the Twentieth was mowed down as usual under fire. Colonel Macy was wounded, Major Abbott (Patten's exemplar and constant friend, whose praises he was never tired of rehearsing) was killed. Patten himself was shot through the hand. Worn out and wounded as he was, he refused to quit the field, but, as senior Captain, took command of the regiment at Spottsylvania, and fought it thenceforth throughout the long road from the Rapidan to Richmond. It was a period of three months of constant march and battle, — march by night and battle by day. Officers and men fell all along by the wayside, with wounds or with exhaustion. He had but three or four officers to aid him in his task, yet he clung to it, marched in every march, led his regiment in every battle, and attracted the notice of the corps and division head-quarters by his extraordinary intrepidity and steadiness. He fought through the Wilderness on May 5th and 6th; through the running fight to Spottsylvania; through the fierce battle of the 10th at the latter point; the battle of the 12th, memorable as "the fiercest and most deadly struggle of the war"; through the murderous battle of the 18th, and all the days and nights intervening. He fought at North Anna, and again at Cold Harbor, where Hancock alone lost three thousand men in less than an hour, — that unmatched charnel-house of the war. When the overland campaign was abandoned, he fought his shadow of a regiment three days before Petersburg, on the 16th, 17th, and 18th of June, and then moved down in the column which attacked the Weldon Railroad. His escape from these perils was amazing, since he was invariably reckless in exposing himself to fire. At length, on the 22d of June, after a score of gallant achievements, he performed the crowning act of his soldierly career and his life.

The Sixth, Second, and Fifth Corps had been extended to the left, to seize the Weldon Road, below Petersburg. By improper tactical dispositions, a gap had been left between the Sixth on the left and the Second in the centre. Mahone saw the error, rushed across the right flank of the Sixth Corps, struck the left of the Second, both in front and on the left, and instantly rolled up Barlow's division like a scroll. The retirement of Barlow uncovered Mott to an attack in front, flank and rear, and he too gave way in confusion. On the right, Gibbon's veteran division alone remained, having a point of support and protection in some hasty intrenchments. It in turn was overwhelmingly pressed on all sides. Regiment after regiment gave way, and the rout appeared universal, till the shock reached Captain Patten. He had a regiment which never had learned to break. Changing front with the greatest rapidity and skill, he disposed his scanty band of heroes to meet the shock. It was met and stayed. For the first time that day the Rebel column was checked, and all that was left of the division and of the day was saved. Thus Captain Patten plucked up drowning honor by the locks, and snatched personal glory from a day of utter and disastrous defeat.

Of this action Major Finley Anderson, soon after of General Hancock's staff, wrote to the New York Herald, and depicting the universal rout and destruction, especially on the capture of McKnight's batteries, said: —

"At this point, however, the tide was turned in our favor by the coolness, courage, and skill of a good line officer. It was Captain H. L. Patten, commanding the Twentieth Massachusetts Regiment, who, taking advantage of an angle of the zigzag line of breastworks, executed a change of front, poured some well-directed volleys into the enemy, and checked his further progress. It is a prevalent opinion that, had other commanders acted as he did, the enemy would have been repulsed in the commencement."

General Morgan wrote afterwards: —

"When nearly all the other regimental commanders seemed to have lost their wits, Major Patten may be said to have saved his regiment from the fate that overtook those adjacent to it."

After this crowning exploit, Patten still commanded his regiment, through battle, march, and skirmish, until the 14th of August, when he was relieved by Colonel Macy. Meanwhile, he had been adjudged worthy of the rank of Major, the assurance of which he received just before his death, — antedated to May 1, 1864. Soon after occurred the series of sanguinary feints at Deep Bottom. Major Patten took his regiment into the fight of the 17th of August, at Deep Bottom, where Gibbon's division suffered greatly, and soon, rushing in to the front, as he always did, he received a rifle-ball in the left knee, — his fifth and final wound. He was carried from his last field, and the surgeons amputated the leg above the knee, —

an operation which he endured with heroic fortitude. But what the soul could bear without flinching was too much for the body. Sent to Turner's Lane Hospital, in Philadelphia, it was soon evident that, in the incessant fatigues of the long campaign, he had poured out his vitality drop by drop. His once vigorous system had broken under the surgical operation, and it was only left for him to bear, as he did with the fortitude of a fearless soldier and a Christian gentleman, his last excruciating agonies.

On arriving at the hospital on August 24th, he wrote to one of his brothers in the gallant vein which always marked him, — a letter designed to relieve anxiety. But its painful handwriting bore witness against it.

"August 24.

"DEAR BROTHER, — Am well still, and improving. We must hope in the future. Of course something adverse may happen at any time. But I have been singularly favored in former wounds. I hope to be all right in this.

"This is a most excellent hospital, and all is done that can be done. Love to all.

"HENRY."

Six days later, he wrote to Professor Child as follows: —

"Your letter gave me great pleasure. We become sometimes almost as weak as children in our exile from home and civilization, and kindly words touch a very weak spot in us.

"I thank you for your interest in the much-suffering Twentieth. I almost weep myself when I think of its misfortunes. Almost nothing is left of it. Colonel Macy, originally a First Lieutenant, is the only officer remaining who came out with the regiment; and he, with Curtis and myself, are the only ones remaining of those who went through the Peninsular campaign; and of the men hardly a corporal's guard of old men remain.

"You have probably seen by the paper that my left leg is off, above the knee, only an apology of a stump remaining. A minié-bullet did the work on the 16th of August at Deep Bottom. I am getting on well, but cannot be moved to Boston yet.

"I must cut short my letter. I have to write lying on my back.

"Very truly yours,

"HENRY L. PATTEN."

On the same day he wrote home that he was "getting along swimmingly"; but the inevitable end drew nigh, and on the 10th of September all that was mortal of him expired.

His last days were consoled by his brothers and by kind friends, among whom was Mrs. A. H. Gibbons of New York, whose presence and motherly kindness were of inestimable comfort to the agonized young soldier. He sent for her a week before his death, and she instantly went to his bedside from Beverly Hospital, fifteen miles distant. She found him "in a very suffering condition," and afterwards wrote: —

"In all he manifested a spirit of resignation and entire submission as to the final result, loving, kind, and considerate to the latest moment; and when he could no longer speak, he took my hand and pressed it to his forehead, giving me a look of recognition and of gratitude for the little I was able to do for him. A very short time before he died, he repeated the names of his brothers, the surgeon at his bedside, who was untiring in his devotion and interest, and my own. I never witnessed more terrible agony than his. He endured it with wonderful patience and fortitude. His manly, heroic bearing was observed by all who were with him."

After his death, the body of Major Patten, clothed in the blue soldier's uniform he had so worthily worn, was taken to Kingston, his home. All the village gathered to the church at the obsequies. "There was universal sadness," writes his brother; "for all had known him, and every one had loved him." Amid tears, his friend, the clergyman, pronounced a simple, tender eulogy, and then all the people looked at his handsome face, still noble and firm as ever, "as he lay in his coffin, every inch a soldier." From Kingston the body of Major Patten was sent to Cambridge, and there buried with impressive ceremonies, with services conducted by the Rev. Presidents Walker and Hill, and the Rev. Dr. Peabody. The solemn procession of the officers and students of the University, the personal friends and admirers of the dead hero, the brother officers of his regiment and other regiments, then bore him to his grave in Mount Auburn.

HENRY AUGUSTUS RICHARDSON.

Acting Assistant Surgeon, U. S. N., August 12, 1861; discharged, on resignation, June 5, 1862; died July 1, 1863, of disease contracted in the service.

DR. HENRY AUGUSTUS RICHARDSON was born in Boston, November 25, 1836, the son of George C. and Susan Gore (Moore) Richardson. In his childhood the family removed to its present residence in the adjacent city of Cambridge. In the schools of Cambridge he received his early education, and commenced his preparation for a college course. Having completed his preparatory studies at Exeter Academy in New Hampshire, he entered the Freshman Class of Harvard College in July, 1854. There his personal traits soon made him a general favorite among his classmates. He had many friends and no enemies in every circle, and in 1858 he graduated, bearing with him the hearty good-will of all.

The circumstances of his life did not drive him to laborious effort, but to a person of his practical nature indolence had no attractions. One of his best inheritances was a desire to be actively occupied amid the busy scenes of the world. Hardly had he left college, when he began his preparation for the labors of life, and chose the practice of medicine as his employment. Indeed, the bent of his genius had been manifest in his boyhood. Before and after he entered college he had enjoyed giving a part of his time, with a few congenial minds, to personal investigations in chemistry and comparative physiology and anatomy. During his Senior year he was a frequent attendant at the lectures of the Harvard Medical School, and treatises upon medicine and surgery constituted a large portion of his desultory reading. The views of his parents and friends coinciding with his own, he became, in October, 1858, a student in the United States Marine Hospital at Chelsea, then under the charge of Dr. Charles A. Davis. Here he remained three years. During this period he devoted himself to the study of his profession with great zeal and diligence. He came regularly to Boston to attend the lectures before the Harvard Medical School, and there received the degree of M.D. in July, 1861. The opportunity which his duties at the hospital presented for exact and certain information was well pleasing to the tendency of his mind, which always inclined toward practical rather than theoretical science. He delighted in close surveillance of disease and remedial experiments, and, though a true student of science in the best sense of the term, was not a great reader of scientific books. His natural self-possession and coolness, his quick sympathy with the sufferings of a patient, and his lively and constant interest in the malady and its development, his reassuring humor and cordial ways, never failed to win the confidence of the rough, warm-hearted men to whom he ministered in the hospital, while at the same time they gave full promise of success among the more congenial associations of civil life. His faithfulness and his natural aptitude for the executive management of the institution soon brought him the principal control of its details; and a formal installation in May, 1861, as the assistant physician of the hospital, was but the recognition of services previously performed.

Dr. Richardson was not a mere student. He preferred the business and activity of the world to the cloister of the scholar. The enterprises of industry, no less than the theories of science, interested him; and upon all affairs of public concern he held decided and intelligent views. He was cautious, but independent and fearless in his conclusions, ready, although never forward, in his avowal of them. The dispassionate and reflective mood in which he considered all questions of duty or policy gave a conservative tendency to his opinions; but when fairly persuaded, he followed his convictions zealously and enthusiastically; for cool and impassive as was his brain, his heart was ardent and impulsive.

This contrast of character was exemplified in his conduct during the great civil strife which agitated the nation. Before the appeal to arms he had shown a strong preference for the security of ancient constitutional landmarks over the hazards of reform, and honestly deprecated much of the action of reformers. Undoubtedly, too, in the remembrance of hospitalities which he had received while sojourning with acquaintances at the South, his ingenuous, grateful nature influenced his mind in some degree. But when the sword became the arbiter of the destinies of the country, he eagerly arrayed himself among the active defenders of his established government. His politics never seduced him beyond the sound of Union music; his prejudices never carried him out of the shadow of the Union flag. When war came, his sympathies, guided by his judgment, led him irrepressibly toward the service of his country. Those who knew Richardson were sure that whither his sympathies tended his devoted action would follow.

In August, 1861, he passed the examination of the Naval Board, was commissioned Acting Assistant Surgeon, and soon after joined the North Atlantic Blockading Squadron as Acting Surgeon on board the United States steamer Cambridge. Thus at the commencement of hostilities he became the first volunteer in his position from New England, and the vessel in which he sailed was the first merchant steamer that left Charlestown Navy Yard, refitted as a gunboat.

Dr. Richardson had often declared naval superiority to be the force which would eventually decide the national conflict, and he entered the service in full expectation of active duty and perilous fortunes. But his steamer was assigned to the monotonous though important blockade off Wilmington and Beaufort. Deeply disappointed that his commander had not received a roving commission, Richardson still applied himself cheerfully and assiduously to the requirements of his position. The audacity of the blockade-runners, their familiarity with shifting channels and fickle currents, the speed of their craft, and the deficiency of the national government in both pilots and vessels, demanded untiring vigilance and constant exposure on the part of our crews. Ceaseless quest and toilsome traversing the same ocean wastes was the lot of the patient blockaders, watching and circling, like scattered sea-gulls, along their prescribed line of coast. When the notorious Nashville was waiting at Beaufort, ready to dart from her refuge and speed once more upon her hazardous voyage, tedious days and anxious nights of sentinel watch, anchored at the mouth of one narrow outlet, formed a part of the duty of the Cambridge. The lively, adventurous temperament of her surgeon chafed under this dreary experience. Gladly would he have sought more stirring scenes of duty, but he would not for a moment contemplate the abandonment of the service.

In consequence of exposure to wet and cold during the wintry season, and the restraint from habitual exercise, Dr. Richardson's health failed. These causes, with the bitter disappointment to his aspirations, induced the development of a disease which had proved fatal to his mother and elder brother. Once, when the Cambridge had put into Baltimore for repairs, he visited his home on a brief furlough. Then his decline was painfully apparent. His figure had become thin, gaunt, and bent, and his system was shaken by a racking cough. Friends and physicians besought him to resign his commission and seek the restoration of his health. But this he steadily refused to do, declaring that while the war lasted he should remain in the service of his country; that he could render the best service in her navy, and there he would stay so long as he had strength to perform his duty.

An incident which occurred at this time illustrates at once the changeless sincerity of his friendship and his uncompromising devotion to his government. Recounting one day the formality and coldness of a recent interview between himself and a Southern classmate, an intimate companion of college days, he said, sadly, regretfully, almost bitterly: "We parted, old comrades as we were, with bare civility, — and both knew that all which estranged us was the uniform I wore." Then in a moment, as if the refluent surge of his patriotic impulses had swept away all memory of personal considerations, he exclaimed spiritedly: "But, friends or no friends, our old flag must wave, and wave it shall so long as there's a halyard to hoist it."

The earnestness and enthusiasm of voice and action showed the determination of the intrepid spirit which was leading his feeble body on to duty, and, alas ! to death.

And so, uninfluenced by the arguments and entreaties of his advisers, Dr. Richardson returned to his ship. He well knew the nature of his ailment, and felt that death was threatening him in a form more terrible than "an army with banners." Yet he did not quail, but went back to his post ; back to the inactivity and exposure of his seafaring life ; back to the fog and spray of ocean ; back to the stormy winds and debilitating climate of the Carolina coast. There, as his friends had anticipated, his condition became daily more alarming. But, steadfast and true to his duties, he would not yield. A few months longer he remained, hoping to render a little assistance to his country. His zeal appeared to gather the strength that his failing vital forces lost, and not until it became manifest, as he sorrowfully said, that he was a hindrance to the cause he would have aided, did he succumb to the irresistible decree.

In July, 1862, he was forced to resign his commission and return home. He was a wreck indeed. His associates hardly recognized in that wan, haggard form their hale companion of former days. In the comforts of home he gained some strength, and then spent the summer months quietly in the salubrious air of Southern New Hampshire. But his health receiving no permanent improvement, he sought a drier climate, and passed the winter and spring in Minnesota. There he obtained small relief. The malady had made too deep an inroad to be stayed by aught that wealth could provide or science suggest. In May, attended by a brother, he returned to his father's house, fully impressed with the certainty of impending dissolution. But the same warm heart and patriot spirit dwelt in his shattered frame. Slowly wasting and dying as the days ran on, he continued constantly happy and sociable. With affectionate invitations he called his friends to his chamber, and in their society the old ardor beamed in his countenance and shone in his converse. When Class Day came, too feeble to participate in the festivities on the College grounds, he assembled a party of his classmates at his own home, and bore himself so bravely that they almost believed his wasted form would rise from its melancholy ruin. Not an impatient syllable escaped from his lips, not a word of regret for his sacrifice. On the contrary, he gloried in the service he had done for his country, and grieved that it was no greater.

But more rapidly and surely, day by day, his decline continued as the summer advanced, and still calmly and firmly he awaited the final catastrophe. As if the very shadows of his friends relieved the gloom of death, one of his latest acts was to obtain the photographs of his College Class. In their silent company he cheered the lonely hours, recalling memories of a brighter and a happier past. To the last he was eager to learn the progress of the war, and enthusiastic in asserting the ultimate success of the national arms. He passed the last day of his life in hopeful discussion of the military movements which three days afterwards culminated in the victory of Gettysburg. In the evening he retired, fell into a deep sleep, and slumbered soundly all night; awoke in the morning languid and weary, conversed a little, then turned and slumbered again, and never more awoke.

And so, on the 1st of July, 1863, emaciated, feeble, and faint, but patient and "forlornly brave" unto the end, died Harry Richardson. In admiration of the fortitude of the patriot, in reverence for the fidelity of the officer, but, more than all, in love of the sterling virtues and endearing qualities of the man, this humble record of his life is placed among the memorials of his classmates and friends. Eulogy his fair memory needs not. All who knew him know the full measure of his worth, and, knowing that, recognize the wealth of the sacrifice, expressed more eloquently to them than labored pages can portray, in his simple epitaph, *Pro patriâ*.

THOMAS JEFFERSON SPURR.

First Lieutenant 15th Mass. Vols. (Infantry), November 17, 1861; died at Hagerstown, Md., September 27, 1862, of a wound received at Antietam, September 17.

THOMAS JEFFERSON SPURR was born in Worcester, Massachusetts, February 2, 1838. His grandfathers were General John Spurr and Dr. Daniel Lamb, of Charlton, Massachusetts; his parents, Colonel Samuel Danforth and Mary Augusta (Lamb) Spurr. Both parents were born in Charlton, but removed to Worcester about 1832 or 1833, having at that time but one child, a daughter. Colonel Spurr pursued in Worcester the business of a merchant until his death, which took place November 3, 1842. Thus in his fifth year Thomas Spurr was left, with his sister, under the sole care of his mother; and it seems well to say here, that perhaps the strongest point in his character was the love which he felt for that mother.

While at school his zeal as a student and his love of athletic sports were equally noticeable. He easily led his class at the Grammar School, and completed, in an unusually short time, his preparation for college, at the Worcester High School. He entered college without "conditions," and took at first a high place in his Class, ranking among the first eight scholars at the first Junior Exhibition. Mathematics proved to be his favorite study, though he was faithful and successful in all. But at the end of the first term of that year he began to suffer from disease of the eyes, and he could only remain a fortnight during the second term. A voyage to Fayal did no good; and though he rejoined his Class, he was compelled to continue his studies with the aid of a reader. This deprived him of rank, although he was chosen by his classmates a member of the Phi Beta Kappa Society, for which rank is usually held to be essential.

After graduation he remained at home for a time in ill health; then entered on his law studies, at first with the help of a reader, and afterwards unaided, as his eyes grew better. He studied for a year in the office of Messrs. Devens and Hoar, in Worcester; and in September, 1860, entered the Law School at Cambridge. His desire was to become a scholar and a lawyer.

"If his life had been spared," writes one of those who knew him best, "it would probably have been respected and useful, though not distinguished. His friends might fairly have hoped for him that he would have become one of the leaders of the bar of his native county; that he would have done his full share to promote all the institutions and schemes for the public good which in our community depend on the voluntary public spirit of the citizens; and that his purity, his generosity, his rectitude of purpose, his friendly and unselfish nature, would have won for him an enviable place in the public regard."

He was ambitious of success, but his standard was a very high one. Speaking about an acquaintance just going into business, he said to one of his companions: —

"I think he will succeed; but I should not wish to succeed by such means as I feel sure he uses. I never could stoop to the little meannesses and deceits which many business men practise without seeming to dream that they are wrong."

He was in every respect thoroughly manly. Strong of body, he was also self-relying and brave. He had, too, a purity and chastity of nature to which no stain of indelicacy ever attached itself. Of his love for his mother, about which a strong statement has just been made, his brother-in-law writes: —

"It manifested itself, not much in expressions of endearment, not at all in any mode which would attract the attention of strangers, but in constantly making her comfort and happiness the predominant consideration in all his plans of life. When he was in College and in the Law School, no week passed without at least two letters from him to her; not letters written as in the performance of a self-imposed task, but full and complete journals of his life and thoughts. This feeling grew stronger with the separation caused by his life in the army. His dying moments were occupied with thoughts for her welfare, and her name was the last word upon his lips."

This strong tie made it peculiarly hard for him to go to the war. His mother was a widow, and he her only surviving child. It was only after a great struggle that he could make up his mind to leave her. He held very strong convictions, and believing that the North was right beyond question in the contest, was fervent in his wishes for its success. He felt, as so many young men felt when the war broke out, that he must do something for his country. He was not moved by the love of glory or adventure, although, being of good constitution, he did not fear hardship. He went because it was his duty to go, feeling, as other noble spirits felt, that he should be ashamed to look his friends in the face, or hold up his head anywhere, if he did not do his part.

When the war broke out he was in Russia, having taken this long voyage, in the spring of 1861, in the hope of thus doing something for the benefit of his eyes. The Russian merchants, to whom he and his companion had letters, received their accounts of the state of things in the United States through the most hostile English sources; and what he heard from them, of course, filled him with alarm and dismay. He hastened home, and after a very short time spent in learning the rudiments of military drill, accepted the position of First Lieutenant in Company G of the Fifteenth Massachusetts Regiment, to which post he was recommended by Colonel Devens, who then commanded the regiment in the field. His recommendation was not sought by him, or by any friend of his for him, but was the result of Colonel Devens's personal knowledge of his qualities.

"His original appointment," says his brother-in-law, "had not been approved by his men or the other officers of the regiment; they thinking that the vacancies should have been filled from among those who had gone through the dangers of Ball's Bluff; and if anything in him had made it possible, he would have encountered serious discomfort, if not hostility. But all this feeling soon yielded to his friendly and courteous manners and his thorough and conscientious performance of his duty; and all persons connected with his regiment agree that he was universally beloved by his comrades, both officers and men."

He was for a considerable time the only commissioned officer in his company, and his devotion to it was invariable. When they were stationed for some weeks near Washington, where he had many friends, he resolutely declined all their invitations, with a single exception, saying that his duty required his constant presence with his men. When he found he was too ill to go into action with his company at Malvern Hill, he burst into tears. He went with his regiment to the Peninsula, returned with it, and received his death wound at the battle of Antietam. The closing scenes of his life are best described by his brother-in-law, George Frisbie Hoar, Esq., who was with him in his last hours: —

"He joined his regiment in the fall of 1861. I never saw him again until I was summoned to Hagerstown after the battle of Antietam. He was dressing the line of his company, about nine o'clock of the morning of the battle, the regiment being under a severe fire, when his thigh was struck by a minié-ball which shattered the bone. Two of his men came where he lay, and offered to carry him to the rear. He ordered them back to the ranks, and refused all assistance. The place where he lay was a short distance in front of a wood, to which the regiment was almost instantly compelled to retreat. The ground where he fell was not again occupied by our troops until after the battle. He lay on the ground where he fell all of Wednesday and through Wednesday night. On Thursday the enemy occupied the ground. Among them was a college acquaintance and contemporary (whom I believe to have been a Major Hale of South Carolina), who treated him with kindness, caused him to be removed to a farm-yard near by and laid on the ground between two haystacks, and gave him a blanket, which we are glad to preserve. Thomas lay in this farm-yard until Saturday, when the ground was again occupied by our forces, and he was then removed to a hospital. On Monday he was taken to Hagerstown, where his mother and I, with Dr. Sargent, found him on Wednesday evening. Early the next morning, Thursday, he was carefully examined by the surgeons, who were able, by extracting the splinters of bone from his flesh, to relieve the agony which he had suffered since he was wounded, but found his recovery hopeless. He said to me after the examination, 'I suppose you will tell me the result when you think it is best.' It would have dishonored that brave soul to keep it back, and I told him the whole truth. He heard it bravely and cheerfully. He said he hoped his company would be satisfied with him, and feel that he had deserved their confidence; that he was not conscious of having had a single thought for himself after the first bullet was fired. He added that he believed he had the confidence of Colonel Kimball. He lay through this day and the next suffering a good deal, and gradually growing weaker, but with his mind perfectly clear and calm. There is too much of a private and personal nature in the conversations of those two days to make it proper to repeat them here. Dr. Sargent, the distinguished physician who kindly and generously left his pressing professional duties at home to give his dying young friend the benefit of his skill, writes: 'I shall consider myself as more than compensated for any sacrifice I have made, by the elevating and purifying influences of that death-bed, — the death of the Christian patriot; of the excellent son and brother, whose translation in the clearness of his intellect, and even in the fulness of wisdom, was such as I never before witnessed.'

"At about half past four on Saturday morning he asked his mother, 'Do you think I am failing?' She said, 'Yes.' He said, 'While my mind is clear, I should like to pray with you.' He then, in a voice as clear and distinct as his usual voice in health, prayed for a blessing on his friends, thanked God for giving him such a kind mother, for the goodness which had followed him through life, and that he had been enabled to pass the last days of his life surrounded by kind friends, without which they must have been days of terrible anguish. He took leave of each of his friends who were present, and sent kind messages to his near relatives who were away. He sent his love to Lieutenant Bigelow, a young officer (then Sergeant) of his own regiment, who lay wounded in the same house, and said: 'Henry (Lieutenant Bigelow) behaved beautifully. I want General Devens to know it. He ought to have a commission. He is so modest and quiet, that I don't think General Devens knows how much there is in him.' He then spoke to Dr. Sargent, and said: 'I have no doubt you have done all you can. I am much obliged to you. I am perfectly satisfied.'

"He then called his man Isaiah, and said, 'I hope I have not been unreasonable with you; I have tried not to be.' The man burst into tears, and replied, 'You have always been mighty good to me, sir.' Thomas then said: 'I believe there are no little things I have left unarranged. I should like to have Isaiah ride in the car beside the coffin, so that it shall not be roughly handled. I have tried to do my duty. I hope my example of devotion to my country may not be lost.'

"After a slight pause he said: 'It may be well for you as surgeons to make a certificate of my death, and send it to Colonel Kimball. His address is, "Lieutenant-Colonel Kimball, Fifteenth Regiment Massachusetts Volunteers, Sedgwick's Division, Washington, District of Columbia."' He then crossed his hands over his breast, and said, 'Now the sooner it is over, the better.'

"He then lay for a few hours quietly, giving occasional slight directions for arranging his position, &c., till about nine o'clock, A. M., when he asked for water, which he could not swallow. He then seemed sinking fast. He opened his eyes once more, and said, 'Don't feel badly; be of good cheer, mother'; and in a few minutes quietly breathed his last."

END OF VOL. I.

Cambridge: Stereotyped and Printed by Welch, Bigelow, & Co.

www.ingramcontent.com/pod-product-compliance
Lightning Source LLC
LaVergne TN
LVHW020933110826
845150LV00004B/852

* 9 7 8 1 4 2 5 5 5 2 3 4 3 *